MANUSCRIPTS AND PRINTED BOOKS
IN EUROPE 1350–1550:
PACKAGING, PRESENTATION AND CONSUMPTION

Emma Cayley is Head of Modern Languages and Senior Lecturer in French at the University of Exeter. Emma has published extensively on late medieval French poetry and its material context. Her first monograph on Alain Chartier and medieval debate poetry came out with OUP in 2006. She published a collection of essays on Alain Chartier in Boydell and Brewer's Gallica series with Ashby Kinch in 2008. Among other projects, Emma is developing an iPad App for use in schools, the 'Exeter Manuscripts App', with Antenna International.

Susan (Sue) Powell is Emeritus Professor of Medieval Texts and Culture at the University of Salford. She has published substantially on late-medieval and Tudor religious culture and cultural products, particularly sermons and devotional texts, with particular emphasis on their dissemination through the medium of manuscript and early printed book. Her current major research projects ar e an edition of the household papers of Lady Margaret Beaufort, a book on the Birgittine order at Syon Abbey, and an edition of the Latin *Manuale Sacerdotis* of John Mirk.

Contributors

Sonja Drimmer, Columbia University, US

Martha Driver, Pace University, US

John Block Friedman, University of Illinois: Urbana-Champaign (Emeritus), US

Anamaria Gellert, University of Pisa, Italy

Carrie Griffin, University College Cork, Ireland

Shayne Husbands, University of Cardiff, UK

Anne Marie Lane, Toppan Rare Books Library, University of Wyoming, US

Anna Lewis, University of Ottawa, Canada

Kate Maxwell, University of Agder, Norway

Mary Morse, Rider University, US

Derek Pearsall, University of York (Emeritus), UK

Matti Peikola, University of Turku, Finland

Yvonne Rode, Fordham University, US

Anne F. Sutton, The Mercers' Company, UK

Manuscripts and Printed Books in Europe 1350–1550

Packaging, Presentation and Consumption

edited by
Emma Cayley and Susan Powell

LIVERPOOL UNIVERSITY PRESS

Front cover: Cloisters Apocalypse, Metropolitan Museum of Art, New York, fol. 16ᵛ: Saint John and the Book. The Cloisters Collection, 1968 (68.174) © 2013 Image copyright The Metropolitan Museum of Art/Art Resource/ Scala, Florence.

First published in 2013 by
Liverpool University Press
4 Cambridge Street
Liverpool
L69 7ZU

This paperback version published 2015

British Library Cataloguing in Publication Data
A catalogue record for this book is available
from the British Library.

ISBN 978 0 85989 870 6 cased
ISBN 978 1 78138 269 1 paperback

Typeset in Sabon, 10 on 12 by
Carnegie Book Production, Lancaster
Printed in Great Britain by
CPI Group (UK) Ltd, Croydon CR0 4YY

Contents

Section II: Consumers:
Producers, Owners and Readers

Section III: Writing Consumption

Figures

Foreword

Derek Pearsall

The conference of the Early Book Society at the University of Exeter in July 2009, organised by Emma Cayley, Martha Driver and Sue Powell, was the eleventh biennial conference of the Society. The Society grew from sessions sponsored at Kalamazoo in 1987 and 1988 by Martha Driver and Sarah Horrall. Sarah died in 1989, and the Society since then has been run by Martha Driver, more or less on her own. She always remembers and makes generous and affectionate acknowledgement of the part played by Sarah in the early days. Martha Driver's determination and energy, and her devotion to the subject, have enabled the Early Book Society to prosper, and the biennial conference has been held punctually every two years since Durham in 1989. In addition, Martha organises the five sessions sponsored by the Society every year at Kalamazoo, sessions which are always filled with good papers, and she edits, in earlier years almost single-handed, the Society's journal. The *Journal of the Early Book Society* has developed steadily since its first annual number, in 1998 (for 1997), and is now a publication of international repute in the field. More recently, she took on the general editorship of a series of publications for Brepols. The general title of the series is 'Texts and Transitions', its subject-matter almost a template of the remit of the Early Book Society, and it already boasts five excellent monographs.

All this activity Martha Driver has kept going, more recently with some help from others, over these many years. Many young scholars owe to her their first introduction to the international world of early book and manuscript studies. Older scholars too have felt the impact of her kindness, inspiration, and unflagging enthusiasm. That so much has been maintained uninterrupted during the last four years of serious illness is a tribute to her stamina and dedication. It was all the more unfortunate that, still in convalescence, she was obliged to miss the Exeter conference. She was well-remembered there on many occasions, and a short service of prayers was held in the University chapel, organised by Emma Cayley, Sue Powell and Linne Mooney, to offer good wishes for her further recovery. She will be back (and has been back, at the twelfth conference in York in 2011), and has even contributed a chapter to the present volume.

Alluding to the headings in the conference title: '*Accipe et Devora*: Packaging, Presentation and Consumption of Manuscripts and Printed Books, 1350–1550', the first group of essays is concerned with material production and presentation, the second group of essays considers consumers—producers, owners and readers—and the final group has more to do, variously, with the contents of manuscripts and early printed books and their reception.

Reading through these essays is an invigorating experience. Many of them are by younger scholars, and they are particularly remarkable for the maturity and precision of their scholarship. Standards are high, perhaps higher than they once were. There may be various reasons for this. There is, of course, the increased attention paid to manuscript and early print studies over the past thirty years, which has been bound to compel a greater sophistication everywhere. Some would also place emphasis on the impact of computer technology on research, sometimes accelerating its progress exponentially, sometimes perhaps getting in the way of thoughtful deliberation. Other factors are the excellence of the cohorts now opting for manuscript and early book studies in their graduate work and the correspondingly more stringent demands of their teachers and advisors. But something must be attributed to institutional changes. The tightening up of regulations for three-year submission of the Ph.D. and the escalating demands on young faculty to produce original publishable research quickly have had some good effects. They have also helped to engineer changes in choice of topic. Where, in the past, the five or six years often allowed for completion of the Ph.D. and the relaxed supervision of faculty research meant that large-scale programmes of research could be undertaken that demanded extensive background reading, now the requirement must be for 'finishable' research tasks. Skill in choosing them has become an essential part of the modern student's armoury.

As to the subject-matter of the papers published in the present volume, it is striking how precise and well-defined they are, perhaps partly for the reasons I have outlined. There is also a great range of topics, many of which completely overturn any of the traditional distinctions between 'literature' and 'history'. 'Food, fleas and folly' would have made a snappy title for the conference and its volume of proceedings, if not, honestly, completely representative. What is printed here is a relic of the many such papers presented at the conference—two complete sessions, two papers in another session, and a plenary lecture. A particular point to be remarked upon is the presence of two chapters on aspects of French manuscript history, a subject which has not in the past been prominent in most Early Book Society conferences. It is a welcome new strength. Much of this can be attributed to the presence at the conference of three experts in the field, Emma Cayley and Yolanda Plumley, both at that time in the Modern Languages Department at Exeter, and Ardis Butterfield, then at University College London. In her plenary lecture, Yolanda Plumley gave a beautiful demonstration of the 'art of citation' in medieval French song—and also the art of listening, because a musical consort was in attendance. Inevitably, this kind of thing does not make its way into a volume of conference proceedings. Ardis Butterfield was there to announce the inauguration of the 'Medieval Song Network', a new interdisciplinary research project of which she is joint co-ordinator.

This account of the Exeter event would not be complete without mention of two plenary lectures which do not appear in the conference volume. One was the scintillating talk by Barbara Shailor, of Yale University, on the manuscript 'mutilator' Otto Ege. Professor Shailor is one of the foremost scholars in the field of manuscript and library studies, and she gave us a most amusing and witty talk. At one point she even managed to air the thought (I think) that Ege's manuscript depredations actually served a public good, since it was his custom to make manuscript portfolios out of the pages he had abstracted in order to provide first-hand material for students to work with. Not many curators of rare books and manuscripts would think this much of an extenuation, or much of an inducement to drop criminal charges! The other plenary talk that must be mentioned is that of Toshiyuki Takamiya, the well-travelled Japanese scholar and manuscript collector. Professor Takamiya is renowned for his splendid collection and also for his generosity in inviting Western scholars to work with his manuscripts at his library in Tokyo, and on occasions for his almost alarming freedom in bringing one or two of his precious manuscripts to conferences for people to look at and pass fearfully around. His talk was highly informative and characteristically modest, and touched with a nice humour. He is a model of professional courtesy and representative of EBS's truly international membership which stretches from Japan across Europe to the UK, the US and Canada.

Derek Pearsall

Preface

Emma Cayley and Susan Powell

This volume has grown from papers delivered at the Eleventh Biennial Early Book Society conference, which took as its theme '*Accipe et Devora*: Packaging, Presentation and Consumption of Manuscripts and Printed Books, 1350-1550'. The focus on books *qua* books has been a particularly fruitful development of the past decade or two, and has enabled EBS to come into its own, revealed as a prescient forerunner of the many conferences, articles and books (but not societies) which proliferate on the subject today.

While focussed on the technical and historical, EBS has always embraced and encouraged (both in its biennial conferences and its Journal) the literary and even theoretical approaches to book studies which are becoming an increasingly common feature of the market today, and it was the hope of the conference organisers that imaginative and inventive uses would be made of the themes of packaging, presentation and consumption. The breadth of the Society is also reflected in its time-span, from Edward III to Edward VI, or perhaps from Chaucer to the Book of Common Prayer, and in its recognition of the variable predominance and importance of the manuscript and/or the printed book during this period.

Traditionally, EBS has mainly focussed on the interests of those in English medieval and early modern studies. Other European languages and literatures are, however, also represented among the membership, and the Exeter conference, organised by a French medievalist (Cayley), aimed to expand the horizons of the Society and to forge further interdisciplinary links between scholars in English and French medieval studies. It was therefore timely, building on current trends for cross-cultural investigation in medieval scholarship. The present volume similarly aims to bring together some of these cross-disciplinary strands, illustrating the richness and diversity of current research being carried out in this field by contributors from a variety of disciplines, including English, French, Art History, Musicology and History.

Finally, before moving to an overview of the volume and its rationale, EBS is also remarkable in that it is an Anglo-American Society. Its Board of Directors consists of two North American, two English, and one Japanese scholar (the exception which proves the rule), and its officers consist of three North Americans (one long resident in the UK), and two British members. Biennial conferences are held in the UK, but several sessions are always held annually at the International Congress on Medieval Studies at Kalamazoo. It is a fruitful and enriching partnership.

'Accipe et devora' ('take and eat') has its origins in the Apocalypse (Revelation 10: 9), where the angel addresses John: 'Take the book and eat it up. And it shall make your belly bitter: but in your mouth it shall be sweet as honey'. Here, in an echo of Christ's words at the institution of the Eucharist ('Take ye, and eat', Matthew 26: 26), we have a central image of the text as food, wholesome and eloquent but at times unpalatable and indigestible, offering uncomfortable spiritual comfort. The Vulgate Latin, introducing as theme the contemporary economic concept of consumption, was intended to reflect the Society's breadth of vision and to encourage both traditional and more daring interpretations. Under the title of 'packaging' we invited papers dealing with the separate tasks of putting late medieval and early modern texts together: writing, abstracting, editing, correcting, illustrating, printing, and/or binding; and also the re-packaging of older texts for contemporary audiences. 'Presentation' included visual and material aspects of the manuscript or early printed book and took account of its particular provenance and reception or trajectory. In book studies the term 'consumption' is frequently used in the context of luxury manuscripts or printed books produced for wealthy owners but, alongside this metaphorical reading, the term was broad enough to encompass literal interpretations: bibliophagia, or consumption by time, worms, fire, or censors. Packaging, presentation and consumption form the essential structure of the present volume of selected proceedings, with the addition of a section on the 'consumers' themselves, those who produced, owned and read these early books.

Section I, 'Packaging and Presentation: The Materiality of the Manuscript and Printed Book', consists of four essays which consider the book as material artefact, both from the point of view of its maker (binding, *mise-en-page*, illustration) and its distributor. In 'How can we Recognise 'Contemporary' Bookbindings of the Fifteenth and early Sixteenth Centuries?', Anne Marie Lane draws on her wide experience as rare books curator at the Toppan Rare Books Library, University of Wyoming. A relaxed and informative conference paper, with a wealth of detail and an abundance of enthusiasm, has resulted in a detailed (and still enthusiastic) essay on the eighty-eight pre-1550 books of the Toppan Library: six manuscript codices from the fifteenth century, three from the early sixteenth century, thirteen volumes of incunabula and sixty-six books printed from 1501 to 1550. Lane's discussion of bindings is from the viewpoint of the curator instructing the visitor to her collection: how to recognise a contemporary binding, why they are few and far between (only 26 per cent of the eighty-eight are in contemporary bindings), where they might come from, what made of, how decorated, and how they can deteriorate. As such, this is an engaging and valuable introduction to a complex subject, and a worthy opener to the 'Packaging and Presentation' section.

The next essay, 'Guidelines for Consumption: Scribal Ruling Patterns and Designing the *mise-en-page* in later Medieval England', takes the reader within the pages of the bound book and investigates a neglected topic, one which Matti Peikola fully demonstrates to have been unfairly neglected, despite the seminal work on ruling practices of Albert Derolez and Denis Muzerelle. Peikola adopts a methodological approach, using late-medieval English, particularly Middle English (such as the Wycliffite Bible and the *Pore Caitif*), manuscripts to discuss the purpose of scribal ruling, first in general terms and then in a detailed examination of the various constraints that could play a role in a scribe's decision to adopt a particular ruling pattern. Demonstrating by numerous examples, the twin principles of function and aesthetics, as well as the situational constraints within which the scribe-ruler worked, Peikola offers a convincing case for the importance of a fully comprehensive research project which might reveal the chronological and geographical scope of the use and distribution of ruling patterns in medieval manuscripts.

In 'The Order of the Lays in the 'Odd' Machaut MS BnF, fr. 9221(E)', Kate Maxwell considers a rather different sort of patterning, the order of Guillaume de Machaut's lays in one of the six manuscripts (five of them presentation manuscripts) which appear to contain his complete works. She argues for the importance and consistency of the packaging of the lays and their presentation on the page, suggesting that the 'package' might almost be as significant for medieval patrons, readers and the author as the contents themselves. It is certainly the case that packaging strongly influenced the readerly interpretation of the contents of a manuscript or early book, and this appears to have been doubly so with Machaut's carefully orchestrated œuvre. In the course of her analysis, Maxwell 'lifts' some of the oddness from Machaut's 'odd' manuscript, and shows how it can be considered alongside its fellow 'complete-works' manuscripts, and appreciated as a work of art. Despite initial appearances, MS E shows considerable internal coherence, and Maxwell further demonstrates how it may be closely linked to the House of France, in common with other Machaut 'complete-works' manuscripts.

While Maxwell argues for the concern for integrity and consistency with which the scribes packaged Machaut's complete works, Sonja Drimmer demonstrates the versatility and ingenuity with which two teams of illuminators packaged different manuscripts of the *Lives of SS Edmund and*

Fremund, one with the focus on the king (Henry VI) for whom the work had been written, and the other on the saint (St Edmund) to whom the abbey was dedicated where the work was written and presented. In 'Picturing the King or Picturing the Saint: Two Miniature Programmes for John Lydgate's *Lives of SS Edmund and Fremund*', she demonstrates Lydgate's fulfilment of his dual agenda, political and hagiographic. The illuminators of the presentation manuscript respond cleverly to this agenda, as Drimmer shows through a detailed and careful study of the two frontispieces, in which, she argues, the saint mirrors Henry whose gaze is not only on Edmund but on himself as saint/monarch. Contrastingly, in the later manuscript prepared for a bourgeois owner, the royal-political agenda is abandoned through re-ordering of text and illustrations in order to package the manuscript as reliquary enclosing as relic the life of the saint. It is Drimmer's achievement to combine a meticulous reading of the illustrations of the two manuscripts with a theoretical critique of their symbolic and iconic significance in two very different contexts.

Finally in this section, the book having been ruled, written, illuminated and bound, Yvonne Rode in 'Sixty-three Gallons of Books: Shipping Books to London in the Late Middle Ages' considers an under-researched element of its distribution. Writing as an economic historian, Rode analyses the import trade as recorded in the overseas customs accounts from 1480 to 1540, which provide quantitative data on the volume, value and shipping units of book imports. While limited in scope and offering some conundrums, the entries provide sufficient information (the name of the importer, the type of book, the container it was shipped in and the custom duty collected) to describe the changes in the overseas trade during these years, as baskets replaced casks and other receptacles, books came to be shipped alone, rather than with other imports, and became a common rather than luxury commodity, and (from 1534) the import of bound books was banned in order to support English binders.

Interest in the consumers of books, whether producers or owners/readers, has been a long-standing topic of book study, certainly not restricted to medievalists. This is reflected in our second section, 'Consumers: Producers, Owners and Readers', which contains two medieval contributions, one from the early modern period, and one much more contemporary, reflecting the antiquarian interest in book-collecting and bibliography which developed from the eighteenth century and is still strong today. Both Anna Lewis and Anne F. Sutton consider the mercantile obsession with books, whether as commodity, status symbol or reading matter. In '"But solid food is for the mature, who ... have their senses trained to discern good and evil": John Colop's Book and the Spiritual Diet of the Discerning Lay Londoner', Lewis focusses on the mid-fifteenth-century religious anthology compiled by the London merchant John Colop for use as a 'common profit' book, that is, to circulate and be shared amongst a group of like-minded, and, as Lewis demonstrates, serious and conventional readers. The strategy of the common profit book has been a topic of discussion for some time, but Lewis' approach is to analyse the contents of one such book in the light of contemporary fears of heresy and what at a later date would have been called 'enthusiasm'. While the texts themselves have the potential for unsafe consumption, the book's overall strategy is to direct the reader towards discreet and careful reading so as to combat dangerous individualism and encourage communal orthodoxy. Colop is set in the wider context of the London mercantile community in Anne F. Sutton's essay on 'The Acquisition and Disposal of Books for Worship and Pleasure by Mercers of London in the Later Middle Ages'. Sutton's knowledge of this community is second to none, and the essay provides a unique and detailed overview of the London merchants, their close networks (in marriage and religious worship), their ownership and bequests of books, and their avid consumption of books.

Martha Driver's absence from the 2009 conference has been mentioned by Derek Pearsall in his Foreword. It was therefore a particular pleasure that we could include in this volume her short essay on women, not as the conventional passive consumers of books, but as active producers. These are the printers, at first in Paris, then Antwerp, and only from 1527 in England, who, after the death of their printer-husbands, engaged in producing books for the early Tudor market. In general, these women were conventional in their choice of titles, publishing service books (perhaps particularly packaged for the female market), although two women stand out, Catherine van Ruremund in Antwerp who moved (perhaps inevitably, given her location) into Protestant publications, and Elizabeth Pickering, Robert Redman's widow, in whom Driver finds an emerging confidence and sense of selfhood, as her essay title suggests: '"By Me Elysabeth Pykeryng": Women and Book Production in the Early Tudor Period'.

The section ends in a very different era, and, once again, male-orientated. Books were a valuable medieval commodity, passed from generation to generation by both the middle and upper classes. In some contexts new books were prized over old—the university and monastic libraries tended pragmatically to replace manuscripts with printed editions, and replace those with newer editions; in domestic contexts old books were treasured for their material worth, often visible in their rich bindings and fine illuminations. This latter interest survived well beyond the Middle Ages and reached its apogee in the founding in 1812 of a society for amateur bibliophiles, the still-extant Roxburghe Club. Shayne Husbands provides a lively and illuminating discussion of 'The Roxburghe Club: Consumption, Obsession and the Passion for Print', unpicking the motives of the collectors, their social background, and, bizarrely, the resentment with which their activities were greeted in the press. The manners of consumption have always tended to a contemporary stereotype, one which the Roxburghe Club was sufficiently wealthy and/or committed to ignore, but at its peril.

EBS's willingness to embrace the literary-critical and literary-historical, as well as the purely bibliographical and codicological, has been noted above. The third and final section, 'Writing Consumption', takes the volume in this direction. Carrie Griffin pursues the literal and metaphorical theme of the conference in 'Reconsidering the Recipe: Materiality, Narrative and Text in Later Medieval Instructional Manuscripts and Collections'. In this she draws on contemporary discussions of miscellaneity and genre to consider the packaging and presentation of culinary and medical recipes. These pose problems for both cataloguers and editors; they also pose more literary problems, differing from their twenty-first-century equivalents in that they are not purely utilitarian and vary considerably in their focus, breadth and language. Griffin argues for a recognition of their complexity and variety and the different consumer models they can represent.

The next two chapters investigate the act of consumption in representations of men and women at table. In 'Fools, "Folye" and Caxton's Woodcut of the Pilgrims at Table', Anamaria Gellert considers the anomalous introduction of a fool into the company of Chaucer's pilgrims in the woodcut to Caxton's second edition of the *Canterbury Tales*. Through a careful study of the fool and folly in contemporary image and text (including the *Canterbury Tales* itself), Gellert investigates consumer expectations and responses to the intervention of this essentially subversive figure into a conventional representation of men and women at table. John Block Friedman also investigates the subversion of convention in 'Anxieties at Table: Food and Drink in Chaucer's Fabliaux Tales and Heinrich Wittenwiler's *Der Ring*'. Extending the scope of the volume into medieval German writing, he traces comparisons between the anti-social behaviour at table in Heinrich Wittenwiler's contemporary *Der Ring* and Chaucer's *Miller's* and *Reeve's Tales*. Both poets explore social class in its relation to anxieties about table etiquette, and both use these class anxieties not only to comment on class divisions and to parody social niceties but as plot devices to trigger subversive dramatic action.

Mary Morse's focus on writing consumption is more unusual. The writing takes the form of an English prayer to Saints Quiricus and Julitta which is found on several late-fifteenth-century English prayer rolls that may have been used by their owners as, or borrowed to serve as, birth girdles. 'Alongside St. Margaret: The Childbirth Cult of SS Quiricus and Julitta in Late Medieval English Manuscripts' considers the history of the saints (barely known in England, where it is Margaret who is traditionally associated with prayers for ease in childbirth) and the tradition of birth girdles, and compares the texts and contexts of the prayer itself in the known manuscripts.

Finally, in her 'Consuming the Text: Pulephilia in Fifteenth-Century French Debate Poetry', Emma Cayley describes a narrative of both literal and metaphorical consumption in the context of medieval flea literature. She traces the origins and salient French literary occurrences of the expression 'avoir/mettre la puce en l'oreille' (to have/put a flea in [some]one's ear). The medieval French phrase, unlike its modern equivalent and the English translation, indicated both disquiet and sexual desire. Cayley investigates the intricate play between desire for intercourse in the fifteenth-century French debate poem—verbal and physical—and consumption. Just as the fleas ravage human flesh, so the interlocutors of these debates desire a 'cannibalistic' union with their lovers, but are kept in a permanent state of irritated frustration as that union is never achieved. As Cayley suggests, consumption for these authors represents the end point of desire, and thus the quelling of voices along with the text. Consumption is always desired by the speakers of her debates, but never achieved, and thus endlessly deferred, just as the text is endlessly perpetuated with the writing of further debates. Consumption or satisfaction of desire (the scratching of the itch) is finally achieved in some way through the material collection of these debates in their manuscript context, via the social and poetic dynamics of the manuscript anthology.

The choice of Exeter as a venue for the EBS conference was the key to the success of our collaborative enterprise. Exeter's Centre for Medieval Studies, run by Professor Yolanda Plumley, and located in the College of Humanities, fosters an interdisciplinary community of scholars. It was among the objectives of the conference to enhance the profile of medieval studies at Exeter, as well as to make an impact on the city. To that end, Exeter itself provided 'material' for the conference: tours of the University Library's Special Collections, Exeter Cathedral Library and Archives, and Devon Record Office's Conservation Studio were conducted, as well as tours of medieval Exeter and sites of medieval interest in Devon and Cornwall.

We are delighted that Liverpool University Press has now taken on the publication of this volume. Our heartfelt thanks go to Anna Henderson, Helen Gannon, and Simon Baker at the University of Exeter Press. Anna in particular has shepherded this project from the early stages with an admirable blend of patience, diplomacy and skill. Thanks must go to Lucy Frontani and Rachel Clarke at Carnegie Book Production and Patrick Brereton and Anthony Cond at Liverpool University Press for their wonderful work on the final stages of this book. We would also like to acknowledge a debt of gratitude to Derek Pearsall, Emeritus Professor of English at Harvard University, and Honorary Professor of English at the University of York, who wrote the Foreword to this volume. It is a Foreword characterised by Derek's considerable intellectual generosity and astute commentary.

Emma would like to dedicate this volume to her children, Oliver and Sophie. Oliver very much enjoyed the croquet at the conference, though he could barely toddle at the time. Emma hopes that both Oliver and Sophie will grow up to appreciate, respect and love manuscripts and medieval literature just as much as their mother does.

Emma Cayley and Sue Powell

Abbreviations

BnF	Bibliothèque nationale de France
BL	British Library
BRUC	Emden, A.B., *Biographical Register of the University of Cambridge to 1500* (Cambridge, 1963)
BRUO	Emden, A.B., *Biographical Register of the University of Oxford to 1500* 3 vols (Oxford, 1957–59)
CC	Commissary Court of London
CCR	*Calendar of Close Rolls*
CHBB III	Hellinga, Lotte and Trapp, J.B. (eds) *The Cambridge History of the Book in Britain III: 1400–1557* (Cambridge, 1991)
CPMR	Thomas, A.H. and Jones, P.E. (eds) *Calendar of Plea and Memoranda Rolls of the City of London*, 6 vols (Cambridge, 1926–61)
CPR	Calendar of Patent Rolls
CUL	Cambridge University Library
CWH	Sharpe, R.R. (ed.) *Calendar of Wills Proved and Enrolled in the Court of Husting, London, A.D. 1258–A.D. 1688*, 2 vols (London, 1889–90)
EETS	Early English Text Society
GL	Guildhall Library
IMEP	*The Index of Middle English Prose*
JEBS	*Journal of the Early Book Society*
JRUL	John Rylands University Library
MED	*Middle English Dictionary*, online edn <http://quod.lib.umich.edu/m/med/>
ODNB	*Oxford Dictionary of National Biography*, online edn <http://www.oxforddnb.com/>

PCC   Prerogative Court of Canterbury
PMLA   *Publications of the Modern Language Association of America*
PROB   Probate
STC   Pollard, A.W. and Redgrave, G.R. (eds) *Short-Title Catalogue of Books Printed in England, Scotland & Ireland and of English Books Printed Abroad 1475–1640*, 2nd edn rev. and enlarged by W.A. Jackson, F.S. Ferguson, and Katharine F. Pantzer, 3 vols (London, 1976–1991)
TNA   The National Archives (PRO, Public Record Office)

Section I

Packaging and Presentation:

The Materiality of the Manuscript and Printed Book

1

How can we Recognise 'Contemporary' Bookbindings of the Fifteenth and Early Sixteenth Centuries?

Anne Marie Lane

Many people, in their haste to get inside a book's contents, do not pay much attention to the way it is bound. But the binding is important, because it is the package in which a book resides and presents itself. While its main purpose certainly is to protect and enclose the text block, its look and feel can also provide an aesthetic and anticipatory experience. Yet Mirjam Foot began her book *Studies in the History of Bookbinding* by stating: 'Even among fellow-historians and bibliographers, bookbinding is considered an eccentric subject, out on a limb, not part of the mainstream of cultural or socio-historical research.'[1] She goes on to explain, however, that the history of bookbinding actually intersects with many different areas of study: religion, art, patronage, collecting, market forces, readership, book production and the booktrade.

Keeping that larger framework in mind, this chapter will focus first on the research scope, intentions and methodologies of a project conducted by the rare books curator at the Toppan Rare Books Library, University of Wyoming, Laramie.[2] Thereafter will be discussed: what is meant by the term contemporary binding; problems caused by later binding alterations; geographical aspects to consider; specific attributes in books that might signal fifteenth- or sixteenth-century bindings. The chapter will conclude with some thoughts on the subject from the curator's perspective.

Research intentions and methodologies

This chapter had its origins in a search of the shelves of the Toppan Library to find all examples of fifteenth- and early sixteenth-century bindings, in order to use them in teaching a new semester-long course in the library on Renaissance book history. But the extent of binding complexity slowly became depressingly apparent when many books with early dates were in obviously later rebindings. To confuse matters, some early aspects continued for centuries (such as wooden boards with metal clasps on German and Dutch Bibles and vellum bindings in Italy and France).[3] Also, before being able to identify what is binding of the time, one must develop an eye for what is not. That involves even more research, as well as intensive visual comparisons with books printed later. For example, Gothic and Renaissance books that were rebound from the seventeenth century on might have their endpapers or covers replaced with marbled papers, which have place and time-specific patterns.[4]

In the course of looking for examples of contemporary Gothic and Renaissance bindings, a question presented itself: what would be their percentage to the total number of pre-1550 books located in the library? Eighty-eight books were eventually located from before 1550 (the end-date of the Early Book Society's scope). While only a small percentage of the Toppan Library's 50,000-plus books (and also a small number compared to the early holdings of other rare book libraries), this made for a manageable sample size. For the study, the pre-1550 Toppan books were physically divided into groups (across a number of tables) by the six centuries of binding styles: those in their fifteenth- and sixteenth-century bindings; those with aspects of 'older' rebindings or restorations from the seventeenth and eighteenth centuries; and those in 'newer' bindings of the nineteenth and twentieth centuries. In determining the category in which to place a book, the extent of any alterations (and how much was left of the original) was a main consideration.

The eighty-eight books comprise six manuscript codices from the fifteenth century and three from the early sixteenth century; thirteen volumes of incunabula; and sixty-six books printed from 1501 to 1550. However, since some books produced in the early-to-mid sixteenth century may not have had their first binding until a little later, the time frame of those particular books was expanded to consider later sixteenth-century binding styles as contemporary to them.

What is meant by contemporary binding?

The binding on a Gothic or Renaissance codex today may not be its 'original' or first covering. That is because text blocks were not usually sold in a publisher's binding like today—rather, they were distributed and warehoused unbound (with the exception of a small number of major printers who offered some bound books).[5] Local booksellers sometimes arranged for small batches to be sold in cheaper or temporary bindings.[6] Usually it was the buyers who commissioned trade bindings, but this might not occur for years or decades.[7] For example, one Toppan Library book was

Figure 1.1   Johannes Eck, *Homiliarum* (Cologne, 1538).
An example of a book with a binding date stamped on it that is twelve years
after its publication. Pigskin over wooden boards with clasps and with tooled
designs: some in blind and some ink-stamped in black. (16½ cm × 11½ cm ×
5½ cm).
William M. Fitzhugh, Jr. Collection BX 4759 E2x.
Toppan Rare Books Library, American Heritage Center, University of
Wyoming, Laramie.

printed in Cologne in 1538 (*Homiliarum clarissimi viri* ..., Johannes Eck,
printed by Eucharius Cervicornus), but its binding date is proudly displayed
as 1550, twelve years later (see Figure 1.1). A book could also have lived
in a sequence of bindings through its lifetime, depending on the desires of
changing collectors. In that case, what we see now is its 'latest' binding.

If book historians do not have specific provenance information to
indicate that a binding is the first or original one, but the style is nevertheless
characteristic of the book's era, then the term 'contemporary' is used instead
to indicate that the binding is from the approximate period of the book's
production.[8] But what is approximate? Carter's *ABC for Book Collectors*
restricts it to within a decade or quarter-century of its production, if before
1700.[9] But because most people are not bookbinding specialists, bookseller

or library catalogue descriptions often encompass the larger context of a century, such as 'contemporary sixteenth-century binding'. That is the view that this study has adopted.

Problems caused by later binding alterations

Many books donated to rare book libraries came from collections of wealthy bibliophiles who had fine binders rebind or restore old-looking books to create a uniformly beautiful display. Today the ideal for the historically minded is to see books preserved as the unique entities they were in their own time. If a book is 'rebound', it has its original binding removed and replaced with one in a different style which reflects the binding interests of the later period.[10] On the other hand, a book is 'restored' if the style replicates the original binding but with new materials. Nowadays, a conscientious conservator will try to retain as much as possible of the original materials, but that was not always the case, and touch-up attempts through the centuries by amateurs to 'repair' any wear and tear can leave a hodgepodge of components.

Contemporary binding is precious because, when books are repaired, rebound or restored, the integrity of the original structures is permanently destroyed. A sad example of this in the Toppan Library is a book from 1511, the *Passion of Christ*. Printed in Nuremberg and illustrated by Albrecht Dürer, it was completely cut-up and cut-down in 1905 (as a gift to the man who later donated it). The woodcuts were matted onto bright white paper and the pages resewn into a modern cover with glaringly bright marbled endpapers. When old endpapers are replaced critical provenance information is lost, such as written notations and dates, signatures and bookplates of early owners. By the fifteenth and sixteenth centuries bookplates with woodcut designs were in use, some even designed by Dürer.[11] Moreover, when a spine is resewn and 'rebacked', early decoration or lettering is lost, as well as the sewing construction, which can be time- and place-specific.[12] Mirjam Foot has observed that even 'well-meaning attempts at replacing binding structures have destroyed evidence that would have been of great value to the binding historian'.[13]

Geographical aspects

Of the Toppan Library's eighty-eight pre-1550 books, two were written or printed in England;[14] two in the Netherlands (exact provenance unknown); four in Spain;[15] six in Germany;[16] six in Switzerland;[17] thirteen in France;[18] and fifty-five in Italy. Of the latter, the majority, thirty-nine, were printed in Venice, almost half by the influential Aldine Press of Aldus Manutius and family.[19] However, it is important to remember that for this period, unless there is some provenance evidence, one cannot presume that the place a book was written or printed is the place where it was bound.

An extensive network of international printers, publishers, merchant financiers and booksellers was active at this time. Florence Edler de Roover describes some books printed in Venice and sent at once on Medici ships to Flanders and London.[20] Thus, if a Venetian book was sent unbound to London for sale, it would probably be bound there in an English style, not an Italian one.[21] Besides what might be considered national styles (bearing in mind, of course, that borders were different then), regional affinities were also strong. E.P. Goldschmidt has said that southern England, Burgundy, the Netherlands and the Rhineland of modern Germany were a more cohesive unit in terms of trading and bookbinding similarities, whereas 'Germanic' styles encompassed southern and eastern Germany, Austria, Hungary and Bohemia (now in the Czech Republic).[22]

What attributes signal that the bindings are from the fifteenth and sixteenth centuries?

It should be noted that this discussion is based on first-hand observations and therefore will not include many characteristic types of book from this time of which the Toppan Library has no examples: girdle books; chained books; chemises; embroidered covers; cut-leather (also called *Lederschnitt*, *cuir-ciselé*, or Jewish binding); deluxe books custom-bound and stamped with the crests, names or mottoes of Renaissance collectors such as François Ier and Jean Grolier. Nor are any of the sample's bindings stamped with the name, initials or monograms of specific monastic or secular binders or workshops.[23] Without such identification, the process of determining whether or not a binding is contemporary becomes more difficult, meaning that one must look at multiple physical clues, including covering materials, structure, decoration and condition.

Covering materials[24]

The books usually have just one type of material covering them, or they are 'quarter-bound' with a different material on just the spine. In the fifteenth century Italian and Spanish books used sheep and also brown or dark red goatskin, whereas Northern European bindings tended to be brown calf or pigskin (though sheep and deer continued there to some degree from the earlier medieval period).[25] In the early sixteenth century goat was popular in France, though it was rarely used before the seventeenth century in England.

Calfskin leather, used for binding from *c.*1450, is the most represented material in both fifteenth- and sixteenth-century Toppan Library books. Its smooth surface (often polished) shows little grain and was tanned in shades from light to dark brown. Two of the examples (Seneca, *Tragoediae* (1517) and Iamblichus, *De Mysteriis Aegyptiorum* (1516), both Aldines from Venice) have paper pages inside. The calf is over pasteboards comprised of pasted layers of either plain paper or waste from manuscripts and printed books. Used in fine Italian bindings from the late fifteenth century, pasteboards were used much earlier in the Islamic world.[26] To produce a sturdier binding, especially when needed to keep parchment or vellum pages flat, calf was stretched over oak or beech wood covers. Since parchment pages were used longer in northern Europe than in Spain or Italy, the use of wooden boards continued longer in the north. The examples in this category comprise a Flemish manuscript (a fifteenth-century Book of Hours); two books printed in Paris, one by Jodocus Badius (Guillaume Budé, *Epistolae* (1520)), the other by Thielman Kerver (a Book of Hours (1500)); and a book (Astesanus de Ast, *Summa de Casibus Conscientiae* (1482)) printed by Anton Koberger in Nuremberg.

Alum-tawed pigskin over wooden boards remained popular in Germany, as evidenced on another Koberger book in the library (Alexander de Hales, *Summa Universae Theologiae* (1481)) as well as the smaller example previously mentioned as printed in Cologne in 1538 with a binding date displayed as 1550 (Figure 1.1). Pigskin can be a light cream to yellow colour; under a loupe, one can sometimes see tiny dots of bristle follicles arranged in threes.[27]

Vellum, the skin of a young animal (traditionally calf, but also kid or lamb), was treated with lime or alum rather than soaked in tannic acid like leather, giving it an ivory or yellow colour. Polishing with pumice produced a lustrous surface, but one that tends to have brown patches of stains from dirty hands over the years. Used from early medieval times, it was cheaper than tanned leather and was sometimes sold on a book as a temporary binding.[28] Though not present on any of the Toppan Library's fifteenth-century books, it is the second most represented material on the 1501–1550 books. One from Basel is in limp vellum; the other four are vellum over pulpboard (a sheet made from pulped paper) and include one from Venice (Seraphino Ciminelli, *Opera*, printed by M. Sessa (*c*.1526)), one from Paris (Strozzi, *Poetae Pater et Filius*, printed by Simon de Colines (1530)), and one from Spain (a little vellum palimpsest from 'Senora de San Martins' (*c*.1530)).

Sheepskin parchment over pasteboards, also untanned, looks different from the finer quality vellum. One Toppan Library example is a school grammar book (1523), which might explain its plainness; it lacks even the vellum spine of the other example, a classical work about Diomedes also printed in Venice (1522). Both have a soft matt surface on one side and are a grayish-white colour (probably from dirt being absorbed into the nap).[29]

Sheepskin leather over pulpboards covers one book from Venice (Jacobus Panis, *Opus in Expositione Psalmi*, printed by Aurelius Pincius (1535)) and another (a three-volume set) from Lyons (Plato, *Operum a Marsilio Ficino Tralatorum*, printed by Jean de Tournes (1550)). Whether tanned or untanned, sheep is the cheapest animal binding because it is so soft and porous (from the fatty cells needed for the wool) that it easily erodes and peels, as on all these examples.

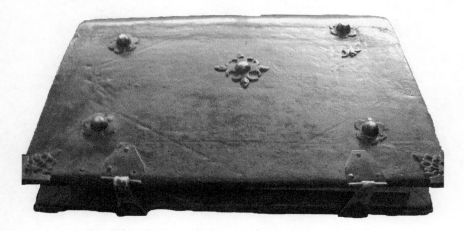

Figure 1.2 Large Spanish choir book from 1504,
over manuscript pages of parchment.
Cowhide over wooden boards with raised metal bosses, corner protectors,
and clasps. Clusters of bookworm holes and simple linear pattern from a
fillet tool. (52 cm × 35 cm × 10 cm).
Toppan Rare Books Library, American Heritage Center, University of
Wyoming, Laramie.

Goatskin, called 'Moroccan leather' if it was imported from the Islamic
world, has a thicker and more richly textured look than other skins
(because it is often hand-boarded to bring up the grain).[30] A strong but
supple material, it can be dyed different colours, but the single example
here (Marulus, *De Institutione Bene Beateq[ue] viuendi institutione*, printed
by Eucharius Cervicornus in Cologne (1530)) is deep brown and is over
pasteboards.

Uncovered pulpboard is at the cheapest end of all covering materials.[31]
The one example (Juan Luis Vives, *Libro Llamado Instrucion de la Muger
Christiana* (1539)) was printed by George Coci in Zaragoza in Spain. Paper
and paper products were produced earlier in Spain than elsewhere in Europe
because of the Islamic papermaking mills there. Finally, thick cowhide
(leather from an adult bovine) is the material over wood on the two very
large Spanish choir books of the early sixteenth century, one from Burgos,
the other unknown (see Figure 1.2).

Structural aspects

Metal 'furnishings' or 'fittings' include raised bosses or flat plates in the
centre and corners, which protected the books in the flat-lying position

Figure 1.3   Printed Book of Hours in Latin by Thielman Kerver
(Paris, 1500).
Calf over wooden boards with broken clasps. Both stamped and roll-tooled designs in blind. The bottom of the lower cover (as well as some of the paper pages inside) shows black charring from an encounter with fire at some point. (17½ cm × 11½ cm × 2 cm).
Lewis Einstein Collection ND 3363 KK4x C3.
Toppan Rare Books Library, American Heritage Center, University of Wyoming, Laramie.

of the time (on desks and in chests) or positioned face-out (on lecterns or shelves).[32] Metal clasps would ensure that a book stayed closed and, along with wooden boards, kept parchment or vellum pages from warping (Figure 1.2). As books became smaller and lighter in the sixteenth century ties of leather or alum-tawed skin replaced metal clasps, although books with paper pages started to dispense with both.[33] With the sixteenth-century increase in new book production there was much reuse of cut-up fifteenth- or sixteenth-century parchment, vellum or paper pages of writing for both the outside of bindings and inside as endpapers or spinal support strips.[34]

Decoration

Some covers are completely plain (such as Martin Luther's *Hauszpostillen*, printed in Nuremberg in 1545).[35] Others have simple linear patterns from a rolling fillet tool (Figure 1.2). For a more ornate effect, small hand-stamp tools produced individual designs, often floral, animal or geometric (Figure 1.1), whereas roll tools, an inch or so wide, covered areas with repeated textural-looking patterns (sometimes with tiny portraits, as in Figure 1.3).[36] The time-saving 'panel stamp' was a large intaglio block

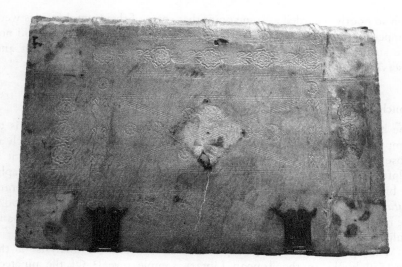

Figure 1.4   Alexander de Hales, *Summa Universae Theologiae*
(Nuremberg, 1481).
Printed by the famous German publisher Anton Koberger, pigskin over
wooden boards with clasps. Fillet and stamped designs in blind. The 'ghost'
shapes on the front and back are from where the metal center bosses and
corner plates were removed by someone in the past. (42 cm × 29 cm × 9 cm)
William M. Fitzhugh, Jr. Collection f093 In2 1481 N932 Ka.
Toppan Rare Books Library, American Heritage Center, University of
Wyoming, Laramie.

usually with a pictorial design for the central area, stamped in with a
press.[37] Motifs were both religious and secular. All the above tools could
be combined to produce three types of designs: ink-stamped, using black or
red for definition; blind-stamped, with designs impressed into damp leather
without gold or ink; and gilt-stamped, from heated tools over gold leaf.[38]
Another decorative technique, gauffering (that is, impressing a geometric
pattern into gilt page edges) started on the Iberian peninsula in the fifteenth
century and became popular elsewhere in the sixteenth century. The Toppan
Library has one example from this time period: a three-volume set of Plato
printed in Lyons in 1550.[39]

Condition

Most of the books are not in the best condition. Clusters of bookworm
holes are fairly common in sixteenth- and early seventeenth-century books
(Figure 1.2). For whatever reason, these particular volumes were either
completely, or mostly, left alone to age naturally, or they might even have

been so poorly regarded at some point that some of their metal fittings were stripped off for reuse elsewhere (Figure 1.4). While most people would not give such humble-looking books a second look, they are significant and deserve attention because they represent 'real' contemporary bindings.[40]

Conclusion

The best way to recognise fifteenth- and sixteenth-century bindings is to compare bindings visually in hand and look for physical attributes such as those mentioned above. In addition to working with original books, it is helpful to read as many reference sources as possible and study photographs of bindings in various collections, such as those in the British Library *Database of Book Bindings*.[41] It is also instructive to look at how books are represented in Gothic and Renaissance book illustrations, paintings and sculptures.[42]

What percentage of contemporary bindings did the analysis of the pre-1550 books in the Toppan Library sample reveal? Of the nineteen manuscripts and incunabula from the fifteenth century, only five bindings are contemporary (26 per cent of the total). Of the sixty-nine manuscripts and printed books from 1501–1550, only eighteen are contemporary (also 26 per cent). Thus, out of a total of eighty-eight books, only twenty-three are still in their Gothic or Renaissance bindings: four of the nine manuscripts; four of the thirteen incunabula; and fifteen of the sixty-six other printed books (including only three of the sixteen Aldines). The ratio is therefore one-quarter contemporary (26 per cent) to three-quarters (74 per cent) rebound or restored.

However, the latter group shows an interesting bell-shaped curve: nine books look as if they were altered in the seventeenth century, and another nine in the twentieth century. Combining the twenty from the eighteenth century and the twenty-seven from the nineteenth century results in forty-seven (72 per cent) for that two-century period. For the Toppan Library books this was apparently the most active period for rebinding and restoration. This high percentage of binding alteration may well be representative of a similar situation in other rare book libraries (informal discussions with other librarians suggest that it probably is). If so, it reflects an unfortunate situation in which people now and in the future will have only a partial experience of the personal connection one achieves by seeing and holding the very same books that people of the past held in their hands.

It is this rare book curator's belief that it is perfectly acceptable for Gothic and Renaissance books in their contemporary bindings to look old and worn. There is nothing wrong with that because such an external appearance is the intrinsic proof of their great age, which we should respect. These books are historic artefacts that were read over and over, carried or transported long distances on carts and ships, and miraculously survived wars, natural disasters, poor storage conditions and other forms of mistreatment for hundreds of years. As John Carter has said: '[C]urrent convention excuses defects in a copy which can truthfully be described as entirely untouched much more readily than it finds merits in one which has been furbished into brightness.'[43]

Yet, while many of the Toppan Library's books show every sign of consumption, the books themselves were not consumed and are still in existence. While rebinding or restoring old books may not be desirable from an historical point of view, one must nevertheless admit that such changes have probably kept many books from being thrown away. Binders of all periods, therefore, have worked in various ways to package books both for presentation and for preservation.

2

Guidelines for Consumption:

Scribal Ruling Patterns
and Designing the *Mise-en page*
in Later Medieval England[1]

Matti Peikola

1. Introduction

Layout, or *mise-en-page*, forms a symbiotic relationship with the communicative purpose of a text, establishing a direct link between producers and consumers of books. When medieval professional scribes set themselves the task of copying a text they had to plan, among other things, how to rule the manuscript page. In addition to the choice of the implements and technique to be used, this involved a decision about the number, relative location and extension of the parallel and intersecting lines that were to be ruled on the page. This decision concerning the ruling pattern was by no means an insignificant one. By ruling the page in a certain way scribes laid the foundation for the design of the *mise-en-page* and thereby inevitably came to take a stand on what the manuscript and its texts sought to communicate. In this chapter I propose that a close study of the ruling patterns adopted by later medieval English scribes will increase our understanding of scribal presentation strategies intended for different contexts of consumption.

Continental codicologists such as Leon Gilissén, Albert Derolez and Denis Muzerelle have emphasised the potential of the study of ruling for establishing production relationships between manuscripts.[2] While important pioneering work on the methodology of studying ruling patterns has been conducted, especially by Derolez and Muzerelle, the research potential of this codicological feature remains largely underutilised. As Derolez observes, 'ruling patterns ... deserve much more study before satisfactory data can be given about the chronological and geographical scope of their use and distribution'.[3]

My main objective here is a methodological one: to examine the grounds on which a scribe opted for a specific ruling pattern when preparing a manuscript for copying. If evidence from ruling patterns is to be used in establishing relationships between manuscripts, including, for example, shared modes of transmission or intended consumption, it is crucial to explore the various situational constraints in operation in the copying process that may have induced the scribe—consciously or unconsciously—to choose a specific pattern. For this reason, the purpose of ruling in medieval manuscripts is discussed first in general terms (Section 2) before an examination is made of the various constraints that could play a role in scribal design of a specific pattern (Sections 3–7).

The issues are illustrated by examples drawn mainly from later medieval English manuscripts, especially from texts written in Middle English. The focus of the enquiry is on religious prose texts, but there are also brief digressions into other genres. My approach combines qualitative analysis of individual copying situations with quantitative observations resulting from a study of larger sets of manuscript data. The latter have mostly been derived from the consultation of manuscripts *in situ*; to a lesser extent, I have made use of digitised manuscript images available on the Internet and printed catalogues containing codicological descriptions of manuscripts. Of the Internet databases offering high-resolution images, *The Digital Scriptorium* and the *Rylands Medieval Collection* have proved especially useful for the present purpose.[4] The technical description of ruling patterns follows the coding system proposed for this purpose by Muzerelle.[5]

2. Purposes of ruling

The purposes of ruling in medieval manuscript books (codices) may be situated under two broad categories, both of which guide the reading experience: functional and aesthetic.[6] The functional purpose pertains to the practical role played by ruling in directing the placement of written text and elements of decoration on the manuscript page.

This feature is most transparently visible in the lines intended to contain the body text (marked (a) in Figure 2.1). Other elements of ruling that can be associated with a functional purpose include, for example, (b) a single or double horizontal line in the upper margin, intended to carry elements of the running title; (c) a double vertical line in the right- or left-hand margin for cross-reference symbols or markers indicating textual subdivisions; (d) a single or double vertical bounding line on one or both sides of the writing area for separating marginal glosses from the body text; in verse texts a double vertical bounding line on the left-hand side of the text-column often contains the capital letter or *littera notabilior* with which each line begins.[7]

Elements of ruling with a functional purpose may at the same time serve an aesthetic purpose.[8] For example, marginal double lines surrounding the writing area on all four sides make the layout symmetrical and thereby create

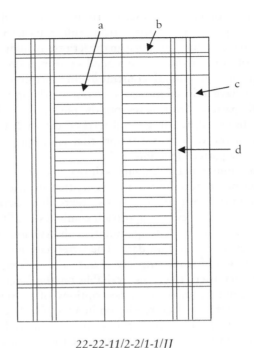

22-22-11/2-2/1-1/JJ
Figure 2.1   Elements of ruling associated with a functional purpose.

a certain aesthetic effect in addition to their possible functional purpose. When elements of ruling originally associated with a functional purpose are used in the absence of the corresponding textual or decorative element they may be viewed as purely aesthetic. This is the case, for example, when the ruling pattern includes a double horizontal line in the lower margin, but catchwords are not placed within it.[9] Not all elements of ruling, however, seem to have served a functional purpose even in the first place. This applies, for example, to double or triple horizontal through-lines at the midpoint of the page (see Section 7).

3. The scribe and the exemplar: a working hypothesis

In philological studies of manuscript transmission the nature of the immediate exemplar and the scribe's way of responding to it are key issues to be considered in accounting for the presence or absence of particular linguistic or textual forms in the copy under scrutiny. Although copying the verbal text itself constitutes the main point of contact between the scribe and the exemplar, non-verbal design features of the exemplar, such as ruling, inevitably also invite scribal attention and response. For the vast majority of medieval manuscripts the influence of the exemplar on the choice of ruling pattern cannot be directly scrutinised, let alone positively determined, as the immediate exemplar has not been identified; it is in fact extremely unlikely that it has even survived down to our time. Based on the economics of professional scribal work it is nonetheless possible to propose some general guidelines as to the direction of influence exerted by the exemplar in the design of ruling.

Evidence as to the recompense later medieval professional scribes received for their work suggests that they expected to be paid not by the amount of time spent on the copying, but by the number of quires, leaves or lines copied.[10] As a general working hypothesis, it therefore seems plausible to assume that unless there were specific situational constraints inducing them to do so, scribes would normally have been unlikely to adopt a more complex and time-consuming ruling pattern than that contained in the exemplar they were copying. Instead, they would under normal circumstances either reproduce the ruling pattern of the exemplar or simplify it by opting for a pattern that was less laborious to execute. Since the pattern would have to be ruled on every page, the cumulative difference in the amount of time spent on simple vs. complex patterns for the whole manuscript could have been a substantial one.

Supporting evidence for this working hypothesis may be found in, for example, the manuscript tradition of Gower's *Confessio Amantis*. In its early manuscripts, copied by professional London scribes in the first quarter of the fifteenth century, the *Confessio* is almost invariably presented with an elaborate Latin marginal apparatus consisting of glosses, names of *auctoritates* and prose summaries of contents of the English text.[11] As Derek Pearsall has demonstrated, accurate reproduction of the marginal apparatus caused considerable difficulties for scribes; in later manuscripts of the *Confessio* the problem was solved by moving the Latin material into the text column.[12] This change is reflected in the simplification of the ruling patterns of the manuscripts. Early manuscripts of the *Confessio* which preserve the marginal apparatus tend to be ruled in complex patterns, with double vertical bounding lines for the writing area and a single vertical line in the margins (see Figure 2.2).

In later manuscripts no longer furnished with the marginal apparatus the vertical lines in the margins tend to be omitted and the double bounding lines replaced by single ones.[13] When the marginal apparatus was no longer a required element in the presentation of a text it was in the interest of scribal economics not to reproduce the time-consuming elements of ruling intended for them, since they no longer had a functional purpose.

As in the *Confessio Amantis*, so too manuscripts of the Wycliffite Bible furnished with marginal glosses show a combination of double vertical bounding lines and single vertical lines in either or both margins (cf. Figure 2.2). These types of manuscript tend to be early copies of the Later

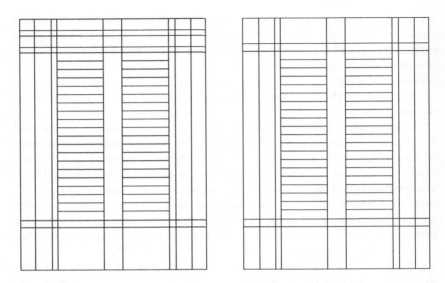

San Marino, CA, The Huntington   Oxford, Bodleian Library,
Library, MS Ellesmere 26.A.17   MS Bodley 902
          12-21-11/2-0/2-2/JJ   *12-21-11/0/2-2/JJ*

Figure 2.2   Ruling patterns in early manuscripts of the *Confessio Amantis*.

Version, stylistically and paleographically dateable to the first or second decade of the fifteenth century.[14] Perhaps partly due to the shortening of the marginal glosses or their relocation into the text column (cf. the *Confessio*), the majority of the ruling patterns found in the manuscripts of the Wycliffite Bible are relatively simple: 69 per cent of those 190 manuscripts whose ruling is currently known to me contain one of the four patterns shown in Figure 2.3 in their single and double column variant, here labelled Types A1/2 to D1/2.[15]

The manuscripts ruled in the patterns illustrated in Figure 2.3 represent both the Earlier and Later Version of the Wycliffite translation, as well as different textual combinations—from complete Bibles to copies of single biblical books. On a very general level, the predominance of such relatively simple patterns in the manuscript tradition would seem to lend support to the working hypothesis that scribes normally tended to reproduce or simplify the ruling of their exemplars instead of making them more complex. It is worth noting, however, that the most complex pattern of the four (Type A), which has a double bounding line both above and below the writing area, is in fact the most frequent one in the material, occurring in 38 per cent of the manuscripts in its single or double column variant. Type C—a simpler frame pattern with single horizontal bounding lines—occurs in 17 per cent of the manuscripts, whereas Type D—an even more basic pattern with a single horizontal bounding line at the top and no lower bounding line—is found in just 7 per cent of the material. Type B, with a double bounding line at the top and a single line below the writing area, has the same frequency as Type D. These findings suggest that, despite the apparent overall tendency towards the simplification of ruling within the textual tradition, scribes only rarely opted for the simplest and least time-consuming pattern (Type D), but preferred the slightly more complex patterns with double (Type A) or single (Type C) horizontal bounding lines. The markedly lower frequency of Types B and D together (14 per cent) in comparison to A and C (55 per cent) may indicate that scribes generally found it aesthetically pleasing to rule the same number of horizontal bounding lines both above and below the writing area.

4. Ruling and standardisation

One way of assessing the role of situational constraints on the scribal design of ruling is to look at the variation in ruling patterns not just within the textual tradition of single works but also between them. Type A occurs frequently in other later medieval English texts as well. It is a common pattern, for example, in the manuscript tradition of the *Pore Caitif*, another popular religious work of the period. My ruling data for this catechetical/devotional compilation are derived from thirty-six manuscripts representing approximately two-thirds of the surviving copies; the data comprise both manuscripts of the complete *Pore Caitif* and miscellanies which include only some of its fourteen constituent tracts.[16] As in the Wycliffite Bible, Type A is by far the most frequent pattern, occurring in twenty copies of the thirty-six surveyed; the corresponding figures for the simpler Types B, C and D are two, six and one respectively.[17] The higher frequency of Type C in comparison to Types B and D corresponds to the findings in the Wycliffite Bible data.

The high frequency of Type A in manuscripts of the Wycliffite Bible and the *Pore Caitif* could be viewed as an analogy of the incipient standardisation of written English in the fifteenth century—a process described by, for example, Jeremy Smith—where scribes replaced local or provincial spellings of their exemplars with 'colourless' forms to enhance the communicative efficiency of texts.[18] Like incipient written standards or focused usages, Type A might be seen as an incipient production standard towards which scribes tended in their ruling of the Wycliffite Bible and the *Pore Caitif*.[19] Even if not present in the immediate exemplar, Type A may have been adopted by scribes because they had commonly come across it in their earlier copying and it provided them with an acceptable, unmarked choice. While pushing the analogy between spelling and ruling further may not be tenable owing to the inherently different (linguistic vs. non-linguistic) nature

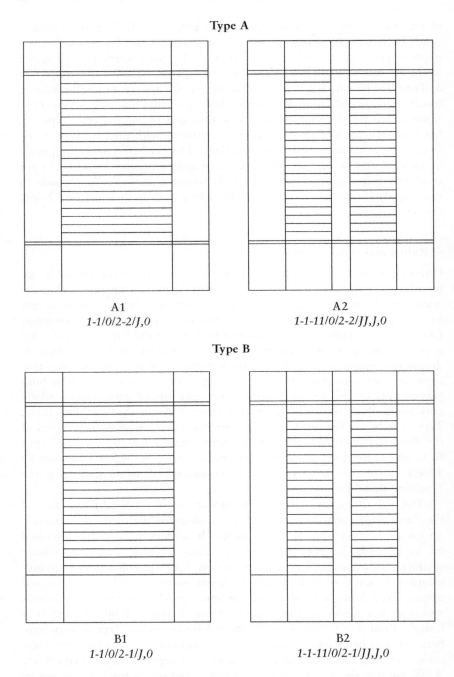

Type A

A1
1-1/0/2-2/J,0

A2
1-1-11/0/2-2/JJ,J,0

Type B

B1
1-1/0/2-1/J,0

B2
1-1-11/0/2-1/JJ,J,0

Figure 2.3   Simple ruling patterns in manuscripts of the Wycliffite Bible.

Type C

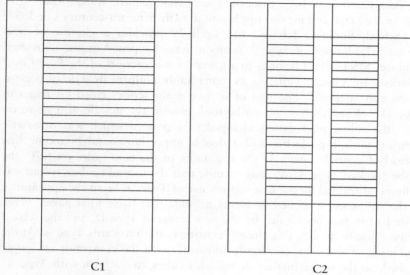

C1
1-1/0/1-1/J,0

C2
1-1-11/0/1-1/JJ,J,0

Type D

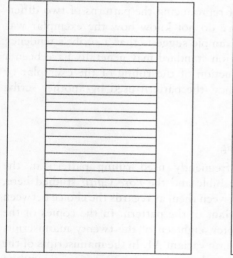

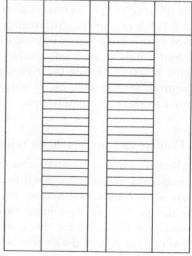

D1
1-1/0/1-0/J,0

D2
1-1-11/0/1-0/JJ,J,0

of these codes, it is worth pointing out that both the Wycliffite Bible and the *Pore Caitif* have been associated with the incipient standardisation of written language and manuscript layout in early fifteenth-century London.[20]

Oxford, Bodleian Library, MS Lyell 29 provides a glimpse of how the scribal adoption of Type A seems to have happened in one individual instance. MS Lyell 29 belongs to a group of manuscripts of the *Pore Caitif* described by Vincent Gillespie as 'remarkably uniform in style of presentation and quality'.[21] The first of its two main scribes ruled his pages in Type D.[22] When the second scribe took over in the middle of a quire on f. 67ᵛ the ruling immediately changed to a pattern which was otherwise identical with Type D but had a double upper horizontal bounding line instead of a single one.[23] At the beginning of the next quire on f. 70ʳ the scribe adopted Type A. We may surmise that the second scribe's ruling was at first constrained by the first scribe's use of Type D. From the appearance of the ruling on ff. 67ᵛ–69ᵛ it seems possible that these final pages of the quire had in fact been ruled by the first scribe in Type D, and the second scribe chose to modify this already existing pattern towards Type A. At the beginning of the next, previously unruled, quire the constraint no longer applied, so the scribe further changed his ruling to conform with Type A.

The example from MS Lyell 29 illustrates a case where two scribes working on the same text in the same manuscript preferred to adopt a different ruling pattern. There appears to be no evidence of a change of a copytext at f. 67ᵛ, so the different patterns adopted by the two scribes cannot be explained simply as instances of reproducing the patterns of two differently ruled exemplars. Although we do not know how the exemplar was ruled in this particular case, the example suggests that a scribe's tendency to conform to an incipient production standard may generally have been a factor working against the reproduction of the ruling of the exemplar or adopting, for the sake of consistency, the pattern used by another scribe earlier in the same manuscript.

5. Double- and single-column ruling

Although Type A is the most frequently used ruling pattern in the manuscripts of both the Wycliffite Bible and the *Pore Caitif* studied here, there is a conspicuous difference between them as regards the choice between the double- and single-column variant of the pattern. In the copies of the *Pore Caitif* inspected for this chapter, eighteen of the twenty manuscripts ruled in Type A have the single-column variant A1. In the manuscripts of the Wycliffite Bible, however, the double-column variant A2 is twice as common as the single-column one (ratio 45:22). The contrast with the *Pore Caitif* is even more striking if we focus on New Testament manuscripts alone rather than including all textual combinations: all twenty-one Wycliffite New Testaments ruled in Type A in the present data adopt A2.[24]

What might explain the difference in the choice of the Type A variant between the Wycliffite New Testaments and the *Pore Caitif*? Let us first consider the role possibly played by the physical dimensions of the manuscripts. Textual and decorative demands placed on the production of a manuscript book by the availability of space are in general also likely to show in ruling. For example, if more text needs to be accommodated on the page than originally planned, the scribe could modify the ruling by increasing the dimensions of the writing area or reducing the space between text lines to fit more of them onto the page.[25] To take another example, the use of decorative ruling elements extending into the margin, such as a triple horizontal through-line ruled across the page, becomes practically impossible when border elements filling up the entire margin space are required.[26]

Readability—the quintessential textual requirement for a book—is also closely associated with spatial concerns. To facilitate the reading process, the adoption of a single-column layout generally tends to become less common when the width of the writing area increases on the manuscript page, especially if there is no corresponding increase in the relative size of the handwriting.[27] In the Wycliffite New Testaments ruled in Type A, the average width of the writing area is approximately 89 mm; in Type A manuscripts of the *Pore Caitif* it is approximately 74 mm.[28] The 15 mm difference between the two texts is a fairly small one and seems insufficient on its own to explain the marked difference between them in the distribution of the single- and double-column variants of Type A.

By way of comparison, among the manuscripts of Nicholas Love's *Mirror*—another popular Middle English religious prose work of the period and also associated with the incipient standardisation of language and layout—it is common to find copies ruled in single columns where the width of the writing area exceeds 120 mm.[29] In fact, of the twenty-one single-column manuscripts of the *Mirror* for which the width of the writing area is currently available to me, there is just a single copy where this measurement is less than the 89 mm average for the twenty-one Wycliffite New Testaments ruled in double columns.[30] The ruling data from a sample of the *Mirror* manuscripts further support the conclusion that the systematic adoption of the double-column pattern A2 in Wycliffite New Testaments does not depend primarily on the size of the writing area.

It would seem that copying a text in double columns was in general more demanding for the scribe; in order to keep the mid-column space blank (for purely aesthetic reasons or in anticipation of a mid-column border), he had to pay careful attention to the justification of the line-endings of the left-hand column while copying a text.[31] The adoption of a single-column layout might therefore sometimes suggest a scribe's lack of expertise in writing in double columns. On encountering an exemplar ruled in double columns, a scribe with little or no previous experience in operating with such texts might have been inclined to copy it in single columns instead.

Even an experienced scribe, however, would under normal circumstances have been unlikely to switch over to the more complex and time-consuming double-column layout if the exemplar was already ruled in single columns.[32] It does not therefore seem tenable to argue that the predominance of single-column ruling in manuscripts of the *Pore Caitif* resulted from the technical inexperience of their scribes in comparison to those of the double-column Wycliffite New Testaments. Such a conclusion is not warranted on the basis of the general appearance of the *Pore Caitif* manuscripts either; on the contrary, Kalpen Trivedi surmises that 'it is quite likely that a number of them were produced in very professional circumstances'.[33]

The markedly different distribution of single- and double-column ruling between the Wycliffite New Testament and the *Pore Caitif* seems most plausibly explained as a feature that was already present in their early exemplars and came to be largely preserved throughout textual transmission by successive scribal copying. Nonetheless, even if the systematic difference in the layout between these texts was already present in their early exemplars, we are still faced with the question as to why precisely these layouts came to be adopted in these texts. An explanation is possibly offered by genre conventions and by the presumed *matere* of the texts. As Malcolm Parkes points out, 'the way in which a text was presented on the page had to be appropriate not only to the needs of ... readers but also to the content of the text'.[34]

The perpetuation of the double-column ruling in Wycliffite New Testaments may therefore indicate that, despite the English language medium of these books, their scribes essentially preferred to present them as biblical texts, imitating the standard double-column layout of Latin Bibles.[35] Some scribes may also have been inclined to preserve the double-column layout because they expected an audience accustomed to using Breviaries. In later medieval England Breviaries were often produced in a double-column layout, and their portable size resembles that of the Wycliffite New Testaments.[36] Many surviving copies of the New Testament are furnished with tables of lessons, which also suggests a liturgical or quasi-liturgical context of consumption for them.[37]

In his discussion of the production features of later medieval manuscript books in the West, Derolez points out that the fifteenth century saw a renewed interest in the use of single-column layouts, possibly brought about by Italian Humanistic imitation of Carolingian *mises-en-page* and the increasing use of cursive scripts as book hands.[38] While these factors must be taken into account in studying fifteenth-century English ruling patterns in general, they seem insufficient to explain the widespread adoption of the single-column layout in the manuscripts of the *Pore Caitif*, which are often written in Textualis (i.e. not in a cursive script) and, at least in terms of their *matere*, can hardly be associated with a Humanistic influence. It is worth noting, nonetheless, that although the majority of the forty-one manuscripts of the *Pore Caitif* for which I currently have information as to their script use Textualis, cursive scripts (types of Anglicana and Secretary) dominate in miscellanies where one or more tracts of the *Pore Caitif* appear in the company of other devotional materials.[39] The distribution of the two types of script, however, does not correlate with the adoption of a single- vs. double-column layout.

Despite the apparent overall increase in the popularity of the single-column layout in the fifteenth century, I would like to argue that in the *Pore Caitif* too the question of the genre of the text should be seen as a probable factor influencing the choice of the ruling pattern. In addition to possible other factors, the adoption of single-column ruling in the *Pore Caitif* is likely to reflect its producers' perception of the text primarily as a representative of catechetical and devotional writing—unlike the Wycliffite New Testaments, ruled in double columns and perceived as belonging to the biblical or liturgical genre. The same argument is applicable to Nicholas Love's *Mirror*, where a majority of the manuscripts have likewise been ruled in single columns, although there the proportion of double-column manuscripts is higher than in the *Pore Caitif* tradition.[40] In the case of the *Mirror*, the contrast with the layout of the Wycliffite New Testaments serves to highlight the promulgation of the work as an anti-Wycliffite surrogate for a biblical text proper, suitable for the consumption of lay readers.[41]

On the whole, Middle English manuscripts falling under the broad generic umbrella of catechetical and devotional writing, including miscellanies of vernacular theology, seem to be very commonly ruled in single-column patterns. While explicating this tendency with systematically collected and comprehensive text-specific data goes beyond the scope of the present chapter, it can be illustrated by means of a cursory survey of the manuscript descriptions available in volumes I–IV of *Medieval Manuscripts in British Libraries*.[42] Among the manuscripts for which information on the number of columns has been provided, there are more than thirty later medieval codices containing catechetical, devotional or other theological material in Middle English (excluding translations of the Bible, biblical commentaries and sermon collections). Only four of them have been ruled in double columns.[43]

The tendency to use a single-column ruling in catechetical and devotional codices is also visible in those manuscripts where individual books of the Wycliffite Bible have been incorporated into a religious miscellany. This is the case, for example, in London, British Library, MS Royal 17.A.xxvi, where the gospel of St John appears in the company of catechetical tracts discussing the rudiments of faith, texts on the visitation of the sick and a non-Wycliffite commentary on the Apocalypse. The manuscript, written by several scribes in Textualis and Anglicana, is ruled in Type D1—a very basic single-column frame pattern without the lower horizontal bounding line.

6. Ruling evidence from miscellanies

As in MS Royal 17.A.xxvi, it would appear that the scribes/compilers of religious miscellanies were often in the habit of regularising the ruling pattern for the whole manuscript to emphasise the textual and thematic unity of the compilation.[44] Imposing a single ruling pattern on all texts of a miscellany irrespective of the possible variations in the ruling of the exemplars used may be compared to the adoption of a single programme of decoration for a manuscript book. In some fifteenth-century miscellanies, such as Oxford, Bodleian Library, MS Douce 322, the unity of the volume is further emphasised by the inclusion of a table of contents.[45] The Douce manuscript is a professionally produced devotional compilation from the third quarter of the fifteenth century which contains both verse and prose items, the latter including one of the constituent tracts of the *Pore Caitif*.[46] Unusually for a devotional miscellany and even more so for a manuscript containing material from the *Pore Caitif*, it is ruled throughout in double columns (Type C2). The physical dimensions of the book, with its writing area of approximately 140 mm in width, may have played a role in the choice of the unusual double-column pattern, although it is worth noting that the manuscript shares production links in the metropolitan area with other anthologies which also contain verse items and include double-column sections, such as Cambridge, Trinity College, MS R.3.21.[47]

Originally commissioned for a lay patron, MS Douce 322 was subsequently bequeathed to a nun in the Dominican priory of Dartford, Kent.[48] Ian Doyle has suggested that it was at Dartford that the manuscript was copied, at the end of the fifteenth century, to form what is now London, British Library, MS Harley 1706 (Section 1).[49] While more modestly decorated than MS Douce 322, the Harley manuscript is sized comparably to it and is ruled—apart from the very first item (Lydgate's poem 'A Calendar')—in double columns, like its exemplar. The faithful treatment of the exemplar, however, did not extend to the exact reproduction of the ruling pattern: instead of the Type C2 used in the Douce manuscript, the pattern adopted in MS Harley 1706 is the more complex A2. The adoption of Type A2 instead of C2 does not seem to have served any particular functional purpose; as suggested earlier, it may reflect scribal adoption of a conventional pattern that at least earlier in the fifteenth century was conceived as an incipient production standard.

Not all professional scribes, however, necessarily sought to impose a single ruling pattern on the texts they copied into a miscellany. Oxford, Bodleian Library, MS Bodley 423 is a composite volume whose Sections B and C also originally belonged together as parts of one and the same devotional anthology.[50] Both sections were copied by the mid/late-fifteenth-century Carthusian scribe Stephen Dodesham.[51] In Section B (ff. 128r–227v) Dodesham uses several different ruling patterns. The first pattern, shown in

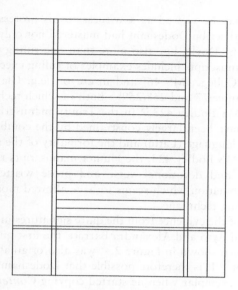

2-21/0/2-2/J
Figure 2.4   Ruling pattern of MS Bodley 423, ff. 128ʳ–132ᵛ.

Figure 2.4, is executed in ink. It is used only in the first quire of Section B on ff. 128ʳ–132ᵛ, an acephalous copy of *Contemplations of the Dread and Love of God*. At a quire boundary on f. 133ʳ the pattern changes to a variant of Type A1, ruled in crayon, where no ruling seems to have been executed for the text lines. There is no change in the text being copied at this point. From f. 133ʳ onwards Dodesham continues using A1 until f. 164ʳ; textually this stint corresponds to the end of *Contemplations of the Dread and Love of God* (ff. 133ʳ–150ʳ), 'an Informacion of Contemplatif lyf and Actyf' (extract from the *Revelations of St Birgitta of Sweden*, ff. 150ʳ–156ᵛ) and two meditations (ff. 156ᵛ–164ʳ).[52] The meditations are followed on ff. 164ʳ–164ᵛ (first leaf of quire 6) by a verse translation of the antiphon *Salve regina*, a short invocation in prose attached to its end and another prayer. No ruling is discernible for these items. About three-quarters of the way down the page on f. 164ᵛ at the beginning of the next item (a unique prose text labelled in the manuscript as 'The mirrour and the mede of sorow and of tribulacion') Dodesham returns to using ink as the ruling medium. He now adopts a variant of Type A1, with all text lines ruled in addition to the bounding lines. This pattern is used until the end of Section B (ff. 164ᵛ–227ᵛ); in addition to 'The mirour', texts ruled in this pattern include a number of devotional items, including several of the constituent tracts of the *Pore Caitif*.[53]

  It is likely that more than one constraint operated in Dodesham's choices concerning ruling in Section B of MS Bodley 423. To begin with, the ruling variation itself may be viewed as a witness to his professional expertise. As an experienced scribe Dodesham had mastered not only more than one script, as shown by Doyle, but also more than one ruling technique.[54] His work in other manuscripts includes examples of ruling executed in ink (e.g. Oxford, Trinity College, MS 46) and in crayon (e.g. Glasgow University Library, MSS Hunter 77 and 258/259)—both of which techniques are used in Section B of MS Bodley 423.[55] In the Trinity manuscript the choice of ink ruling may have been largely constrained by the combination of genre (liturgical texts), language (Latin) and the formality of the script (Textualis Quadrata). Like MS Bodley 423, the Hunter manuscripts represent Middle English didactic and devotional verse and prose written in Anglicana Formata—a combination which seems to have allowed more freedom as to the choice of ruling technique.

On the basis of the evidence from the quire signatures in MS Bodley 423, discussed by John Ayto and Alexandra Barratt, the first quire of Section B, ruled in the pattern shown in Figure 2.4, was also originally the first quire of the manuscript.[56] It is therefore possible that Dodesham reproduced this pattern from the exemplar when he started copying *Contemplations of the Dread and Love of God*. In any event, the adoption of the pattern—either in the exemplar or as an independent choice by Dodesham—may reflect (para)-textual concerns prompted by the presence of notes identifying biblical and other *auctoritates* in the margins of the *Contemplations*. For their accommodation in the *mise-en-page*, a combination of double vertical bounding lines and a single vertical line in the margin would have been a conventional choice for a professional scribe (cf. the use of these elements in the *Confessio Amantis* and the Wycliffite Bible discussed above).

Dodesham's abandoning of the pattern after a single quire may have been constrained by scribal economics. Importantly, the boundary between ff. 132 and 133, where the ruling pattern changes, corresponds to a conspicuous simplification in the overall decoration of the volume—a process which continues in a more subtle and gradual way to the end of Section B.[57] In the words of Ayto and Barratt, 'the decorative scheme became progressively less ambitious in Section B'.[58] Conceivably the less ambitious decorative scheme adopted after the first quire made Dodesham reduce the amount of time to be spent on the execution of ruling in the subsequently copied quires by opting for a simpler pattern.

The next change in the pattern, on f. 164^r, may for its part reflect a generic shift. It seems possible that the variant of Type A1 used on ff. 133^r–164^r for the copying of prose was judged by Dodesham to be inadequate to accommodate stanzaic verse, so he copied the verse items on ff. 164^r–164^v with no visible ruling. His return to Type A1 (the second variant) three-quarters of the way down f. 164^v may similarly have been triggered by the return to prose at this point of the manuscript. The rest of the texts in Section B, ruled in the same pattern, are all in prose.

7. Rare patterns

As shown by the data discussed in this chapter, quantitative information on the occurrence and distribution of ruling patterns will not only help to identify the most conventional or commonly used patterns for different genres and texts but will also enable the spotting of deviations from the usual practice. While the frequency of the ruling patterns and their elements discussed so far varies between individual genres and texts, none of them can be regarded as highly unusual or rare in English manuscripts between the end of the fourteenth and the early sixteenth century. Especially among the manuscripts of the Wycliffite Bible, however, there are some patterns that appear to be quite uncommon in books written in English during this period. I have briefly discussed some such patterns in an earlier study addressing the *mise-en-page* of the Wycliffite Bible more generally, but it is worth returning to the topic here, where the focus is on the contextualisation and interpretation of ruling evidence.[59]

In the Wycliffite Bible material there are a few manuscripts in which the ruling pattern includes a double or triple horizontal through-line across the middle of the page. This feature is found in just seven manuscripts of the total of 190 copies investigated. It occurs in five different patterns, the most common of which, found in three manuscripts, is shown in Figure 2.5.[60] The manuscripts are all parchment codices in the Later Version of the Wycliffite translation, probably dating from the first quarter of the fifteenth century. Of the seven, five are New Testaments, one a gospel book and one a copy of the gospel of St John occurring on its own. The Textualis bookhands, running titles and illuminated or decorated initials found in these codices suggest that they are professional products.

As an element of ruling, the double or triple horizontal through-line in the middle of the page seems to have been relatively common in thirteenth-century Latin Bibles and biblical commentaries.[61] It is also found in thirteenth- and fourteenth-century English and French Psalters, although apparently less frequently than in Bibles.[62] Derolez regards it essentially as a purely decorative High Gothic feature—something that for its part contributed on the manuscript page to 'a complicated grid of horizontal and vertical lines, which evokes the buttresses, flying buttresses and pinnacles of Gothic architecture'.[63] By the early fifteenth century, in any event, its use appears to have become quite rare and may even have been felt to be an archaism.

It is possible that the adoption of the feature in some manuscripts of the Wycliffite Bible may reflect scribal intention to present the English text in an authoritative guise traditionally characteristic of Latin biblical texts. The interpretation is supported by textual evidence from Manchester, Chetham's Library, MS Mun.A.2.160 (*olim* MS 6723). In this early fifteenth-century Wycliffite New Testament, ruled with triple horizontal through-lines (see

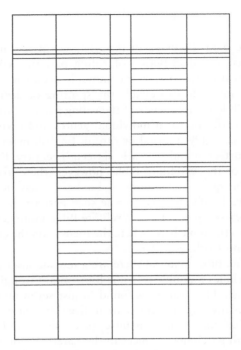

1-1-11/0/3-3-3/JJ

Figure 2.5   Ruling pattern found in three manuscripts of the Wycliffite Bible: Manchester, Chetham's Library, MS Mun.A.2.160; Manchester, John Rylands University Library, MS English 79; Princeton University, MS Scheide 13 (pattern 2).

Figure 2.5), chapters open with their Latin incipit, underlined in red ink; the English translation of the whole chapter then follows the incipit.[64] This feature is unusual in manuscripts of the Wycliffite Bible, where new chapters normally begin directly in English. The presentation strategy adopted by the scribe clearly signals the precedence and authority of Latin over the vernacular. By ruling the triple horizontal through-lines at the midpoint of the page the Chetham scribe may even have wanted to make the text look older than it really was to avoid potential problems resulting from Archbishop Arundel's ban on recent biblical translations into English. Whatever the precise motives in this particular case, it seems likely that the scribe was familiar with earlier Latin texts ruled in triple horizontal through-lines and derived the design of the ruling from their sphere.

8. Conclusion

Relying on data mostly provided by later medieval English texts, this chapter has briefly touched upon various situational constraints that may have influenced the scribe's adoption of a specific ruling pattern when copying a manuscript. Governed by the functional and aesthetic purposes of ruling, such constraints include scribal economics; scribal expertise/professionalism; individual scribal preferences and the influence of texts earlier copied by the scribe; the ruling pattern of the exemplar; incipient standardisation of the *mise-en-page*; the physical size of the manuscript in the making and spatial requirements; the genre/*matere* of the text being copied; the language of the text being copied; the script chosen for the copying; archaising motives.

It is obvious that more than one of these (and possible other) constraints always operated in a given copying situation, sometimes no doubt pulling the scribe in different directions as to which pattern to adopt. Although most decisions concerning ruling were made *in situ* by scribes at the producing end, they essentially anticipate different forms of consumption of the manuscript book, as both text and artefact.

As demonstrated here, understanding the role played by the various constraints on ruling requires the combination of quantitative and qualitative methods. Macro-level data on the distribution and frequency of ruling patterns in different periods, genres and texts forms an interpretive frame within which the micro-level analysis of the unique situational features of any given copying situation takes place. Interpreting the use of ruling patterns in later medieval English manuscripts will help us further understand scribal strategies for the packaging and presentation of texts, thereby revealing both continuities and discontinuities between individual manuscripts and manuscript traditions. I hope to have been able to show that Derolez's important call for the tracing of the chronological and geographical scope of the use and distribution of ruling patterns in medieval manuscripts is highly relevant to the English context of book production and consumption as well.

3

The Order of the Lays in the 'Odd' Machaut Manuscript BnF, fr. 9221 (E)

Kate Maxwell

Ne say comment commencier
Un tres dous lay ...
[I don't know how to begin a sweet lay ...][1]

Guillaume de Machaut's lay output is considerable and spans his entire career. In many ways his lays can be considered to represent the apex, or at least the concretisation, of the genre. Machaut was singled out in the fifteenth century in a well-known anonymous source as 'le grant retthorique de nouvelle fourme, qui commencha toutes tailles nouvelles et les parfais lays d'amours' [the great rhetorician of the new form, who began all new forms, and the perfect lays of love].[2] More recently, David Fallows in *Grove Music Online* states that 'Machaut's lais [*sic*] must be regarded as the highpoint of the form's history'.[3] Certainly, after Machaut, very few examples survive which combine both words and music, and prior to Machaut the form was more fluid, with examples ranging from Marie de France's narrative lays through the troubadours and trouvères to the lays set to music in the *Roman de Fauvel*.[4] Indeed, in the view of at least one of Machaut's readers, the beloved Toute Belle from the *Voir Dit*, 'c'est chose de dit et de chant qui onques plus me plaist' [it is words set to music which I always like most of all].[5] For, while Guillaume de Machaut was a prolific writer, it is his skill with both words and music which still sets him apart from his contemporaries.[6] In terms of the lay, Machaut stands out as the most prolific composer of both words and music in this form.

In this chapter I will analyse the ordering of Guillaume de Machaut's lays as they are presented in one of the six manuscripts which appear to contain his 'complete-works'. That we have so many is testament to Machaut's popularity during his lifetime and thereafter.[7] All but one are elaborate presentation manuscripts, and even the miniatureless sixth, being for the most part a full-scale paper copy of one of the others, is not without visual appeal. Finally, all these manuscripts stand out for the consistency of the works they contain in both content and the order in which the works are presented. It is almost as if the packaging of Machaut's oeuvre was on a similar scale of importance to medieval patrons and readers—and, indeed, perhaps the author—as the works themselves.[8]

Although the detailed relationships between these manuscripts remain essentially unclear, some links can be drawn between them. C has been dated as the earliest of the group, and its narrower range of contents supports this view. A and F–G are closely related in content and layout, but divided in time. Vg and B are so closely related that the latter is for the most part a less elaborate copy of the former. Finally, E stands on its own, the 'odd' manuscript which bears no direct relation to any one of the others but is indirectly related to all them.[9]

E is the largest of the group, and without doubt the manuscript which displays the highest degree of scribal virtuosity. Its large format and careful layout shows that the *mise-en-page* of each work was scrupulously planned. The *Voir Dit*, for example, is laid out in three columns, yet space was left for the forty-six letters to be written in cursive hand across the width of the folio, like 'real' letters, and also for the music to be notated across all three columns, without any 'waste' of text space. (For comparison, the two other 'complete-works' manuscripts to transmit this tale do so in two-column format throughout, without music, and with the letters written as prose within the columns.)[10] Virtually all the works in E were copied into separate gatherings, so that the order in which the whole manuscript was presented could be decided at a later stage, with an index then drawn up.[11] As one of the two posthumous 'complete-works' manuscripts, these differences have meant that E has been subject to charges of 'unauthorised' activities, and of deviating from the 'official' ordering and presentation of Machaut's works. While it is also acknowledged that this does not diminish E's value as a source, it is essential to remember that the homogeneity of the other Machaut sources is unusual for the time. Whatever can be argued for and against the poet-composer's concern for the ordering and presentation of his works, the extent to which E follows or deviates from the format of the other 'complete-works' sources can be fruitfully analysed not as the product of a rebel workshop but as the careful arrangement of later scribal compilers working on an elaborate collection of the works of an illustrious and revered 'poète'.[12]

The position of the lays in the 'complete-works' manuscripts, and within Machaut's works, implies the importance of the genre to both the poet-composer and to the manuscript compilers (and therefore, presumably, also to the audience). In one of Machaut's earlier works, the *Remede de Fortune*, the lay takes pride of place as the first and most accomplished (and also arguably the most important) of the lyric genres to be presented within the tale. In the later *Voir Dit*, a lay forms the central, pivotal point in the story, as a punishment imposed upon the author-narrator figure by the allegorical figure of Hope for his perceived neglect of her in this tale. Likewise, another lay plays a role alongside two of Machaut's other works, the *Jugement dou Roy de Behaigne* and the *Jugement dou Roy de Navarre*, where the poet is commanded to write a lay ('Qui bien aimme') as a penance for the former tale in which the judgment goes in favour of a knight against a lady.[13] In the music sections of the majority of the 'complete-works' manuscripts the lays take their place at the head of the lyrics set to music, just as the genre did in the *Remede de Fortune*.

It is worth dwelling a little on the fact that, although not all the lays are set to music, they still appear as a group in the music section in all the 'complete-works' manuscripts. (Those lays not set to music are marked as such in Tables 1 and 2 below.) This is in contrast with Machaut's other lyric poems not set to music, now known as *La Louange des Dames*, which form a section in their own right and whose position in the manuscripts is less static. This suggests the conferring of equal status, in the minds of the manuscript compilers (and perhaps the author and audience), on all Machaut's lays, whether or not they were set to music. Thus the music, while far from incidental, does not define a lay, even in the music section of the manuscripts. Analysis of the music of the lays neither supports nor distorts the arguments presented here: in terms of the ordering of the lays in the manuscripts, it was the texts which held sway.[14]

There are twenty-five lays in total across the 'complete-works' manuscripts. Twenty-three of them appear in E, and nineteen of these are grouped together in the music section and form the primary subject matter of this article. The others are: the lay from the *Voir Dit*, 'Longuement me sui tenus' (entitled in E 'Le Lay d'Esperance'), which in E is presented within that tale; the lay from the *Remede de Fortune*, 'Qui n'aroit autre deport', likewise presented within the tale; and 'Qui bien aimme', the poet's penance doled out in *Le Jugement dou Roy de Navarre*, which is placed after that poem in E. Finally, E is alone in transmitting the lay 'Malgré Fortune' (presented as a text-only lay, despite being set to music in other sources) immediately following the *Voir Dit*.[15] This lay, on the wiles of Fortune, provides an unusual but fitting commentary to the end of the *Voir Dit*, which sees the beloved Toute Belle (and, though significantly less negatively, the lover) cast in the image of Fortune.[16]

With the lays holding such an important position, both in Machaut's oeuvre and in the 'complete-works' manuscripts, we would expect to find a carefully structured presentation and internal ordering within the section of each manuscript devoted to the genre. While four of the six 'complete-works' manuscripts employ an order for the lays which is virtually consistent and probably chronological, two manuscripts do not fit this pattern. The first of these is the early manuscript C, which for half of its lays does not follow the order which became standard in later manuscripts. The order of the lays in this manuscript has been analysed by Sylvia Huot and, like all Machaut scholars since, I am indebted to her analysis (on which Table 1 is dependent).[17] The second manuscript not to fit the 'standard' pattern is the posthumous E, already 'odd' in terms of its materiality (it is significantly larger than its fellows, as previously mentioned), contents and layout, and for its high number of variant readings. E diverges from the other manuscripts from the second lay onwards, and until now an analysis of its ordering of the lays has not been undertaken.

Table 1. Order of lays in the manuscripts (except E)

C (c.1350)	A, Vg + B (c.1370), F–G (c.1390)
Each individual lay headed by a miniature. Only ms in which lays not at head of music section, though they were possibly intended to complete it.	A + F–G: One miniature for all lays. A: man honouring a lady, implication of offering of works from Prologue— link to author. F–G: Author at lectern writing words to first lay (Vg + B: no miniatures)
1. Loyauté que point ne delay (*inspiratio* from Loyalty) *no music, but staves provided for first stanza	1. Loyauté que point ne delay (service to love)
2. J'aim la flour (*meditatio*)	2. J'aim la flour
3. Pour ce qu'on puist (creative act, image of scroll)	3. Pour ce qu'on puist
4. Aus amans (appeals to audience— lovers) *no music	4. Aus amans *no music
5. Nuls ne doit (poet-protagonist, though this is not highlighted in imagery)	5. Nuls ne droit
6. Par trois raisons (poet-protagonist, again not highlighted in imagery)	6. Par trois raisons
7. Amours doucement (love lay)	7. Amours doucement
8. Amis t'amour (love lay)	8. On parle de richesses *no music
9. Un mortel lay ('Lay mortel') (death of poet-protagonist)	9. Amours se plus *no music

C (*c*.1350)	A, Vg + B (*c*.1370), F–G (*c*.1390)
10. Qui bien aimme ('Lay de plour') Lady mourns death of her lover. Subject matter: discussion between man and woman.	10. Amis t'amour
11. Ne say comment commencier un tresdoulz lay (figures in margins, man and woman)	11. Se quanque Diex *no music
12. Se quanque Diex (figures in margins, man and woman) *no music	12. Un mortel lay ('Lay mortel')
13. Maintes fois (female protagonist addresses audience as to the proper way to love, miniature is male) *no music	13. Maintes fois *no music
14. On parle de richesses (voice changes: clerkly male with long lines, then courtly female with shorter lines. Subject matter: clerk writing, lady in castle. Last appearance of scroll motif in C—a weight restricting the protagonist.) *no music	14. Ne say comment commencier un tresdoulz lay
15. Amours se plus (neutral voice, image of a female figure. Lover-protagonist is erased, just like music in opening lay.) *no music	15. Contre ce dous mois de may
	16. Je ne cesse de prier (entitled in F–G 'Le Lay de la fonteinne')
	17. S'onques doleureusement
	18. Longuement me sui tenus (also in the *Voir Dit*, without music, in A and F–G)
	19. Malgré Fortune (not in Vg/B) entitled 'Le Lay de Plour'
	20. Je ne me say (not in Vg/B) *no music
	21. Pour vivre joliement (not in Vg/B)
	22. Qui bien aimme (not in F–G) ((also) entitled 'Lay de plour'): Lady mourns death of her lover. (After *Navarre* in Vg and B)

Before presenting an analysis of the order of lays in E we should first consider the patterns from which it deviates (see Table 1 above). The early 'complete-works' manuscript C (which, we must remember, was compiled when the poet-composer was around fifty, certainly not young for the time) follows an evidently carefully planned order of both lays and illuminations, with each lay bearing its own miniature (perhaps elevating them to a similar status as the longer works, a status unique to this manuscript). Huot has analysed this programme as being in two sections, the first opening with what she terms an 'extended prologue' of four lays and miniatures depicting the creative act of writing and its performance. The lover-protagonist of the lays, thus established, speaks first as a poet in the fifth and sixth lays and then as a lover in the seventh and eighth. The ninth lay in C, 'Un mortel lay', holds a similar position in both C and E, closing the end of the first section devoted to the genre (as Huot explains in detail, this may indicate a break in C's production precipitated by the death of Bonne de Luxembourg, who was perhaps the manuscript's intended recipient). This lay depicts the death of the poet-protagonist. At this point in C we have therefore come full circle: from poetic inspiration from loyalty to death through *mesdis* (slander).

Following this possible break comes 'Qui bien aimme', in which a female voice mourns her dead lover. The accompanying image of male and female figures in conversation seems to provide a link to the other manuscripts (as yet unmade when C was being compiled) in which this lay is the poet-protagonist's penance at the end of the debate poem *Le Jugement dou Roy de Navarre* for finding against ladies in the *Jugement dou Roy de Behaigne*. In the two following lays the iconography of C extends for the first and only time into the margins of the page. The principal miniature accompanying each lay depicts the object of love, and the poetic voice stands to one side: the 'new', post-death arrangement of lays here seems to focus less on the lover-protagonist than on his (or, indeed, her) audience. In the thirteenth lay, 'Maintes fois', a female voice instructs her audience on the proper way to love. The fourteenth, 'On parle de richesses', is the only lay to change voice within the poem. The male voice speaks in long, grand lines of verse with even syllable counts, whereas the female voice speaks in shorter lines of uneven syllable counts, with their corresponding variation in stress offering more flexibility and fluidity. Here, then, the courtly lady's freedom provides a contrast to the clerkly lover-protagonist. Rather than the scroll shown in the accompanying miniature elevating our male lover to the status of author, he is here bound by it, restricted by its weight and alienated outside the courtly lady's castle and her world. The final lay in C is in a neutral voice, but the accompanying miniature, the last miniature in the manuscript, is of a lady addressing other ladies, encouraging us to read it as female. Thus, at the end of the lays the male author-figure, normally concealed behind his persona of lover-protagonist, is not in evidence. The author is present behind the works in C—it is, after all, a single-author collection—but here he is invisible, speaking only through his creations, themselves brought to us through a series of personae portrayed in both words and image. In C, in the lay section as well as the whole, it is the creation, rather than the creator, which we admire.

In contrast to C, the 'complete-works' manuscripts other than E place more emphasis on the author-creator figure. In the lay sections this is particularly apparent from the accompanying miniatures (when present), the order of the lays (which appears to be broadly chronological) and the exceptional clarity of the music presentation. In A the miniature shows the male lover-protagonist honouring ladies, as the first lay describes. Yet in this manuscript the protagonist is not as subservient as he appears. The manuscript contains an index which, in a rubric which is now well known, claims to reflect the order of works desired by the author himself.[18] In the grand opening miniatures to A, Machaut the author promises Nature that he will write poems in honour of ladies: this miniature represents the fulfilment of that promise. In addition, this miniature introduces all the lays (and thus the music section), even those in a female voice, reminding us that they are the work of a single author. They are his to give.

In F–G the authorial presence in the lays is made even more explicit. In the opening miniature, the only miniature in the music section, there can be no doubt that the figure, seated at a lectern with an open book and a pen, is the author. The coat-of-arms of the newly identified patron is relegated to the background, and the curtain implies that we, the admiring audience, are being offered a privileged glimpse into the author's private sphere through the manuscript transmitting only his works.[19] Add to this the clarity of the musical presentation and the chronological order of the lays, and we can see that this manuscript presents the lays as a lifetime's work to be appreciated.

Vg does not have an opening image in the lays section, although the elaborate initial letter (which occupies a space large enough to contain an image) and the condition of the folio suggest that the lays once began a separate volume.[20] The miniatureless B, whose layout is in many ways virtually identical to that of the elaborate Vg, is missing the folio which would have opened the lays section, implying a similar degradation due to layout or (if it contained basic decoration) perhaps even a misappropriation by an avid collector. In both of these manuscripts the order of the lays is essentially the same as that in A and F–G.

It is against this background, then, that E is considered 'odd'. One important aspect which E shares with the other 'complete-works' manuscripts (with the exception of C), however, is the placement of the lays at the head of the music section, although in E the music section is placed centrally within the manuscripts, framed on either side by narrative dits, rather than at the end of the manuscript (or indeed as a separate volume), as in the other 'complete-works' sources.[21] This leads us to view its opening lay and

Table 2. The order of the lays in E (c.1390).

1. Loyauté que point ne delay	Opening dedication
2. Aus amans (declamation to an audience, masculine) *no music 3. Amours se plus (declamation to an audience, feminine) *no music	masc./fem. pair, audience
4. Se quanque Diex ('le lay du mirouer amoureux', title in E only) (private declamation, feminine) *no music 5. J'aim la flour (private declamation, masculine) *no music	fem./masc. pair, private
6. Nuls ne doit (masculine lament, poet) 7. Amours doucement (masculine lament)	masc. pair, laments
8. Pour ce qu'on puist (masculine poet) 9. Amis t'amour (feminine love)	masc. poet, fem. love

Section 1

10. Un mortel lay ('Lay mortel') (death of protagonist)	Death of poet
11. Ne say comment commencier (masculine lament) 12. Contre ce dous mois de may (Marian lay, entitled in E 'Un Lay de nostre dame')	new beginning masc. lament, Marian consolation
13. S'onques doleureusement (feminine lament) 14. Je ne cesse de prier (entitled in E 'un lay de nostre dame')	fem. lament, Marian consolation
15. Par trois raisons (masculine lament, poet) 16. Pour ce que plus (*unicum*, entitled 'Un Lay de consolation') (masculine praise).	masc., to audience, lament then praise
17. On parle de richesses (clerkly/courtly male/female exchange) 18. Maintes fois (female protagonist addresses audience as to the proper way to love)	courtly, audience present

Section 2

19. En demandant (*unicum*, depicts the death of a 'valiant' and 'hardi' king)	Closing dedication, death

Lays contained elsewhere in E:

Qui bien aimme (entitled 'Le Lay de Plour', after *Le Jugement dou Roy de Navarre*)
Qui n'aroit autre deport (in the *Remede de Fortune*)
Longuement me sui tenus (in the *Voir Dit*)
Malgré Fortune (also entitled 'Le Lay de Plour', after the *Voir Dit*, presented in E without music)

miniature not just in the light of the lays which follow, but also in the light of the music section as a whole, which contains no further miniatures. This opening miniature portrays a group of men singing from or discussing the bound book held by their apparent leader. This reading, this performance, is clearly a group activity in which the participants engage with one another under the guidance of the book, and it is a fitting image for a manuscript, particularly one that contains music. However, there is no author-figure in this image, not even in his guise as lover-protagonist. Unlike the equivalent miniatures in other manuscripts, in this image the author is present, if indeed he is present at all, only through the presence and presentation of the material object of the book.

Certainly, the authorial presence attested by the chronological ordering of the lays in the other manuscripts (apart from C) is not present. I would like to argue here that rather than this order being essentially random, as has been presumed (since the large format and virtuoso *mise-en-page* of E all but rule out the possibility of spacing issues), in fact a careful programme is at work.

Like the other manuscripts, E begins with the lay 'Loyauté', suggesting that its compilers may have been aware of the other programmes. Indeed, the rubric which accompanies this lay reads 'Explicit le premier lay de Machaut' ('here ends Machaut's first lay') (f. 108ᵛ). This lay is a particularly fitting opening to the music portion (or volume) of a manuscript:

> Loyauté,
> Que point ne delay,
> Vuet sans delay,
> Que face un lay;
> Et pour ce l'ay
> Commencié [...] (Lay 1 (E1))

> [Loyalty, who never waits, wants me to write a lay straight away, and so I have begun ...]

Indeed, the poet-persona speaking through the lay dedicates himself to love, with certain death—or at least certain melancholy (often bemoaned as a crueller fate for the courtly lover)—awaiting him at the end of every half stanza should his love (his work) be neglected. At the close of the lay, both his work and life are over: 'Car ma vie et mon lay define' ('for I end my life and my lay'). In E alone does the stark singularity of the poetic voice contrast with the plurality of the miniature: we may choose to read and hear the lays, most of which are monophonic, as the work of an individual, whereas the miniature reminds us of the collective nature of making music and indeed manuscripts. It is arguable here that it is not in fact E which is 'odd', but the other 'complete-works' manuscripts, whose persistent emphasis on the author-figure of Machaut contrasts distinctly with their contemporaries.

The remaining eighteen lays in the music section of E fall into two groups of nine, each group comprising four pairs and a concluding lay, as depicted in Table 2 above. The first pair of the first group continue in the 'public' sphere, since they are both declaimed to an audience, the first from the masculine point of view, the second from the feminine. In the first of these, 'Aus amans', the poetic voice is once again a masculine poet writing a lay in the shadow of death:

> Aus amans pour exemplaire
> Vueil un lay retraire
> De celle qui traire
> Me fait tout contraire
> Par un soustil regart traire
> Qui a li amer m'amort
> Que je ne m'en puis retraire
> Eins m'en lay detraire
> Pour s'amour attraire
> Que me vuet deffaire
> S'autrement ne li puis plaire
> Dont jugies me tieng a mort. (Lay 4 (E2))

> [To lovers, as an example, I wish to write a lay of reproach
> to her who holds me against my will with a wily look that
> commits me to enduring love of her. Rather I grow distracted
> by trying to win her love which seeks to undo me. If I
> otherwise cannot please her I will be condemned to death.]

Like 'Loyauté', this lay ends with a death-bed appeal to the lady, and the repetition of the 'lay/delay' rhyme only serves to accentuate this:

> Receves mon lay ...
> Sachiez que vous estes celle
> Pour qui je muir sans delay. (Lay 4 (E2))

> [Receive my lay ... Be aware that you are she for whom I
> am about to die.]

In contrast, the feminine voice of the third lay, 'Amours se plus', proclaims to her audience her joy: in this manuscript, the first joy that we have seen or heard in a lay.

The next pair move from the public arena into the private chamber, beginning with 'Se quanque Diex', in which a female voice endures the bittersweet nature of being in love yet separated from her lover. This lay is given a title only in this manuscript through the following rubric: 'Explicit le lay du mirouer amoureux Machaut' [Here ends the lay of Machaut's Mirror of Love], f. 110ʳ. Such a title immediately brings to mind the subtitle of that medieval 'best-seller', the *Roman de la Rose*, even if the imagery of the lay itself does not explicitly reference this work.[22] The second lay in this pair, 'J'aim la flour', is a private masculine lament. In the other manuscripts this lament follows 'Loyauté', yet, despite rhymes on '-ay', it does not reuse the imagery of the poet writing his lay. Indeed, its placement in second position in the other manuscripts could be argued as representing the *meditatio* stage of poetic composition, which follows immediately after an *inspiratio* from the allegorical figure 'Loyauté'.[23] Whereas the depiction of poetic creation fits with the author reverence as portrayed to a greater or lesser extent in the other manuscripts, this is not the case in E. By putting in second place a lay which shares the imagery of 'Loyauté', and moving this lay into the private sphere, the author-figure and his process of creation are even further displaced.

This trend continues into the third pair, which are both masculine laments: 'Nuls ne droit' and 'Amours doucement'. The first nine stanzas (of twelve) of 'Nuls ne droit' bemoan the necessity to lament, and in the tenth stanza we find that the speaker in fact rejects poetry: 'Pour ce entrelais/ Chans et lais ...' [Consequently I forsake songs and lays ...]. Of course, this statement is essentially contradictory, since readers and listeners, particularly of a 'complete-works' manuscript, know very well that there is an author present; yet, when taken within the emerging author-effacing context of E, a more literal reading is encouraged. This continues in 'Amours doucement', a lay which Huot has described as 'a pure articulation of love'.[24] Like 'J'aim la flour', this lay plays with concepts of loyalty and death, but avoids any mention of the protagonist's métier, thus estranging itself from the authorial dedication to duty of the opening lay.

However, the author-figure, the first-person poet, can never be far away in the works of Machaut, and the final pair of lays in the first section opens with 'Pour ce qu'on puist'. This lay is headed with the rubric 'Item un autre lay Machaut', and is a lay which Huot describes as depicting the creative act.[25] The claim in the opening stanza that 'Je vueil faire avant me mort/ Un lay dou mal qui me mort' [Before I die, I wish to write a lay on the evil which afflicts me] is accompanied in C by a miniature of a figure writing on a scroll. In all the manuscripts other than E this lay takes its place as part of what Huot terms the 'extended prologue' which establishes Machaut as the poet-composer behind the collection.[26] Nevertheless, by dividing and separating this opening series of lays in the other manuscripts, E displaces as far as is possible the notion of the author. (Once again it can be noted that, while this displacement of the author-figure makes E 'odd' among the Machaut manuscripts, the net result of such comparative effacement is by no means 'odd' for the late fourteenth century.) The partner to 'Pour ce qu'on puist' in E is a relatively uncomplicated lay about love in a feminine voice, 'Amis t'amour'. While one must hesitate to overlook the subtleties in any of Machaut's works, the comparative simplicity of this feminine lay serves to quell, as far as is possible, any authorial curiosity aroused in its predecessor.

At the halfway point in the lay section E continues its efforts to efface the author-figure by, literally, killing him off. The idea of the wronged lover wishing to die from grief is one which occurs frequently in Machaut's lays, yet only in 'Un mortel lay' (entitled 'Le Lay mortel' in A and F–G) is it taken to an extreme, as its opening and closing lines show:

> Un mortel lay vueil commencier
> Et a tous amans annoncier
> Comment Amours me vuet traiter ...
>
> S'en chant en mon jour darrenier
> 'Dame, mort m'ont, sans menacier
> Vostre dous oueil, vostre dangier
> Et vostre amour que chier compere.' (Lay 12 (E10))
>
> [I wish to begin a mortal lay and tell all lovers how love chooses to treat me ...
> ... Yet on my dying day I sing 'Lady, this is no threat. Your sweet gaze, your domination and your dearly bought love have killed me.']

Whereas in C this lay completed the circle from the establishment of the figure of the poet-lover figure practising his art, in E it retains a central position but acquires quite a different function. Following the dismantling of the 'extended prologue' and the consequent attempt to efface the author, the death of the protagonist in E can be taken much more at face value. E is, after all, and in contrast to C, a posthumous collection which belonged to a living patron, Jean, duc de Berry, bibliophile and son of the French king.[27] In addition, and perhaps more significantly, this break in the lay section is reminiscent of the (purported) death of Guillaume de Lorris at the end of the first section of the *Roman de la Rose*, whereupon the narrative is taken up by Jean de Meun.[28] As Huot has noted, the death of the author 'reflects the lyric identification of singer and song, extended to the lyrical writer and his corpus'.[29] Unlike in C, where the break in the lay section may indicate the death of the manuscript's intended recipient, here in the posthumous manuscript E (which has thus far sought to eliminate the author-figure as far as possible) the 'death' is much more along the lines of the equivalent event in the *Rose*. Although the authorial change in the *Rose* could be fictitious, the death of Machaut in 1377, some ten to fifteen years prior to the compilation of E, was not. Thus E seems to have quite a different agenda from its fellow 'complete-works' sources.

The opening lay to the second group clearly suggests new beginnings:

> Ne say comment commencier
> Un tres dous lay
> Pour bon Amour mercier
> De l'espoir qu'ay
> Et pour ma dame au corps gay
> Glorefier
> Et loer
> Car trop po scay
> Pour telle ouevre edifier. (Lay 14 (E11))

> [I don't know how to begin a sweet lay to thank kind Love
> for the hope I have and to glorify and praise my blithe lady,
> for I know too little to construct such a work.]

Even though there is no new author, unlike in the *Rose*, the author-figure appears to have taken a new direction: instead of melancholy, we have joy in hope. Indeed, this lay promises in its closing lines that this is now the author-figure's métier:

> Or li vueille Amours noncier
> Que porteray
> Dedens mon cuer sans trichier
> Et serviray
> Sa douce ymage et l'aray
> Plus que moy chier
> Et tant com durer porray
> Ne feray autre mestier. (Lay 14 (E11))

> [Now I wish to proclaim the love that I will carry faithfully
> in my heart, and serve the sweet image which I will cherish
> more than myself. And for as long as I can survive, this will
> remain my work.]

Like the first group of lays in E, this second group proceeds in pairs. This opening lay, then, is answered by the first of the Marian lays in the manuscript, 'Contre ce dous moi de mai' (entitled in E 'Un lai de nostre dame'). Instead of praising an earthly lady, the poet-composer in his new guise praises the Virgin Mary, 'Dame, digne d'estre honnouree' ['Lady, worthy of being honoured'] [Lay 15 (E12)]. Although this lay ends on a note of death, it speaks of the hope of heavenly pity in response to faithful service to the mother of God. We have come a long way from the languid self-pity of 'Un lai mortel'.

The second pair of lays in the second section reflects the previous pair, with the essential difference that this time it is a feminine poet who is answered by a Marian lay (again, in E the Marian lay is highlighted by the title 'Un lay de nostre dame'; in F–G this lay is entitled 'Le Lay de la fonteinne'). Indeed, these two lays, 'S'onques dolereusement' and 'Je ne cesse de prier', can be read together as a contrast between Fortune and the Virgin. Whereas the feminine poet in 'S'onques dolereusement' takes comfort from Fortune in Hope, the (presumably masculine) poet in 'Je ne cesse de prier' begins as if praising an earthly lady, only revealing in the third stanza the true object of his devotion and ensuing joy. The reader (or listener) to both of these pairs of lays does not have to dwell very long to understand that the Virgin brings comfort like no other lady.

The third pair of lays in the second section contrasts two facets of a masculine poet speaking to an audience: lamentation ('Par trois raisons') and praise ('Pour ce que plus'). Whereas 'Par trois raisons' can be found in all the 'complete-works' manuscripts, 'Pour ce que plus' is the first of the two *unica* lays in E.[30] While 'Par trois raisons' sees the author-figure wavering in his promise of praise, the effect is immediately negated by 'Pour ce que plus', which is entitled 'Un lay de consolation'. This tension continues in the final pair of lays in E, which, as we have seen, also occur together in the same penultimate position in C: 'On parle de richesses', with its clerkly/ courtly contrast, and the feminine, didactic 'Maintes fois'. Therefore, the second group of lays moves from love and comfort in Marian devotion to a lamenting poet, before obliterating any remaining trace of the author-figure by turning to the feminine, courtly voice, as in C.

The concluding lay to this section is the *unicum* 'En demandant'. Like 'Un mortel lay', which ended the first section, its voice is that of a poet writing, and the opening stanza tells of grief and sorrow such as have never before been written about:

> En demandant
> Et lamentant
> Vueil commencier un lay
> Triste et dolent
> Chanter d'un chant
> Par droit tel le feray
> Quar je ne scay
> Escript en vray
> Qu'onques cuers eüst tant
> De grief esmay
> Si comme j'ay
> Ne de dueil si pesant ... (Lay 24 (E19))

[Entreating and lamenting I wish to begin a sad and
sorrowful lay, to sing a fitting song, such that truly to
my knowledge its match has not been written, for no
heart has ever had as much grief as I have, nor such heavy
sorrow ...]

The insistence on the novelty of the writing of such sorrow elevates the
grief of this lay above that of 'Un mortel lay': the mourning here is of
greater magnitude even than that for the author-figure. In the second stanza
we learn that the grief is caused by the death of 'le roi de fierte/Fleur de
chrestiente' ['the proud king, flower of Christianity']. He is described in
the stanzas which follow as 'Asseüre et hardi' ['assured and brave'], 'Lion
de nobilite' ['lion of nobility'], 'Sanglier hardi et creste' ['brave and proud
warrior' (signified by a tufted or razorback boar in heraldry)], and as the 'roy
de droiture' ['king of righteousness'] who is imbued with 'vaillance hardi'
['courageous valour']. These descriptors could indicate a reference to that
great epitome of chivalry, Jean de Luxembourg, who was Machaut's early
patron. Jean was the father of the likely recipient of C, Bonne de Luxembourg, and grandfather of Jean de Berry, the known owner of manuscript
E. If this is a lay in Jean's honour, then this would be the only mention in
Machaut's works of the death of the king at the disastrous battle of Crécy in
1346. Perhaps towards the end of Machaut's life, after the death of Bonne's
husband king Jean II of France in 1364 and three years later the definitive
return to France from England of the hostages, including his son Jean de
Berry, the time was finally right to honour the chivalric king whose family
could hope for brighter times ahead. Indeed, this lay closes with expressions
of service, of the ageing of the poet and of dedication to God:

Me fault et convient devourer ...
Mon hault chanter
Mettre en plourer
Mon bel parler
Et mon rimer
Laissier et tourner a rebours ...

Par naturel port
Sui si fort
Que je port
Cheveux gris
Et Fortune a tort
Me remort
Quar l'un mort
L'autre pris.

Voy trebuchant
Le [sic] gent ...

Les biens que j'ay
Ou que j'aray
Fortune, or as fait tant
Que tout lairay
Et chanteray
'Joie, a Dieu te commant'. (Lay 24 (E19))

[I must turn my high song to tears, desist from fine speech
and abandon my muse ...
Nature wills it that I am strong enough to have lived to turn
grey. And Fortune is wrong to torment me as one dies, the
other is taken captive, I see sturdy people stumbling ...
Fortune, you have ensured that I will renounce all the gifts
that I have or ever will have and sing 'Joy, I bid you Adieu'.]

In this ending, our author-figure is abandoned again and renounces his
gifts, this time in favour of his grief for, and service to, the house of France.
Certainly, a more fitting conclusion of the lays in this manuscript cannot
easily be imagined.

It has been my intention in this analysis to demonstrate the considerable
internal unity of the lays of E, and to go some way towards lifting the weight
of 'oddness' from this manuscript. The complex relations between E and
the other 'complete-works' manuscripts, together with its high number of
variants, mean that it remains the son of many fathers, *pour ainsi dire*, yet
it is far from being compiled without careful consideration of its contents. It
thus stands out from its fellows through the reasoning behind its structure as
much as through the structure itself. I have shown here how, like C, E can be
linked to the house of France, having been designed, to paraphrase Deborah
McGrady, to attract the patron's gaze, albeit at the cost of the author.[31] The
presentation of the lays in this manuscript seems to be a concerted attempt
to subdue the author-figure in favour of the patron, as far as is possible in
a single-author 'complete-works' manuscript. For E is first and foremost
a presentation manuscript, with great importance throughout placed on
the visual beauty of its contents, even at what might be considered as the
cost of accuracy and authority. However, if we leave these two supremely
problematical concepts to one side, as it seems did E's compilers, then it can
take its place alongside the other 'complete-works' Machaut manuscripts,
no longer the unreliable 'odd one out', but a carefully presented and finely
constructed work of art.

4

Picturing the King
or Picturing the Saint

Two Miniature Programmes
for John Lydgate's
Lives of Saints Edmund and Fremund[1]

Sonja Drimmer

The efficacy of a hagiography lies in its ability to move devotees to venerate and emulate its protagonist.[2] This end is achieved through radically different pictorial means in two manuscripts of John Lydgate's *Lives of Saints Edmund and Fremund*, a double hagiography based on two royal saints.[3] The *c*.1434–39 dedication manuscript (London, British Library MS Harley 2278), a gift to King Henry VI containing a cycle of 120 miniatures, has been described as 'one of the most remarkable surviving illustrated manuscripts of Middle English verse in the fifteenth century'.[4] In contrast, the producers of a copy made in the 1460s for an East Anglian family (London, British Library MS Yates Thompson 47)[5] have been compared unfavourably with their predecessors, referred to as 'cruder and brash in their drawing and use of colour',[6] having created fifty-three images whose backgrounds are 'rendered with relentless dullness'.[7] Yet the close associations between the two copies—and the ease with which illuminators copied from models— indicate that, far from originating in technical inequality, their differences in execution are due to the circumstances of their commissions. The aim of this essay is to demonstrate how two different pictorial cycles for the same poem could radically alter audiences' receptions and experiences of the subject of that same poem.

It is now widely accepted that the notion of an ideal text is inapplicable to the medieval and early modern eras; rather, the text was an embodied thing, bearing the marks of its moment(s) of (re)-inscription. In essence, each time a text was composed, it was 'packaged' in its unique physical form and temporal circumstance. The pictorial content that accompanies much of later medieval literature can be understood as a further (and further-removed) layer of this packaging, not in subservience to the text, but rather as an equally powerful partner in shaping the reception of a story or idea. What we find in the two manuscripts addressed in this essay is evidence for precisely how the same narrative took on new meanings and orchestrated different experiences by dint of its distinct visual packages.

In particular, I will show how the later copy of Lydgate's *Lives* presents motivated and strategic alterations to an earlier, equally motivated illustrative cycle for the poem.[8] For an abbey whose right to land and self-rule hung in the balance, sumptuous manuscripts recounting the *Life* of its patron saint were a crucial tool in fortifying his cult as a bulwark against royal encroachment and local resentment.[9] Of course, a project with appeal to both royal and local audiences demanded sensitivity to the individuality of these audiences: an exact replica of a manuscript originally designed for a specific royal recipient could not be counted on to rouse the desired response from a different, non-royal audience. Charged with making the subject of Lydgate's hagiography compelling to distinct audiences, the illuminators of this poem confronted a crucial question of packaging centred on the saintly and royal identity of its main protagonist: to picture the king or to picture the saint? In answering this question, the illuminators modelled their manuscripts on two very different paradigms, each suggested by the poem itself: the prince's mirror, and the saint's relic.

Lydgate's *Lives of Saints Edmund and Fremund*: the poem and its commission[10]

In 1433 Abbot William Curteys commissioned John Lydgate, a monk of the Abbey of Bury St Edmunds,[11] to write an English version of the *Life* of their patron saint as a gift to Henry VI for his visit from Christmas of that year to Easter 1434.[12] Lydgate records this commission in the prologue to the poem, writing that:

> Thabbot William, his humble chapeleyn,
> Gaf me in charge to do myn attendance
> The noble story to translate in substaunce
> Out of the latyn aftir my kunnyng,
> He in ful purpos to yeue it to the kyng. (I. 108–12)[13]

The occasion promised to be mutually advantageous. For Henry's part, the sojourn constituted a 'cost-saving measure for the royal household'[14] as well as a deft show of accord between the monarchy and one of England's wealthiest and most influential religious institutions.[15] For a king whose claims to the thrones of England and France were under threat, the significance of the latter should not be underestimated.[16]

From the perspective of the abbey—or, more accurately, of Abbot Curteys[17]—the event offered a chance to showcase its impressive grounds, architecture, significance to the local community and, by extension, its right to self-rule. Just twelve years prior, Henry V had issued a strong assertion of religious subordination to royal authority. In a direct confrontation with the Benedictine Order, he summoned its leaders to Westminster in May 1421, demanding a number of reforms that included the suppression of personal accumulation of wealth and a curtailment of the number of days abbots could dwell outside their convents.[18] Henry VI's extended visit thus presented a rare opportunity to redress such encroachments and impress upon such a young king (he was twelve years old at the time) the abbey's vital role in the nation's spiritual and political well-being. The composition and gift of an illustrated *Life* of their patron saint must be seen against this background of royal and religious competition and interdependence.

Lydgate's task, then, was to compile, compose, translate and embellish his sources in a way that would resonate with both its intended recipient *and* its donors. Recounting the lives of, and successive miracles performed by, SS Edmund and Fremund, the narrative is a collation of various oral and written versions of the two legends.[19] The earliest known record of St Edmund, included in the ninth-century *Anglo-Saxon Chronicle*, is remarkably terse, relating the following under the year 870:

> Her rad se here ofer Mierce innan Eastengle and wint[er] setl namon aet Þeodforda. and þy wint[re] Eadmund cyning him wiþ feaht. and þa Deniscan sige namon. and þone cyning ofslogon. and þaet lond all geeodon. (and fordiden ealle þa mynstre þa hi to comen) (þara heauod manna naman þa ðane cing ofslogon waeran Igware and Ubba).

> In this year the army rode across Mercia into East Anglia and settled at Thetford for the winter. King Edmund fought against them that winter, and the Danes were victorious. They slew the king, completely conquering the land. (Also, they destroyed all the monasteries they came to.) (The names of the chieftans who killed the king were Ingware and Ubba.)[20]

Over the ensuing five centuries the legend became the subject of great elaboration as the figure of St Edmund rose to the status of national saint, trumped only by Thomas Becket. Collectively, the Edmund corpus 'reflect[s] an abiding concern to foster the cult [of St Edmund] and spread its influence',[21] and in Lydgate's rendition, as well as in a Latin version by Abbot Curteys himself, there appears 'that familiar theme of the Abbey's traditional exemptions from outside control'.[22] Bury St Edmunds's objective to affirm its legitimacy as an independent organisation is thus evident in the steady additions to the mass of Edmund literature, as well as in the content of these two most recent accounts.

While the addition of St Fremund's *Life* might strike one as 'puzzling',[23] there is reason to consider it as one of these additions intended to affirm the abbey's pre-eminence. The earliest extant record of Fremund's history is in a Latin poem of about 1220, but he is not linked to Edmund until the literature of the late thirteenth century, in which he assumes the role of Edmund's nephew and avenger.[24] Although Lydgate's reason for joining the biographies of these two saints is unknown, there are several aspects of Fremund's narrative that suggest that its inclusion may have resulted from a desire to glorify further the reputation of Edmund. First, Fremund is a secondary protagonist to whose biography are devoted fewer verses than that of Edmund. Second, his story is something of a sequel to Edmund's, as he takes up the earlier martyr's cause and retaliates against his assassins. Furthermore, because so many episodes in Fremund's legend are similar to incidents in Edmund's history, they provide a retrospective spotlight, bringing Edmund's story to the minds of those reading or hearing the tale of Fremund. It is important to point out this aspect of the *Lives* because, in echoing the legend of Edmund, it champions, both implicitly and explicitly, the monastery in his name. By reiterating the miraculous history of the saint whose relics it houses, the legend embellishes its own miraculous history, enhancing its own reputation.[25]

What the text of the *Lives* presents, then, is a dual agenda to which Lydgate was admirably suited. As the perennial 'poet-propagandist'[26] for the Lancastrians (or, at the very least, a 'regal ideologue')[27] he was the obvious choice for the author of this work.[28] Renoir and Benson observe that, throughout the work, 'Lydgate ... takes the opportunity to discuss proper political rule as well as sainthood'.[29] In a general sense Lydgate uses the narrative of the *Lives* to convey the most estimable traits in a monarch: he devotes large sections of the work to descriptions of the noble characters of Edmund and Fremund, both kings before they were martyred and beatified. More pointedly, Lydgate manipulates his sources to advocate, both implicitly and explicitly, Henry VI's legitimacy. The poet is dexterous in attending to several contingencies, ensuring that Henry is portrayed as the natural, genealogical heir to the thrones of England and France, asserting that adoptive heirs are equally legitimate and insisting that a king's legitimacy is evidenced by the numerous virtues he espouses.[30] At the same time, as a representative of Bury St Edmunds, Lydgate takes ample opportunity to prioritise pious obligation over royal prerogative. And he is especially keen to praise a monarch's respect for monastic self-determination. As in many royal hagiographies, it is the conflict between a king's duties to his people and to God that predominates in this text.

The prince's mirror and the saint's relic

Like Lydgate, the team of scribe and book artists charged with producing the presentation manuscript took into account the desires of both donor and recipient. As John Lowden has argued, it is this presence of a double agenda that defines the 'royal-imperial book [which], if going to the ruler, presents us with the perceptions that others had, or wished to promote'.[31] As I will show, the combination of Lydgate's text and the manuscript's illustrations achieves this end by deploying a specular paradigm that encourages Henry to envision himself as Edmund and to match both the monarchic and saintly ideals he embodies.

The dedication manuscript, henceforth referred to as Harley, contains two frontispieces that initiate this process of conflation between reader/viewer and protagonist. Emblazoned on the verso of its first folio is one of Edmund's two standards, a token 'that no vices never maad hym erre' (General Prol. 28). Within a vertically oriented, rectangular, unframed space, Adam and Eve stand against a deep crimson ground. They flank the Tree of Knowledge, whose shape is transformed by the surmounted Agnus Dei into both a Holy Cross and a Eucharistic monstrance. It is significant that this, the first image in the manuscript, is placed on the verso of the first folio, leaving the recto blank. Presumably, this placement was chosen to allow the frontispiece to face its accompanying text. Indeed, allowing the king to find, upon opening the volume, an image of Original Sin might have set for the legend an unduly pessimistic tone.[32] Instead, the manuscript's producers positioned the frontispiece alongside the opening lines to the prologue, which declare:

> Blyssyd Edmu[n]d/kyng martir and vyrgyne
> hadde in thre vertues/by g[ra]ce a souereyn prys
> & which he venquysshed al venymes serpentyne
> Adam baserpent/banysshed fro paradys
> Eua also/be cause she was nat wys
> Eet off an appyl/off flesshly fals plesance
> Which thre figures/Edmund by gret auys
> Bar in his ban[n]er/for a remembrance
>
> (General Prol. 1–8)

The words are visualised later in the manuscript, where we see Edmund warring under this very standard and sporting over his armour a tunic bearing the same image (f. 50ʳ). Because the frontispiece is likely to have been a late addition to the manuscript,[33] it seems that the artist was inspired by the miniature of Edmund charging into battle: as a result, he devised a frontispiece that attempts to reify the very object that the miniature describes. In lacking a frame, the frontispiece draws attention to itself not

Figure 4.1   Second Frontispiece: Edmund's Standard.
John Lydgate, *Lives of Saints Edmund and Fremund*.
Bury St Edmunds, *c.*1434–1439.
London, British Library MS Harley 2278, fol. 3ᵛ.
Copyright © The British Library Board.

as an image but rather as an object, intimating the shape and scale of an actual banner. As Victor Stoichita writes, 'All picture frames establish the identity of the fiction. To give a painting a painted frame, in addition to its actual frame, indicates that the fiction has been raised by the power of two'.[34] Conversely, to deprive the image of a frame, particularly when it is surrounded by a gallery of images within frames,[35] is to *un*-mediate it and insist upon its object-hood. Thus, while the verses accompanying the frontispiece pledge protection for the king who fights under such a standard, the manuscript itself provides the audience—that is, Henry—with a facsimile of the material with which to do so.

The following image relies even further upon interpictorial citation to consolidate the identities of Edmund and Henry (Figure 4.1). Replicating the shape of the first frontispiece, it shows three crowns in a descending triangular formation against an azure ground. Also a standard borne by Edmund, the crowns, we are told, signify Edmund's martyrdom, virginity and royal dignity (General Prol. 50–54); they served, in fact, as the arms of the Abbey of Bury St Edmunds. At the same time, they prognosticated the future, prophesying Henry's destiny and right to wear the crowns of England and France in this world and the crown of heaven in the next (General Prol. 65–72). As before, the image reappears later in the manuscript, hung from the trumpets of attendants who lead Edmund to his coronation. Once again, the manuscript presents the audience with a simulacral prop whose use is illustrated in a later, narrative scene.

But the frontispiece truly derives its force from its allusion to imagery that was central to Lancastrian propaganda during the king's minority. During this precarious period in the monarchy, poster art, poetry and a rash of newly minted coins comprised a public relations campaign aimed at convincing the English and French public of Henry's right to both thrones.[36] Key among the emblems were the twin crowns, the twin arms and the double-branched lineage converging in the single figure of Henry. Lydgate himself deployed this imagery widely, penning an exhaustive supply of verse that invokes the double crown. Among such works is his piece commemorating Henry's return from France in 1432:

> The [pe]degree be iuste successioun,
> As trewe cronycles trewely determyne,
> Vnto the Kyng ys now dessended dovn
> From eyther partye riht as eny lyne;
> Vpon whos heede now ffreshely done shyne
> Two riche crovnes most sovereyn off plesaunce
> To brynge inne pees bitwene England and Fraunce.[37]

Verbal genealogies such as this were given pictorial form as well, as in an illumination that copies poster art meant to accompany Lawrence Calot's poem on Henry's legitimacy.[38] In this illumination from a manuscript given to Margaret of Anjou (London, British Library MS 15 E vi, f. 3^r), a column of roundels runs down either side of the folio: on the left, against a ground of fleur-de-lis, is the French royal line; on the right, against a ground of leopards, is the English. At the bottom of the folio the two lines converge in a point over which is a roundel framing the figure of Henry VI. An angel hovers on either side, each holding a crown over Henry's head. In this instance, it is the figure of Henry who completes the triangular formation of crowns imaged on the Harley frontispiece. Likewise, among the new coins minted early in his reign was the *blanc aux deux écus*, featuring the two arms of England and France side-by-side, centred above which is Henry's name.[39] What all these pieces of propaganda share is a strong visualisation of Henry as the locus of unification. Moreover, in a brilliant fusion of royal support and monastic self-promotion, the Bury illustrators have subsumed the icons of Henry VI's monarchic lineage under the aegis of St Edmund. The frontispiece of the three crowns flags the recipient of the manuscript through potent visual allusion to the abbey's support, while predicating that support on Henry's commitment to their monarchic ideal.

The manuscript's producers, in appending the two frontispieces, promote this ideal effectively through a manipulation of specular politics. Lydgate's poem, certainly, positions Henry as the rightful heir to Edmund and his legacy, but the two frontispieces, as quasi-props, encourage Henry to *be* Edmund, not just succeed him. Such a precedent guarantees that, in every mention of Edmund's name, Henry hears his own name implied; in every picture of Edmund, Henry sees a reflection of himself. According to Lacan's famous formulation, the mirror stage

> is experienced as a temporal dialectic that decisively projects the individual's formation into history: the mirror stage is a drama whose internal pressure pushes precipitously from insufficiency to anticipation—and, for the subject caught up in the lure of spatial identification, turns out fantasies that proceed from a fragmented image of the body to what I will call an 'orthopedic' form of its totality—and to the finally donned armor of an alienating identity that will mark his entire mental development with its rigid structure. Thus, the shattering of the *Innenwelt* to *Umwelt* circle gives rise to an inexhaustible squaring of the ego's audits.[40]

A formative phase in the development of the self, the mirror stage occurs when the child identifies himself with the image reflected back at him in the mirror. This identification causes a startling rupture in the child's experience of the world, as he becomes aware that it is experienced not only first-hand, through his own eyes, but also second-hand, as the world looks back at him. What he finds in the mirror is himself, but not himself, a version that differs from his own perception of himself but which offers the possibility for curatory practices that shape how he might appear to the world. Lacan's notion is, in essence, a twentieth-century update of the Augustinian conception of the *speculum* as a paragon, in which the viewer sees both what she should be and what she is.[41]

In the hands of its intended pre-adolescent recipient, the Harley manuscript of the *Lives* functions perfectly according to this paradigm. Edmund does not merely represent himself but he also mirrors the prince who, in gazing upon him, is made to understand that he is gazing too upon himself. The artists of these two frontispieces crafted images that would reflect back at the twelve-year-old Henry a promise of the perfectibility of his present imperfect self: and if the cult that sprang up around Henry after his death is any indication of the identity that he himself cultivated, the Harley illustrators were successful in their efforts.[42]

When, approximately thirty years later, another team collaborated to produce a manuscript of the *Lives*, a vastly different set of expectations shaped its appearance. Yates Thompson 47, henceforth referred to as YT, was probably made at Bury St Edmunds between 1461 and 1465.[43] There is no internal evidence identifying its original owner, but I believe there is sufficient information pointing to Elizabeth Fitzwalter of Attleborough.[44] As a member of a wealthy family with deep roots in Essex, her ownership of a manuscript of a local saint's life would have been entirely typical. The absence of a patron portrait or even the Fitzwalter arms suggests, further, that this manuscript was not specially commissioned, but rather purchased by or gifted to Elizabeth shortly after the death of her first husband.[45] Though this final suggestion cannot, at present, be proved, there is every reason to believe that its destination (whether via commission or speculative production) was for a wealthy local family with ties to the abbey.

Equally unverifiable is the relationship between YT and Harley 2278. The text of the majority of the poem is largely unaltered from Harley, but its order differs from the prototype and the poem has been expanded. Apart from minor discrepancies in orthography, the text proceeds almost entirely unchanged from Book I to the final line of Book III in Harley.[46] Forty-one additional stanzas (1521–62) are appended to Book III, and accounts of miracles occurring between the time of the completion of the presentation manuscript and 1444 are included in fifty-eight eight-line stanzas. These later miracles are composed in the style of Lydgate, although their authenticity has been questioned.[47] Significantly, the *General Prologue* was moved to the final pages of the manuscript, where it is followed by the envoy.[48] Although the illustrations of YT and Harley are drastically different in style, their shared images and a number of remarkably similar compositions suggest some affiliation, whether via another copy of Harley, a set of preparatory drawings for it or a maquette. Furthermore, it is probable that Harley 2278 left the royal collection once Henry VI had reached adulthood: it was during this time that he gave away many of his books in acts of largesse. Perhaps the subsequent owner of Harley showed the manuscript to the producers of YT.[49]

Of YT's fifty-three images, forty-nine depict episodes represented in Harley, with minor variations in composition.[50] Only the four pictures that accompany the additional miracles in YT are not illustrated in the earlier manuscript. As Kathleen Scott has shown, five miniatures in particular exhibit the strong influence of Harley over the later copy, as they are near duplicates in their compositions and minutiae:

1. John Lydgate kneels at the shrine of St Edmund, beseeching the saint's aid in composing the legend (Harley 2278, f. 9ʳ; YT 47, f. 4ʳ).

2. The scene of Alkmond's pilgrimage, with the widow's prophecy and the king genuflecting at the feet of the pope (Harley 2278, f. 12ʳ; YT 47, f. 6ᵛ).

3. Edmund's arrival in Eastern England, with the miraculous five springs (Figs 6, 7).

4. Edmund shot with arrows (Harley 2278, f. 61ʳ; YT 47, f. 49ᵛ).

5. Fremund and cohorts, travelling as pilgrims (Harley 2278, f. 79ᵛ; YT 47, f. 65ʳ).[51]

The remarkable similarities between these images indicate not only that the deviser of YT had access to images in the earlier manuscript (whether from the original manuscript itself or in an intermediary volume or maquette form) but also that the lack of correspondence between other miniatures resulted from the artist's decision not to adhere to the model.

Perhaps the most profound distinction between Harley and YT is the latter's rejection of the earlier manuscript's royal-political agenda.[52] Here the alliance forged between Henry VI and St Edmund in the presentation manuscript is entirely absent, an omission achieved not through emendation of Lydgate's text but rather through the manipulation of its order and illustration. As mentioned above, the *General Prologue* was moved to the end of the manuscript, a sign that the manuscript's producers were sensitive to the influence of narrative order and the powerful precedent set by this introductory text. After moving the *General Prologue*, the production team reduced the overwhelming frontispieces to final insignias (Figure 4.2). Cast as escutcheons and located centrally at the foot of the page, Edmund's standards have been assimilated to marks of ownership. In so doing, the arms proclaim that this is not merely a book *about* Edmund but that it is also a book *of* Edmund, one that he in some manner possessed and declared as his own. As Hans Belting has argued so eloquently, the coat of arms, as a proto-portrait, assumes the status of a place-holder, which in this instance articulates a rhetoric of saintly presence.[53] The simulation effected here enacts the 'indwelling personality' of the medieval image, manifesting the divine person in his material representation.[54] In transforming Edmund's standard into a mark of ownership, the illustrators of this manuscript liken the book not only to Edmund's own possession but also, like contact relics, to a prosthesis of his self. As such, the book becomes a reliquary, the flesh of its folios proxying the body of the saint whose story they relate.[55]

Reader response confirms the reliquary nature of the manuscript. Beneath Edmund's arms the second-generation owner of the manuscript included her own name and dedication of the book to her daughter, writing: 'thys boke gyftan to my lady beaumoun[t] by har lovfynge moder margaret

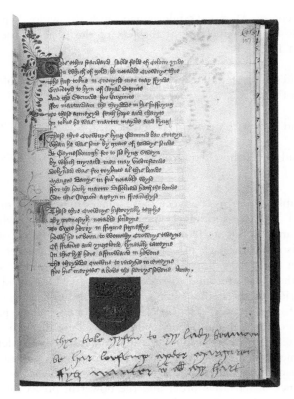

Figure 4.2   Edmund's Standard.
John Lydgate, *Lives of Saints Edmund and Fremund*.
Bury St Edmunds, *c*.1461–1465.
London, British Library, MS Yates Thompson 47, fol. 107ᵛ.
Copyright © The British Library Board.

ffytz wauter w[i]t[h] all my hart'. Margaret Fitzwalter's decision to write
this dedication beneath Edmund's arms is telling. While the Fitzwalter arms
are nowhere to be seen in this manuscript, the space beneath the heraldic
insignia of its holy protagonist has become the site of its owner's personal
stamp. Making contact with St Edmund's surrogate body, his marks of
ownership have become her own. Structurally, this process of imitation and
transference parallels Eucharistic absorption, so that, partaking of the body
of the saint, Margaret herself shares a measure of the divine.

In comparing the two treatments of Edmund's standards we see how
changes in shape, placement and frame dictate the visual references they
deploy and, in turn, the reader's/viewer's encounter with the saint: for Henry
VI the manuscript functions as a hand mirror in which he sees himself and

as a prop with which he broadcasts that image. For Margaret the manuscript functions as a relic and the vehicle through which she unites her own self with the object of her devotion. While Lydgate's text lends itself congenially to both the specular and the reliquary models, it is the text's appearance in an illustrated manuscript that determines which of these models is at work.

The saint's shrine and the king's throne

With these two paradigms established, I would like to observe figural representations of Edmund to assess how they further orchestrate the viewer's experience. Because, generally speaking, the manuscript that is considered technically 'inferior' plays second fiddle to its 'superior' counterpart or model, I want to reverse the trend and analyse YT first, outside the Harleian shadow.

Lifting the cover to the volume, it is an iconic image of King Edmund that first confronts the viewer (Figure 4.3). The image corresponds to the verses it precedes, which declare the subject of the poem, 'the noble story ... of saint Edmund martyr, maide, and king' (l. 1). It likewise conforms to an audience's expectations by figuring the object of interest according to compositional conventions of iconic frontality: Edmund is both at the front of the book and frontally facing the viewer. Furthermore, the miniature's frame evokes the shape of a triptych, with the canopy to Edmund's throne extending above the border and creating a tripartite space. The crowned figure enthroned before the viewer is undoubtedly a king, but, with the instrument of his later martyrdom—an arrow—in his right hand, the depiction has a memorial resonance. Unveiling this first folio of the manuscript, we are not so much looking at an illustration as contemplating an altarpiece.

What is most conspicuous about this image is a certain lack. Far from filling the stage of space in which he sits, Edmund is flanked by a figural absence. He is the sole occupant of the picture plane, accompanied by neither attendants nor devotees. Viewed within the common visual context of the donor portrait—often seen on lateral wings of triptychs similar in shape to this miniature—this absence is so prominent that it demands to be filled. A favoured prefatory miniature in several Lydgate manuscripts, other images of Edmund unanimously include supplicants, usually Lydgate himself.[56] In light of the commoner format, I would argue that this space is a lacuna meant for the reader/viewer to fill.[57] Corresponding to the simulacral relationship between hagiography and reliquary, this gap assimilates the *foramina*, or portals, common on saints' shrines such as Becket's and Osmund's at Salisbury.[58] These apertures were designed to allow worshippers physical access to relics, enabling bodily contact with the saint's body. Certainly, in a visual sense, the wings of this miniature do *not* imitate *foramina*, but rather they rest on an embedded material

Figure 4.3   Edmund Enthroned.
John Lydgate, *Lives of Saints Edmund and Fremund*.
Bury St Edmunds, *c*.1461–1465.
London, British Library, MS Yates Thompson 47, fol. 1ʳ.
Copyright © The British Library Board.

infrastructure that motivated supplicants to insert their bodies where a gap presented itself. Lacking any kind of hermetic encasement, the image begs the viewer to draw near.

Once again, reader/viewer response indexes the saint's magnetism. The manuscript remains in excellent condition, although erosion on the present miniature and deliberate damage to three others record an early audience's visceral connection to the subject of this hagiography.[59] The opening miniature shows heavy signs of wear and rubbing in isolated and pictorially significant locations. The gold filigree on either side of Edmund has flaked off, the paint over his shins and the adjacent drapery over the throne is completely absent, revealing the pencilled underdrawing, and the paint over his face, chest and shoulders has likewise worn away. The erosion of paint in these locations discloses the kind of digital engagement that mimics how a devotee would kneel in reverence before a holy statue.[60] Placing her fingers beside Edmund, embracing his legs as a supplicant, and daring even to caress his face, the pious audience's tactile response to this tiny altarpiece attests to its irresistible allure. Three other miniatures in the manuscript reveal a further consequence of this allure: a devotee appears to have indulged in an emotional outburst against Edmund's aggressors, smudging and rubbing their faces, even tearing at the page.[61] This act of aggression was, as I am arguing, encouraged by the 'packaging' of Lydgate's text in YT, which through visual associations made the saint's presence seem to inhere in the folios of this book.

A very different set of associations is sparked by the page on which the same introductory verses appear in the dedication manuscript. Text, image and graphic intertwine here to conflate the subjects of our, or, more accurately, Henry VI's, gaze. A half-page miniature (Figure 4.4) that intromits Henry VI into the narrative itself rests above the opening lines to Book I, which declare:

> The noble story to putte in remembraunce
> Of saynt Edmund martir maide & kyng
> With his support my stile I wil auaunce
> First to compile aftir my kunyng
> His glorious lif his birthe and his gynnyng
> And be discent how that he that was so good
> Was in saxonie born of the roial blood (I. 81–87)

While the verses announce Edmund as their focus, the image illustrating them displays *Henry* enthroned. Seated against a chancel screen, or perhaps within a chapter house, the king is surrounded by both retainers and the Black Monks of Bury. In his analysis Nicholas Rogers has argued that the scene 'embodies features of presentation iconography ... [and] should rather be interpreted as a depiction of the admission of the king and leading courtiers into the confraternity of St Edmund's, just before their departure, an event described in the poem'.[62] Rogers is right to note both aspects of this miniature, but, rather than insisting that it represents only a single moment, I would argue that the miniature is much more (deliberately) ambiguous. Henry rests his right hand on a book extended to him by a kneeling monk, a tell-tale feature of presentation iconography.[63] At the same time, the book being presented to Henry is doubled in the form of the blue codex flanked between two officiating monks and lying on precisely the same vertical axis that Henry himself occupies on the picture plane. Collapsing the activities of indoctrination and presentation into a single visual event, the image suggests that it is Henry's very acceptance of the book which guarantees his absorption into the brotherhood.

Figure 4.4   Presentation of the Book / Henry's Admission to the
Confraternity.
John Lydgate, *Lives of Saints Edmund and Fremund*.
Bury St Edmunds, *c.*1434–1439.
London, British Library, MS Harley 2278, fol. 6ʳ.
Copyright © The British Library Board.

More than that, an image found further on in the manuscript asserts
that such an induction cements more than fraternity and launches a
transformation whereby *Henry* becomes the subject of the lines his image
illustrates. The presentation/induction scene reappears in a modified form
several folios on, in the coronation ceremony of Edmund (Figure 4.5). As
before, Henry is confronted with an enthroned king beneath a pink-and-
white patterned canopy, surrounded by attendants and officials of the faith.
However, while a distinction between clergy, nobles and king is maintained
in the image of Henry VI, an affinity between these groups is forged in the
depiction of King Edmund. With almost all members clad in white, with
the scene set in an ambiguous locale and with no participants kneeling,

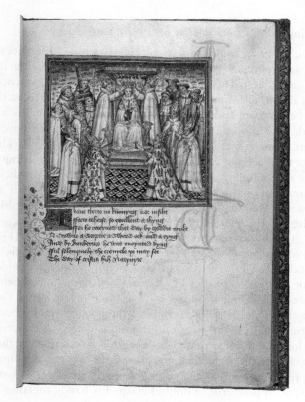

Figure 4.5   Edmund's Coronation.
John Lydgate, *Lives of Saints Edmund and Fremund*.
Bury St Edmunds, *c*.1434–1439.
London, British Library, MS Harley 2278, fol. 31ʳ.
Copyright © The British Library Board.

the relationship between monarch and clergy is imaged as one of equality and harmony. Moreover, the scene is set at eye level, entreating the viewer to enter the space, whereas the image of Henry enthroned is viewed from a disembodied eye hovering above the scene and set off from it by a stone wall, submitting it to a colder and less inviting form of inspection. Through the visual cross-reference between the presentation/induction ceremony and Edmund's coronation, Henry is encouraged to embrace the Bury monks' idealised vision of kingship and led to believe that it lies entirely within his grasp. In exchange he is, in the words of Sartre, relieved of 'the burden of imagining his divine right'.[64]

The five springs: a monarch's right or a saint's miracle?

Finally, I would like to compare a set of images whose differences mobilise the specular and reliquary paradigms established early in each manuscript's programme in order to inspire two different kinds of reverence. In the episode they illustrate Edmund arrives in East Anglia to accept the crown and sceptre bequeathed to him by his deceased uncle, Offa. As a token of His approval, God causes the earth to become verdant and flow with five springs where once there was only barren earth (II. 747–59). The images that illustrate this scene in each manuscript are so similar in composition as to intimate a direct line of influence from Harley to YT. Yet their stylistic differences and minor discrepancies speak volumes about their respective attitudes towards Edmund's sanctity and his supernatural faculties.

The artists of the Harleian manuscript illustrated this scene with an image that carefully avoids over-empowering its protagonist (Figure 4.6). At the top of the miniature God emerges from within a cloud in the sky, His hand raised in a gesture of benediction, and with golden beams radiating out from His form towards earth. Edmund, just below, gazes in His direction, guiding the viewer's eye not only towards God in the heavens but also towards the verses above the image, which open with the words, 'thoruh goddis myht' (l. 666). Edmund is placed at the centre of the miniature's lower register, situated between his attendants on the left and the five streams on the right. His gestures, pose and garb distinguish him particularly from his companions: donning a gold crown and a sumptuous black surcote with gold trim, Edmund clasps his hands together in prayer. Divided from him by a sliver of negative space between their heads, his six companions, all clad in white, gesture variously in surprise and conversation. To the right each of the five springs gushes forth independently from the land, compartmentalised by the vertical axis stretching up the outline of the hill and culminating in the face of God. To the left of this line Edmund kneels with his left knee bent and his right knee touching the ground. The significance of this pose is clarified throughout the manuscript's miniature programme where figures kneel in such a manner before those of higher rank, whereas those at prayer kneel with both knees touching the ground.[65] It is clear that King Edmund, as he is here portrayed, bends not as a pious devotee but rather in fealty, as a vassal to his Lord, God. This image, made in the awareness of its recipient's gaze, is cautious to maintain the distinction between monarchic and divine pre-eminence, expressing it in the gestural conventions of courtly service. In short, Edmund is the lord of his men, but the man of his Lord.

While the image of the five springs in the Henrician manuscript negotiates the sovereign's position between two worlds, its later counterpart situates Edmund confidently as the fulcrum of an earth kinetic with an autochthonous divinity (Figure 4.7). Preceding, and visually above the

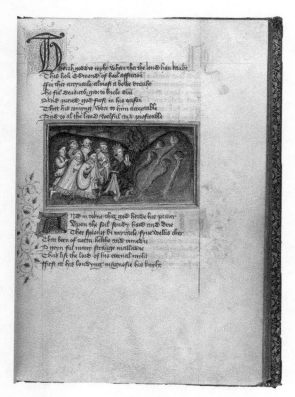

Figure 4.6   Edmund and the Five Springs.
John Lydgate, *Lives of Saints Edmund and Fremund*.
Bury St Edmunds, *c*.1434–1439.
London, British Library, MS Harley 2278, fol. 28ʳ.
Copyright © The British Library Board.

verses that declare 'thoruh goddis myht', the miniature of the five springs
omits God's face, focusing instead on the kneeling figure of Edmund.
The distinction between him and his companions is less pronounced in
the mundane details of rank and wealth, hinging instead on one attribute
in particular: the proleptic blue halo around his crown, anticipating his
beatification before the fact.[66] Beyond this, the colours of the patterned red
and gold robe he wears are picked up and echoed in the garb of his four
companions. There is no negative space between them, so that, while it is
clear that Edmund is king, the terms of his kingship are attributive only:
the crown and the pattern on his garb. In gaze, pose and comportment he
is a member of a group. Cynthia Hahn has remarked upon the importance
of a royal saint's identification with his subjects in 'divorcing [him] from his

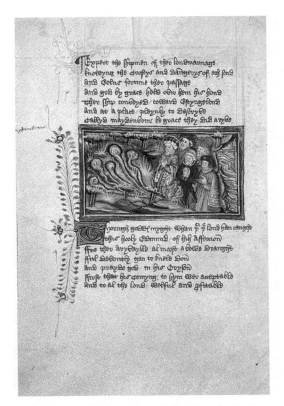

Figure 4.7   Edmund and the Five Springs.
John Lydgate, *Lives of Saints Edmund and Fremund*.
Bury St Edmunds, *c*.1461–1465.
London, British Library, MS Yates Thompson 47, fol. 19ᵛ.
Copyright © The British Library Board.

aristocratic origins', an effect that was achieved in an earlier depiction of St Edmund, also made at the Abbey of Bury St Edmunds and still housed there in the fifteenth century.[67] Moreover, in addition to minimising mundane distinctions of rank, the miniature denies naturalistic incidentals in favour of an almost hallucinatory vibrancy and symbolic view of this realm. Vivid swatches of emerald, sapphire, ruby and canary yellow cover the surface of this image and burst beyond its frame, suffusing it with frenetic brushstrokes of technicolour. And, while in the earlier image the number of companions joining Edmund lacks value, the number here, along with Edmund, totals five, duplicating the number of springs flowing from the land. All five of these springs have their source, visually, in Edmund himself, whose body divides the spatial plane in three. Behind Edmund, and to the right of the image, his boat floats in the salty water over which he sailed. At first this might appear to be a superficial detail added for narrative content, but it plays a figurative role here, reminding the viewer of the undrinkable water and the sandy terrain that were. As a result of these features, the land is transformed into a map of divine signs: at its axis is Edmund and his retinue, rending the fierce and inhospitable from the fresh and pure. This image typifies the aims of the pictorial programme, staging Edmund as the embodiment of sanctity, the cause of miracles and the object of devotion.

King Edmund the Luxurious; St Edmund the Crude

At the beginning of this chapter I proposed that we look beyond style in order to penetrate the differences between two miniature programmes for the same poem. But in concluding I would like to return to style, itself a potent carrier of meaning. In demanding an imitative response the Henrician manuscript depended upon mimesis as far as possible in order to convince the king that he is, in these pictures, seeing a more perfect picture of himself. At the same time, the mirror-images, resting on the mundane, ensure vigorously that the image on which the king models himself is always an earthbound one, whose power never exceeds that with which a religious institution could remain comfortable. Utterly transforming this naturalism into a visual language of inspecificity, stylised gesture and supernal jewel-like colour, the reliquary manuscript insists upon the ever-present possibility of divinity in this world, a divinity that erupts forth through contact with the saint. Far from reliable indicators of skill, the naturalism of Harley and the supernaturalism of its later counterpart direct their respective readers to evaluate their own position in relation to St Edmund. Wrapping the same hagiography in two very different visual and codicological packages, the producers of these manuscripts ensured that each of their respective audiences would have very different experiences of St Edmund's legend. And so, in answering the question 'to picture the king or to picture the saint?', the illustrators of the *Lives of Saints Edmund and Fremund* choreographed how the audience would picture himself or herself.

5

Sixty-three Gallons of Books

Shipping Books to London in the Late Middle Ages

Yvonne Rode

This study aims to contribute to our understanding of the early book trade in England by analysing the first importation of books into the port of London, a focus that is particularly pertinent given the inability of printers in England to meet a rising demand for books in the late fifteenth and early sixteenth centuries. Of the eighty books which Don Fernando Colón purchased in London during June 1522, 90% were printed outside England.[1] The import trade can be tracked in some detail in the overseas customs accounts, which survive in sufficient number to provide quantitative data on, for example, the volume, value and shipping units of book imports up until 1540. The focus here will be on the types of books imported and the containers in which they arrived in London, England's capital, which dominated the county's overseas trade, particularly traffic by aliens.[2] Many aliens were able to become leading members of the early book trade due to favourable regulations given to them.[3] In addition, London was the centre of political, cultural and social life in England, along with nearby Westminster, and its citizens were major consumers of books.[4] A review of customs accounts available in print for other ports shows very few book imports outside London.[5] Further information on the merchants, printers and publishers involved show that the trade developed from a craft to a business within a few decades of the development of movable type and the printing press.

Previous scholarship on the early importation of books into England has drawn on several different types of evidence. Bibliographic studies by Lotte Hellinga, Nicholas Barker and Margaret Lane Ford have focused on determining the place of production and have examined extant collections to determine the date and origin of imprint, particularly for the institutional collections of monasteries or universities.[6] Other scholars, such as Carol Meale, have examined wills and inventories of individuals for similar information that could be gleaned from title lists.[7] Although these sources list specific titles, they do not show when they were brought to England nor whether they were imported by a bookseller on speculation or purchased abroad by an individual.

A few scholars have looked at customs accounts for evidence of the early imports of books. Henry Plomer briefly examined four London customs rolls from the fifteenth and sixteenth centuries before abandoning his research due to the 'monotony' of seeing the same names over and over again.[8] Plomer chose to emphasise the merchants involved, particularly those already well known in the book trade (such as Francis Birckman and Wynkyn de Worde) and included only a few sample entries from the rolls. Paul Needham has discussed how the customs accounts can be used for research on the early book trade, but he has focused on explaining how the custom system functioned and the kind of information to be found in the accounts.[9] Julian Roberts has drawn on London customs accounts and port books as one of his sources when researching book imports for Oxford University in the sixteenth and early seventeenth centuries, but he mentions only the names of the merchants involved and does not discuss any other information found in the accounts.[10] Probably the most comprehensive approach was taken by Nelly Kerling, who examined all extant London customs accounts from 1460 to 1492 and offers considerable detail on, for example, all the imports by a Dutch merchant named Peter Actors.[11] For the most part she gives only a handful of specific examples and mentions the names of a few other merchants who imported books, and she provides no systematic analysis of the data.[12]

By examining a larger collection of customs accounts for London, I hope to augment the data available on the book trade from 1450 to 1540 and provide the big picture that is currently lacking. Using an Access database in order statistically to analyse information systematically culled from the accounts, it is possible to find patterns in changes to the various containers used in shipping and the different terms used to describe the books; this helps to illuminate parts of the business side of the book trade overlooked by recent scholarship. The Access database helps show how early printers— now faced with large numbers of texts—had to find an economical way to distribute those works over long distances to a bigger consumer base, otherwise the savings made by producing multiple copies would be lost. The terms used to describe books can show us how these commodities were viewed by those outside the world of print and scholarship: men who viewed these items as another piece of merchandise to be accounted for and accorded a value.

Book imports in the customs accounts

The national customs accounts kept track of imports and exports in order to determine the value of the merchandise and impose a duty that went to the king.[13] Customs duties were an important source of royal revenue, accounting for more than 50% of all crown revenue in the late fourteenth century.[14] The summary accounts that record the total customs revenue survive in an almost continuous series from the mid-fourteenth century into the eighteenth century.[15] The accounts that record book imports, however, are the particular accounts for individual customs jurisdictions, which were used as the basis for the summary, enrolled accounts. Although the survival of particular accounts can be patchy, they provide more detail, including the date the ship entered the port, information on its shipmaster (and occasionally the ship name and home port), its cargo and merchants, and customs valuations. There are two types of particular accounts: those kept by the collectors of customs tend to be fuller than the audited accounts, which were compiled by the controller.[16] There were different types of accounts depending on the specific type of customs duty assessed: some duties, for instance, targeted only alien (foreign) merchants, not natives (English merchants) or denizens (former aliens who had acquired rights similar to natives). Other duties were applied only to certain goods, such as wine (called tunnage accounts), wool, hides or cloth.[17] For our purposes, the most important particular customs accounts were petty accounts and poundage accounts (both customed a large range of goods based on an *ad valorem* tax that was usually 3*d.* on every £1 worth of goods).[18] Survival of petty and poundage accounts for London is erratic in this period.[19] I was able to examine eleven different accounts, most of them petty customs accounts, for evidence of book imports.[20] These accounts make up roughly 28% of extant customs accounts of ten membranes or longer (i.e. likely to cover a full year).

The diverse and usually consistent information offered by customs accounts makes them a particularly useful source for an economic study of the book trade. A typical customs account entry from 1504 reads: 'Item: In the ship of Peter Busse, entered on the 8th day of July [...] Frederick Vanegmond, alien, for one basket of *libris impressis* 40 shillings'.[21] There are limits to what information the entry offers: we are not told what ship this was or where it came from, or much about the merchant. In addition, we do not know what books were in the basket, or even how many there were. What we are told is the name of the importer, a description of the type of book, the container it was shipped in and the custom duty that was collected. Although this type of cursory information restricts the kinds of questions we can answer, enough information is offered to establish a picture of the trade.

I found no book imports in the earliest two London accounts examined

(1457/8 and 1471/2).[22] This so far confirms Nelly Kerling's statement that no imports of books can be found in the London customs accounts before 1477,[23] although commercial importing of books must have begun by the 1450s because of evidence of books in English being printed on the continent in that decade.[24] This paper thus focuses on book imports to London from 1480 to 1540.[25]

The nine accounts surveyed that do contain book imports allow us to get a good picture of the movement of books over time (Table 1.a). During the period surveyed there were fluctuations in the number of book consign-ments, the most significant occurring between 1507/8 and 1514/15, where the figure fell from twenty-six to eleven cargoes containing books (42%). This substantial decrease could be attributed to England's war with France during the early 1510s, which may have affected imports from overseas.[26] In addition, there was civil unrest elsewhere on the continent at this time, making trade difficult or impossible. Anton Koberger writes several times to Basel printer Johann Amerbach that trade has come to a standstill and he is unsure whether the Frankfurt book fair will take place. 'We are beset with terrible war and costs to us grow greater every day. There is absolutely no trade at all, and nobody can do any business because of the war.'[27] Imports rose more than four-fold by number from the mid 1510s to 1520 (eleven to forty-six consignments), but decreased again over the subsequent decades. Studies of additional accounts and other commodities can show whether these fluctuations followed periodic disruptions in trade (for example, as a result of war or unrest making trade difficult) or whether there were sporadic slumps specifically in the demand for books from overseas owing to competition with local printers.[28]

Changes in how books were shipped

Books were shipped in a range of containers which varied over the decades (Tables 1.a and 1.b). Although it is difficult to know what many of these containers might have been, Paul Needham believes they were easily distin-guished by those involved in shipping at the time.[29] In the early decades books were shipped in baskets, barrels, fardels, fatts, pipes, vats, hogsheads, chests and maunds, with cases, trusses, hampers and coffers in the middle decades. Scholarly experts on medieval measures, however, show there is no consensus on the capacity of many of these units. Casks, such as the pipe, hogshead and barrel, seem to have been the only units with clearly defined measurements, as they were based on the tun, or *dolium* (252 gallons), and linked with the assises of wine and ale.[30] Those used to ship books were not necessarily expensive water-tight oak casks, as the letters of Anton Koberger to the printer Johann Amerbach show. Koberger was originally a printer but eventually focused his energy on publishing and distributing books throughout Europe.[31] In correspondence spanning seven years Koberger

Table 1.a. Types and Number of Shipping Units of Cargoes Containing Books Imported into London by Year

Container	1480/81	1490/91	1502/3	1507/8	1512/13	1514/15	1520/21	1534/35	1537/38	Totals
Half-Basket	1 (5%)				1[b] (6%)			9 (26%)	9 (37%)	20
Basket		2 (10.5%)	15 (47%)	8 (31%)	10 (58%)	11 (100%)	19 (41%)	13 (37%)	11 (45%)	89
Fardel	1 (5%)	2 (10.5%)		1 (4%)	3 (18%)		1 (2%)			8
Fatt	1 (5%)	1 (5%)	7 (22%)	3[a] (11%)	1 (6%)		18[d] (39%)	13 (37%)	2[f] (8%)	45
Pipe	1 (5%)		2 (6%)	6 (23%)			3[e] (7%)			12
Vat	1 (5%)									1
Hogshead	3 (16%)	9 (47.5%)		2 (7.5%)			3 (7%)			17
Maund			2 (6%)				1 (2%)			3
Chest	12 (63%)	3 (16%)	3 (9%)	1 (4%)	1[c] (6%)					20
Barrel		2 (10.5%)							1 (4%)	3
Case			2 (6%)	1 (4%)	1 (6%)					4
Coffer			1 (3%)							1
Truss				1 (4%)			1 (2%)		1 (4%)	3
Dolia				2 (7.5%)						2
Hamper				1 (4%)						1
Totals	19 (100%)	19 (100%)	32 (100%)	26 (100%)	17 (100%)	11 (100%)	46 (100%)	35 (100%)	24 (100%)	229

Sources: PRO, E122/194/25 (1480/81); 78/9 (1490/91); 80/3 (1502/3); 80/5 (1507/8); 82/9 (1512/13); 82/3 (1514/15); 81/8 (1520/21); 82/8 (1534–35); 81/18 (1537/38).

Notes: Not all books were shipped in containers. The accounts for 1507–9 and 1512–14 apply the term *parvus* (small) to some containers, while the 1520–21, 1534–35 and 1537–38 accounts used *dimidiatus* (half). I considered these terms to mean the same thing. [a]Includes one small fatt. [b]Entered as small basket. [c]Entered as small chest. [d]Includes one half-fatt. [e]Includes one half-pipe. [f]Includes one half-fatt.

Table 1.b. Types and Number of Shipping Units Containing only Books Imported into London by Year

Container	1480/81	1490/91	1502/3	1507/8	1512/13	1514/15	1520/21	1534/35	1537/38	Totals
Half-Basket					1[b] (9%)			8 (23.5%)	9 (37.5%)	18
Basket		2 (10.5%)	15 (51.7%)	7 (31.8%)	10 (91%)	10 (100%)	18 (51.4%)	13 (38.2%)	11 (46%)	86
Fardel	1 (6.7%)	2 (10.5%)		1 (4.5%)			1 (2.9%)			5
Fatt		1 (5.3%)	5 (17.2%)	3[a] (13.6%)			13 (37.1%)	13 (38.2%)	2[d] (8.3%)	37
Pipe	1 (6.7%)		2 (6.9%)	5 (22.7%)			1[c] (2.9%)			9
Vat	1 (6.7%)									1
Hogshead	2 (13.2%)	9 (47.4%)		2 (9.1%)			2 (5.7%)			15
Maund			2 (6.9%)							2
Chest	10 (66.7%)	3 (15.8%)	3 (10.3%)	1 (4.5%)						17
Barrel		2 (10.5%)							1 (4.1%)	3
Case			1 (3.5%)	1 (4.5%)						2
Coffer			1 (3.5%)							1
Truss				1 (4.5%)					1 (4.1%)	2
Hamper				1 (4.5%)						1
Totals	15 (100%)	19 (100%)	29 (100%)	22 (100%)	11 (100%)	10 (100%)	35 (100%)	34 (100%)	24 (100%)	199

Sources: See Table 1.a.

Notes: Not all books were shipped in containers. [a] Includes one small (or half-) fatt. [b] Entered as small basket. See note in Table 5a about use of 'small' and 'half'. [c] Includes one half-pipe. [d] Includes one half-fatt.

continually pleads with Amerbach to ship his books in better barrels to avoid damage and insists that he has seen 'good barrels' coming from Amerbach's home town of Basel.[32] In a letter of 9 May 1506 an exasperated Koberger writes, 'Later it rained and half the books in the three barrels were drenched and damaged. There went my profit.'[33] The letters clearly show that the barrels were being made to order and not reused.[34] Amerbach also received a complaint about pages being damaged by the nails which were used to fasten metal hoops to the barrels.[35]

The sizes of the other measures used for shipping are less exact. The fatt seems to have been an unofficial measure of nine bushels used in fifteenth-century London.[36] Zupko believes that the fatt was equivalent to a half-maund, with a maund holding forty reams of paper.[37] Paul Needham argues that a maund contained twenty-four reams of paper, basing his estimate on the 1582 *Rates of the Custom House*, which listed a maund of unbound books as containing twenty-four reams of paper.[38] Since the rate (£2 per half-maund) was unchanged from the 1545 *Rates of the Custom House*, he assumed maunds and baskets of previous decades to have held the same quantity. In the Antwerp privileges of 1446, granted to the Merchant Adventurers of England, several items in the tolls list are charged per maund or fatt, implying that these are the same size, and elsewhere in the toll list they are equated to two pipes.[39] Zupko describes the maund as a basket of wicker with handles, similar in construction to the hamper, but a 'large basket'.[40] The fardel was a bundle weighing approximately 150–180 lb but varying by commodity.[41] The truss was also a unit of capacity, equivalent to about 56 lb of hay, although it is not clear what this term meant as a container or measurement for books.[42] The truss and fardel were probably not containers at all, but referred to a bundle of items either tied with rope or wrapped in leather. They may be similar to what Anton Koberger was describing when he asked Johann Amerbach to stop shipping books in barrels and have leather bought so that the books could be shipped in bales.[43] The chest, which appears to be one of the most popular shipping containers for books in the earlier decades, also seems to have had no standard size.[44]

The preferred shipping container for books changed over the years. In the 1480s the chest was used 63% of the time. Casks were often used up to 1507/8, making up as much as 58% of the shipping containers in 1490/91 for book-only shipments and over 31% in 1507/8. The hogshead, containing 63 gallons, accounted for nine of nineteen cargoes containing books in 1490/91, but quickly fell out of favour. Beginning in 1502/3 the basket started to dominate as the choice shipping unit, with 47% of book-only cargoes, although only 31% in 1507/8. That number rose to 64% of all cargoes in 1512/13. The basket continued to be the preferred shipping unit by 1534/5, where it (and the half-basket) accounted for two-thirds of the shipping containers. In that year books were shipped only by the basket, half-basket and fatt, and they make up almost 92% of containers in 1537/8.[45]

Merchants were also shipping cargoes of mixed goods, not containers filled entirely with books, particularly in the earlier decades (compare Tables 1.a and 1.b). One-third of the shipments in 1480/81 included other goods materials (e.g. cloth, metal goods and religious items). In contrast, for the later years there were only a few occasions when other goods are imported along with books, a sign that the book trade has moved out of the hands of the general merchant completely.[46] A few of the later mixed consignments included other printing-related items such as paper and 'bordes for bokes', presumably for binding.[47] Most of the later mixed cargoes were for primers which were imported by the dozen or gross and fell outside the purview of the Stationers, and were thus imported and sold with other cheap goods (Table 2).[48]

Table 2. Shipments of Books Combined with Other Cargoes Imported into London by Year

Years	Book importers	Book shipments	Shipments incl. other goods	Shipments excl. primers incl. other goods
1480/81	10	20	7 (35%)	7 (35%)
1490/91	8	11	1 (9%)	0 (0%)
1502/3	18	28	3 (11%)	3 (11%)
1507/8	8	17	2 (12%)	2 (12%)
1512/13	6	11	5 (45%)	1 (9%)
1514/15	5	8	1 (12%)	1 (12%)
1520/21	20	39	10 (25%)	7 (18%)
1534/35	10	26	1 (4%)	1 (4%)
1537/38	5	22	0 (0%)	0 (0%)
Totals	89[a]	182	30 (16%)	21 (11%)

Sources: See Table 1.
Notes: [a] The number of individual importers was 73.

The basket became the predominant unit for shipping from 1502/3 on, accounting for about one-third of the containers in each account. By 1512/13 even more standardisation in shipping units took place and we find the basket and small (*parvus*) or half-baskets dominating, with the addition of fatts. After 1507/8 we rarely see books shipped in casks (hogsheads, pipes or other containers that were originally designed to ship liquids). It seems that merchants discovered that the basket and fatt was the ideal way to move their product.[49] In addition, the low numbers of mixed cargoes, particularly for books other than primers, shows that there were merchants specialising in the importing of books to London.

There is no scholarly consensus about the size of these containers and, since books were printed in various sizes, it is impossible to estimate how many books could fit in them. Evidence of this variation can be seen in the book imports recorded in the 1480/81 account, the only one examined which notes the number of books in each container. For that year chests were recorded with any number from twenty-nine to ninety-six volumes, proving that it is unwise to try to estimate an average size for a book or guess at how many may fit into any particular container.[50] François Regnault was one of the major importers in the 1520s and 1530s, specialising in English primers.[51] His editions ranged in size from deluxe quartos to tiny sextodecimos, so it is reasonable that there could be books of various sizes in a single container.[52] This is especially relevant as Regnault accounted for one-third of books by value in 1534/5.[53] Regnault was even printing deluxe editions on vellum, so we cannot even assume that all his imports were paper books.[54] Business correspondence from importers could discuss individual shipments and shed further light on this matter, including whether they shipped their books bound or unbound (and if unbound as sheets or quires).

Descriptions of books

Although the customs accounts do not tell us what specific titles are in any given shipment, they do give some descriptions, albeit not particularly clear ones (Table 3). The books are described in Latin, English or a mix of the two languages (e.g. *libris impressis unbound*).[55] In 1480/81 only a single shipment (of five books) was described specifically as printed. Three-quarters of books from 1480/81 are described as *diverse histories*. One of these was imported by John van Acon, who Henry Plomer believes is the Belgian printer John of Westphalia.[56] It is reasonable to assume that his cargo of *diverse histories* were printed, not only because it was being imported by a printer but because manuscripts would not be produced in large numbers to be shipped overseas. By the next decade ten of the eleven shipments (91%) were described as printed, either as *diverse libris impressis* or *libris impressis*; only the primers are not fully described. That percentage decreases for 1502/3, with twenty-three of twenty-eight cargoes (82%) printed. Of the five remaining shipments, three were for *bokes* while two are for *libris*. These terms could signify differences (for example, manuscript or print) because on 15 December 1502, on the ship of Martin Cosyn, four fattes and one chest of *libris impressis* were charged a duty of £20 while two fattes of *bokes* were charged £10.[57] *Bokes* appear again in 1507/8, with one shipment qualified as printed and rated at £4 to the basket.[58] The second shipment was by Francis Birckman, printer and member of a well-known bookselling family.[59] His consignment of *bokes* was rated at £5 per basket, higher than the average for printed books. In addition, for that year there was one entry for *bokes printid* and charged at the same rate as *libris*

Table 3. Cargoes of Books Imported into London by Description and Year

Descriptions	1480/81	1491/92	1502/3	1507/8	1512/13	1514/15	1520/21	1534/35	1537/38	Totals	Per cent
Bokes			3	2					1	6	3.2%
Preyntyd Bokes	1			1						2	1.1%
Unbound Bokes								3	3	6	3.2%
Diverse Histories	15									15	8.2%
Libris, Parvis Libris	2		2	2		6	1	2		15	8.2%
Libris Depictus	2									2	1.1%
Libris Impressis		5	23	12	7	2	33	19		101	54.8%
Libris Unbound									6	6	3.2%
Diverse Libris Impressis		5					1			6	3.2%
Libris Impressis Unbound								2	13	15	8.2%
Libris Impressis Bound & Unbound								1		1	0.5%
Primers		1			4	4				9	4.9%
Totals	20	11	28	17	11	8	39	27	22[a]	184	100%

Sources: See Table 1.a.
Notes: Book descriptions are as they appear in the accounts (mixed Latin and English). [a] Includes one cargo of *Libris Impressis* and *Bokes* shipped together.

impressis.[60] The accounts for 1512/13 and 1514/15 are much simpler, with an increase in descriptions again in 1520/21, including one shipment of *iiij gross borded primers.*[61] A single entry in 1537/8 is for *libris impressis unbound and bokes,* implying that there was some distinction between these terms.[62]

In 1534/5 there began two new distinctions for *libris impressis:* unbound and a mixed cargo of bound and unbound.[63] In total the printed books accounted for 84% of the number of shipments, while *unbound bokes* and *libris impressis unbound* accounted for 5.2% (five shipments). In 1534 the importing of bound books, along with the privilege to sell books retail by those outside the Stationers' Company, was revoked by Henry VIII with *An Acte for Prynters and Bynders of Bokes,* which included the additional provision that books were required to be imported unbound as English binders were 'destitute of worke and lyke to be undon, except somme reformacion here in be hade'.[64] It seems that English printers could not keep their binders busy, so Parliament had to step in to assure them of future work.[65] This was in contrast to the early years of print, when the need for their skills led to favourable regulations for aliens involved in the book trade.[66] The French printer François Regnault complained to Thomas Cromwell about this act because he had imported bound books and was now unable to sell them.[67] Only a single cargo for 1537/8 was not identified as being specifically all unbound: the mixed cargo of *libris impressis unbound and bokes.*[68]

As the customs accounts are a mix of English and Latin, it is possible that there is no difference between *bokes* and *libris.* Of course many (if not most) of the *diverse histories* and primers were probably printed, but those books were classified by subject matter in the accounts.[69] François Regnault was importing books described as *libris impressis, libris impressis unbound* and *unbound bokes.*[70] He printed *horae* (Books of Hours) for all price ranges, so perhaps the *bokes* were deluxe editions. They may have been manuscripts or perhaps even printed books on vellum. The percentage of books described as *libris impressis* decreased over the decades as there was an increase in the number of terms available for describing the different types of books.

Obviously *libris impressis* refers to printed books. If *bokes* refers to manuscript books what could *libris* mean, if there is any difference? It could merely denote *libris impressis* when it did not seem as if enough space were available in the accounts. In many of these instances, however, there was plenty of room to fit a longer description. Although printed books were the main import, if we examine them by value we get a slightly different picture for our final years—that is, if the term *bokes* does refer to manuscripts. It might, on the other hand, refer to deluxe books printed on vellum. Two importers of *bokes,* Francis Birckman and François Regnault, were both having deluxe Books of Hours printed, including one edition jointly.[71] Regnault was known for editions printed on vellum, and it is possible that Birckman was also.

Evidence in the account book of the Oxford bookseller John Dorne, who records transactions at his shop through 1520, suggests that Birckman's editions were somehow special.[72] Few of the transactions note the printer of the text, but Birckman's name appears again and again, implying that books he printed deserved to be noted. Books printed by Richard Pynson, Richard Faques and Wynkyn de Worde were also noted by John Dorne in his account book. In addition, Birckman's texts were some of the more expensive books: a bound *Sarum Missale* sold on 17 May 1520 for 6s. 4d., while a similarly described copy by Faques sold eleven days earlier for 4s. 6d., only two-thirds the price.[73] While it could be that Faques' edition was printed in England and was therefore cheaper, it does show that people were willing to pay considerably more for a text printed by Birckman. Further research into printing on vellum and paper by these printers along with related information from booksellers' accounts identifying specific editions could help clarify if there are any real differences between the various classifications found in the accounts.

Custom officials were merely concerned with collecting the revenue for the kind, so why did they see the need to distinguish between types of books? Was there some reason for collecting this information? Books did not appear in any official customs rate book until 1545 and even then were only classed as either books (imported by the basket or maund) or primers (imported by the dozen or gross), not by any other features (e.g. bound or unbound).[74] Other sources relating to the customs systems may reveal what, if any, distinction there was between *libris impressis, libris, diverse histories* and *bokes*.

Conclusion

A systematic analysis of a wide range of overseas customs accounts helps to illuminate and extend our understanding of the early trade in books in England. The first entry for the import of books in extant London customs accounts was in December 1477 and by 1480/81 there was already a lively book trade with merchants who were specialising in importing books.

One of the questions that remain is whether there were any significant differences in meaning of the different descriptive terms for books used in the customs accounts. Because of their production method, manuscripts would not have been produced in large enough quantities to have been imported the way printed books were. It is possible that *libris* and *bokes* were not printed books or were deluxe editions printed on vellum, although *libris* could have been an abbreviation for *libris impressis*. Further research on importers of *libris* who printed on vellum could solve this question. In addition, there were now distinctions between cargoes of bound and unbound books. It is possible that the customs officials began making this distinction as a way to collect evidence to support the ban before Parliament passed the Act forbidding the import of bound books.

Beginning in 1512/13 we see fewer types of shipping units, with baskets and fatts making up over 88% of containers for book-only consignments and often 100%. This shows that importers had discovered that the basket and fatt were ideal for shipping books, probably both as a physical unit and economically. They quickly gave up using casks such as the hogshead and pipe, which were more expensive to produce and not an ideal shape. This specialisation in shipping containers went along with the increase in the numbers of book-only cargoes, showing that there was a merchant group specialising in the trade in books. Of the mixed consignments in later decades, many of them included printing- and binding-related items such as paper and binding boards.

This study also adds to our understanding of how the English demand for books was supplied by continental Europe in the late fifteenth and early sixteenth centuries. In particular, the customs accounts give us a view into the business side of the book trade, as printers had to discover the best way to distribute their product over long distances, information that is not obtainable through bibliographical or textual studies. By examining accounts over ninety years we can see the emergence of an industry that evolved a growing specialisation in the import of books. Further research examining changes in the duties applied to books can show how books moved from a luxury item in the beginning of the age of print to a common commodity within a few short decades. Even though a set customs rate was not official until 1545, a change from an *ad valorem* rate (applied to each item) to a standardised rate began to be applied by the early sixteenth century. This shows that customs controllers had become familiar with printed books and no longer viewed them as unique items, instead assigning them a general value per cargo. Studying the importers can also show patterns in specialisation over time. A group emerged specialising in the importation of books alone, members of which were often involved in the book trade in other ways. Some were responsible for publishing texts, many specifically for the English market. Others were printers themselves, either in England, supplementing their own stock, or on the continent. Secondary sources show printers, publishers and agents working together to locate and ship desired texts and make recommendations.

Looking at these few accounts and analysing the data quantitatively has made it possible to see some large-scale patterns in the importation of books in the late Middle Ages. A picture of the book trade from an economic perspective has been overlooked by scholars researching early book history, who have been mainly focused on bibliographic surveys. It adds to information about trade for a commodity not yet studied by economic historians. In addition, information in the accounts helps to show the beginnings of the book industry, as the printing of large numbers of texts forced its practitioners to change from craftsmen to businessmen.

Appendix A: The Sources

This study draws on eleven fairly complete and legible overseas accounts of petty custom or poundage for the port of London from 1457 to 1535. The accounts were chosen largely on the basis of which were likely to contain information on book imports, and which could be most easily filmed in the Public Record Office. Only one of the accounts is in print: that edited by H.S. Cobb for 1480/1.

Using the National Archives database a list was created of accounts that could possible contain cargoes of books (petty customs and tunnage and poundage accounts). All accounts 5 membranes or less were eliminated, as they were unlikely to cover a full year. Accounts were selected at intervals of 5 to 10 years, although there are no extant accounts between 1523 and 1533.

All but two accounts (E122/203/4 and E 122/81/8) are petty customs, by either collectors or controllers of the accounts. There were usually two collectors for each port who kept account, as well as one controller who kept a separate account as a way to audit the collectors' accounts.[75]

E122/203/4. 36 Hen. VI. The first legible date is 12 November, 1457 on f. 2, the last legible date is 4 August, 1458 on f. 29r. It is the beginning of the account that is greatly damaged, which also makes it difficult to read the account header. It is possible to make out that it covers up to (*usque*) Michaelmas, so this account seems to cover a full year. Bound in book form containing 36 folios, all of them recording imports. This account is the only one not petty customs, but of tunnage and poundage. Much of it is badly damaged and large parts of it are illegible with blotchy leaves and faded ink, while other pages are in very good condition.

E122/194/19. 11–12 Edw. IV. Covers 10 ½ months, from 29 September 1471 to 4 August 1472. Consists of 18 membranes, imports cover mm. 1–17d. Petty Customs, particulars of account. In very good condition. The ink is very dark and the hand very clear although small and cramped.

E122/194/25. 20–21 Edw. IV. Covers 12 months, from 29 September 1480 to 29 September 1481. Consists of 27 membranes, imports cover mm. 1–11d. Petty Customs, controllment of account. Although I worked mainly from Cobb's edition of this account, I checked several entries in the original account to see how he was translating the different terms for books. Membranes good, although some dark areas, hand was easy to read.

E122/78/9. 6–7 Hen. VII. Covers 12 months, from 29 September 1490 to 29 September 1491. Consists of 18 membranes, imports cover mm. 1–6d. Petty Customs, controllment of account. Membranes in very good condition, very light with a clear hand.

E122/80/3. 18–19 Hen. VII. Covers 12 months, from 29 September 1502 to 29 September 1503. Consists of 29 membranes, imports cover mm. 1–13d. Petty Customs, controllment of account. Membranes in good condition, the ink was dark and the hand was very easy to read.

E122/80/5. 23–24 Hen. VII. Covers 12 months, from 29 September 1507 to 29 September 1508. Consists of 32 membranes, imports cover mm. 1–15d. Petty Customs, particulars of account. Account in fairly good condition, a few small holes. The bottoms of some membranes were dark and sections were sometimes difficult to read because the ink was faded.

E122/82/9. 4–5 Hen. VIII. Consists of 46 membranes, imports cover mm. 1–30d. Petty Customs, controllment of account. The first legible date for 1512/3 is in the middle of membrane 1 for 4 October, while the last legible date is 5 September on membrane 29d, with membranes 30 and 30d also containing exports, so it seems to have a full year, or almost a full year. There is damage to the bottom and right side, but what isn't damaged is legible. It looks like some of the damage to the membranes occurred before the accounts were recorded, as they were squeezed in and follow the contour of the damage on the sides. The damage to the bottom must have occurred later and often only the beginnings of lines are visible. It looks like a fairly consistent amount of each membrane is missing from the bottom, so it is hard to know how much is gone. None of the legible names in the damaged sections were found importing books in other entries, but it is certainly possible that entries were missed. On a few occasions the prices of cargoes were missing due to damage on the right side, but fortunately they were all baskets of *libris impressis*, which were listed elsewhere and used to estimate values.

E122/82/3. 5–6 Hen. VIII. Probably covers 12 months. First legible date on m.3 of 6 Nov. 1514 to 25 September 1515. Consists of 36 membranes, imports cover mm 1–14d. Petty Customs, described as view/controllment of account. Some sections were faded and hard to read. There were many holes and some damage, mainly along the edges. Similar to E122/82/9 some of the damage must have occurred before being used to record the entries, as they often followed the damaged edges.

E122/81/8. 11–12 Hen. VIII. Covers 11 months, from 3 October 1520 to 22 August 1521. Tunnage and Poundage, particulars of account. Consists of 44 membranes, imports cover mm. 1–43d. Nearly half of membranes 11–15 are missing. There is considerable damage and holes on many membranes. In addition there was considerable fading in sections which made some areas difficult if not impossible to read. Account is not catalogued as Tunnage and Poundage, but includes imports by *indigena* so it cannot be Petty customs.

E122/82/8. 26–27 Hen. VIII. Covers 12 months, from 29 September 1534 to 29 September 1535. Consists of 48 membranes, imports cover mm. 1–22d. Petty Customs, controllment of account. The membranes were in good condition, but the hand was the most difficult to read.

E122/81/18. 28–29 Hen. VIII. Covers 11½ months, from 6 October 1537 to 26 September 1538. Consists of 17 membranes, imports cover mm. 1–16d. There was quite a bit of damage to the left side of membranes 3–8, which cut off mainly the values of imports, but on the dorse side means quite a bit of information on importers and cargoes are missing. The hand is otherwise clear and easy to read although faded in areas.

Section II

Consumers:

Producers, Owners and Readers

6

'But solid food is for the mature, who … have their senses trained to discern good and evil'

John Colop's Book and the Spiritual Diet of the Discerning Lay Londoner

Anna Lewis

In a sermon on the subject of acquiring knowledge, Bernard of Clairvaux distinguishes between good and bad approaches to learning. Drawing on Paul's warnings that 'knowledge puffs up' and that a man should 'not think more than he ought, but [should] think with sober judgment', Bernard compares knowledge to food that should be consumed in 'the right amount in due order' to ensure it is beneficial to one's health. He clearly has in mind biblical imagery such as that of Hebrews 5: 13–14: 'For everyone who partakes only of milk is not accustomed to the word of righteousness, for he is an infant. But solid food is for the mature who because of practice have their senses trained to discern good and evil.'

Just as the physical well-being of the body depends on 'a right choice in the taking of food, what to take first, what next, and the amount of each kind to be eaten', so spiritual health is determined by the Christian's ability to pursue the right kind of knowledge (matters related to salvation first and foremost) in the right 'manner' (with godly motives). This is the difference described by St Paul between those who 'think they know' and those who know as they 'ought to know'. Those who exercise 'sound judgement' and 'prudence' will desire knowledge only for the sake of edifying themselves or blessing their neighbours. Knowledge that is 'cooked on the fire of love' can be 'digested' by the soul and converted into a godly life, but the man who stuffs the memory, the 'stomach of the mind', with a 'glut of knowledge' will discover in his conscience the 'inflammations and torments' caused by undigested food. Bernard's choice of language clearly indicates that the 'well-read man' who fails to learn responsibly is guilty of a form of gluttony, a vice that contrasts with the prudence or temperance of the one who learns correctly.[1]

Bernard's sermon was incorporated into the late fourteenth-century Middle English tract known, from its opening words, as *The Holi Prophete David Seith*, which was almost certainly written by a Lollard. The writer of this tract presumably felt that, at a time when the consumption of religious literature by the laity was increasing, Bernard's guidance on developing a spiritually healthy approach to learning was worth hearing. We know the identity of at least one recipient of this advice because *The Holi Prophete* is found in the mid-fifteenth-century religious anthology that bears his name, John Colop (CUL MS Ff.vi.31). Colop was a London merchant with notable responsibilities in the city and connections to the senior stratum of civic society.[2] In Colop's anthology, *The Holi Prophete* keeps company with a rather 'remarkable' combination of material of a spiritually advanced and controversial nature, in particular tracts on the contemplative life by the author of *The Cloud of Unknowing* and texts composed entirely of Bible translation accompanied with authoritative commentary.[3] In the fifteenth century this was deemed to be exactly the kind of reading material that required 'sober judgement', 'prudence' and 'care' if it was to be digested correctly and not produce the 'irregular and harmful humours' described by Bernard.[4] It may then seem surprising that this potentially hazardous volume was not compiled for private use but was produced as part of a book-sharing scheme; an inscription (also found on four other manuscripts) designates the book as intended for the 'comyn profite', to be passed from 'persoone to persoone, man or womman as long as the booke endureth' (f. 100ʳ). In fact, as this paper will demonstrate, the network or community that the common-profit book scheme both assumes and perpetuates offers the safest place for the reading of difficult or dangerous religious material. As so much of the content of Colop's manuscript itself suggests, the communal dimension of the common-profit book scheme could have provided an environment conducive to the prudent and sober learning described by Bernard.

Late medieval England seems to have been marked by an acute suspicion, or even fear, of religious 'enthusiasm' and the unique or 'singular' behaviour, the individualism, it bred. Excesses in behaviour, acting in ways that set oneself off from the crowd and claims to out-of-the-ordinary spiritual experiences were seen as possible preludes to, if not outright symptoms of, heresy. Of course, this was nothing new: in a tradition of teaching going back to the earliest monastic communities, error was associated with extremes of behaviour, rejection of counsel and a reliance on one's own thoughts and opinions, all of which were rooted in pride. According to the Desert Fathers, those guilty of acting in such ways failed to exercise discretion, the 'mother[,] … guardian, and the guide' of all virtues.[5] Nevertheless, there are good reasons to think that in the fourteenth and fifteenth centuries England experienced renewed anxiety about the dangers of 'radical religious individualism'.[6] In part, this anxiety was contracted from the Continent, where heavy-handed responses to disconnected and sometimes nebulous expressions of autotheism and antinomianism had created the terrifying spectre of 'Free Spiritism', a threatening heresy to be guarded against at all costs. The term 'Free Spiritism' was a loose one, embracing 'eccentrics who had picked up a few mystical terms'; consequently it is not easy to establish the doctrine and character of the movement, if we can even define it as such.[7] Nevertheless, as Robert Lerner points out, many of those accused of the heresy drew the hostility of the authorities because of their extreme piety, asceticism and 'insubordinate zeal' manifested in behaviour that set them apart from others and from the authority of the church.[8] Given the link between Free Spiritism and the mystic Marguerite Porete, the heresy presented a challenge to orthodox mystics in particular, who consequently went to great lengths to define and reject 'false' or erroneous forms of the contemplative life while defending their own teachings as 'true'.[9]

As Kathryn Kerby-Fulton has recently made clear, England was well aware of the dangers of Free Spiritism, the consequent suspicion of mystical and revelatory theologies and the legislation and literature designed to forestall error and heresy.[10] Indeed, Kerby-Fulton argues that this awareness helped to shape England's own mystical and visionary writers and the readers who responded to their texts. For anyone interested in mystical experience, guides to the testing of that experience through the processes of *discretio spirituum* and *probatio* became required reading. Thus *The Chastising of God's Children*, a text written for female contemplatives sometime around the start of the fifteenth century, incorporates instruction on discerning true and false visions taken from Alphonse of Pecha's defence of Bridget of Sweden and, notably, renders it more conservative and less 'enthusiastic'.[11] As Rosalynn Voaden has pointed out, the rigorous process of the discernment of spirits gave spiritual directors an authoritative tool with which to counsel, but also control, the visionary, limiting her independence and keeping her accountable.[12] Considering a slightly different but related context, Vincent Gillespie argues that the Carthusians, usually assigned a 'dominant role' in the production and circulation of vernacular religious texts, were in fact anxious to keep a tight control on the dissemination of mystical texts, preventing their 'leakage into a potentially more volatile readership in the wider community'.[13] As the fifteenth century wore on the Carthusians seemed to lose confidence in the abilities of a lay audience and became increasingly cautious and conservative in their book-making.[14] This desire to limit the readership of mystical texts to a reliable group is also apparent in the writings themselves: *The Cloud of Unknowing*, for example, begins with careful instructions about who can, and who cannot, read the book. For both mystical writers and the communities that read their work this desire to regulate access came from a keen awareness of the potential perils of pursuing the contemplative way, of how easily the inexperienced may go astray.

Pride, disobedience and singular behaviour were also identifying characteristics of England's homegrown heretics, the Lollards. In particular, Lollards were guilty of prioritising the individual's engagement with scripture and rejecting the counsel of church and tradition. Arundel's Constitutions were an attempt to reduce the opportunity for such independent reading and interpretation; however, writing in the mid-fifteenth century, Reginald Pecock described how Lollards still 'cleuen and attenden over vnreulili to the Bible' and refuse to countenance the arguments or expositions of 'clergie of Goddis hool chirche in erthe'.[15] Pecock, the century's most vocal opponent of Lollardy, described the heretics' refusal to submit to the church (disobedience) and their over-dependence on the Bible (a lack of discretion) as the two central errors of the sect. In *The Repressor of Overmuch Blaming of the Clergy* Pecock tellingly compares the Lollard obsession with relying on scripture to the exclusion of all other texts to the gluttony of children:

> bi cause children louen sweete meetis and drinkis ful miche, therfore whanne thei comen to feestis thei feeden hem with sweete stonding potagis and with sweet bake metis, and leuen othere substancial and necessarie metis ... and therfore at the laste thei geten to hem therbi bothe losse of dewe nurisching and also sumtyme vilonie. Certis in lijk maner y haue wiste suche men, that han so ouer miche ʒeuen hem to reding in the Bible aloone, haue gete to hem losse of sufficient and profitable leernyng which in other wheris thei miʒten haue gete ...[16]

Pecock makes the Lollard dependence on the Bible childish and the Lollards themselves children, an image that denounces the heretics' refusal to be properly governed by their superiors as nothing other than immaturity. Children lack all sense of measure, they lack 'sober judgement'; discretion is clearly a mark of the mature. Pecock was not opposed to the laity reading scripture as long as they invited the assistance of the clergy; by withdrawing from this authoritative community the Lollards fell victim to the perils of misinterpreting vernacular scripture.

Colop's volume contains texts on the contemplative life and texts containing vernacular scripture. The book therefore furnishes the reader with ample opportunity to run foul of both sets of perils described above: the peril of going astray on the contemplative path and the peril of misinterpreting scripture. These are dangers, however, that the contents of the book, both in and around these particular texts, seem to address. The following survey of the volume's contents reveals recurring instances of warnings of the dangers of singularity. These warnings are complemented by an equally insistent focus on the need to counter the urge to individualism with integration in spiritual community and the humility to be subject to that community. The presence of this emphasis connects Colop's book to contemporaneous teaching on 'safe' and responsible reading.

Given their customary titles, *A Tretis of Discrescyon of Spirites* and *A Pistle of Discrecioun of Stirings*, these tracts traditionally ascribed to the *Cloud* author seem the obvious place to look for teaching on discerning learning. They are not given these titles in Colop's book but are described, respectively, as an account of 'iii dyuers thoughtes ... [and how] to withstond hem' and a 'good reule' (ff. 43ʳ, 53ʳ). While dealing in part with the nature of contemplation (the centrality of love above all and the possibility of union between God and soul), both texts focus more on practical advice for the preparation of the contemplative. The opening of *A Tretis*, describing how there are 'diverse' kinds of spirits and invoking St John's warning that we are not to believe them all, may lead us to expect a manual on the formal testing of visionaries of the kind being abundantly produced during the fourteenth and fifteenth centuries (f. 43ʳ). In fact, as the description of the text in Colop's book suggests, it is rather a treatise on thought management, treating 'thought' as a synonym for 'spirit' or 'demon' in the way that monastic writers such as Evagrius Ponticus and John Cassian had done. Providing instruction on how to recognise the source of one's thoughts, the treatise warns of the dangers of mistaking virtue for vice and of falling into extreme behaviours and pride. It is the devil, the author says, who leads men into 'singuler holynes, passing the comon statute and custom of here degre, as is fasting, wering [the wearing of coarse garments], and other many deuoute observances and outward doyngis,' and into 'open reprouyng of other menys defautis, the whiche thei have not of office to do' (f. 47ʳ). Desiring to be 'singular,' seeking to surpass the actions of other men by going beyond the 'comon ... custom' and demonstrating contempt for others all indicate an abandonment of measure, moderation and humility in favour of extreme behaviour and pride. Such 'unsemely singulertees' are seen to cause dissension and division within a 'deuout congregation', planting seeds of 'bitterness and discord' and damaging the reputation of an entire community: 'wher so euer that any oon or two ben in any deuout congregation, the whiche any oon or two vsith any siche outward singulertees, then in the sight of alle fooles alle the remenant been ensclaundrid bi them' (ff. 47ʳ⁻ᵛ). The way to avoid this dangerous individualism is to refuse to 'consente' to deceptive stirrings of the enemy by opening oneself up to others: giving oneself 'meekly' in all humility, to 'prier and to conseil' (f.48ᵛ). The quality of humility and the process of accountability are key to preventing a falling away from 'right amount and due order'.[17]

This teaching is expanded in *A Pistle of Discrecioun of Stirings*, written as a personal letter to a novice who wants to know how he should respond to the 'stirings' within him that prompt him to take upon himself certain disciplines such as fasting, silence and the solitary life.[18] The answer laid out by the author indicates that the disciple must know the source of his stirrings in order to know how to respond to them, and that this knowledge comes from self-knowledge. Self-knowledge, in turn, is a product of 'gostly wisdom ... ful dyscrecioun and ... perfeccioun of vertu' (f. 56ʳ). With these qualities the student 'sittith quietely in himsilf, as a kyng crowned in his rewme ... goodly gouernyng himsilf and alle hise thoughtis and sterynges' (f. 55ᵛ). The author describes how the contemplative can reach a state where he will not only take the actions of fasting, being in silence, or being solitary, but will know when and how to do these things. While 'kinde' or nature directs us in the simple physical carrying out of the deeds, 'to kun do all theese' is a gift granted only by 'grace of discrecioun' allowing the disciple to 'govern' himself 'discretly' (ff. 65ʳ, 66ʳ). This distinction between doing and knowing how to do can be compared to the distinction between just 'knowing' and knowing how one 'ought to know' made in *The Holi Prophete David Seith*. In both cases the superior knowledge is a product of discretion.

It takes hard work and trial to acquire this ability to govern oneself, however, and the disciple is as yet only at the beginning of this journey. Consequently, he is warned against being overhasty in his own responses to 'the senguler steringes' of his 'yong hert' (f. 57ᵛ). Instead, the youth will benefit from a distrust of himself and his own desires and a willingness to submit to the wisdom of his superiors. Addressing the young man, the author states that he can come to perfect life if his soul:

> is so disposid [to] ... besili, night and day, meke it to god & to good counseil & strongli rise & martir it silf, with casting doun of the owne witt and the owne wille to alle siche sodeyn steringes & singulere and sey scharply that it wol not folow suche steringes, seme thei never so liking, so high, ne so holy, bot if it have therto the witnes and the consentis of some gostli techers. (ff. 58ʳ⁻ᵛ)

At this early stage in his spiritual walk, therefore, the disciple shows his discretion by being obedient: the beginner should not worry about discerning the right from wrong of his thoughts but should submit them all to the judgement of a superior.

The short, penultimate text in the book, 'teching hou a man owith to haue him in alle temptacions', is an English translation of a Latin text (unlikely, in fact, to be by Hugh of St Victor) possibly circulating via the Carthusians.[19] It also deals with thought management and governance of the self. It asserts the need to have control over one's thought-life by understanding the distinction between the 'feeling 'or 'stirring' of a temptation and the consent to it, and between 'reason', 'feeling' and 'fleshly liking.' It stresses the need for self-knowledge and understands that this knowledge is grounded in humility: the man who has truly 'enserchid' himself is aware of his own 'freelte and ... vnperfeccioun'; trust in the self comes about through ignorance of the self (f. 95ᵛ). Finally, in the battle for the mind, the Christian should open himself up to the counsel of the wise: 'if foule thoughtis comen: thoo schulen be schewid soone to sum discreet man' (f. 98ʳ).

We have already noted the presence of Bernard's instruction on learning in *The Holi Prophete David Seith*. The tract goes on to extend this teaching on right kinds of knowing to the reading of scripture. Humility and obedience are described as the goals of study: a man should study holy writ in order to discover his 'owene freelte and defautis' and to 'kepe wilfulli the comaundements of god' (f. 4ᵛ). They are also, however, the necessary foundation of study. *Holi Prophete* describes six steps for attaining a 'trewe vndirstondying' of the Bible (f. 9ʳ). Notably, these are all grounded in humility before God and before others. Praying devoutly before God, Christians should 'meke hem silf' to God and 'sugette hem self' to God's will but they should also 'meke hem self' to their brethren and 'enquere mekeli of every lerned man and speciali of wel-wellid men and weel lyvynge the trewe vndirstondyng of hooli writ, and be thei not obstinat in ther owne wit but gyue stede and credence to wiser men that han the sperit of wisdom and of grace' (ff. 9ᵛ–10ʳ). Additionally, they should 'studie the trewe and opyn exposicion of hooli doctours and othere wise men as thei may eseli and goodly come therto' and presumably submit themselves to such teaching (f. 10ʳ). Instructions on acquiring a 'trewe vndirstondying' of scripture are also given at the end of Colop's book in the brief text entitled 'foure errours whiche letten the verrey knowyng of holi writ' (f. 98ᵛ). The four errors are revealed to be worldliness, fleshliness, covetousness and pride. Like *Holi Prophete*, this text does not offer intellectual or academic advice but emphasises the need for godly living and humility in the pursuit of a 'trewe vndirstondying' of scripture.

What we see in these tracts is a definition of a 'right', we might almost say 'safe', way of knowing, of growing as a Christian. This emphasis on 'discretion', on sober judgement and accountability, is certainly nothing new—late medieval readers of spiritual literature were accustomed to calls to exercise 'discretion' when reading—but, as we have seen, these qualities held renewed appeal in the fifteenth century. Legislation against heretical groups and the formalisation of processes to determine the authenticity of mystics and their experiences were the more obvious manifestations of a desire to contain 'enthusiasm' and inhibit individualistic behaviour. Recent work by Kerby-Fulton and Marleen Cré has demonstrated how strategies of control and containment are also evident in a less public but no less potent form, namely within textual communities: that is, communities tied through the production, dissemination and consumption of texts, whether real and active or only planned or envisaged.[20] Focusing on Carthusian communities reading and writing mystical texts, both Kerby-Fulton and Cré have drawn attention to the 'safe reading' strategies and methods of 'reader guidance' that they cultivated.[21] Kerby-Fulton concurs with Gillespie in pointing to the essentially conservative and cautious attitude of the Carthusians towards lay access to mystical writings and argues that it led them to attempt to rein in the 'enthusiasm' of future readers through annotation and benign censorship of texts.[22] Looking in detail at the case of the glossing of Porete's *The Mirror of Simple Souls*, Kerby-Fulton suggests that the annotator M.N. mounts a series of 'safeguards' throughout the text to promote a balanced and orthodox response to it among readers, a response based on making sound judgements and accepting M.N.'s guidance.[23] She suggests that M.N.'s main goal seems to be 'to teach a style of "safe reading" that will protect the reader's orthodoxy throughout the book'.[24] The role of prudence or 'discretion' in this 'safe reading' is more fully articulated by Cré in her analysis of the Amherst Manuscript, which contains *The Mirror of Simple Souls* as well as other mystical texts. Cré argues that the collection has been structured in such a way as to emphasise the need for discretion in the reading and experience of the contemplative. She points out how more extended discussions of mystical experience are placed in a context of shorter texts promoting humility (the foundation of discretion) and submission to the counsel of elders. The manuscript, then, contains its own form of 'reader guidance ... in the shape of insistently repeated descriptions of the basic tenets of the contemplative life which, if practiced, constitute the spiritual attitude that precludes a mistaken reading of ... texts'.[25]

I believe that this discussion about the implementation of 'safe' reading strategies can be extended to other textual communities such as those envisaged by Reginald Pecock and described in his works, and also to the common-profit book scheme. The combination, identified by Kerby-Fulton and Cré, of appropriate reading matter and an interpretive community around it is in evidence in Reginald Pecock's plans for 'safe reading' by the laity. Though it is unlikely that these plans were ever realised (many of them depended on a plentiful supply of Pecock's own books, something that became an impossibility after his trial for heresy), they are sketched out in his writings. As we have seen, Pecock was critical of Lollards because they 'singulerli' kept themselves to the Bible and focused on the individual, rather than community, as interpreter.[26] In contrast, Pecock envisions the use of several comprehensive texts (mostly his own) to supplement, or even replace, the use of the Bible. These texts do not shy away from dealing with difficult and challenging aspects of the faith for fear that such discussions will provoke dangerous questioning.[27] In fact, Pecock considers that this is exactly the kind of material that will draw the laity into communion with the clergy. Faced with hard concepts and ideas, Pecock argues, the laity will not only realise how they need the assistance of knowledgeable clerks but will also desire to dwell in friendship and acquaintance with them.[28] Pecock envisions lay reading operating under the instruction of the church but emphasises fellowship rather than authority. Wise and discreet readers read within this safe and responsible community.[29]

As these examples suggest, strategies of safe reading based on the exercise of discretion are strategies firmly embedded in community. The tracts in Colop's book iterate the teaching that the meek soul practises discretion by submitting to the counsel of others and accepting the 'comon statute and custom' while the soul which errs acts 'withouten auysement of counseil' and follows 'the steringes of the gredy hert by [its] owne witte and [its] owne wyll' (f. 58ᵛ). Renunciation of self-will in favour of the 'common will' is, in fact, the subject that opens Colop's book. The short text entitled *Propur Will* celebrates the forsaking of one's own (or 'propur') will and states that submitting to the 'comon will' is a most precious offering to God (f. 1ᵛ). The common will is identified with obedience and humility on the part of the individual; it is 'meke men' who 'be counceyl' bind themselves 'unto comyn will', 'for obedience is the tresoure of the trinite' (ff. 6ᵛ–7ʳ). Judas, who gave into his 'propur wille', is contrasted with Jesus, who was 'fre of will and comen to all' (f. 8ᵛ). Notably, those who refuse to let go of their own will are identified as those who 'forsakys the conceyl ... [which is] the ordenaunce and techyng of discrete men' (f. 7ᵛ).

It is perhaps appropriate that a book that claims it has been written for the 'common profit' should open with a bitter attack on self-will and a praise of 'common will'. Like the persistent textual emphasis found in Colop's book on the need for subordination of self to community, for openness and accountability, the theme of *Propur Will* could presumably have been used to affirm the values and the authority of the very real community to which these common-profit book readers belonged. For it seems likely, given what we know of his associations and activities within the city, that Colop was part of a network of social, spiritual and literary connections that formed something of a spiritual elite.[30] This is the kind of grouping that Mary Erler has recently described as a 'devout society'.[31] It is also likely, given the (albeit limited) reader history of the common-profit books, that those expected to benefit from Colop's book were also members of this group.[32] Membership of these informal networks could transcend convent and monastery walls, and Vincent Gillespie has suggested that Syon Abbey, with many of its nuns coming from high-born and well-connected families and a high number of its brethren recruited from the London clergy, was a 'metropolitan centre for such networks'. As Gillespie shows, Colop had connections with Syon because of his involvement in the fraternity of the Chapel of All Angels at Syon, and it is possible that the abbey was the source of a number of the texts found in the common-profit books.[33]

Rather than travelling far, then, the common-profit books circulated within the bounds of a small, devout community composed not only of laity but also of clergy and religious. Such a community could supply the environment for the realisation of the model of reading practice that the teaching in Colop's book promotes: namely, reading with discretion. Books that were transmitted within spiritual associations or 'devout societies' served, as Erler states, as markers of 'affiliation with others, of an identity more inclusive and more complex than the personal'.[34] In the case of the common-profit books, even though there is some room for personal response to any one book (it can be temporarily kept by one person; it can be read in private), reading is always performed with awareness of the volume's greater communal or 'public' form; reading and response become accountable. Furthermore, among the book's readers are members of religious orders and the ecclesiastical hierarchy; their commanding, if silent, presence offers other readers the reassuring (or cautionary) spiritual authority of those 'lerned' and 'wel-wellid' teachers described by *Holi Prophete*. As the inscription in Colop's book explaining the common-profit book scheme suggests, this is a book that is lent out, borrowed, but never actually owned by any one person. A consequence of this is that the book disassociates itself from the dangers of privacy and the creation of secret or 'singular' readings; it can never be wholly received nor wholly consumed by one individual. If the texts in this anthology are a spiritual meal which the reader is being given the chance to enjoy, then the message of both its content and its packaging is that it is a meal that has to be shared with others.

In both its form and its content, then, Colop's book manifests the same concern with safe reading and regulated access to knowledge expressed by other writers and readers of the period. On the one hand, there is regulation and restraint. The presence of past, current and future readers becomes a force for 'reader guidance' and therefore a force of control. After all, this is a period in which there is heightened sensitivity to the danger of individualists (those who, at a later date, would be labelled religious 'enthusiasts'), a danger likely to be only more critical among a lay reading audience. On the other hand, there is access and opportunity. This reading community creates a space within which the 'safe' reading of a variety of texts can take place; it sets some 'safe' boundaries for limited exploration of difficult material, including tracts on the contemplative life and vernacular scripture. Colop's book shows us that such 'solid food' could be an acceptable part of the diet of the discerning lay Londoner of the fifteenth century.

7

The Acquisition and Disposal of Books for Worship and Pleasure by Mercers of London in the Later Middle Ages

Anne F. Sutton

Very few mercers of late medieval London did not have a good basic education, often with Latin grammar, and few lacked the means to buy some books; in their wills they passed these possessions to others. The friends of a young man destined for apprenticeship with a mercer of London in the fifteenth century had to pay a premium for his indenture, up to £10 with a mercer of middling standing, and probably £20 to someone like Richard Whittington. When they were sent abroad in the last years of their apprenticeship they learned the basics of Dutch and French. If they had linguistic facility, like William Caxton, they could make themselves a career abroad, as a factor for others, or even in diplomacy. Lesser mercers rarely ventured into overseas trade and contented themselves with a shop in the capital, visiting country fairs or distributing via provincial chapmen, and might be content with apprentices who had only basic reading, writing and arithmetic and the Latin picked up from a primer and the liturgy. In other words, the need of mercers for learning varied, and consequently their need for books.

The skills of all mercers with account books and business papers, and their use of scriveners, who supplied business and legal writing on order, have already been examined;[1] this paper describes the books they acquired for devotion and pleasure and aims to include all references to surviving books as well as those mentioned in wills and inventories.[2] Mercers shared the same texts available to other English people of similar education and means: many owned books as a matter of course, a few took an exceptional interest, and, as their trade of mercery included books among other small luxury items, they were interested in their consumption from a purely commercial angle (but about this nothing is known).

Education, religious debate and common profit

That mercers were educated was borne witness to by Reginald Pecock, that supporter of lay education and opinion. He was rector of St Michael Paternoster Royal and master of Whittington College from July 1431 to 1444, appointed through the influence of John Carpenter, common clerk and chief executor of Richard Whittington, the greatest mercer of them all; he was given the duty of selecting books from Carpenter's collection for Guildhall Library. For these years Pecock was at the centre of the Mercery, and it was then he wrote most of his books, choosing to write in English and engage the laity in his arguments promoting the church's authority and combating heresy. He thought that the capacity to understand and reason on theological matters was not confined to the clergy. Mercers were 'right great witted lay men being of great reputation';[3] he also recorded that some servants of mercers had read one of his books and reproved him—in other words, they had not refrained from argument with him.[4] The brightest and most inquiring of lay minds, avid for sermons and argument and all new ideas in the busy concourse of a great city, needed more sophisticated guidance, as Pecock recognised, to keep them under the control of the clerics who considered themselves to be their superiors. Not only was Pecock one day to be arraigned as a heretic and condemned to be deprived of books and writing materials, but some mercers came close to investigation in the 1420s. Education and cleverness in business, quite apart from an inquiring mind (not always an adjunct of business flair), made it almost inevitable. The aged and wealthy John Shadworth's dinner table in St Michael Bassishaw parish was the location of some dangerous conversations. Shadworth's chaplain, Thomas Garenter, was an associate of Richard Mungyn, a priest sentenced to perpetual imprisonment because of his obduracy in heretical opinions in the heresy trials of 1428–29. Men sitting at Shadworth's table in February 1428 who heard Mungyn's heretical opinions included Alderman William Estfeld and John Russell, both mercers, and priests from nearby churches who gave evidence at the trial. Both Estfeld and Russell were examined. Thomas Garenter had to formally abjure at St Paul's Cross on 5 December 1428,[5] and Estfeld became mayor for the first time nine months later. It was for Estfeld's mayoralty that John Lydgate was commissioned to write a mumming for Twelfth Night 1429, performed apparently by and for the Mercers. Guests could have included Bishop Alnwick of Norwich, close friend of Estfeld and the presiding bishop at the trials of the year before. Lydgate's complex text complimented the city and merchants for their wealth, and the courage that made them trade in exotic lands across the sea.[6] Wealthy mercers, therefore, had access not only to the latest religious debate but also to the best of contemporary literature and books, if they wanted them, and that access should not be underestimated.

The company also had a certain religious standing, and, like all companies of London, they encouraged communal worship. They had their own chapel, and from 1442 were in full charge of the considerable Whittington estate which supported an impressive almshouse and chantry college. Although the company did no more for the latter than hand over funds, the college clerics were there for those mercers who wished to converse with them, including the first master, Reginald Pecock. The dispersal of Whittington's bounty had also involved lesser men such as John Colop, a fellow parishioner who benefited from the great man's beautification of St Michael Paternoster.[7] Colop was employed as a minor dispenser of funds on the instructions of the executors and has been shown to have been involved in a scheme to make religious texts more widely available. The texts so designated were often called common-profit books. The mercers were thus part of this milieu and method of thinking—anything to do with Whittington interested them. Persons associated with a surviving common-profit book include John 'Killum', a grocer who died in 1416 and made John Colop, described as his servant, his executor.[8] Killum was very variously spelled but the name was shared by a well-known mercer, Martin Kelom, and the possibility of a relationship remains an intriguing possibility. John Killum's will is the first reference to John Colop, who was presumably a grocer, like his master; he became ubiquitous as a conscientious disposer of estates left for charity, often involving considerable sums: Killum's precise charitable bequests amounted to at least £100, there was his residuary estate, and another 200 marks fell due ten years later. Colop was later an administrator of the will of one of Killum's executors, John Sudbury, and associated in the administration of others. In 1423 his most prestigious task was the disposal of Whittington's estate under the directions of Carpenter. Colop also had close family relations with a stationer, which helped in the creation of common-profit texts.[9] The deliberate transfer of worthy texts between pious persons in order to gain prayers for the donor and promote learning and devotion free from the taint of heresy has been particularly linked to the first half of the fifteenth century, but it did not begin or end there. It can be understood to have become a standard means of disposing of charitable residuary estates, almost on a par with the repair of bridges and poor maidens' dowries. The church was especially eager to combat the circulation of heresy in the aftermath of the Wycliffite and Hussite controversies, but there remained a solid desire to assist poor clergy who could not afford books and to promote education generally. Books could be expensive to buy if they reverted to the retail market, so bequests to a worthy recipient contributed to the common profit and spiritual welfare of the community. It is not impossible that this type of bequest was favoured by Whittington as well as by others of his circle, including his chief executor, John Carpenter, common clerk of London, who left his many books to worthy men. Pecock is known to have supported similar projects, and may have picked up the idea from his time at Whittington College, to which he was appointed by Carpenter. It has also been noted that the concept of common profit—the common weal—should not be limited to those books specifically designated and inscribed by the donor with its purpose as a common-profit book that was to pass from hand to hand until it fell to pieces. The foundation of libraries and the promotion of education were other more expensive and laborious good works created by the same convictions.[10]

During his lifetime, in 1411, Whittington contributed £400 and books to the Greyfriars library, and his posthumous estate assisted a library at Guildhall, probably the result of a deathbed wish expressed to his executor, John Carpenter. The estate of another mercer, William Bury, who died within months of Whittington, was also pressed into the service of the Guildhall library by his executors, who included Thomas Chaucer, the son of the poet.[11] The re-establishment of the library of St Paul's Cathedral by Canon Sherington (d. 1449) and his successor Thomas Lisieux (d. 1450) provoked the mercer William Haxey to leave it his *Gesta Romanorum* in 1460.[12] A similar interest made the mercer families of the Frowyks and Sturgeons draw into the Mercers' Company in 1452 the clerk Roger Merssh, an administrative colleague and an executor of Sherington. Merssh's will of 1459 specifically endorsed Sherington's chantry and endowment of the library.[13] We know nothing of Bury's books or, more importantly, of Whittington's books, but a magnificent Italian-decorated Bible now at Wolfenbüttel can be suggested as once Whittington's. There may also be a hint of Whittington's books in the fact that Thomas Roos, an apprentice of the great man, bequeathed copies of the *Prick of Conscience* and *Piers Plowman*.[14] Was Whittington's household a place where *Piers Plowman*, a poem so closely concerned with matters of the common weal and good works and with so many references to London, circulated and was read aloud? We can be certain that the household was devotionally literate, and we can compare the wide-ranging conversation at the table of Whittington's long-term associate, John Shadworth.[15] Certainly Whittington's concern to chastise and control brewers during and after his last mayoralty and his attendance at the usury trials of 1421 (in which William Bury was not the only mercer prosecuted) may indicate a man determined to conform to the 'good mayor' described in the poem.[16]

Was the poem also known to his executors, the scrivener John Grove, the common clerk John Carpenter, and John White, master of St Bartholomew's Hospital (1418–23) after a period as rector of St Michael Paternoster, Whittington's parish church? White resigned as master and became a brother in Whittington's chantry college of priests, where he died shortly after Whittington in 1424. The poem was certainly known to John Cok, a clerk working for a former master of St Bartholomew's Hospital from 1418, who became a brother of the hospital in 1420 and thus overlapped with Master John White; he spent the rest of his life working for John Wakering

(1423–66), a master whom he grew to admire greatly. Whittington's estate was to pay for the great gate of the hospital and for a window depicting the seven corporal works of mercy, a commonly used device but one emphasised in *Piers Plowman*.[17] Cok had the useful habit of annotating books in his care and the Wolfenbüttel Bible is one of them.[18] Among his annotations in the Bible is the note that John White, who died 15 January 1424, had given this Bible by the means of (*mediante*) his successor, John Wakering, to remain in the hospital for ever (f. 501ʳ). This elegantly and extensively decorated Bible (with little historiation, however) is of Italian workmanship and would have found a perfect owner in Whittington, the greatest supplier of Italian silks and luxuries to the English royal court; his Italian contacts could have sold him this book and he could afford it. Did he give it to John White, his friend and executor, while he was master of St Bartholomew's, and did White then take it and other items to his retirement home? The Bible was an item over which John Wakering had to go to law in order to retrieve it from Whittington's executors after the early death of White in Whittington's College had confused his goods with those of the mercer to whom he was an executor; the items were a cross, an antiphoner, two breviaries, a psalter and a large Bible worth £16.[19]

One other aspect of the common profit idea needs mention: education. Whittington's estate did not provide for a school, and, as his wishes guided his executors, it is likely that the provision of more schools for the capital was an issue only for the next generation. Whittington was certainly in his seventies, possibly his eighties, when he died in 1423, but his younger executor, John Carpenter, was passionately interested in the promotion of education in the capital and founded what was to become the City of London School. Fellow enthusiasts who received books from Carpenter included William Bingham who founded Godshouse, Cambridge, to teach young men to become schoolmasters, and John Neel, Master of the Hospital of St Thomas of Acre, who founded what was to become the Mercers' School. No mercer, great or small, could have been unaware of the interests of the charismatic John Neel, master for over forty years (1420–63) of the Hospital where the Mercers' Company had its hall and chapel.[20]

Bequests for the common profit of giver and recipient

The notion of the common spiritual profit can be said to have pervaded everyday life. Everyone attended a church service and a sermon on Sundays. The parish dominated social life and linked every pursuit to itself. It can therefore be suggested that 'common profit', in its widest possible sense, underlies all book ownership and bequests, not merely of mercers but of all people. It was expected that everyone should promote orthodox piety. It is not surprising, therefore, that devotional texts dominate the wills of all testators. To bequeath an item of spiritual value was a meritorious act which also conferred benefit on the recipient, and it was eminently suitable to record it in the last document of one's life before facing one's Maker.

The wills of mercers studied for this essay come from those proved in the city's court of husting from 1259, the commissary court of the bishop of London from 1374, the court of the archdeacon of London for the brief period during which they survive, 1393 to 1415, and the Prerogative Court of Canterbury from 1383. This survey stops in 1536, simply because the Reformation provides a suitable end point. The husting court produces a total of 193 mercer wills, including those of widows, possibly a slightly high figure as identifications of trade in the early years is not always certain. Of these, 147 fall between 1259 and 1399 and only forty-five between 1400 and 1536, largely because the husting court increasingly attracted only wills concerned with land.[21] Books were rarely mentioned before 1400 (only three mercer wills mentioned books), perhaps because chattels were less emphasised than later and testaments tended to be brief; and of the five husting wills of mercers which mentioned books after 1400 four were also proved in the court of the archbishop of Canterbury. It is certain, for example, that a mercer such as Nicholas Picot, who served as chamberlain (1300–1304) and was almost certainly a member of the London Puy, and who instructed in his husting will that his sons should be taught to 'compose in prose and verse reasonably well', had plenty of books in his house, but they are not in his will.[22] The archdeaconry court produced twenty mercer wills, including those of widows, between 1393 and 1415, with only one book mentioned, a psalter.[23] The Prerogative Court of Canterbury from 1383 and the Bishop of London's Commissary Court from 1374 produced a total of 432 mercer wills, including those of widows, before 1536; of these, 48 testators mentioned books (37 PCC and 11 CC).[24] As is well known, few probate inventories survive for this period, and any books found have been noted, but statistics concerning books in wills cannot be precise and are rarely of any real use.

Bequests for clergy and churches

Two of the earliest mercer wills illustrate the wealth of some mercers and the dominance of religious books, and show the common profit element already at work in its simplest form of the meritorious bequest of a religious text to a church or a clergyman. John de Worstead, a mercer born in Worstead, Norfolk, died in 1368 leaving a portiforium, a missal, a Bible and a Legends of the Saints to his son for life, with instructions that they were then to serve in the church of St Laurence Jewry.[25] Ten years later, in 1379, Walter de Berney, another Norfolk-born mercer of great wealth, left his books of canon and civil law, as well as a portiforium, to William de Norton, a Norfolk rector and an advocate of the court of Canterbury; unfortunately he does not mention why he had the law books. His *Summa de abstinencia* went to Friar Thomas de Elsing along with his Legends of the Saints.[26] The books bequeathed by both these mercers illustrate what a rich mercer might acquire. He could own texts he might never use or read, but he could be aware of their value in terms of learning and money, often perhaps because they had come to him as a pledge or to pay a debt.

The books most likely to be left to churches or priests were the books used daily at mass. Four missals were bequeathed by mercers in this period, all of whom had their own chapels (and chaplains) and the appropriate books and furnishings. William Bury, whose patronymic was probably Church and who came from Bury St Edmunds, left a missal, a chalice and the apparel from what was probably his own altar to his kinsman, Thomas Church of Bury, a chaplain. John Wells left the vestments and missal of his personal chapel to the church of Milding, Suffolk, on the death or remarriage of his widow.[27] Another missal was to serve at the altar of the Virgin in St Michael Bassishaw, along with the chalice and vestments of his private chapel, under a bequest from Elias Davy, who was a benefactor and founder of almshouses at Croydon; the residue of Davy's estate was to provide books for Croydon parish church in 1456. Henry Frowyk left his best missal (of two) and breviary to his widow, Isabel, in 1460, for she continued to use the family's altar.[28] One missal of a mercer alderman survives, that of William Melreth (d. 1446), with an image of him as an alderman kneeling before the Trinity.[29] A missal was essential for any household that could afford its own chapel and chaplain—and the wardens of the Mercers had a block papal licence to have private altars from 1479–80, organised, it seems, during the mastership of Henry Colet.[30] The only printed missal mentioned by a mercer was the 'new massebook prynted of the use of Sarum with all the new festys' left to the parish church of Hernhill, Kent, by William Tenacre in 1498 (see below). A single example of a manual, a collection of rules for priests, was bequeathed by John Denton in 1432 to Robert Rash, chaplain.[31] John Woodcock, a wealthy associate of Whittington, died in 1409 and directed that books and other ornaments were to be bought for his parish church, St Alban's Wood Street.[32]

Another book particularly suitable for a cleric was the *legenda*, the compilation of readings and lessons including extracts from the scriptures and lives of saints used in church services (not to be confused with the *legenda sanctorum*, Legends of the Saints). In 1400 William Sonningwell bequeathed a *legenda* to William Prittewell chaplain, along with a portiforium and £10.[33] Parish connections and duties led Thomas Berby to lend money to his parish of St Stephen Coleman Street, taking as a pledge 'a certain *legenda*', and this he returned on his death in 1468 with a request for prayers.[34] In 1515 William Weston left his great 'legent' with two silver clasps to the master of the Maison Dieu at Dover, stipulating that, if it was sold, the house should have the money and a suite of vestments of blue velvet powdered with angels and stars made with Venetian gold thread, and orphreys.[35]

Most of these bequests represented the simple passage of possessions with the expectation of prayers. Gifts to churches, such as that of Thomas Dunton, who had once served as governor of the Merchant Adventurers, were more elaborate. Thomas left £20 to his parish of St James Garlickhithe so that graduals (large books containing the text and music of the sung parts of the mass) might be bought, the fabric of the church repaired and his tomb paid for. His widow married a fellow parishioner and mercer, Thomas Kent, clerk of the king's council, who endowed a house for the chantry priests of that parish and left it a substantial number of his books in 1469.[36] Equally appropriate gifts were the gospel and 'pystell' (readings from the epistles) left in 1518 by John West, alderman, to the parish church of Millington, Yorkshire, where his father was buried and he had been born, along with three copes; a duplicate set was left to the church of Everingham.[37]

A more common possession of pious and prosperous households was the portiforium or portuous, a compendium of divine service including the hours of the Virgin. The very first book recorded as left by a mercer, Roger Madour, in 1349, was a portiforium (along with a vestment) to a priest.[38] Mercers left a total of seventeen portiforiums. In 1384 the wealthy John de Hellesdon, from the Norfolk village of the same name, left a portiforium (as well as a psalter and chalice) to the parish church of his birthplace.[39] John Sibille, another prosperous mercer whose career was clouded by a spell in the Tower, left 'my two books', a portiforium and a missal, to his son in 1400.[40] In the same year Sibille's contemporary, William Sonningwell, left a portiforium to a chaplain.[41] William Marchford distinguished between his best portiforium left to his kinsman, Simon Marchford, and another covered in green left to another kinsman, John Avery.[42] John Bally, the first husband of Dame Isabel Frowyk, left his portiforium to Edward Fleet if he took on the task of executor with Isabel.[43] Thomas Tickhill, a benefactor of Reading Bridge, left a portiforium and a primer to his kinsman Thomas Cook, an apprentice of Sir William Estfeld. Tickhill's patronymic was Cook and Tickhill, Yorkshire, was the birthplace of Estfeld, and presumably of the Cooks as well.[44] Sir William Estfeld, twice mayor of London and one of the wealthiest Londoners of the fifteenth century, left a portiforium to a favoured apprentice, John Middleton, which he had himself received from his own master, Robert Trees.[45] Substantial gifts from master to apprentice were not uncommon. Katherine, widow of Richard Rich, left a two-volume 'portuos' to her priest, William Love, presumably her household chaplain, described as being already in his possession, and another 'great' portiforium of hers was to be sold. Sir John Stokton left his son William 'my portenar with rings of silver and gilt', as well as his mass book covered with purple velvet upon velvet; another 'portener' with rings not gilt went to his son, John, along with his psalter covered with black velvet. In 1479 John Sutton left his 'best portuous' to Master John Thoresbutte, clerk, to pray for him.[46] William Shore, divorced husband of Edward IV's mistress, left a printed 'portuus' to John Dayll, a priest, in 1494, and lastly, 'my written portous' was the only book mentioned by name in the 1503 will of Sir Thomas Thwaites, mercer and royal official at Calais, the well-known commissioner of books. This he gave to the abbess of Barking, while Master Morgan Hawes might choose eight books.[47]

Common profit dominated the gift of the most ubiquitous and personal of books, the primer (the book of hours, the Little Office of the Blessed Virgin Mary), to which a favourite devotional text might be added. No mercer or his wife would have lacked this essential aid to prayer and devotion; a second-hand manuscript could be found to suit the poorest pocket and printed ones were available for a few pence. Their closeness to the donor made them perfect bequests for favourite relatives and children, and they should perhaps be likened to christening or confirmation presents, status accessories to be carried to church, which often became heirlooms.[48] A minimum of twenty-eight can be found in mercer wills. To the primer must be linked the psalter, which can usually be assumed to mean the psalter of the laity, containing 150 psalms in numerical order.

The best example of this familial inheritance of primers and other religious books in daily use comes from the wills of Henry and Isabel Frowyk. Henry died in 1460 and left his son Thomas his primer, psalter, small red breviary, second best missal and the everyday furnishing of his chapel; he and his wife had been licensed to have a portable altar in 1441. To his wife he left what were the most sumptuous of the furnishings of their chapel and his best breviary and best missal. Isabel was the widow of three mercers and an eminent silkwoman in her own right throughout her life; when she died she left precious religious jewels, such as her tablets of gold and silver-gilt, one depicting the Virgin Mary and the other the Salutation of the Virgin and the Passion of Christ, but she also valued her best primer and her pair of gold beads, both given her by her third husband, Henry Frowyk. These last items she left to Joan (born Sturgeon), the wife of her son Thomas. Thomas received all the furnishings of her chapel, including, no doubt, all the service books she had had since her husband's death. Another primer covered in blue velvet went to her daughter Isabel, wife of the grocer John Warde, along with her best coral beads. Beads were a natural accompaniment to a primer. It is certain that her household contained many more books, but the religious texts were the most valuable and precious items for favoured female relatives.[49]

To turn to more mundane examples: in 1439 John Wells left his three sons, Edward, Erkenwald and Eborard, two psalters and a primer; his daughter received no books.[50] Richard Syff left his sole child, Elizabeth, his primer covered in blue velvet with clasps of silver gilt, which had been her mother's.[51] Elias Davy left a primer to Idonea, daughter of Henry Ruislip, provided she marry with the consent of his executors; perhaps she was his granddaughter. Primers also went outside the family: Richard Wise left his godson, Richard Fabian, his 'better' primer in 1485.[52] William Kirkby, whom his kinsman, John Kirkby, wanted as executor, received one, and Elizabeth, the wife of John Shelley, received a primer from Thomas Chatterley in 1483.[53]

John Sutton, originally from Gnowsall, Staffordshire, died in 1479 owning several primers. His young gentry wife, Beatrice Cokayne from Derbyshire, was to do extremely well out of his estate and be snapped up by a gentry husband. She was, however, specifically excluded from having any of Sutton's books, described as 'alle myn English bookes, ij primers covered with blak velvet, one of thaim with ij claspes of silver ovir gilt and the other with oon clasp of silver enameled' (f. 283ᵛ). To the countess of Oxford, Katherine Neville (whose husband, John de Vere, the thirteenth earl, was in prison at Calais) went the primer with the two clasps and £10 (her priest and each of her two gentlewomen received 50s.); Edmund Cokayn, a relative of Beatrice, received the other primer with one clasp. His English books and all his business books were to be equally divided between his three brothers and two sisters and their families.[54] Comparable in many ways to John Sutton's long will is that of his executor Hugh Brown, mercer and wool stapler, who died in 1503. He lived close by the Crutched Friars, to whom he was a considerable benefactor. He had neither children nor wife, so he left his 'newe written portatyfe sawte', his legends of the saints written on parchment in English, 'the sege of the Regell of Troye', and all his other books 'in papir written' to William Brown, the fifteen-year-old son of Richard Brown, his kinsman.[55]

A young adventurer and mercer, John Ripon, who died in his thirties in 1485, had made use of his time in the Low Countries to buy himself a primer covered with black leather 'of Bruges making', bequeathed to his master, Alderman John Matthew. His panel of the Day of Judgment ('painted table of the Dome which I did make beyond the sea') was left to Henry Smith, his father-in-law.[56] Ripon's comparative informativeness underlines how little is told us by mercers, who were so often adventurers travelling to the Low Countries and the fairs of Antwerp and Bergen op Zoom.[57]

Scarcely ten years after Ripon bequeathed his manuscript hours, a mercer very familiar with the printed book (although there is only one in his will) left 'my new massebook prynted of the use of Sarum with all the new festys' to the parish church of Hernhill, Kent, where he had property. This was William Tenacre, who would certainly have known Caxton well for he had been an apprentice of William Pratte, Caxton's close friend, and had as his apprentice John Colyns, that unsuccessful entrepreneur in the book trade. Tenacre had completed his apprenticeship four years before Caxton came back permanently to England, but his contact with the Prattes remained close for he acted as executor to Pratte and then his widow, Alice.[58] In 1506 Nicholas Alwyn, a past mayor with plenty of expensive items to give away, left his parchment primer covered with black damask with silver clasps to his granddaughter, Joan, wife of Oliver Wood.[59] The last two primers found in mercers' wills are one left to Eleanor, daughter of Humphrey Carvile, in return for her prayers, by Robert Carvile, who had neither child nor wife in 1506, and the 'primer limned with gold with the register of silver belonging' left to Anne, the daughter of his master, William Brown, by Thomas Compton in 1536.[60]

In total seventeen psalters, which were so often bound with primers, were mentioned by mercers. A psalter was left to the church of his birthplace by John de Hellesdon, a mercer of the top rank in 1384. Another was left by Elizabeth, widow of Robert Burley, to one of her executors, Thomas Dane, along with some silver in 1403. Her will was modestly proved before the archdeaconry court, but in fact she owned considerable property in the parishes of St Mary Wolchurch and St Mildred Poultry, including The Saracen's Head, and could be addressed as 'Lady'.[61] In 1417 Margery Nerford, who lived not far from Mistress Burley, left to her eminent and pious executor John Whatley her two-volume glossed psalter, the gloss possibly by Richard Rolle.[62] William Thake left a psalter and 'j prikyng palet' to the supervisor of his will, another mercer, John Olney, in 1422.[63] The prosperous mercer and stapler Thomas Cressy left his son, Thomas, his psalter and primer in 1423.[64] Thomas Aleyn (alderman 1415–22) left all his books (unspecified) and personal adornments as remembrances to his friends in 1438. His widow Margery retained his 'primer and psalter of David that my devout late husband had as a particular memorial (*in special' memoria*) during his life', and this she passed on to Thomas, son of another Thomas Aleyn, kinsman of her husband.[65]

Isabel Street came to London from Cheshire to learn to be a silkwoman and marry William Fleet, a mercer, at the shop-owning craft end of the mercery trade. They had no children who survived to be mentioned in their wills; William died first, and in 1455 Isabel left their great psalter to her kinsman, John Pikton, once an apprentice in her household, with careful remainders. Pikton managed to move higher up the social scale within the Mercers, and over forty years later his will made no reference to any psalter. His widow Margaret survived him by another twenty years and in 1525 left her 'best primer but one' to her daughter, Alice, wife of Piers Starkey, draper. As she had a private chapel there must have been other service books, such as the by then hundred-year-old psalter, but they were not mentioned.[66]

John Donne left his former apprentice and executor, Thomas Mustell, his large psalter, the sole book in the long will of a man who was keenly interested in education and frequently acted as an executor and trustee for the charities of others, including the school in Guildhall Chapel founded by John Carpenter. Mustell left 'my wicked deeds to my ghostly enemy', but he did not mention the psalter in his will.[67] When sons and daughters had already been provided for, treasured texts could be left to others: Maud Muschamp, widow of Thomas who had died many years before, left her primer to Canon Peter Muschamp and her psalter to his brother William in 1498. The Muschamps were a cultivated family: not only was Maud a silkwoman but Thomas had lands in Surrey and the city, served as sheriff, and as warden of the Mercers had ordered new vestments for their chapel in 1449, including altar cloths embroidered with the maid's head device of the company. He also designated in detail the brass for his tomb, even the size of its border and its texts: it was to include his arms 'departed' with his wife's, images of him and his wife and their seven sons and seven daughters, all with appropriate texts above their heads, including a text from Job 19:12 *Miseremini mei, miseremini mei. Saltem vos, amici mei, quia manus Domini tetigit me* and several Biblical texts from the *Dirige*.[68]

As noted, inventories of medieval mercers are hard to find. An inventory of the goods of William Ferris (admitted to the company 1453) was taken when he fell on hard times about thirty years later: it included a primer and a 'portuous' among his household goods.[69] To conclude on primers and psalters, one of the most exemplary practitioners of the common-profit principal was William Pratte, the life-long friend of Caxton: he bequeathed a psalter-primer in the approved manner and encouraged the printing of a text specifically designed to improve the moral and devotional life of his contemporaries. In 1486 he left the psalter-primer to his daughter, Alice, wife of Richard Bull, a mercer. She died after her father but before her mother and had no surviving issue; she left the book to a priest, Richard Phelip, who in his turn passed it to another mercer, John Stile, who recorded the history of the book in his will of 1505 when he left it to John Overton, a chaplain of the company's chapel, on the understanding that he would also pass it on 'as in the said book ys expressed by writtyng, dewly to pray for the sowles theryn expressed by writing'. Enough is known of Stile, who vehemently disapproved of the practice of taking interest, to conclude that he was an appropriate person to share in this book.[70] It was Pratte who persuaded Caxton to translate the *Book of Good Manners* which gave advice on how to live moderately, devoutly and according to one's station. Caxton published it shortly after Pratte's death, paying tribute to his friend in his prologue and mentioning their long friendship, which had begun during their apprenticeships fifty years before. Pratte was therefore a book owner and reader of considerable influence, a fact no one would guess from his will or from that of his widow in 1490: neither mentioned books, and certainly not this common-profit bequest.[71]

A few exceptional religious texts were owned by mercers. As mentioned, John de Worstead left a Bible, and the only other one was owned by Anne, widow of Roger Bonyfaunt, in which she had recorded the only debt she owed that she considered to be more than 'small'. It was owed to a Johanne Baret, she had written it in the Bible herself, and it was to be paid first of all her debts. As her husband Roger had been a successful mercer and adventurer, it is unlikely that this was the family's only book.[72] Mercers also recorded their ownership of other edifying texts: the *Summa de abstinencia* of Walter de Berney (above), the *Prick of Conscience* of Thomas Roos (below) and the *Musica ecclesiastica* of Richard Rich (below). John Trussbut left his *Bonaventur in Anglice descript'* in 1439 to his sister, Dame Eleanor Trussbut, a nun at Crabhouse: the popular Life of Christ in the translation of Nicholas Love was an ideal gift for a nun. Trussbut was a member of the well-connected Norwich and Norfolk family among whom there were several nuns, all remembered by him.[73] John Burton, who came originally from Wadworth, Yorkshire, died in 1460 possessed of property in London and Twickenham, Middlesex. He left his 'great English book called *Legenda sanctorum*' to his second daughter, Katherine, a nun at Halliwell, and specified that it was to belong to the prioress and convent after Katherine's death. Burton and his family were older members of the circle of William Pratte, friend of Caxton, who was to compile his own version in English of the Lives of the Saints and publish it in November 1483.[74] Roger Glasier in 1507 left a copy of the *Pupilla oculi*, which he held as a pledge, to be delivered to Master Harte, a priest of his parish church, St Magnus, and he was to have the 20s. for which it was in pledge or keep the book. This was a manuscript copy because John de Burgh's adaptation of William of Pagula's guide for priests in matters of the confessional went into print only in 1510. Glasier also left instructions for an altar cloth decorated with the Mercers' maid's head to serve at the altar of the fraternity of Our Lady of Gracechurch and he can be understood to have had an appreciation of things both beautiful and religious.[75] Lastly, William Bromwell, a pillar of the Guild of the Holy Name of Jesus in the Crowds of St Paul's, left his English book called *Vitas Patrum* (undoubtedly Caxton's translation) to the wife of Michael Dormer.[76]

Mercers who loved books

For some mercers books were an integral part of their lives. Martin Kelom was not only a mercer but had a good hand and and could cope with an Anglo-Norman text: he wrote up the Mercers' new ordinances of 1404, incorporating those of 1376 into the parchment volume kept for the fair copies of their annual accounts. He undertook this in order to preserve the secrecy of the ordinances and was paid 3s. 4d. Unfortunately it is not known to whom Martin was apprenticed, and he was admitted to the company before the wardens' accounts start in earnest in 1390. He was certainly married before 1401, and his marriage sets him in an interesting context, for he married Joan Cumberton, niece of the notorious John Cumberton (usually known as John of Northampton), who led the opposition to Nicholas Brembre's faction in the city and was nearly executed for his activities.[77] Certain groups within the Mercery were deeply and dangerously involved in the controversies, and it would be interesting to know the part played by a literate young man such as Kelom, probably then in his early twenties, who might have been capable of composing the famous Mercers' petition to parliament of 1386.[78]

A contemporary and possible relative of Martin was John 'Killum', grocer, already mentioned as a man whose estate was used in part to pay for a common-profit book in 1416. So far no certain connection has been found, but, since John was an apprentice and then servant of Nicholas Brembre (the main antagonist of John of Northampton, uncle-in-law of Martin), hostility may have ensured that there was no reference to Martin in John's will. Martin was generally well thought of and acted in several responsible capacities: in 1413 he served as renterwarden of his company and was an arbitrator that year with fellow mercer, Alan Everard, in a dispute; he was an arbitrator again in 1422 with the eminent John Whatley; and he was later on a jury inquiring into aliens acting as brokers in the city without licence.[79] In 1425 he was one of the many feoffees chosen by Whatley to convey property left by Margery Nerford to endow a chantry in St Christopher at Stocks. Margery's feoffees who had made the original grant to Kelom and Whatley had included John Wakering, master of St Bartholomew's Hospital, Richard Osbarn, clerk of the city's chamber, and David Fyvyan, rector of St Benet Fink (recipient of books from Carpenter). Whatley was close to Margery and was bequeathed her glossed psalter (see above); he also took an interest in the provision of a new lectionary for the chapel of St Thomas on London Bridge during his term as a warden of the Bridge (1404–18).[80] Margery was a contemporary of Richard Whittington and part of a devout and 'theologically questioning, yet finally loyal assemblage'[81] of persons who had many links to Reginald Pecock and the executors of Whittington, notably the common clerk, John Carpenter. The same phrase could be applied to similar circles of mercers in other parishes.

It may be that Martin's parents had intended him for a clerical career before his apprenticeship to a mercer. He came from a seemingly affluent background in Writtle, Essex, a manor held by Anne, daughter of Thomas of Woodstock, whose first husband was Edmund, earl of Stafford. In 1427 Kelom handled plate bearing the arms of Suffolk and Stafford, which was apparently in pledge and eventually returned to the then earl of Suffolk.[82] Martin's will was composed in the parish of St Mary Aldermanbury on 1 February 1426, presumably by the notary, John Bungay, clerk of Norwich diocese, who witnessed it: he did not, however, die until 1431. He was to be buried in the same grave as his first wife, Joan Cumberton, but by then was married to Margaret, who was to receive all the goods she had brought to the marriage, his goods at Herfeld and a third part of his property in Old Fish Street for life, the other two-thirds going to his two children. If there were any dispute, matters were to be settled by her oath. He owned to *parentela* in Lincolnshire. To his son, James, who was of age, Martin left not only his defensive armour, sword and dagger but also all his grammar books, his books of philosophy and theology and 'all my English books', but not his primers (in the plural); of these the 'worst' was to be given to his daughter, Joan, who was still a minor. A John Covyn, who appears to have been his step-son, was to have all the books which Kelom had given him during his lifetime. Martin's widow, Margaret, died in 1434 and established a ten-year chantry for her two husbands, John Covyn and Martin Kelom; she chose to be buried with the latter in St Mary Aldermanbury with no 'festis superfluous or pompous'.[83] Martin's son, James, went on to be employed in the office of the privy seal, and for twenty-eight years as a chancery clerk, a striking witness to his family's book-learning. He was associated with Richard Sturgeon, clerk of the crown, who lived in St Bartholomew's Hospital Close and whose family had close links to mercers. He maintained his family's lands in Essex and died in 1458 leaving a widow and heirs.[84]

Thomas Roos, a mercer contemporary of Kelom, also loved books. He benefited from apprenticeship in the household of Richard Whittington, a place which would have widened his cultural aspirations. He was apprenticed in 1391–92 and issued in 1396–97, achieving the livery in the same year; his brother Richard Roos was apprenticed to John Woodcock, another eminent mercer, and admitted and liveried in the same years.[85] All of this argues substantial family capital as well as possible favour from their masters: certainly Richard's son was to receive a gift from John Woodcock. Thomas Roos's will suggests that they were connected with the Hamlake or Helmsley and Belvoir family. A famous master such as Whittington attracted well-connected young men: a fellow-apprentice with Whittington was William Cavendish, grandson of Chief Justice Cavendish, who was to remain an associate of Roos all his life.[86] Cavendish mentioned no books in his will, but Roos left his one son, Guy, a primer with red rubrics and its bag, another small primer with its bag, and also his *Prick of Conscience* and his *Piers Plowman*—Roos is the first known layman-Londoner to bequeath a copy of this work. It can be profitably asked once more whether *Piers Plowman* circulated in the Whittington household? The poem was certainly circulating in Thomas Roos's parish of St Alphage Cripplegate, for the first known bequest of this text had been made by William Palmere, rector of that parish from 1397 to his death in 1400.[87] Roos could have known Palmere personally, and it is also possible that he knew Agnes Eggesfeld, who was the recipient of the book. Roos served as a warden of the Mercers 1401–2 when Whittington was master, and again in 1410–11, when he acted as a feoffee for the company's estate; he also acted regularly in transactions concerning Whittington's property.[88] He does not, however, appear to have prospered quite as well as Cavendish, who was to become the heir of his family estate and establish the fortunes of the dukes of Devonshire. Thomas's brother, Richard, died about this time, leaving two sons who were minors, and the widow married Elias Davy, another up-and-coming mercer. In 1412 one of Richard's sons, Thomas, died, making his uncle, Thomas, an executor along with his step-father Elias Davy.[89] When Thomas Roos died in 1434 he was a widower. Apart from *Piers Plowman* and the other books, he left his son, Guy, land which he had bought in Beverley (perhaps his home town), his armour and 100 marks. There were also three grandchildren by his daughter, Elena, and a Roger Gerebray who had proved an unsatisfactory husband. Roger was a mercer and it was to him that Guy had been apprenticed in 1430–31.[90] Thomas attempted to make some provision for her and her children, avoiding her husband, and in a codicil to his testament set up an exhibition of £12 for one of the boys, whom he described as 'Bernardus Roos de Gerebray'. The emphasis on the Roos name seems to be significant. He also left Bernard his psalter, his old primer, his 'quire of prayers' and an old satchel of grammar books. Had the satchel remained unopened ever since Thomas Roos had abandoned his study of Latin and departed for his apprenticeship in London? Roos and Martin Kelom were the only mercers to mention their grammar books. Appropriately enough, one of Roos's executors was William Brampton, a writer of the court letter or scrivener.[91]

Book-owning families

The Riches of Ironmonger Lane were a book-owning mercer family, but they were as careless of recording their books as anyone else. In 1464 the seventy-two-year-old Richard Rich left his son, Thomas, his psalter, and his son-in-law and executor, Thomas Urswick, the recorder of the city (1454–71), his copy of the *Musica ecclesiastica*, part of the work of Thomas à Kempis, usually called *Imitatio Christi*. Urswick and his fellow executors were to dispose of Richard's other books for the good of his soul, and as a consequence none of the books was named.[92] What books passed to the surviving son, Thomas, at the division of the estate between himself and his mother, Katherine, is not known. She was as old as her husband and had not been made his executor, and her long will of five years later contained some confusions about books: she asserted that her husband had wanted a priest, John Robert, to have the use of a mass book and all the vessels for mass for his life and then return them to their son, Thomas. In fact the priest's name was Robert Love, he had been Richard's chaplain, and had been left an annuity by her husband and made one of his executors. William Law, Katherine's own chaplain, received a bed and her two-volume 'portos'. She also instructed that her great portiforium and all the other books which had come to her as her share of her husband's estate should be sold and the proceeds used for charitable works. Clearly neither Richard nor Katherine Rich, nor, it must be thought, their son, Thomas, or their three well-married daughters, Katherine (widow of the mayor and grocer, William Marowe, and her mother's executor), Margaret (wife of the alderman John Walden (d. 1464), supervisor of Richard Rich's will) and Anne (Urswick's wife), cared to have these books. The only son-in-law to be left a book was Thomas Urswick; the list of the six books in his chapel at his country estate did not include the *Musica ecclesiastica*. Perhaps the elderly Riches had disposed of their best books in their lifetimes, and only the oldest and least regarded remained.[93]

Beatrice, widow of William Melreth, took more care over her well-known bequests of books, but she must be classified as a gentry wife rather than a true mercery wife (although it can be said that mercer wives generally came from families which taught their daughters to read and write).[94] Beatrice was one of four co-heiresses of John Wallis, and her first husband was Reginald Cokayne, who held the manor of Burre Hatley and other property in Bedfordshire; by him she had two daughters and two sons. Her life estate in the manor made her an attractive second wife for William Melreth, a wealthy London alderman (1429–46) and MP (1427, 1429, 1432). He was proud of his status and bequeathed the missal in which he had himself portrayed in his robes before the Trinity to serve in St Laurence Jewry for ever. Beatrice was even-handed in her bequests to her sisters, her children and Melreth's two daughters. Her sister, Agnes Burgh, perhaps a nun or vowess by the time Beatrice died, received a wide selection of pious texts: a book of 'merce and gramarce' written with gold letters, a roll of the Passion of Christ, the Letters of Nicodemus in French, a French and Latin book unspecified, a French primer and, lastly, a roll of the Fifteen Joys of the Virgin. Henry Bardolf received a combined primer and psalter, his son Edward was left 40s. for his schooling, and Robert Mawdisley, an executor, received a gold tablet of St Katherine and her black primer. If Beatrice's books are added to her husband's missal, their households in Bedfordshire and London contained a substantial number of pious texts of a varied character.[95]

Mercers' wills prove that some mercantile families had a considerable store of books, but the facts are few. It is clearly of no significance that a mercer such as the extremely wealthy Geoffrey Boleyn made no mention of books in his long and detailed will; he had plenty of sons and daughters and a wife, and they received his property in blocks, often delineated only by value.

Mercers' interest in history and literature

Finally, something can be said about mercers' interest in history (for which the evidence continues to be limited to bequests) and in what is now called literature (for which the evidence is the few surviving texts once owned by mercers). The history ranges from the *Gesta Romanorum*, which William Haxey left to St Paul's Cathedral (above), to Hugh Brown's gift of his 'sege of the Regell of Troye' (Guido delle Colonne's *Historia Destructionis Troia* or Caxton's *Recuyell of the Historyes of Troye*) left to a fifteen-year-old kinsman in 1503, to William Bromwell's Froissart left to Oliver Leder, gentleman, in 1536.[96] London households had a tradition of keeping chronicles, and a few survive, but it was a tradition that his contemporaries had failed to keep up to his satisfaction when Caxton was looking for material to bring up to date the texts of the *Brut* in his *Chronicles of England* in 1480 and *Polychronicon* in 1482.[97] There survives only one chronicle certainly associated with the household of a mercer, albeit the son of a mercer mayor and a silkwoman who had moved on to be an administrator of great estates. The Frowyk family exemplify once again how rarely testators referred to their books. Sir Thomas Frowyk, mercer by patrimony, son of Henry Frowyk and his second wife, Isabel Bally-Otes-Frowyk, was steward of Westminster Abbey and Syon Abbey, and died of the sweating sickness on 28 September 1485.[98] He mentioned no books in his will, but he certainly owned books for he and his wife were left several by his parents. His household possessed and partly compiled a small volume (now BL Harley MS 541) which contains, among other things, a very simple chronicle for 1483–97 preceded by a list of mayors of London (the earliest section of which was probably supplied by the stationer who sold the original gatherings), the Frowyk swan marks and some prayers and snippets of useful information. The few chronicle entries were added by three persons, and the subjects of the entries can be linked to the Frowyk family's distant but certain kinship to Anne Neville, queen of Richard III, whose death is accorded special attention with a prayer. The death of Richard III is also carefully detailed, and he too is accorded a prayer.

The Frowyks were an ancient family of London and Middlesex and had plenty of property to transmit, as well as traditions of education and culture. Sir Thomas's father, Henry, twice mayor of London (1435–36, 1444–45), has been suggested as a possible commissioner of the *Libelle of English Policy*, the famous poem which promoted a policy of active sea-keeping by the English government. The evidence suggests rather a civil servant who had a good theoretical knowledge of trade but lacked a deep appreciation of Londoners' opinions and desires regarding trade, but it remains certain that Frowyk was capable of such patronage.[99] Sir Thomas's wife, Joan, was the only daughter of Richard Sturgeon, clerk of the crown and inhabitant of St Bartholomew's Hospital Close, which is known to have housed a flourishing literary community during Sturgeon's lifetime; one of Sturgeon's brothers was a mercer and chamberlain of the city and another was a musician and canon of Windsor. A combination of Sturgeons and Frowyks had made the promoter of St Paul's library, Roger Mersshe, a member of their company in 1452 (see above). Sir Thomas's cousin of the half-blood was Sir Thomas Charlton of Middlesex, an inventory of whose books survives in Westminster Abbey; Sir Thomas's son, another Sir Thomas, became one of the youngest chief justices of England. There is thus no doubt that Frowyks of all generations valued learning and owned books, but from their wills we know only of the few devotional texts which were carefully passed from one generation to the other as keepsakes.

The greatest English chronicle circulating in mercer circles (there is no sign of the *Brut*, apart from Caxton's publication) was Higden's *Polychronicon*. Robert Scrayningham, a mercer from Lincolnshire, owned many good things when he died in 1468 and left 'my great English book called Pellycronycon' to Thomas Thirland, a merchant.[100] This was a manuscript copy of Higden's great work in the English translation by Trevisa which William Caxton was to print. One copy of Caxton's edition bought by a mercer survives: William Purde inscribed his copy *Presens liber pertinet ad Willelmum Purde emptus a Willelmo Caxton Regis impressore vicesimo Novembris Anno Regni Regis Edwardi quarti vicesimo secundo* [1482].[101]

Caxton's career is well known. He was proud to be a mercer,[102] but it was undoubtedly during his illustrious career as governor of the Merchant Adventurers of England 1462–70 that he decided to become a printer and supply his fellow countrymen with books. His experience of trade, as both mercer and adventurer, helped him to survive in the perilous new world of printing and leave a flourishing concern to his successor. He had admirers among his fellow mercers, as Purde's inscription proves, and also emulators: Roger Thorney, apprentice, nephew and heir of John Pickering, Caxton's successor as governor of the Merchant Adventurers, and John Tate III, who founded England's first paper mill; and others were not slow in importing foreign printed books.[103] Thorney emerged from apprenticeship in 1474 but is only regularly traceable in the Low Countries in the 1490s, especially during the last months of his uncle's governorship. It was in these years and as Pickering's heir after 1498 that Thorney apparently gained the means to finance Wynkyn de Worde's 1495 edition of Caxton's first book, the encyclopaedia of Bartholomew Anglicus, a folio production of nearly 500 pages in Latin printed by Johann Veldener in Cologne and paid for by Caxton as he learnt the craft in 1471,[104] as well as the 1495 edition of Caxton's 1482 *Polychronicon*. Thorney's involvement in both projects is proved by de Worde's verse preface to the former, which heaped praise on Caxton, Thorney and Tate. John Tate III, of the short-lived paper mill, was investing the resources inherited from his mercer father, John Tate I, and of his heiress wife, Elizabeth Marshall, who came from a family well known for its books.[105] Thorney also owned what appears to have been the copy text of de Worde's edition of Lydgate's *Siege of Thebes* (Oxford St John's College MS 266), suggesting that his involvement with de Worde may have been of some duration.[106] He was involved in an abortive scheme for Henry VII's tomb and may also have dealt in such luxuries as carvings from the Low Countries, but these were one-off commissions suitable for an adventurer with wide connections overseas and did not represent his day-to-day trade.[107]

History was serious and didactic, but some mercers owned more frivolous material. The evidence lies in their surviving books, not their self-righteous wills, and brings this survey to a conclusion. The Fyler family had an autograph copy of Hoccleve's poems, now Huntington Library HM MS 744, and used it to enter the births and deaths of their children. Thomas Fyler was from a well-to-do Bristol family and married Beatrice, daughter of Robert Fitzandrew, draper. Their eldest daughter, Joan, married Thomas Rawson, mercer, and there were seven other children; some died before their mother and all save Joan died before the death of their father in 1482. The family also owned a *mappa mundi*, kept at their country house at Great Baddow, Essex. The Fylers were literate and cultivated, backed up and paid for by their trade: Beatrice was a successful silkwoman all her life, and Thomas sold English cloth in the Low Countries in 1439 and to the Salviati of Florence, whose bank flourished in London 1445–66; he also had dealings with Hanse merchants.[108] William Fetiplace owned some Chaucer and Lydgate, now at Magdalene College, Cambridge.[109] John Keme seems to have owned some at least of Gower's *Confessio Amantis*, now in the Bodleian Library,[110] and Thomas Crisp put his name into an early fifteenth-century copy of the same text, asserting the book *pertinet Thomam Cryspe Civem et Mercerum Londiniarum[sic]* (Oxford, Corpus Christi College MS 67, f. 209).[111] His merchant's mark was drawn on a shield hanging on a tree (f. 207ᵛ). Thomas was admitted a mercer in 1506, which places his birth in 1480, and he died in 1531 as a parishioner of St Martin Pomary, Ironmonger Lane. He mentioned no such text as his *Confessio amantis* in his will, and asked for 'no pompous array no other superflious charge' at his burial. He wondered if any of his six children might opt for a religious life and provided chantries in the traditional manner. His cousin, Robert Packington, was an executor and guardian of his children with Walter Marsh, and both these men, Packington in particular, were advocates of the reformed religion. The wording of Crisp's will and choice of executors were both extremely careful and not surprising for 1531. To accuse Crisp of being conservatiive in his religion because of the traditional wording misses the significance of his reformed executors: a correct reading must acknowledge the depth of religious feeling of all three men.

Crisp and his executors show that the underlying preoccupation of all mercer book-owners was the same as it had been over a hundred years before. Curiosity about the latest religious arguments was still a characteristic of mercers in the 1530s as it had been in 1428 at John Shadworth's dinner table. Mercers and their wives were still passionately involved with religious debate and in the early 1500s became key figures in the import and spreading of the new religion and its books.[112] This preoccupation continued to make them careful of mentioning more frivolous texts in the serious confines of a will, and those disappeared under the blanket of 'my English books'. Mercers of London were always aware of books, serious, moral and entertaining; the greatest reached the height of a William Caxton, who translated and published books for consumers throughout England, while the lowest treasured his primer as a bequest for a child.[113]

8

'By Me Elysabeth Pykeryng'

Women and Book Production
in the Early Tudor Period[1]

Martha W. Driver

During the early Reformation printers were a powerful force, helping to shape religious and political change. While male printers were busily engaged in commercial self-promotion, women worked alongside fathers, husbands, brothers and sons to produce books in the shop. As in other small family-based businesses in the late medieval and early modern periods, women actively engaged in the 'domestic mode of production [which] had come to dominate the industrial economy', performing their customary roles as managers in the family-based business 'under the supervision and for the benefit of the usually male household head', as David Herlihy points out.[2] While the earliest women printers did not even mention themselves by name, later printers in France and England often had several identities which appear in the colophons, or sometimes on the title pages, of the books they produced. As widows, women published books themselves, usually retaining their husbands' devices, or printer's marks, and adding 'Widow of' to the family name of the publishing house (although in some cases the printer reverted to her maiden name). This essay briefly examines named women engaged in printing or publishing books for the early Tudor market—several of them working in Paris and Antwerp—during a period when printing and publishing became political acts (with women, who produced texts orthodox or reformed, and sometimes both, on several sides of the argument).

The earliest women printers of English books were not English but French. Two important examples will suffice. Yolande Bonhomme was the widow of Tilman Kerver, whose shop in Paris produced some of the most beautiful printed Books of Hours in the early part of the sixteenth century. After her husband died on 24 November 1522 Yolande continued their business at the sign of the Unicorn, the family's shop address in Paris, until her death on 15 July 1557. Her Sarum primers and breviaries were sold in London at the shop of John Growte, or Groyat, a Norman bookseller and bookbinder. She also printed a number of books for the London stationer Francis Birckman, who, like Bonhomme's husband, had been born in Germany. In her colophons she describes herself as 'the matron Yolande Bonhomme, widow of Tilman Kerver', using both her maiden and married names. As a daughter of Pasquier Bonhomme, who was one of the four appointed book dealers of the Sorbonne, Yolande Bonhomme had grown up in a print shop, and her use of both names points to her connections not only with her husband but with her father, who himself published illustrated Books of Hours at the end of the fifteenth century.[3]

Similarly, Madeleine Boursette continued the family business after the death of her husband, the printer François Regnault, in 1541. Although her publications were mainly for the French market she produced a number of English service books at the sign of the Elephant in Paris from 1552 until her death in 1556, along with a dictionary in eight languages. Toward the end of her printing career she returned, like Yolande Bonhomme, to her natal name. After her death in 1556 her daughter, Barbe Regnault, also the widow of a printer, then took over, and the family business passed from mother to daughter.[4]

The French women printers tended to produce Sarum service books in small formats ranging from octavo to trigesimo-secundo (32mo, sized about 5.5 × 3.5 inches), which may suggest that their books were intended for a female readership as well as a male one; their books are readily portable and are sometimes printed in red and black. Such packaging seems to suggest an audience mainly female, able to hold a little book in one hand, and also young, as the type can be deciphered by an older person only with a magnifying glass.[5] Books printed by Yolande Bonhomme and Madeleine Boursette for the English market tended to remain orthodox and they did not enter into the religious controversy that began in England in the 1530s.

This was certainly not the case with Catherine van Ruremund, a printer in Antwerp from 1532 to 1546. She was the widow of Christopher van Ruremund, who between 1527 and 1530 produced Sarum missals, Books of Hours, a Sarum processional, Sarum hymnals and an English almanac. In 1531 he came to England to sell New Testaments in English to the bookbinder John Row, but was thrown into prison at Westminster, where he died.[6] His widow continued publishing orthodox books for the English market, including processionals, hymnals, Books of Hours and other Sarum books, throughout her printing career. But she also published the third and fourth editions of Tyndale's New Testament (in 1534 and 1535) with commentary and unauthorised changes by the evangelical theologian George Joye. In the latter books she identified herself by name as 'Catharyn wydowe of C. Ruremond'. She further published many tracts by Joye, sometimes under the name 'widow of C. Ruremund' but also using a number of pseudonyms with unlikely place-names. For example, her edition of Joye's translation of Philip Melanchthon's tract defending the marriage of priests was purportedly published in 'Lipse' by a person named 'U. Hoff'.[7] In other Protestant works, however, she named herself openly as 'the widow of C. Ruremund', as in Matthew Coverdale's paraphrase of David's Psalms and in other works by Coverdale, and in John Bale's *Christian Exhortation*, among others.[8] Like other printers, Catherine used the press to promote her views even as she maintained commercial success by printing orthodox books alongside books with radical content.

The first named woman printer in England was a Widow Warwick who worked in York about 1527 and, according to the Chamberlains' Account Book, gained ten shillings for the printing of 'a thowsand breyffes', as Stacey Gee finds.[9] We know more about Elizabeth Pickering, the widow of Robert Redman, who printed law books in a shop formerly owned by Richard Pynson, one of the successors of William Caxton. After Redman died in October 1540 Elizabeth issued about a dozen surviving titles before marrying William Cholmeley, a lawyer at Lincoln's Inn and councilman of the city, and transferring the business to William Middleton, who continued to publish law books.[10]

There is some evidence that Elizabeth began printing even before her husband's death: the British Library copy of *The Treasure of Poore Men* has the colophon: 'Imprinted by me Robert Redman 24 Jan 1539', but the printer's initials 'E.R.' are presumed to stand for his wife, Elizabeth. This was a variant of Redman's original device. After Redman's death the next year, in 1540, Elizabeth issued three books (according to *STC*), including John Standish's *Little Treatise against Robert Barnes*, and eleven books the following year, most of which retain Redman's printer's device, presumably to attract the same customers who had bought books printed by her husband.[11]

Although there is no way to date precisely the books Elizabeth published within this two-year span, because most of the works are undated, a profile of the woman printer and her changing sense of identity might be constructed from their colophons. In Thomas Moulton's *Myrrour or Glasse of Helth*, a book of remedies, the printer describes herself as 'Elysabeth late wife vnto Robert Redman'. This formula is also found in the *Abregement of the Statutes*, a legal work which is undated.[12] In the colophon of the undated edition of the Magna Carta in the Harvard Law Library, Elizabeth continues to describe herself conventionally, as 'Elisabeth wydow of Robert Redman', and supplies the usual details of her address where a prospective buyer might wish to purchase a copy: 'dwelling at the sygne of the George next to saynte Dunstones churche'.[13] Elizabeth's Magna Carta edition is particularly interesting, however, because a preface explains that the text has now been corrected against Redman's previous edition of its 'sundry apparent faultes, which nowe in this second prynt are well weedyd out'.

In the double-dated edition of Anthony Fitzherbert's *Boke of Justices of Peas*, which has the date 1540 on the title and is dated 1541 in the colophon, we are told the volume was printed 'by me Elysabeth Pykeryng late wife to Robert Redman'.[14] The name 'Pykerynge' also occurs in other, possibly later works printed by Elizabeth. In *The Maner of Kepynge a Courte Baron* the colophon reads 'by me Elisabeth Pykerynge widow of Robert Redman',[15] while in the *Offyce of Shyreffes* the colophon states that the book was printed 'by me Elysabeth Pykerynge wydo to Robert Redman dwellynge at the synge of the G[e]orge nexte to saynt Dunstones Churche'.[16] It is interesting to note that the formulaic and emphatic identification of the book's maker, 'by me', which was also conventionally employed by male printers in colophons of this era, was used by Elizabeth when she gave her maiden name or when she identified herself by her first name only as 'Elysabeth late wife to Robert Redman', as she did in the *Abregement of the Statutes* (tentatively dated 1541).[17]

Whether Elizabeth thought of herself as Elizabeth, late wife, or Elizabeth, widow, or Elizabeth Pickering, as a kind of progression, or perhaps simultaneously as all three, cannot be told. After running the business on her own for two years, in 1541 Elizabeth married the wealthy lawyer William Cholmeley and the printing house passed to William Middleton, who then took over the sign of the George in Fleet Street. The transfer of the shop to Middleton was apparently achieved through William Cholmeley, who was not himself a printer but, according to Barbara Kreps, purchased his freedom as one of the stationers on 31 May 1541, presumably in order to transfer Elizabeth's business to Middleton.[18] Like Robert Redman and then Elizabeth before him, Middleton specialised in the printing of law books. Several of Middleton's books are nearly exact copies of the editions previously put out by Redman and Elizabeth Pickering, using the same title pages and ornaments, which is not particularly surprising, given the tendency, prevalent in early printing as it is still today, to copy a successful original.[19]

Unlike the books and tracts printed by Catherine van Ruremund, Elizabeth's publication list is fairly conservative, although for her first publication she printed Standish's *Treatise against Bankes*, which describes the burning of the Protestant martyr Robert Bankes at Smithfield. She did not, however, reprint any of the books printed by her husband that might have been deemed controversial in 1540; these included prayer books and a Bible in English, an edition of Erasmus's translation of the New Testament in English and Latin (which was to be placed on the *Index Librorum Prohibitorum* during the Counter-Reformation) and some ballads about Thomas Cromwell, attributed to Redman, about which fellow printers Richard Bankes and Richard Grafton were questioned by the Privy Council in 1540. As Kreps further points out, 'In a period when Henry VIII's stance on religious writings was far from trustworthy, she issued only the non-polemical books of health ... and the kinds of law books her husband had specialised in.'[20]

Marriage to William Cholmeley did not, however, seem to end Elizabeth's interest in the London printing business. After William's death in 1546 Elizabeth married William's brother Randolph, also called Ranulf or Ralph, who was, like William, also a lawyer.[21] This second Cholmeley brother was actually Elizabeth's fourth husband, as shown by the fact that William provided in his will for two girls named Luce Jackson and Elizabethe Jackson, described as 'my wyffes daughters', along with Elizabeth's child by Robert Redman, Alice Redman, who was still a minor.[22] William's will also made provision for a large debt owed him by Middleton (to whom Elizabeth's shop had been transferred), which indicates continued interest in the shop. William Cholmeley further drafted an early charter of incorporation for the yet-to-be-formed Stationers' Company and, as Peter Blayney suggests, 'it is distinctly possible that [the Stationers' Company] was his idea (or perhaps his wife's?) in the first place'.[23] This initial attempt was not successful, but in 1554 Ranulf Cholmeley, Elizabeth's fourth husband, became Recorder of London and pushed through the first successful draft of the incorporation of the Company of Stationers. As Blayney points out:

> We know of only two occasions on which the Company had sought a charter, and each time a City lawyer who probably orchestrated the application was married to the same former [woman] printer. It is therefore difficult to avoid the suspicion that the Stationers may owe more to Elizabeth Pickering Jackson Redman Cholmeley Cholmeley than they have hitherto realised.[24]

In the first half of the sixteenth century, when women's social, economic and legal status was subordinate yet intimately tied to that of husbands or of male relatives, women did useful and productive work in the new public medium of printing. The work of these women was regulated by powerful male-run guilds which stipulated that a working woman have a close connection, whether as a wife or widow, with a man in the book trade. As we have seen, the earliest examples of books printed by women for the English market issue from French presses. These books tend to be orthodox, while those coming from the press of Catherine van Ruremund in Antwerp, a comparatively tolerant city under the rule of Charles V, were more radical. The titles from Catherine's press suggest a personal interest in reform along with a well-honed business sense of just what might sell in London. The bright, if brief, printing career of Elizabeth Pickering may not have entirely concluded with her marriage out of the trade. In her case, as in some others, we also begin to see in Elizabeth's use of her own printer's mark and in the wording of her colophons an emerging sense of self, a self separate from that of her dead husband, and the beginnings of a separate female identity marking the book, the product, as her own.

9

The Roxburghe Club

Consumption, Obsession
and the Passion for Print

Shayne Husbands

In 1812 a group of wealthy bibliophiles founded the Roxburghe Club in order to dine, celebrate rare books and, eventually, publish their own editions and facsimiles of rare items. This was an era renowned for its ostentatious aristocratic consumerism and extravagant enjoyment of life, but also one that saw society tormented by tides of moral, financial and political anxieties.[1] This was also the year in which the first steam-driven press was being given its trial run and the mass production of books was becoming a reality, causing men of letters to voice their concerns about the quantities of books that were threatening to overwhelm the discerning reader and reduce the claim of erudition to a hollow boast. The members of the Roxburghe Club revelled in the printed word, and the more labour-intensive and antiquated its method of production the better in their eyes.

As harmless and wholesome as this pastime may appear to modern eyes, their Club met with almost instant hostility and ridicule to a degree that was seldom directed towards other, less salubrious clubs and pastimes. Many in this period were disgusted by the extravagances of the times and criticised the moral turpitude of the aristocracy. The upper classes stood accused not only of being morally insolvent at a time when England itself was perceived to be vulnerable to calamity but also of setting a corrupting example for the lower orders, who could not be trusted to exercise self-control in the face of fluctuating economic conditions, especially when revolution in Europe was likely to reach Britain at any moment. Few critics would have been naïve enough to question why a man should fritter away his fortune on clothes, mistresses, drunken parties, hunting or gambling: it was considered too self-evident to require comment. However, many questioned the propriety, integrity and even sanity of the men who wished to lay out large sums of money for rare books. In this chapter I wish to examine what it was that some members of Regency society perceived to be the 'crimes' of the early nineteenth-century bibliomaniac, and the Roxburghe Club as its most visible representation of obsessive book collecting.

The Club members were typical enough examples of wealthy men of the period: they consisted of a mixture of aristocrats and affluent middle-class professionals, many of them admired and respected members of fashionable and influential society. Interestingly, although the Roxburghe Club is perceived as an 'aristocratic' society, of the eighteen men who were present at the first dinner only two were peers and a further two were baronets (and therefore technically classed as commoners). At that dinner they 'co-opted' a further six members (of whom three were peers), and by the time the Club numbered thirty-one, a year later, it contained seven hereditary titles (if one includes Egerton Brydges, an eccentric whose right to any title was a matter of dispute),[2] only five of which were aristocratic. This would indicate that the aristocratic members were in a definite minority who were equalled in the Club by the five clergymen and far outnumbered by practitioners of law. They were content to expend large sums of money on their pastimes, and few of them appeared to feel the need to make savings in one area to balance out their spending in another. They dined lavishly and, while their excesses were no greater than those of many other clubs of that time, they certainly seemed to believe that if a thing was worth doing, it was worth doing with a laden table and a full glass. While their carousing created a handy 'peg' on which to hang disapproval, it was not the only, or even the predominant, aspect of their activities that was criticised: their choice of books and dedication to the early printers, in opposition to the dictates of early nineteenth-century taste, also attracted a considerable degree of censure among their contemporaries. These were men who were in love with typography and the early technology of the printing press. They celebrated the medieval innovators of movable type and the practical workmanship of the artisan. It was not the idealised chivalric dreams of Romanticism that inspired them—such an interest would perhaps have led them instead to idolise manuscripts and the illuminated page in preference to their chosen bibliophilic drug. One member, Thomas Frognall Dibdin, certainly wrote in an over-heated romantic style when he was gushing about 'book-knights', or indeed in virtually anything that he wrote for the bibliomaniac market,[3] but this was his own literary tic and not indicative of the general interests of the Roxburghe Club. Instead, their interests seemed to lie in the discovery and appreciation of an authentic talent, both literary and artisan, that largely went unrecognised by their contemporaries. They combined this with an enthusiasm for the technology of printing which verged on what might frivolously be called 'boys and their toys', even to the extent of running printing presses of their own. This was not a politically and socially reactionary notion of recreating romanticised visions of feudal times, but a highly personalised reaction to the literature and technology that came together in the black-letter volumes.

The Club was founded in what has been regarded as the golden age of book collecting; its name commemorated a dinner held to celebrate the auction of the Duke of Roxburghe's library at which the record price that had ever been paid for a single volume was attained—that of £2,260 for the famous Valdarfer Boccaccio. It was won by the Marquess of Blandford, beating his cousin, Earl Spencer, in the bidding and laying another stone in the path to Blandford's financial destruction. They were both to be early members of the Roxburghe Club, but the Marquess was a spendthrift in all areas of his life and by 1819 was forced to sell his library, at which point Lord Spencer was able to buy the Boccaccio for the bargain price of 875 guineas. This perhaps demonstrates how quickly the high tide of book prices fell away during this period (although it is also possible that there is another explanation, such as an inexperienced auctioneer allowing items to be sold at prices far below their value).

While most of the Club's founders were capable of laying out huge sums of money to form their collections of rare books,[4] one member, Richard Heber, still manages to stand out, even among such a profligate group, as the most obviously obsessive bibliophile in the Club. In modern terms he was probably a compulsive shopper who, although he was a scholarly man, seemed driven by obsessive impulses beyond those usually experienced by even the most 'completist' of collectors. His collection was not an organised library, since it was without the catalogues, classes and indexes that characterise and make coherent most large collections, and it is doubtful that he himself fully knew what he owned. He was unable to pass by any choice item, even one that he already owned many copies of, and he found excuses for buying duplicates, asserting that 'no man can comfortably do without three copies of a book. One he must have as a show copy, and he will probably keep it at his country-house; another he will require for his own use and reference; and unless he is inclined to part with this, which is very inconvenient, or risk the injury of his best copy, he must needs have a third at the service of his friends'.[5] This creed goes some way towards explaining the eight houses full of books that were sold after his death at auctions that required five thick octavo volumes to contain the sales catalogue.

Lord Spencer also bought books on a prodigious scale, but in his case it was a purposeful and orderly process of acquisition, aided and abetted by T.F. Dibdin, which saw him hold a number of sales to dispose of duplicates when necessary, retaining only the best copies each time he bought yet another entire library. Mainly he collected early printed items, and his collection contained entire series of the works that had proceeded from many of the early presses. By 1864 these included fifty-seven separate works by Caxton, a figure which included three items believed to be sole surviving copies. This was at a time when twenty-seven Caxton items in unique copies were known to be extant, of which the British Museum (which had fifty-five Caxtons) owned eleven.[6]

The Roxburghe members' collections did, of course, contain many rare and beautiful manuscripts[7] and other examples of technologies that preceded or existed alongside movable type,[8] but the main focus of collecting for most of the members was the early printed books which were often scorned by their contemporaries and yet have since proved their value beyond the narrow confines of collecting. Tellingly, the first items that they chose to reproduce were not manuscripts but these early printed volumes and, if the point needed underlining, the Club toasts were dedicated to the memories of the pioneering printers: Valdarfer, Caxton, Aldus, Wynkyn de Worde, Gutenberg, Fust, Pynson and Notary.[9] The Club's fascination with both consuming and reproducing the works that had caught their imagination did not come, however, without an unanticipated social price.

Bibliomania had already been declared a mental disorder by Dr John Ferriar in his poem *The Bibliomania*, written in 1809 and addressed to Richard Heber.[10] The condition described by Ferriar may be defined as the collecting or hoarding of books to a degree where actual damage to social relations or personal health is incurred: in the public imagination this obsessive-compulsive disorder gradually expanded to include book collectors in general. Dibdin acknowledged the dim view taken of bibliophiles in his answering work, also titled *Bibliomania*, which is part satire, part warning and part celebration of the obsessive collecting of books.[11] First published in 1809, it was later extended and its format altered to consist of a series of discourses between a group of friends who discuss various aspects of book collecting and collectors.[12] This later version contains a wry exchange between the collector Lysander (Dibdin) and the more scholarly Philemon in which Lysander asserts: 'I am an arrant BIBLIOMANIAC—that I love books dearly—that the very sight, touch, and more the perusal ...', at which point his friend interjects to say: 'Hold, my friend, [...] you have renounced your profession—you talk of *reading* books—do BIBLIOMANIACS ever *read* books?'[13] This was a criticism often to be levelled against the Club: that they cared more for the appearance and rarity of the books that they collected than for the literary contents, although, as will be shown, it could be said that their critics undermined their accusations by showing a lack of interest as to what those contents might be. This accusation of superficiality was, in any case, unfair, because, as Jane Campbell points out, most of the Roxburghe members were part of the group of book collectors who actually did read the books they amassed, and the Club was particularly rich in men who were profoundly connected with literature in a variety of ways.[14] In other words, they were consumers not only in the economic sense but also of the contents of their books, and their desire for rarity and fine bindings was supplementary to their literary tastes rather than the only focus of their collecting habits. Rarity value and technical admiration created intellectual curiosity about the texts, leading to the formation of a literary taste for the 'barbaric' works of earlier times, which in turn inspired the desire to preserve, reproduce and ornament the texts that had been discovered.

Surprisingly, given the apparently low opinion held by many of their critics regarding the literary worth of what they produced as a club, they were also criticised for not making copies available for purchase by the general public. A letter from the *Gentleman's Magazine* of September 1813 asserted that

> the honourable members of the Roxburghe Club have, no doubt, persuaded themselves that they are aiding the diffusion of useful knowledge, and promoting the interests of literature. But, instead of diffusing knowledge they selfishly cut off the springs which should feed it; and, instead of promoting the interests of literature they materially injure them.[15]

The judgement would seem both harsh and a little premature, as the Club was only just over twelve months old at this point and had not yet printed anything; in fact, it would be another twelve months before William Bolland presented the Club with its first volume.[16] It also seems doubtful whether the diffusion of the springs of literature would have been as gratefully received as the letter-writer seemed to believe. The Scottish Bannatyne Club, while emulating the Roxburghe example in most matters, decided to avoid the accusation of withholding literature from the reading public by making its volumes available for sale outside the Club; the Club secretary admitted that it 'always proved a complete failure'.[17] It is difficult to avoid the conclusion that the public tended to desire the option to purchase such books on principle, perhaps from a fear of being excluded from an 'elite' purchasing opportunity rather than desiring the books themselves. Also, as the Victorian book-collector John Hill Burton noted, there was no restriction placed on other publishers creating editions of these texts if they so wished in order to cater for a less wealthy readership (although there is little evidence that this occurred in most cases).[18] Valued by the general public or not, the gentlemen of the Club were undaunted and continued to present the membership with their reprints of printed books, and it is not until the nineteenth item, *Balades and other Poems*, presented by Earl Gower in 1818, that an edition based on a manuscript appears.[19]

Returning to the question of the motives of the Club's founder members, it is common for them to be dismissed in print as 'dilettante' in their inter-actions with the books that they gathered and disseminated. While it is true that most of the members of the Roxburghe Club were not scholars in the modern, professional sense, the majority of them were deeply involved with books—the reading, writing, editing, commissioning, printing, illustrating and, of course, collecting of books. Their friends and acquaintances were authors, critics, poets, booksellers, editors and printers; they created literary magazines, wrote books and reviewed the works of the writers of the day; they set up printing presses and acted as patrons. It is difficult to imagine how a group of individuals could have had a closer relationship with the printed word than that enjoyed by the men who made up the early Roxburghe Club. And yet still they were accused of having no knowledge of, or taste for, literature. As David Matthews and Alice Chandler have demonstrated, the Roxburghe Club displayed an interest in early English literature at a time when it was receiving relatively little attention, and they were instrumental in preserving and giving value to many early works that might otherwise have perished under the weight of public indifference or even hostility.[20] As one of their detractors, writing in December 1813, phrased it:

> If an old work is truly valuable, it will not be necessary to search monasteries, dive into vaults, pore over bookstalls, or grub up all the trash which has been consigned to the silence of centuries, and which, but for their officious zeal, would have been of much more service in the shops of cheesemongers.[21]

The depth of animosity can be surprising and perhaps indicates that the Club's members were doing something that was unusual enough in the early nineteenth century to seem threatening to many people.[22] After several years of such accusations Samuel Egerton Brydges eventually answered this point with a well-reasoned article in which he asked: 'If it be true that great intrinsic beauty or sublimity cannot obtain, even for a day, the public favour to many productions which are candidates for fame, may it not equally happen, that the same capricious insensibility may throw back into the shades several of those which have obtained it?'[23] Unfortunately, once the Club's vociferous detractors had put forward their opinions, in some cases before the Club had actually produced any books, the situation seemed to become circular in its logic—the Roxburghe Club printed items that nobody else valued, therefore nobody valued the Roxburghe Club's judgement, which meant that whatever the Club printed was considered by many to be without value.

Even beyond the requirements of their commitment to reproduce a rare item, many of the Club members were not content merely to be consumers of books; the Roxburghe Club contained among its early attendees three men who were drawn to the ownership of a private printing press and the freedom that it gave them to pursue their own literary interests, both in terms of printing their own original work and of reproducing rare, largely forgotten works of early literature. As John Hill Burton said: 'Much as has been told us of the awful scale in which drunkards consume their favored poison, one is not accustomed to hear of their setting up private stills for their own individual consumption'.[24] The best-known of these presses was probably the Lee Priory press, owned by Sir Samuel Egerton Brydges, who seems to have found the experience an expensive mixture of vanity publishing and patronage during the short time the press was running. It was founded in 1813 at a house belonging to his eldest son at Ickham, near Canterbury,[25] and it remained in production until 1823, printing 'forty-odd' books and pamphlets during that time.[26] Works from the Lee Priory were usually limited to 100 copies or fewer. The first book printed at the Lee Priory Press was *Poems of Margaret, Duchess of Newcastle*, but it was not made available for purchase. It was a royal octavo edition, and only twenty-five copies were printed to display the quality of production from the press.[27] *Two interludes: Jack Jugler and Thersytes* was printed at the press for Joseph Haslewood; he presented it as his contribution to the Roxburghe Club in 1820.[28]

Sir Alexander Boswell famously owned the Auchinleck press and was by his own admission 'infected with the *type* fever'.[29] It was in operation from 1815 until 1818 and was initially set up to print a facsimile of *The Disputation between John Knox and the Abbot of Crossraguel*, a black-letter item from Boswell's own collection; it also produced a number of other publications before the press was officially established.[30] At first Boswell owned a 'portable press' which he chose to exchange in 1815 for 'one of Mr. Ruthven's full sized ones', a change that was necessitated by the wish of his brother, James Boswell, to have his Roxburghe Club contribution printed at the Auchinleck press.[31] This item was Richard Barnfield's *Poems*, a reproduction of a number of poems, including *The Encomion of Lady Pecunia, or The Praise of Money*, which had first been printed in 1598 and which was considered to be an accurate reprint of the earliest impression of the work.[32] Many works followed and would no doubt have continued to do so if not for Alexander Boswell's untimely death in a duel in 1822.[33]

The third printing press owned by a Roxburghe member at this time was the Beldornie Press, which was the property of Edward Vernon Utterson, a well-known barrister, book editor and accomplished artist as well as an ardent antiquarian book-collector.[34] The Beldornie press was largely used by Utterson to reprint rare pieces of sixteenth- and seventeenth-century poetry (Payne Collier described them as 'highly curious poetical tracts, of dates between 1590 and 1620')[35] which he presented to his friends, rarely producing more than twenty copies of each item. These were 'highly valued by the possessors, not only for their rarity, but also for their intrinsic value', and a manuscript was produced entitled *Catalogue of Books Printed at the Beldornie Press*, which lists sixteen printed items plus 'a number of pamphlets and other minor pieces'.[36] Of the sixteen items printed at the Beldornie Press in total, seven were a series of reprints of works by Samuel Rowlands (1598–1628), a writer of pamphlets, mainly in the form of satirical verse, which were all printed in the first year.[37] Perhaps Utterson's most controversial choice of text was *Micro-cynicon: Sixe snarling satyres*, first published in 1599 and sometimes attributed to Thomas Middleton.[38] In all three cases, these activities, which lay outside the confines of the Roxburghe

Club, fed back into the complex literary current which affected the interests and products of the Club.[39]

One event in particular has seemingly had a lasting and invidious effect on the way in which the Club has been perceived. In 1834 a virulent attack was made on the Roxburghe Club following the death of one of its founder members, Joseph Haslewood, and the discovery of notebooks among his papers that contained a light-hearted account of the Club's meetings, including copies of the menus from their dinners, personal letters and other ephemera. The manuscript was bought by a bookseller named Thorpe who immediately offered it to Haslewood's friend and fellow Roxburghe member, T.F. Dibdin, who with admirable strength of moral conviction but perhaps a degree of naivety declined to buy it, viewing it as tantamount to blackmail.[40] Eventually, through a series of sales, it came into the possession of the editor of the *Athenaeum* magazine, C.W. Dilke. Shortly afterwards, a vitriolic article appeared serialised in the *Athenaeum*. It was published anonymously but generally believed to have been written by James Silk Buckingham[41] (if so, almost certainly at the behest of the editor who, as will be seen, had reason to bear personal animosity against Haslewood). While Haslewood, as Cathleen Hayhurst Wheat has stated, 'carried on no literary quarrels but seems, for the most part, to have been on the best of terms with fellow antiquarians like Bliss, Park and Singer',[42] it would nevertheless appear that there had earlier been a brief and somewhat unfriendly correspondence between Haslewood and Dilke. A letter exists in which Haslewood recounts to another correspondent how he had previously encountered Dilke in a professional setting which had led to his criticism of Dilke's abilities and taste as an editor. Haslewood writes that Dilke

has stuck my name at the head of those from whom he derived assistance, having answered a letter of his on the subject of Marston and which answer, had he duly considered, he might have discovered was a most palpable sneer at his work, by telling him the volume he enquired about was 'neither of sufficient rarity to keep as a curiosity, or of any value to an editor'.[43]

Whatever the catalyst that caused the article to be written, the late Joseph Haslewood was erroneously and maliciously portrayed in print as an illiterate, vulgar and dishonest fool who had fraudulently insinuated his way into the Roxburghe Club and, once there, had damaged its reputation and poisoned its atmosphere. The Roxburghe Club itself was also criticised, and the piece jeered at the members for having allowed such a man to belong to their assembly, saying that

such men as the Duke of Devonshire, Lord Spencer, Lord Gower, Lord Morpeth, Sir F. Freeling, Mr Baron Bolland, Mr. Justice

Littledale and others, must have felt themselves very ill-assorted, cheek-by-jowl, at a dinner-table at the Clarendon, with such a man as Mr Haslewood.[44]

The article was later reprinted, along with a rebuttal of its claims, under the title *Roxburghe Revels and other Relative Papers; including Answers to the Attack on the Memory of the late Joseph Haslewood, Esq. F.S.A. with Specimens of his Literary Productions.*[45] An article from the *Gentleman's Magazine* at that time also defends Haslewood, and among a number of other arguments points out that 'although it is true that, like many other more eminent lawyers, he failed (as it is generally thought) in framing his own will so to convey precisely the import of his wishes', he was, however, 'shrewd and prudent' as a collector and

> with respect to his personal manners, he was perfectly quiet and unobtrusive in society; and therefore the gentlemen of rank and education who have composed the Roxburghe Club had no cogent reason (as his slanderer has pretended) to dismiss from their society a man possessed of very extensive information on subjects connected with their favourite pursuits.[46]

The damage was done, however, and, although spirited, the defence put forward by his friends failed to undo the harm caused both to the memory of Haslewood and to the reputation of the Roxburghe Club itself. Thirty years later and the Haslewood affair was still being raked over, with Edward Edwards in his generally very even-handed book *Libraries and Founders of Libraries* saying of Dibdin that

> when you read his *Reminiscences* of the men with whom he had mixed in life, you are left in considerable doubt whether or not he quite understood the difference between two men, both of whom were 'Roxburghians' and editors of black-letter rarities—Walter Scott and Joseph Haslewood.[47]

This may bring us to the heart of many of the objections arrayed against the Roxburghe Club: its members' willingness to overlook differences of class and wealth in the interests of a specific class of antiquarian book.

While Phillip Cornell and others have argued that the antipathy towards the bibliomania of the early nineteenth century was a symptom of the fear that control over learning and the 'correct' way of reading would be lost by the seeming avalanche of books appearing at this time, it can also be read as the fear of the loss of social boundaries. The Roxburghe Club was certainly extremely elitist at this period—in fact it was considered to be 'easier to get into the Peerage or the Privy Council than into The Roxburghe'[48]—but this exclusivity did not necessarily adhere to typical class boundaries as closely as would perhaps be supposed.[49] Many members were lawyers, schoolmasters or clergymen, the typical 'scholarly' or passionately curious bibliophile such as Henry Drury, Joseph Haslewood or Thomas Frognall Dibdin. The idea that a commoner (albeit one with the means and knowledge to amass a collection of expensive rare books) should be able to fraternise with members of the aristocracy on equal terms, or as near to equal terms as English society at that time would allow, simply on the basis of a shared passion for books, must have seemed daring coming, as it did, on the heels of the French Revolution and at a time when the British were uneasy and distrustful of social change. This was also a time when the aristocracy, with their aura of glamour and authority, were considered demonstrably superior to the lower orders. While we may despair at the modern ubiquity of celebrity culture, the magazines of the Regency period often contained letters arguing over the minutiae of aristocratic titles, noble family trees and forms of address—pedigree mattered, and these hereditary titles were often viewed as indicating moral fibre and intrinsic personal qualities which set the bearer apart from the *hoi polloi* and bestowed on them a God-given suitability to govern. It would therefore appear to be a singular decision on the part of an aristocrat to ignore this hierarchical chasm between the classes and to condescend to socialise with his inferiors for the sake of books. The apparently overtly elitist nature of the Club would have made this oddity appear even more threatening as inevitably many men who considered themselves to be eminently socially suited to this aristocratic company may have been black-balled in favour of a socially inferior but bibliophilically more committed postulate. Ironically, what would appear to be a bastion of the social hierarchy might, during its early years, have appeared to be frighteningly radical and egalitarian, if not downright perverse, to outsiders if not to its members. To its members it may have seemed obvious that a commoner with the right sort of bibliophilic obsession, one with whom they had attended auctions and engaged in bidding wars over the same coveted books, should take precedence over an aristocrat who possessed all the social prerequisites and a certain liking for books or for collecting but without the necessary depth of passion for the particular types of books that he chose to collect.

John Hill Burton described the Club as consisting of 'affluent collectors, some of them noble, with a sprinkling of zealous practical men, who assisted them in their great purchases, while doing minor strokes of business for themselves'.[50] This would perhaps be a fair enough assessment, although really only Haslewood and Dibdin could be said to have carried out any sort of regular business within the confines of the Club and it is not obvious how much of this business was motivated by money and how much by friendship. However, Burton goes on to say that 'these, who in some measure fed on the crumbs that fell from the master's table, were in a position rather too closely resembling the professionals in a hunt or cricket club'. So we see that even as late as 1863 the mixture of classes contained in the Club was still causing disquiet and a certainty that Club relationships between nobles and commoners must have been those of master and servant (or paid expertise) rather than those of fellow enthusiasts. Dibdin in his *Reminiscences* of 1836 had already pointed out in answer to similar accusations in the Roxburghe Revels affair that his accuser 'may as well be informed that I am not the Secretary—that I receive no emolument—that the office of Vice-president is one of no trouble and no indignity'.[51] Dibdin, through his often penurious state and the unfortunate necessity of needing to make a living, often found himself criticised or ridiculed essentially for the crime of not being wealthy and of needing to support himself and his family while in other respects being a 'gentleman'. For instance, the reviewer of Dibdin's *Library Companion*[52] in the *Quarterly Review* of 1825 is critical of his use of 'booksellers' slang' and contemptuous of what is described as his willingness to 'lower himself into a walking puff for booksellers and book-collectors, engravers and auctioneers',[53] thereby presumably associating himself too closely with the perceived sordidness of mercantile life. Again we see that dangerous propensity to ignore social boundaries for the love of books.

The discussions about, and criticisms of, the Roxburghe Club continued over a number of years and were carried out predominantly in books, articles and the letters pages of magazines, but the overriding feeling that one is left with is that their contemporaries continued to criticise the Club for its members' failure to adhere to a set of literary objectives and social standards that the Club itself had never professed to be working towards or upholding. The Club was, beyond the usual bibliomaniac preoccupations, conscious of, and focused towards, the appreciation of books as artefacts that contained important information for the reader beyond and in addition to the text itself. This consideration of books as artefacts is perhaps a common-place idea in the modern world but did not have such widespread currency in the early nineteenth century. The Roxburghe Club might, from that perspective, be seen as the intellectual forerunners of modern projects such as Google books and similar digital facsimile projects. During the Club's dawn its members were the focus of much criticism regarding their reprints and facsimiles of early printed books; their critics were unable to understand their desire to reproduce these works in forms that were as close as possible to the originals, and it was considered by many to be a sign of their lack of scholarly discipline and knowledge of literature that they would waste their time doing this rather than producing modern editions of the early printed works or, better still, manuscripts. However, as Edward Edwards pointed out, early printed books often represent the only surviving evidence of 'many precious manuscripts'.[54] That was certainly so in the case of Lord Spencer's first offering to the Club, which was *The First Three Books of Ovid De Tristibus*, translated into English, by Thomas Churchyarde, dating from 1578 and believed to be the only surviving copy.[55] Its future survival certainly became more assured once another thirty-one copies had been printed, however limited that number might appear.

From the Club's point of view there would have been little point in producing standard modern editions that could easily have been provided by the normal publishing channels. The opportunity was still there for mainstream publishers to print modern accessible editions of any of the works if they believed that the readership existed to make it worth their while, and the Club members were mostly very generous in lending items from their collections to authors, editors and publishers who needed access to the original texts. Richard Heber, with his massive collection, was an especially generous lender of rare volumes to needy scholars and black-letter editors. For their own publications Club members were interested in doing something very different, which was very often to reproduce the books as they had first appeared.

In this pursuit the Roxburghe Club was embracing and celebrating the printer's art while insisting on retaining the individuality and personal eccentricities of each volume and maintaining an artisan approach to the creation of a book, in contrast to the methods of mass production that were just coming into existence. Each book had its individual personality which was to be maintained and reproduced as far as possible. The literary content might be important but so too were the typography, the woodcuts, the mistakes and the oddities, and the Roxburghe Club was willing to give full rein to these idiosyncrasies.[56] Why produce a copy in a modern, uniform roman type when you could have all the personality and emotional impact of black-letter? Why force the text into uniformity when with a little effort you could experience the book almost as its first readers experienced it in all its idiosyncratic glory, printer's contractions, errors and all? And when the Roxburghe Club reproduced their rare volumes they also usually attempted to reproduce as much information from the original item as they could, given the restrictions imposed by the technology available to them.

If their facsimiles were considered eccentric and self-indulgent, the fact that they were reproducing black-letter items put them completely beyond the pale. John Payne Collier, for instance, had a particular dislike of their activities, writing that

> while all investigations of the origin and progress of printing must almost necessarily be productive of some useful information ... this excuse ... will not apply to the mere divers into the depths of black-letter darkness, who exhaust those lives that might have been devoted to valuable acquisitions, in employments to which they blindly attach an imaginary and factitious importance.[57]

As a critic one might have expected Collier to have an appreciation for the activities of the Roxburghe Club, especially as he was happy to receive copies of rare items printed at the Beldornie Press by E.V. Utterson, but, as another commentator put it, 'a very profound and loud-speaking critic is not always, and of necessity a much wiser man than the writer, or even than the editor, of a poor black-letter ballad'.[58]

As shown, the depth of emotion displayed in many of these polemical exchanges often appears disproportionate to a discussion of the actions of a small number of book-collectors who were spending their own money on private interests, and it is difficult to believe that such vitriol was purely the result of a disagreement regarding the correct way to reprint minor works of early literature. There was a small but vociferous segment of early nineteenth-century society that was determined to disapprove of the Roxburghe Club for its own reasons. Whether they were being criticised for their compulsive buying or their lack of buying power,[59] their elitism or their want of social discernment, their lack of seriousness or their pretensions to scholarship, it would appear that the Roxburghe Club's main offences were to place the love of books above social conventions, and to prefer the early printers and their works to contemporary critical opinion. Perhaps society was just not ready for that most unexpected of radicals, the egalitarian aristocratic bibliophile.

Section III

Writing Consumption

10

Reconsidering the Recipe

Materiality, Narrative and Text in Later Medieval Instructional Manuscripts and Collections

Carrie Griffin

This chapter is a reconsideration of the cultural, material and historical importance of late medieval recipe texts, collections and manuscripts, and a reinterpretation of how modern scholarship consumes and receives 'texts' that are short, apparently formulaic, and that constitute examples of 'non-literary' textual genres.[1] I consider how the modern scholar who deals with recipe texts is usually informed by a specific definition of the word 'recipe' and by conventions in cataloguing and recording. Significantly, the term 'recipe', and indeed the terms 'text' and 'collection', are rather more loosely applied to early and early modern writings than to modern ones. The word 'recipe' now indicates a text that is usually culinary, easily recognisable and formally predictable; yet recipe texts that circulated in England in the later Middle Ages manifest such variety that they challenge our lateral, strict and frequently unhelpful classifications as well as our sense of how and why they were consumed.

What follows, whilst acknowledging the excellent work carried out to date on medieval and early modern recipe categories and collections,[2] reconsiders the nature of the medieval recipe in order to demonstrate the earlier fluidity of what has in modernity become a relatively stable, fixed form. Moreover, it argues that recipes frequently respond well to analysis which explores them in the contexts of narrative or performance. Recipes are generally imagined to have been 'consumed' by those with culinary aims; I contend that their consumption contemporaneously may have been more varied than might be imagined. Significantly, that consumption has a dual aspect: we can consider how recipes are to some extent a record of bodily consumption, but we can also examine how recipes are consumed as texts and how their manuscript contexts, as well as their co-texts, offer insights into some of the ways in which that consumption occurred or was conceptualised.

There are several issues that face scholars of recipe texts that survive in manuscripts from the later Middle Ages in particular. These issues can limit the ways in which we interpret and receive these texts in modern scholarship. First, many studies of recipe texts and recipe collections from the late-medieval and early modern periods tend to emphasise their utilitarian function, or their potential to offer insights into 'everyday' life, or their relationship to conspicuous consumption; in other words, recipes are considered valuable mainly in terms of their revelations about eating habits, commercial activity or medical and social practices. Consequently, since they are not always viewed as fully relevant to, or representative of, late medieval textual culture, they are frequently discussed out of context, divorced from their companion texts and from their material forms. Second, modern cataloguers, often bound by the conventions of publishers and editors, face problems when recording recipes. They are often preserved in manuscripts of different kinds, and frequently in ways that are unfamiliar to modern consumers of similar texts. We can expect to encounter early recipes inscribed on flyleaves, in margins and in other blank spaces, as well as assembled with other recipes in collections or manuals or subsumed into longer tracts. Equally, their contexts—commonplace books, miscellanies, surgical manuals and other apparently randomly compiled books—challenge expectations of where recipes are and should be located. Third, recipes as texts are not stable, predictable or generic: rather, they record instruction of a variety that rarely conforms to modern expectations of what a recipe should look like or the type of information or instruction it should transmit. And finally, recipes manifest narrative and literary qualities that are often missed by modern cataloguers and readers. These qualities suggest that their consumption was in no way standard or predictable. Reconsidering medieval recipes and recalibrating our thinking regarding their consumption, both bodily and textual, requires a reassessment of what is inferred by the term 'recipe' as well as another look at the ways in which medieval recipes are packaged and presented in their contemporary manuscript contexts.

Recipes: recording and function

Although not all these issues have been directly expressed in scholarship and literature, some scholars have addressed the conventions for cataloguing medieval English recipes in ways which inform and steer the arguments of this paper. Kari Anne Rand Schmidt, for example, points out that the cataloguing procedures of the *Index of Middle English Prose* (*IMEP*) 'consider recipes a special case' to which 'separate rules apply'.[3] *IMEP*'s editorial guidelines recommend that a distinction be made between collections of recipes and instances of the occurrence of individual recipes. A collection is to consist of six or more recipes; if there are fewer than six, it is recommended that the recipes be recorded individually. As Rand Schmidt explains:

> [C]ollections are to be indexed by transcribing at least fifty words, including the first ten or twelve of each of the first three recipes. One should then transcribe the lines which conclude the collection, giving some indication of the recipe in which they occur, and also indicate in one's notes the approximate number of recipes in the collection as well as their subject matter, i.e. whether they are medical, culinary, or general. Individual recipes occurring in isolation are to be transcribed. (pp. 423–24)

The work of Henry Hargreaves, and in particular his advocacy of the consideration of the medical recipe in relation to the collection (rather than singly), has been simultaneously influential and detrimental, since it encourages the recording of recipes based on an organisational principle that may or may not be present.[4] Rand Schmidt questions his assumptions, asserting that, even with regard to *materia medica*, 'collections of recipes are much more heterogeneous than Hargreaves would have us think'. In addition, Hargreaves based his recommendations on the assumption that there would be consistency of variation across recipe collections: something which seems not to be the case. If recipes were considered only in terms of the collection, as *IMEP* demands, that would leave 'large quantities of prose text unaccounted for' (pp. 424–25).

Although these difficulties were first addressed and debated over thirty years ago, the conclusions reached have been influential and are still relevant. It must be acknowledged that recipes present significant problems for cataloguers and indexers, occurring as they do in vast numbers and in varying contexts, and the concerns of the *IMEP* editors to find ways in which best to represent them in relation to their manuscript contexts are fully explicable. However, a number of further issues relevant to the concerns of this paper emerge from the points argued by Hargreaves and Rand Schmidt. To begin with, Hargreaves considered medical recipes *only* when outlining his schema to deal with recipes to be indexed, arguing that, where these are concerned, collections were rarely assembled casually; rather, the medical recipe collection follows a *cap-à-pie* system that is indebted to classical traditions. Consequently, Hargreaves believed that variants of the same recipe occur over and over again with some variation in order. Rand Schmidt argues that, even within the realm of medical recipes, 'what [Hargreaves] describes is much more orderly and predictable than the groups of recipes one actually encounters in MSS collections' where 'repetition turns out to be very rare' (p. 425). Irma Taavitsainen agrees, noting too the tendency of recipes in remedybooks 'to follow one another in some kind of order', while the *cap-à-pie* structure is shown to apply, in manuscripts, 'to a limited extent only'.[5] Both Taavitsainen and Rand Schmidt agree, then, that Hargreaves' conclusions are too general and that, in reality, recipes in manuscripts are much more variant and unpredictable than his work suggests. Rand Schmidt's conclusions are also concerned with the intended utility of *IMEP* as a research tool and as a facilitator of further work: she highlights a concern that the guidelines leave vast numbers of recipes unaccounted for and ignored, despite their importance for fields of study such as lexicology and dialectology (p. 427).

Rand Schmidt's concerns are highly relevant, particularly since short instructional texts respond to investigation on many levels and because attitudes to medieval recipes and to how they ought to be recorded comment at a fundamental level on their status as texts. *IMEP* volumes are, of course, primarily handlists which, theoretically at least, treat the recording of all texts, whether a version of the prose *Brut* or a fairly unremarkable instructional text, in roughly the same manner: that is, a portion of the *incipit* and the *explicit* are recorded.[6] However, the guidelines also prescribe that, where individual recipes occur in isolation, they are to be transcribed. Thus, implicitly embedded into these guidelines, and evident too in wider scholarly trends, is a lack of consistency in terms of how we deal with recipes. Where they occur individually they are treated as texts, but when grouped or copied alongside five or more other (not necessarily similar) items in what might be described as a 'collection' the individual text somehow is stripped of its boundaries and becomes dependent on the wider collection for identification and definition.

There is, however, general agreement in scholarship about the value of incorporating these culturally significant sub-genres into late-medieval and early modern studies. In fact, recent scholarship on medieval textual genres has been concerned to explode the canon insofar as works of science, information and instruction are concerned, and the resulting models of classification allow us to catalogue, describe and theorise works that may in the past have been ignored simply because they are instructional or 'non-literary'. Despite some issues and problems, such as those outlined above, more aids to research are available: handlists, models and bibliographical surveys such as Keiser's *Manual*,[7] which (rightly or wrongly, since, as we know, categories of medieval writing were relatively fluid) pay close attention to generic classifications and at least attempt meaningfully to describe or contextualise individual texts. Over the last twenty-five years scholarly work has begun to foreground 'writings that had once seemed marginal and deserving of concern for their philological value ... [and] that are now being shown to be central to an understanding of literary, social, intellectual, political, and cultural history'.[8] Increasingly recipes are treated as culturally and textually important, and the variety and scope of individually preserved recipes and recipe collections from late medieval Europe are evidence of impulses to record not just personal and private tastes and requirements but also more general popular trends and developments.

Terms and variance

It is necessary at this point to explain the use of the terms 'recipe' and 'text' in this particular context, since evidently both are issue-laden and remain open to interpretation and interrogation. Because recipes are mostly expected to be formulaic, and since they are often collected together to form longer works, they tend, as we have seen, not to be examined as individual short texts but instead are frequently considered as constituent parts of a longer work or collection. We generally expect 'recipe' to relate in some way to food or drink: a formula that instructs us how to make something that we can ingest or consume; it is usually formulaic and accurate, and not subject to great formal variation. If a recipe is *not* culinary (for example, if it deals with a medical remedy), we still expect it to conform to a formula or standard type. In relation to medieval and early modern recipes, Taavitsainen reckons that 'the overall structure of recipes is fairly regular: it consists of a title or rubric, indications of use, ingredients, preparation and dosage, application, and the efficacy may be assured at the end'; however, she acknowledges that '[n]ot all components need be present'.[9] Her example of a 'typical' medieval recipe, after Edmar, is as follows:

> For to hele þe festere: Tak betis and stampe wiþ barly mele. And tempre hit wiþ white of eyren and make a plastre þer of. And ley hit þer to. And ȝif þer be eny ded flesch hit wele detrie hit.[10]

Although this is a medical rather than a culinary recipe it conforms well to the formula identified by Taavitsainen, who goes on to point out, after Görlach, that

> the contents and function of recipes are well-defined, and it has been stated that genre conventions of recipes were standardised early so that the formal and structural characteristics have undergone only minor modifications according to period styles up to the present time.[11]

Contemporary definitions, especially those that emerge in the early modern period, tend to relate to culinary recipes at the expense of other short instructional texts, and mostly emphasise the utilitarian or instructional functions of those recipes. The *Oxford English Dictionary* (OED) defines 'recipe' as 'a statement of the ingredients and procedure for making something, [now] especially a dish in cookery'; etymologically, the term seems to have entered common use in this regard in the mid-seventeenth century, and the *OED* cites one of the earliest recordings as occurring in Jonson's play *New Inne* (1631):

Tipto: ... thou are rude, and dost not know the Spanish composition.

Burst: What is the Recipe? Name the ingredients.[12]

However, it is of course also used in the later Middle Ages and early Renaissance to denote a 'formula for the composition or use of a medicine, a prescription; a medicine prepared according to such a formula; a remedy'. Closely linked, and often substituted in this sense, is the word 'receipt', which stems from the same root, the Latin *recipere* (to receive), which was used by physicians to head prescriptions. 'Receipt' comes to English *via* Anglo-Norman: one of the earlier recordings is in Trevisa's translation of Bartholomaeus Anglicus, *De Proprietatibus Rerum* (1398), and it also occurs in Lanfranc's *Science of Chirurgie* (1400).

Today the word 'recipe' is used in a fairly specific sense: we expect recipes to be formulaic, arranged in a particular way and leading to a precise outcome. Furthermore, we know where to locate them (we can buy books full of recipes) and where to store them (we can also buy blank books to fill with recipes, either handwritten or taken from elsewhere and pasted in). However, interrogating the *OED* definitions a little more closely throws up the possibility that these definitions do not fully allow us to appreciate recipes as texts. Rather, recipes are statements of the ingredients and procedure; or they are formulae that are prescriptive. They are therefore predictable, conforming to prescriptive structures that are not subject to great variance. By extension, though they may be malleable and may of course manifest variety of content or type, they do not have the fluidity that we might expect of other genres of writing or composition, and they seem to defy or resist definition as individual texts precisely because of their sameness and predictability. Taking a bibliographer's view on text, such as Machan's assertion that it is simply 'the order of words and punctuation, as contained in any one physical form, such as a manuscript, proof or book',[13] would certainly allow us to admit recipes as text, but this view is perhaps reductive and sterile and removes the necessity for the discovery of meaning in a text.

The problem remains that recipes are routinely regarded either as marginalia, and thus incidentally or situationally recorded, or as part of larger collections that form an amorphous text-like mass that resists definition or deconstruction. They are not often classified as individual texts in and of themselves, and are usually treated collectively simply because they have one or two features in common. This situation is not helped by the fact that, because of the sheer numbers that survive, and their dispersal across various manuscripts in sometimes sporadic fashion, recipes are not well treated by catalogues, handlists and databases. As discussed above, recipe texts are not fully recorded by handlists such as the *Index of Middle English Prose* and in many library catalogues recipes may be approximately counted and their matter (medicine, cookery and so on) briefly, and sometimes inaccurately, described. However, this situation exists not only because of cataloguers and their grapple with the large numbers of extant short texts but also because of the practices of medieval scribes and compilers and the consequent instability of, in particular, longer works comprised of shorter texts. Keiser notes, for example, the complex textual history of *The Herbal of John Lelamour of Hereford*, which, he comments, 'is actually a conflated copy text of Lelamour's translation of the Macer herbal with the herbal known as *Agnus Castus* and the *Anonymous Prose Treatise on Rosemary*'; similarly, a tract like that attributed to John of Burgundy was 'frequently interpolated into remedy books' such as Robert Thornton's *Liber de Diversis Medicinis*.[14] Because of this fluid textual landscape, as well as their variability, portability and close relation to charms and incantations, we do not have anything approximating a full perspective on the corpus of Middle English recipes, and we know even less about their consumption and attitudes towards them.

Recipes: modern attitudes

Modern conceptions or expectations of recipes and their consumption are often transferred onto medieval texts, in particular onto those recipes surviving in manuscript collections in what Carroll describes as cultural and temporal 'biases'.[15] Coupled with the ways in which we investigate and record recipes, this has resulted in a perception of medieval recipes as short and mundane, of interest only to the social historian, as well as in preconceived ideas about the purpose of recipes. Carroll's work, some of which challenges the perceived opacity of medieval culinary recipes, makes the point that modern readers are accustomed to being given 'exact measurements' and therefore assume that recipes are 'written for the same purpose and the same audience. Some recipes written as *aides-mémoires* by a cook for his or her own use thus may be very imprecise indeed.'[16] The presumption of predictability, utility, functionality and brevity produces a misleading view of medieval recipes. Rather than thinking of them as a single category, relevant only in terms of a collection, we need to recognise that their subject matter varies even within a collection: they can be alchemical or medical; they can instruct readers on how to make ink, lace, paper, parchment, dyes and so on; they can even relate closely to charms and prayers. Moreover, it is apparently the very signifiers of the linguistic text-type 'recipe', such as semantics, structure, prescription and length, that produce such resistance to the definition of a recipe as a *text* in and of itself. In other words, the presence of the indicators of a text-type has a standardising effect and allows us to consider recipes more easily as part of a collection of similar pieces of writing.[17] This view of recipes that are transmitted in manuscript as instructional units, forming part of a larger work or 'discourse colony' (that may or may not be possessed of a discernible structure), actually masks their variety of subject matter and form and narrows our sense that they may have been consumed in variable ways.[18]

Nevertheless, the impulse to classify these works inevitably privileges the literary-historical, and instructional texts are still treated as occupying a very particular space. This is despite the widespread recognition that it is misleading to attempt to distinguish 'literary' works in the Middle Ages, a point stressed by Tim Machan's discussion of generic categories. Machan identifies an ambiguity that relates to the definition of late-medieval and early modern *belles lettres*, evoking a textual landscape in which genres such as biblical paraphrases and historical chronicles displayed cultivated rhetorical strategies and effects that modern readers typically associate with fiction, and when poetry, not prose, was a common medium for technical and scientific works. Works such as saints' lives and the Wycliffite sermons thus seem to be generically excluded from modern conceptions of belletristic writing, even though in medieval terms such works have as a primary purpose the cultivation of literary effects.[19]

It is my contention that medieval recipes—not just those that are culinary but recipes for cures, remedies, inks and dyes, as well as the closely related charms—display features that relate less obviously to utility than we might expect. In terms of their forms and functions, their intended audience or actual consumers and, perhaps most importantly, the material contexts in which they survive they can manifest a surprising variety which complicates the view that recipes 'have maintained their function throughout the history of English and they can be readily identified even in the early periods'.[20] Thus recipes have the potential to be more complex than simple and ought not to be fully imagined as instructional or thought completely to reflect 'real life': the food described in culinary collections, for example, was intended for those who could 'afford the services of both chef and scribe ... and who indeed took a certain pride-of-place in committing to posterity a record of ... the best of their dining principles'.[21] The fact that recipes may relate to what Terence Scully calls 'conspicuous consumption', or may be intended to indicate the wealth or status of a household, need not, according to Carroll, 'negate other functions'.[22] Recipes may be performative, and in this respect they may not always represent an accurate record of what people ate and drank; rather, they may have functioned as fictions, narrative wish-lists of delicacies and combinations that may or may not have been realistically accessible.

Recipes in manuscript: some examples

The material records of medieval recipes must contribute to any analysis of how these texts were preserved, accessed and consumed, and for the remainder of this chapter I examine some pertinent examples of manuscripts from the later Middle Ages containing medical, herbal and culinary recipes. Cambridge, Trinity College, MS R.14.51 contains what may best be described as a medical herbal, constituting recipes for ailments and wounds as well as charms that protect and cure. The 'collection', generally known as 'In Hoote Somere', contains directions for the gathering of herbs, the preparation of medicines and the application of treatments to patients.[23] It was written on vellum in the mid-fifteenth century in an East Midlands dialect and an *anglicana formata* script. According to Linne Mooney, the manuscript is composite; however, the two parts are similar in script and decoration and were bound together some time after copying.[24] The collection described here occupies the first forty-five leaves and is notable for the high proportion of verse recipes, as well as the intermingling of charms and prayers with those recipes. 'In Hoote Somere' has been copied with some scribal consideration for ease of consultation and access: the recipes are visually demarcated with the use of blue and red ornate initials, ensuring that each component of what is treated of as a complete text is taken separately and can be located relatively easily. The layout that we might expect of a prose text is thus interrupted visually. This practice will be familiar to many students of manuscripts: Taavitsainen records that in another recipe collection, that preserved in London, British Library, MS Sloane 2378, the items are listed and enumerated up to 154. The titles of recipes are underlined in red; some are inserted in a box and the layout indicates where new items begin, although this marking is not consistent throughout the book. Similarly, in the recipe collection found in London, Wellcome Historical Medical Library, MS 405, titles are in red ink, initial letters in blue and against what would have been black ink each item stands out clearly.[25] 'In Hoote Somere' is notable also for what Elaine Miller calls the 'superstructure',[26] a *cap-à-pie* movement through the human body with some digressions in between.

Despite this carefully marked structure, however, the individual recipes can function as separate texts: thus they are significant both as part of the collective and as individual, portable and transmutable pieces of text that can be removed whole from the collection and inserted into another context without losing their integrity. The collection as a whole has been described as a single text by modern scholarship, which takes the first line of the first recipe (or text) and assigns this as the title: 'In Hoote Somere'. Such a manner of assigning a title is not unusual, as scholars need to find ways in which to refer to texts that are unnamed. However, in the case of a whole that is constructed of smaller, shorter and self-contained texts which are demarcated scribally and thus recognisable as individual texts, this act of labelling conceals more than it reveals.

I reproduce here the first recipe, a verse prescription for clear eyes, after Miller (p. 1):

> In hoote somere these erbes thou take,
> And styllyd watre of them thou make,
> Thys ys prouede for the sight,
> To clere yen and make hem bright.
> Here ys for yen that watter or renne,
> For gretande yen and waterne.
> Take rewe, aisell, and faire hony,
> Stampe hit togeder all by dene,
> And wrynge hit thorouʒe a clothe clene,
> And that drynke sone anone,
> Schalle sclake alle the watery teres ilkone.

This recipe, describing the fabrication of a mixture of distilled water, honey and herbs to soothe irritated eyes, has been packaged to be memorable and thereby more readily consumed by a wide range of readers or hearers. The audience is advised to consume the simple tincture 'sone anone' to 'sclake alle the watery tears ilkone', so that consumption—both of the remedy and the recipe—is beneficial and profitable. However, the nature of consumption implied by this text is more profound and complex. This is due to the narrative quality of the text, an aspect of many medieval recipes that is seldom theorised.

By virtue of its construction in verse, the recipe has a lyrical quality that elevates it beyond the level of the strictly informative, nicely illustrating Machan's point that divisions between instructional and literary texts are not always clear-cut in the medieval tradition. The recipe, which could be much shorter, more imperative and more to the point, has an impulse to narrative that adds another dimension to the consumption of the text by the audience: the possibility that the text may delight as well as instruct. This intermingling of the lyrical and the instructive is something that is largely absent from modern recipes, which mostly privilege the imperative mode and which tend to abbreviate.[27] Of course, recipes sometimes needed to be recalled from memory, and verse functions mnemonically in many cases. But here there is also a strong sense of narrative, not just in the individual recipe texts but through the collection as whole, whose structure is supplied by the imagined form of the human body in a manner comparable to that of medical treatises and visual *aides-mémoires* from the same period, such as vein or astrological men.[28]

It is easy to see how a text like that just quoted might have survived and been consumed, like many charms, prayers, recipes and incantations, independently of the collection, and how it might have transcended its presumed utilitarian function. It is not dependent on the superstructure for meaning, relevance or survival and, although it has most of the elements prescribed by Taavitsainen and others for the identification of the text type 'recipe' (ingredients, directions on preparation and on application, statements on how the medicine might work and a given title or rubric), it lacks the instructional, strictly imperative tone that is evident in the example quoted earlier (after Taavitsainen and Edmar). There are, of course, imperative directions such as 'take', 'stampe', 'wrynge', but these are framed and softened by a more soothing, advisory tone that we do not usually find in the text-type identifiers. Those identifiers are formulaic, requiring the text to operate within fairly strict parameters, and what we have here cannot reasonably be described in simple terms: it is indeed a recipe, but it is also a complete piece of verse.[29] Moreover, by our modern standards of dealing with such materials, this verse also functions as the prologue to a long text comprised of smaller units. When recorded in a handlist or a catalogue, the nature of that record will be dictated, generally, by the type of text found. In other words, this text is first a recipe and second a piece of verse, but, since it is strictly speaking 'non-literary', it is perhaps unlikely to find a home in the standard canon of Middle English verse works. It is a complex phenomenon, then, that should lead us to question the ways in which we describe and record texts with protean generic features.

How texts are presented in manuscript can indicate form, and even a cursory glance at the first recipe of 'In Hoote Somere' in Cambridge, Trinity College, MS R.14.51 reveals that it is a verse text. Manuscript witnesses to recipe texts, particularly collections, frequently follow the material patterns described above: there is usually evidence of the efforts of the scribe/compiler—or indeed of owners and readers—to distinguish between individual texts. The sophistication of these material statements ranges from marginal titles, enumeration and crude maniculars or asterisks to more elaborate forms of demarcation such as rubrication, underlining, the use of paraphs and boxes and decorated initials, often quite ornately rendered. However, these too impose a frequently false uniformity on a set of texts and, materially, it would seem that the majority of 'recipe collections', by their *mise-en-page* and through the various interventions of the scribe(s) or other agent(s), disguise rather than reveal narrative impulses. However much they are disguised, both by the *schema* of the books containing them and by the constraints of the modern catalogue, it is my contention that there is clear evidence of literary and narrative elements in recipes and collections from the later medieval period.

The well-known medieval herbal the *Treatise on Rosemary*, attributed to Friar Henry Daniel, is extant in almost twenty manuscripts; it is preserved in one version in London, British Library, MS Royal 17.A.3, ff. 13ʳ–17ʳ, dating from c.1400.[30] The *Treatise* is generally considered to be a single work and is mostly described specifically as a herbal: it prescribes different uses for the herb rosemary, 'paying attention to the cultivation of the plant'.[31] Indeed, the *Treatise* displays many of the features that we look for in something that announces itself as a complete work, including a discernible theme and an elaborate prologue which claims that the text is a translation of one sent by the Duchess of Hainault to Queen Phillippa, the wife of Edward III. However, this work comprises not only instructions on how to cultivate and care for rosemary but also instructions on its uses, framed in a similar fashion to the shorter recipe-type texts that have already been discussed. Taavitsainen notes the close relationship between herbals and groups of recipes, stating that 'some parts of [herbals] are ... inserted into recipe collections'.[32] It seems likely, however, that the reverse also occurred. The following instruction occurs at f. 16ᵛ of BL MS Royal 17.A.3:

> Also take þe flouris of þat herbe *and* drye he*m*, *and* make poudir þerof; *and* bynde in a ly*n*nen clooþ vndir þi*n* ri3t arm put *and* þou schalt be li3t *and* myrye al þat while þat it is þer (my punctuation).

Here, within a herbal, we find a short instructional text that might be described as a recipe and that was able, presumably, to be adapted into many contexts. However, aspects of the *Treatise* manifest themselves as something other than instruction and recipe. Another example occurs at f. 15ʳ:

> Also if a ma*n* stonde vndir a brau*n*che of þis tre, þu*n*dir ne leyt schal hi*m* not derene smyte. And þis same dooþ lorer [laurel] a3ei*n* þe þu*n*dir, but not a3ei*n*s leytny*n*ge. We redden þat þe e*m*por*er* of Rome, Tyberye, dredde þu*n*dri*n*g moor*e* þan ony ma*n*, *and* bi cause þer of he dide make a gro*u*e of lorer trees; *and* in ech a þu*n*dri*n*g he hid hi*m* þer y*n*ne (punctuation mine).

The presence here of what might be described as anecdotal information, side by side with authoritative citation, introduces a quality that is somehow Other and asks us to reconsider the ways in which such a text is packaged and may have been received contemporaneously. This additional information is perhaps designed to render the instruction more interesting, memorable and authoritative, and ultimately more easily transferable from reader to listener.

The prologue to the *Treatise on Rosemary*, mentioned above, functions rather like an explanatory preface; it does not necessarily describe the individual texts themselves nor the information they purvey, addressing instead the tradition and the authorities to which the collection—or at least the impulse to collect—is indebted, as illustrated from f.13ʳ:

> Rosemarye is boþe þe tre *and* herbe, *and* is hoot *and* drie in þe

þridde degre *and* þese ben hise *ver*tues, as it is fou*n*den by diu*er*se
aucto*ur*s *and* in books of ffisyk *and* as seith þe litil book þ*at* þe scole
of Sallerne wroot to þe Cu*n*tasse of Henowd *and* sche sente þe copie
to hir dou3t*er* Philip þe qu*e*ne of Yngelond *and* bigynneþ þ*us* ...

The text announces itself as a treatise, paying due attention to authority
and sources, and gives little indication that what follows is a compilation of
shorter recipes; rather, the material is treated holistically, despite the references to 'diuerse auctours' and 'books of ffisyk'. Examining how the *Treatise*
and its short texts are materially structured, however, reveals a desire to
ensure that the constituent elements of the collection remain somehow
separate: each distinct section is demarcated by a rubricated paraph and
most parts begin with the word 'also' or 'take', forcing a reader to pause,
or at least creating a division between parts. Moreover, the rubric which
precedes the prologue, 'Here ben þe virtues of rosemarye', does not use the
word 'treatise', suggesting rather that the work is a compilation of 'virtues'.
In fact what is found is a compilation of varied instructional texts suitable
for consumption in a variety of settings and linked not thematically or
generically but by the common concern with the herb rosemary.

What is significant here is the mapping of a structure onto discrete
shorter texts. They are organised so that the reader can readily access
them, either separately or as part of a larger work. It is clear that within
the collection not all the texts are recipes: they defy the definition demanded
by that term. However, the term 'herbal' is also problematic as a descriptor
for the so-called 'treatise', and it is difficult to assign one term—and thereby
one function—to the work. If we choose one term we run the risk of
concealing, as opposed to revealing, the surprising blend of genres, styles
and elements. The materiality of the manuscript demonstrates that the texts
can be accessed separately by offering a reader easy access to individual
items independent of context, but it also packages the individual texts in
ways that allow readers to consume them as part of a collection.

Longer works like this not only invited selective readings and discerning
copying at the time, but they also serve today to confound the distinctions we might want to make between short, individual instructive pieces
and larger collections. Shorter texts can stand alone, or function within a
collection with or without a thematic focus, or, somewhat paradoxically,
stand out from that collection as having variant or unexpected elements.
Our terminology seems unsuitable to describe genres that behave in these
unpredictable ways. Since recipe texts, broadly speaking, manifest considerable variation, textually as well in their material forms, it is difficult to
theorise generally about meaning, purpose and audience. When they are
divorced from their material contexts (the physical material, paper and ink)
and from the works that surround them, recipes, both individually and
collectively, make less sense to modern readers.

The scribe-compiler of New Haven, Yale University, MS Beinecke 163 (the Wagstaff Miscellany), which can be dated c.1450–75, thought to organise his recipes in a different manner from the scribe or compiler of British Library, MS Royal 17.A.3, using a table of contents that precedes the text and giving each recipe a title that is offset with red ink underlining. The culinary collection of London, British Library, MS Additional 5467 (located at ff. 25ʳ–64ʳ), a manuscript linked to John Shirley,[33] is differently divided into sections for fish, meats, sauces and vegetables. The manuscript is given running titles and each individual recipe has its own title, offset in a Gothic script from the text of the recipe, and is numbered in the same hand. The collection is divided from the rest of the manuscript by menus, detailing the dishes served at a feast attended by Richard II and John of Gaunt in 1397 (ff. 23ʳ–25ʳ), along with a numbered index to the recipes copied at the end (ff. 65ʳ–66ᵛ). Many of the recipes outlined in the menus correspond to texts in the collection, and it is tempting to imagine that the recipes here, clearly and spaciously copied and supported by different types of finding devices, were intended for the table of the household who commissioned the manuscript. It is easy to imagine that the consumption of the dishes described here was not restricted to the act of reading: the detail in, and length of, the texts suggest that they are realisable in the kitchen of a large noble household. However, the inclusion of menus that relate to a royal feast of the previous century may suggest that there is a certain performativity inherent in the copying and preservation of the recipes. Since many of the recipes included in the collection correspond directly to dishes mentioned in the royal menus, their co-location may indicate that not all recipe collections were copied for practical reasons or should indicate records of actual bodily consumption. In this case the menus can be seen to function rather as a wish-list: they are less a preface to the recipes and more a performance of possibilities. Read in conjunction with the royal menus, the recipe collection can be viewed as a fiction or, more accurately, a fantasy; accessed from the other end—the index—it becomes a functional, utilitarian collection of texts. Side by side, however, with *Le Livre de Bonnes Meures* and *The Gouernance of Prynces* in a volume that promotes good living and appropriate reading, the culinary collection becomes part of the identity of a household and part of what it consumed and valued. The recipe texts here may have only had a limited application or realisation, but they represent, in context, a record of aspirations.

The materiality of the witnesses is key to understanding how these texts and collections were consumed, whether that consumption was strictly textual and imaginative or whether the texts led to actual consumption of both instruction and product. As the Middle Ages progressed so too did the sophistication of the organisation of knowledge, and we see this manifest in the gradual introduction of the paratextual elements that make it easier for us to access and assess books: indices, titles and title pages, running headers, prefaces, explanatory notes and numbered lists.[34] But the levels and sophistication of organisation and *mise-en-page* vary quite considerably even in later medieval manuscript copies, and they must, when they exist, point to increasingly diverse audiences and increased levels and ways of consumption. The more structured and orderly a recipe collection the more likely that it enjoyed a wide readership, even within one household. Moreover, such a collection can frequently be understood in terms of its co-texts, a matter for another paper but worth noting since there has been a tendency in the past to divorce texts and works from their companions in manuscript. Recipes—fluid in movement and in type—circulated in books of many sorts until the printing press encouraged the disentangling of genres of writing and knowledge, and early printers such as Richard Pynson and Wynkyn de Worde printed *The noble boke of festes ryalle and cokery* (STC 3297, 3297.5, 1500, 1510) as stand-alone works.

In conclusion, what I suggest is that we can learn much from these compelling shorter texts, not just about society and culture but significantly about the consumption and organisation of knowledge and information. We should refrain from transferring onto them modern expectations of text and genre, expectations that reduce them to the incidental and secondary. We should acknowledge the fluidity of textual genres and the elements of narrative that find their way into medieval recipes. Editorially, we should not separate them from the material forms in which they survive and from their companion texts, since in so doing we mask not only their individual variety but the many ways in which they were transmitted, packaged and consumed. Much excellent work has been conducted on recipes, but a movement away from categorising them 'among utilitarian genres'[35] and towards a wider appreciation of their potential may ultimately prove more rewarding.

11

Fools, 'Folye' and Caxton's Woodcut of the Pilgrims at Table

Anamaria Gellert

But to assemble these Foles in one bonde.
And theyr demerites worthely to note.
Fayne shal I Shyppes of euery maner londe.
None shalbe left: Barke, Galay, Shyp, nor Bote.
One vessel can nat brynge them al aflote.
For yf al these Foles were brought into one Barge
The bote shulde synke so sore shulde be the charge.
                              S. Brant, *Stultifera navis*
                              (STC 3545 sig. b2ᵛ, 1509)

The unexpected figure of a fool with his traditional ass's ears and coxcomb depicted among the twenty-three pilgrims seated at table in the woodcut from Caxton's second edition of the *Canterbury Tales* (1483) raises a series of questions concerning the implications of his presence as well the consequences it had for the late fifteenth-century reception of the *Tales*.[1] Since the consumption of a literary work is always mediated by the form in which it is transmitted, such material aspects as the layout of the page, the decoration and the illustration, as well as the typographical conventions, have an 'expressive' function and help to shape the text's meanings.[2] Therefore, the woodcuts in Caxton's edition function both as a threshold to and as a comment on the text. If one accepts the notion that the rendering of words into pictures is a translation from one semiotic system into another, one must also bear in mind that *translatio* and *interpretatio* are strongly interconnected. As Schapiro has pointed out, besides the disconnections between text and picture which may arise from the resources peculiar to each single medium, there are differences marked by historical factors. Among these factors two are particularly significant: the new meanings texts acquired for later illustrators

Figure 11.1   Pilgrims at Table, *Canterbury Tales* (1483).
Oxford, St John's College, MS 266/b.2.21, sig. c4ʳ.

and the new styles of representation, which, being the products of a specific
Weltanschauung, revealed how and to what extent ideas, thoughts and values
changed in the course of time.[3] Early editors' interpretations of given literary
works were thus reflected in their editorial choices.

The fool in Caxton's woodcut

The image of the pilgrims at table, presumably at the Tabard Inn, is one
of Caxton's most widely known and frequently reproduced woodcuts
(Figure 11.1). The woodcut is placed at the top of page c4ʳ, above the single
text-column which begins with the lines:

> Gret chere made our ost to vs euenrychon,
> And to soupere sette he vs anon.

He serued vs wyth vytayll at the beste
Strong was the wyne & wel drynke vs lyste.[4]

These lines, as well as the woodcut which illustrates them, help to shift the focus from the description of the pilgrims as individuals to the representation of the community of storytellers, a fact also confirmed by the number of pilgrims contained in the woodcut. As is well known, only twenty-three tell stories, although Chaucer mentions thirty pilgrims including himself. In Caxton's woodcut the storytellers are accompanied by a twenty-fourth figure which critics have largely disregarded: a fool with his traditional ass's ears and coxcomb. Hodnett has argued that the woodcuts in Caxton's edition are not copies of foreign blocks but represent examples of original English woodcutting.[5] Yet the courtly lady seated at the monk's right side wears a stylish fifteenth-century Burgundian hat and the figure with ass's ears and coxcomb is reminiscent of the fools in the works of German artists such as Master E.S. (active 1450–67) and the Master of the Housebook (c.1470–1500), as well as in Albrecht Dürer's (1471–1528) woodcuts which illustrate Sebastian Brant's *Stultifera Navis* (Ship of Fools).

The question which arises is whether the woodcut borrows single figures from an international iconographic stock and places them together to represent the pilgrims, or whether the whole image is copied from a foreign model. While the second hypothesis cannot be proved in the absence of a woodcut which can be indisputably shown to have been the printer's source, it is reasonable to conjecture that the artist borrowed from a stock while paying particular attention to textual details such as the number of storytellers.[6] Caxton was known to have acquired stocks and he sometimes had his artist copy foreign models for his illustrated books. Moreover, in the 1480s the Frankfurt Book Fair was gaining momentum, and many well-known fifteenth-century printer-publishers are attested to have sold and bought books at the fair.[7] So Caxton may have secured some of his iconographic stock there, or he may have re-elaborated figures and garments which he had used elsewhere.

In the dedicatory engraving from the presentation copy of the *Recuyell of the Historyes of Troye* (STC 15375, 1473/74) he is depicted in the act of kneeling deferentially and presenting the book to Margaret, duchess of Burgundy, whose coat of arms and motto appear on a canopy in the background. His connection with the duchess's household is well documented. In fact, in the prologue he attributes his decision to complete the translation to Margaret's patronage and encouragement. The duchess and her waiting maids are represented wearing hennins (i.e. steeple-shaped bonnets with veils draped over them) and dresses with v-shaped or round collars, just like the courtly lady depicted in the woodcut of the pilgrims at table. Moreover, the young man, with his wavy hair, plumed bonnet and Burgundian gown, who is represented next to the monk, is reminiscent of the male figures in the dedicatory engraving as well as of the Squire in the woodcuts which precede his description in the *General Prologue* (sig. a4ᵛ) and his tale (sig. n8ᵛ). The anachronistic costumes of the courtly figures in the woodcut of the pilgrims at table reflect the artist's attempt to render the characters as people of his own time and to attenuate the sense of estrangement, provoked by the chronological distance, that late fifteenth-century readers of Caxton's edition may have experienced.

Among the fifteen extant copies of the 1483 edition of the *Tales*, the copy in St John's College Library, Oxford is an illustrative example of how the 'consumption' of Chaucer's text also involved its material adaptation to the commissioner's tastes and interests. In this *Sammelband*, prepared for Roger Thorney, the *Canterbury Tales* (STC 5083) are bound with Chaucer's *Troilus and Criseyde* (STC 5094), John Mirk's *Quattuor Sermones* (STC 17957)—all published by Caxton in 1483—and a manuscript of Lydgate's *Siege of Thebes*.[8] One of the distinctive features of the volume is the considerable effort invested in making these incunabula look as similar to a manuscript as possible. All the pages were ruled in purple ink. Illuminated initials and red or blue paraphs mark the major divisions in the text. The woodcuts in the *Canterbury Tales* were washed in ink, and details such as irises, trees and heraldic shields were added. According to Edwards, it would be tempting to see the volume 'as a final vestige of some very specific in-house interest in enhancing the products of his press for a particular purchaser or prospective patron, as Thorney may have been'.[9] The escutcheons depicted next to the pilgrims may reflect the aspiration of a middle-class patron to have a coat of arms, a privilege which was reserved for the aristocracy. Interestingly enough, heraldic shields appear even in the woodcuts of pilgrims from the lower classes, such as the Cook (sig. i5ʳ) and the Miller (sig. b7ᵛ).

Since Chaucer did not explicitly include a fool among the pilgrims he portrayed in the *General Prologue*, the explanation for the fool's presence must be sought elsewhere. In the *Canterbury Tales* the words 'fool' and 'folye' (with the variant spelling 'folie') appear thirty-four and forty-two times respectively.[10] A survey of the contexts in which these words appear and the range of meanings they acquire in the tales will help to establish if and to what extent Chaucer's use of these words influenced Caxton's decision to include a fool. In order fully to understand how and why Chaucer employed these terms, it is important to try and reconstruct the medieval concept of folly as it emerges from the religious, medical and literary discourses that formed the cultural context of the poet's work.

Categories of the medieval fool and folly

In the Middle Ages the word 'fool' indicated a wide spectrum of intellectual disabilities and mental disorders as well as different forms of spiritual and bodily corruption. What emerges from the definitions provided by the

Middle English Dictionary (hereafter *MED*) is that there were four main types of fool:[11]

1. the natural or congenital fool, or a person who is temporarily foolish because of a momentary loss of his/her intellective powers caused by drunkenness

2. the impious or unchaste person

3. the court jester kept by kings or noblemen for their amusement

4. the madman or pathological fool

The natural and pathological fools were mainly the objects of medical and legal descriptive and normative discourses, whereas the impious or lecherous fool was predominantly dealt with in theological discourse. The wise fool or jester often finds a prominent place in medieval literature, where he is less the object of a discourse than a speaking subject. Nonetheless, he is allowed to express his own point of view only when he temporarily reacquires speech and reason. Moreover, literature also gives voice to melancholy lovers afflicted by the aristocratic malady of *hereos*, which occupies an intermediate position, halfway between sinful and pathological folly. As Fritz has shown in his acute analysis of twelfth- and thirteenth-century religious, legal, medical and literary discourses about folly, theological treatises tended to identify the fool with the *insipiens* of Psalm 52, the man who ignored or denied God's existence.[12] Folly was thus often perceived in negative terms as the absence of reason, as the morphology of so many terms shows: *in-sania, in-sipientia, de-sipientia, a-mentia, de-mentia*. In his *Summa Theologiae* Aquinas distinguishes between *stultitia*, characterised by apathy in the heart as well as dullness of the senses (*hebetudinem cordis et obtusionem sensuum*), and *fatuitas*, whose distinctive feature was the person's deficiency in judgement or sense (*totaliter spiritualis sensus privationem*) (II^a–IIae q. 46 a. 1 co.).[13] Moreover, he makes a further distinction between a sinless type of stultitia, provoked by natural disposition, as in the case of congenital fools (*amentibus*), and a sinful one, which can be found in human beings who, by plunging their senses into earthly things, are incapable of perceiving divine things (II^a–IIae q. 46 a. 2 co.). Even if the various terms used to refer to folly in the medical (*frenesis, mania, melancholia, lethargia*) and religious discourses were not always charged with negative connotations, what strikes one is the extraordinary proliferation of words used to refer to folly. The unity of *sapiens* was thus contrasted with the discord and multiplicity of folly. According to Fritz, in the Middle Ages the term *alienatio mentis* [alienation of the mind] is the closest one can get to a generic definition of folly.[14]

The proverbs and proverbial expressions offered by the *MED* help to outline two of the main characteristics associated with the medieval fool: his frantic, aimless wandering ('A fool cannot be still. A fool must show his folly.') and his excessive talkativeness or obstinate taciturnity ('A fool is known by his tongue. A fool's bell is soon rung.'). The lack of moderation which characterises his peregrination, gestures and speech find a counterpart in his physical appearance. The rich iconographic evidence and, in particular, the representation of the *insipiens* in the historiated initial 'D(ixit)' of Psalm 52 in twelfth- and thirteenth-century manuscripts indicate that by the end of the thirteenth century there was a well-established repertoire of pictorial signs which were used to create a conventional image of folly.[15] Nakedness and/or torn, scruffy clothes were two of the most evident signs of alienation. The idea of estrangement was often reinforced by the fool's dishevelled or tonsured hair, which contributed to creating two sets of associations. On the one hand, the figure of the fool was modelled upon that of the *homo silvester* with whom he shared the locale of his wanderings (the forest) and the weapon necessary for his self-defence (the club), as well as physical features such as the hairy body and the muscular build. On the other hand, the tonsure connected the fool with clerks and saintly people through a reversal of the function of the sign. If, in the case of clerks and saints, tonsure was perceived as a sign of humility or voluntary self-defacement, in the fool's case it was a mark of infamy, denoting humiliation and derision. In the initial 'D(ixit)' of Psalm 52, the fool's head is often shaved.[16] The practice of head shaving was widespread among the mentally insane who went on pilgrimages to sanctuaries. As Fritz has pointed out, the fool of medieval romances resembles a pilgrim in his wanderings, with the difference that he is on his way to a non-existent sanctuary.[17] The collocation of romance fools in wild, uncivilised settings outside the court, but at the same time not far from it, reflects the condition of real-life people suffering from *alienatio mentis*, whose wandering in the countryside in the proximity of the medieval cities made them 'prisoners of the threshold'. Set in a highly symbolic position, the interior of the exterior and inversely, the fool was at the same time a marginal and an emarginated figure.[18] As a marginal figure, he was both the person who did not correspond to the model that society constructed of itself and the individual who did not identify himself with the norms and conventions imposed on him.[19]

As Guglielmi has shown, in the Middle Ages the Christian ecumene, intended in a geographical and spiritual sense as the land inhabited by the *corpus mysticum cuius caput Christus* [mystic body whose head is Christ], was the space and social body against which marginality was defined.[20] The fool depicted in the initial 'D(ixit)' of Psalm 52, who says in his heart 'non est deus' [there is no God], because he is either unable or unwilling to believe in God's existence, sets himself outside the Christian ecumene. In a miniature (f. 43ᵛ) from Oxford, Bodleian Library, MS Rawl. G. 185, a fourteenth-century Psalter, he is depicted in the act of disputing with a monk. The whole scene is dominated by the towering presence of God, whose head is emerging from a cloud. The scrolls issuing from their mouths and the posture of the monk's and fool's hands are conventional pictorial signs which indicate that they are engaged in conversation. God's scroll reads 'Ecce dixit insipiens' [behold what the fool said]. The fool's proposition 'Non est deus' is confuted by the monk, whose scroll reads 'Tu menteris aperte' [you lie openly]. The particularity of this miniature lies in its drama-tisation of a dialogue which sets in contrast the fool's irrational speech with the monk's authoritative rational discourse, which is reinforced by the book he is holding, presumably the Bible, and by God's authorising presence. It is interesting to note that the monk's statement, 'tu menteris aperte', plays upon the meanings of the verb 'mentire', which derives from the Latin *mens* (mind), and the adverb 'aperte', which means 'openly', 'in a straightforward and clear way'. Thus the sentence 'you clearly lie (tell untrue things)' was underpinned by the idea that the fool's mind, just like the empty bag he is holding, was full of air. The limner was evidently exploiting the etymology of the word 'fool', which derives from the Latin *follis* (i.e. windbag or bellows) and is applied, by extension, to 'empty-headed' people. As Kolve has shown, in the Middle Ages the statement *non est deus* was an example of a self-evidently untrue proposition used to teach the nature of false logic in the schools.[21] An illustrative example of teaching material is the collection of six *impossibilia*, composed by Siger of Brabant between 1266 and 1276, which posits the statement *non est deus* as the first impossibility, followed by such absurd statements as 'The Trojan war is still in progress' or 'Things infinite are finite'.[22]

The miniature also enacts the biblical opposition between *sapiens* and *stultus*: 'verba oris sapientis gratia et labia insipientis praecipitabunt eum' [the words of the mouth of a wise man are grace: but the lips of a fool shall throw him down headlong] (Eccles. 10: 12); 'initium verborum eius stultitia et novissimum oris illius error pessimus' [the beginning of his words is folly, and the end of his talk is a mischievous error] (Eccles. 10: 13). The fool's irrational *multiloquium* is often contrasted with the wise man's silence. In his rendering of the vice of Folly in the Scrovegni Chapel in Padua Giotto offers a symbolic as well as ingenious solution for the fool's loquaciousness: *Stultitia* is depicted with mouth and lips sealed with a padlock. Giotto's departure from the representation of the Psalm fool, who was allowed to speak in order to give voice to a self-evidently impossible proposition, reflects a gradual change in attitude towards folly, anticipating in an embryonic form what Foucault has called 'the great internment', when fools were no longer permitted to wander freely and express their insensate discourse. If the padlock is an original contribution to the traditional repre-sentation of fools, *Stultitia*'s club, tunic with torn sleeves and dagged edges and feather crown decorated with bells are conventional pictorial signs used to denote folly.[23] Yet the inclusion of the allegorical figure of Folly among the traditional set of vices was an innovative element by itself.[24]

In the medieval system of Vices and Virtues Folly occupied a marginal position. Neither Prudentius's fifth-century *Psychomachia* nor Gregory the Great's sixth-century *Moralia in Job*, two of the most authoritative works on the topic, include Folly among the traditional set of vices.[25] Both authors consider pride (*superbia*) the root of all deadly and venial sins. Moreover, in the twelfth-century tract *De fructibus carnis et spiritus*, attributed to Hugh of Saint-Victor, neither *stultitia* nor *insipientia* appears on the *arbor vitiorum* [tree of vices], which is set in contrast to the *arbor virtutum* [tree of virtues].[26] Lackey has recently argued that Giotto's ensemble of virtues can be traced back to the traditional system of Vices and Virtues and, in particular, to St Thomas Aquinas's works, whereas the cycle of vices is original.[27] Thus the traditional vices of Pride, Avarice, Lust and Gluttony are displaced by Folly, Inconstancy, Infidelity and Injustice. The representation of Prudence, which faces Folly on the opposite wall, contains, however, some less conventional aspects. She has two faces, one looking into the past and the other into the future, and is depicted standing behind a lectern on which an open book is placed, holding a pair of compasses in her right hand and a mirror in the left. If, as Lackey has argued, Giotto intended to emphasise the 'intellectual dimension' of Prudence as opposed to Folly,[28] the relationship between the two images may be interpreted more as a re-enactment of the contrast between *sapiens* and *insipiens* than as the traditional antagonism between virtues and vices.

If, in the twelfth and thirteenth centuries, the *insipiens* or *stultus* of the intitial 'D(ixit)' of Psalm 52 shared characteristics with the wild man and the natural fool, by the mid-fourteenth century limners often represented him as a court fool or jester.[29] An early example is offered by a miniature from Bodleian Library, MS Laud Lat. 114, a thirteenth-century English Psalter (f. 71ʳ). The fool is wearing a parti-coloured costume with bells and has ass's ears. He is holding a bauble in his left hand and an inflated bladder attached to a stick in his right hand. The social marginalisation of fools through norms which restricted their access to the sacraments and their right to self-determination, as well as subjecting them to public mockery and imprisonment, was counterbalanced by the partial rehabilitation of folly in the courtly milieu, where the function of the fool was not only to entertain but also to give voice to unutterable truths or to be the king's counsellor. The court fool was both a flatterer, who made the king laugh, and the king's unsettling double, a relationship symbolised by the fool's bauble, which was a reversed replica of the royal sceptre.[30] When the fool is not depicted as a solitary figure or engaged in conversation with the devil, he appears in the company of a king, presumably David, who admonishes him with his raised finger. What strikes one in the initial from the English Psalter mentioned above is the jester's aloofness (he is not even looking at the royal figure) and the absence of any pictorial sign which could indicate a rebuke on the part of the king. The latter seems absorbed in watching the fool's performance (dancing), and is reminiscent of the mad King Saul rather than of the wise David.[31] Saul's madness (actually a form of possession by an evil spirit) was God's punishment for his excessive pride and despotism.[32]

The medieval tendency to interpret folly in a moralising key by associating it with sin, and in particular with lust, is well reflected in an early fifteenth-century historiated initial from the Great Bible (London, British Library, MS Royal 1 E IX, f. 148ʳ). The jester is depicted in a courtly milieu in the act of wagging his index finger mockingly at God. He is also pointing at his own mouth, a gesture which is indicative of the sins of the tongue. Just like the *insipiens*, the jester is one of the talkers of 'ydel wordes of folye or of vileynye' (X, 377) that Chaucer's Parson warns against in the *Parson's Tale*. One of the courtiers is pointing at an elegant young couple engaged in an erotic embrace and kissing passionately. God's gesture of rejection is indicated by the posture of his hands. Here, the negation of God's existence is associated with the 'fol-delit' of sexual love. The courtiers' smiles, as well as their complacent attitude, denote the impiety of those who are not aware of, or choose to ignore, the fact that they 'shal yelden acountes of it at the day of doom' (X, 377). According to Aquinas, the type of *stultitia* which causes man's senses to be dulled is sin. Moreover, since man's senses are chiefly plunged into earthly things by lust, which is the greatest pleasure, folly arises above all from *luxuria* (IIᵃ–IIae q. 46 a. 3 co.).

Folly in the *Parson's Tale*

In his treatise on the Seven Deadly Sins Chaucer's Parson follows his *auctoritates* in setting Pride at the root of the *arbor malorum*, whose branches are Ire, Envy, Sloth (*Accidia*), Avarice or Covetousness, Gluttony and Lechery.[33] The Parson points out that, since lechery 'is ful displesaunt thing to God', he punished sinful people with the deluge and 'putte grete peynes agayns this synne in the olde lawe' (X, 837). The first finger of the hand the devil uses to imprison man's soul is 'the fool lookynge of the fool woman and the fool man' (X, 852) which derives from the covetousness of the heart. The second finger is the 'vileyns touchynge in wikede manere' (X, 853), the third the 'foule wordes, that fareth lyk fyr' and burn the heart (X, 854), the fourth is the act of kissing, for 'trewely he were a greet fool that wolde kisse the mouth of a brennynge oven or of a fourneys' (X, 855), the fifth is the sexual act (X, 861). The scene depicted in the historiated initial enacts the first four stages which plunge man's soul into the vice of lust. The fifth is left to the reader's imagination.[34] The fact that the limner chose a courtly milieu for the location of the scene is indicative of a trend in medieval thought, exemplified by the *Roman de la Rose*, towards an unmasking of the artificiality of courtly love conventions and unveiling of the lovers' false pretences of Platonic love. After all, the 'feestes', revels and 'daunces' which took place at court were often occasions for flirtatious conversations and 'folye' (VI, 64–66). Moreover, the four stages of love described in Andreas Capellanus's influential *De amore* overlap with the five fingers of Lechery condemned by the Parson: arousing of hope (*spei datione*), offering kisses (*osculi exhibitione*), the enjoyment of intimate embraces (*amplexus fruitione*) and the abandonment of the entire person (*totius personae concessione*) (I, 7:60).

In discussing the sin of Lechery, the Parson distinguishes between various subtypes: fornication between husband and wife, adultery, the prostitution of the 'fool women, that mowe be likned to a commune gong, where as men purgen hire ordure' (X, 884), the fornication of priests and other religious figures, as well as the sinful dreams provoked by an imbalance of the four humours, malady, excessive eating and drinking or wicked thoughts. As may be expected, Chaucer's use of the words 'fool' and 'folly' in the *Parson's Tale*, whose form and content is similar to that of a religious tract, has a moralising function. Folly is constantly equated with sin, whether it be the sin of Pride, Lechery, Gluttony, Ire or Sloth. Thus it is a 'greet folye' for human beings to feel pride in the goods of nature (health, beauty and strength, wit, sharp understanding, good memory), in the goods of fortune (wealth, high social position) or in those of grace (virtue, the power to suffer spiritual distress and resist temptation) (X, 450–55). The man who values excessively the goods of fortune is a 'greet fool' because he ignores the levelling power of the wheel of fortune, which can unexpectedly turn a great lord into a 'caytyf' (X, 470). Fools are also those who, like King Saul, give free rein to their wrath, for 'manace' is an 'open folye' (X, 645). Within the wider topic of *Ira*, the Parson also discusses the sins of the tongue: swearing, flattering, chiding and reproaching, scorning, jangling (speaking idle words) and mocking. He calls the sinners who indulge in mocking 'japeres, that been the develes apes, for they maken folk to laughe at hire japery as folk doon at the gawdes of an ape' (X, 650). There is an obvious affinity between the japer and the court jester, with the difference that the latter made people laugh as part of his professional entertainment. Another category of fools mentioned by the Parson are those who, like the courtiers in the historiated initial, are guilty of *tarditas* (a form of *accidia*) in amending their ways and turning to God. The high frequency of the words 'fool' and 'folye'/'folie' in the *Parson's Tale* is equalled only by their occurrence in the allegorical *Tale of Melibee*, which is a close translation of the *Livre de Melibée et de Dame Prudence*, written by Renaud de Louens around 1336.

Folly in the *Tale of Melibee*

This 'moral tale vertuous' (VII, 2130) told by Chaucer the pilgrim emphasizes the importance of patience, wisdom, prudent action and taking good counsel, as opposed to the folly of uncontrolled wrath, sorrow and reckless, hasty action. In the Ellesmere manuscript the rubric of the tale reads: 'here bigynneth Chaucers tale of Melibee'. Since in the Middle Ages the distinction between author and narrator was not as sharply defined as it is in modern literary theory, medieval readers may have been easily led to identify Chaucer the pilgrim with the author himself. It is, therefore, reasonable to conjecture that the riding pilgrim depicted in the niche of the foliate bar border on the folio containing the incipit of the *Tale of Melibee* (f. 153^r) was believed to be the poet's life-like portrait.[35] This assumption is supported by the reproduction of the bust in a picture from Hoccleve's *Regiment of Princes* set in the margins of the stanza in which the poet claimed that the 'peynture' was a life-like rendering of the real Chaucer:

> Al thogh his lyfe be queynt the resemblaunce
> Of him hath in me so fressh lyflynesse
> That to putte other men in remembraunce
> Of his persone I haue heere his lyknesse
> Do make to this ende in sothfastnesse
> That thei that haue of him lest thought and mynde
> By this peynture may ageyn him fynde.[36]

In the miniature the poet is holding a rosary in his left hand while pointing with the index finger of his right hand at the word 'sothfastnesse' in the text. In both the Harley and Ellesmere portraits Chaucer is represented as a venerable elderly man whose profession is indicated by the penner hanging from his neck. In his attempt to create an authoritative *auctor*, the Ellesmere limner departed from Harry Bailly's portrayal of Chaucer the pilgrim in the *Prologue to Sir Thopas* as a rather shy and reserved man whose physical appearance was similar to that of a 'popet in arm t'enbrace/For any woman, small and fair of face' (VII, 1891–92). Moreover, the decision to place the portrait at the beginning of the *Tale of Melibee* instead of the *Tale of Sir Thopas* was part of the artist's or the commissioner's attempt to construct a venerable author figure by associating it with the moral tale in prose rather than with the romance told in the obsolete doggerel rhyme. The oversized proportion of the pilgrim's bust may be read in terms of the hierarchical perspective of medieval art, in which the size of the figure denoted the degree of the character's importance.[37] The insertion of a rosary in the Harley portrait also played an important part in constructing the author's persona in accordance with the early fifteenth-century notion of the *auctor*. Hoccleve's reference to Chaucer as 'mayster dere and fadir reverent' contributed to setting the basis for the process of canon formation through which Chaucer was transformed into the father of English poetry, the poet laureate, whose works were described by Caxton in terms of 'holynesse and virtue', 'noblesse', 'wysedom' and 'gentylesse'.[38]

That Chaucer the *auctor* was a fifteenth-century creation is proved by the poet's description of himself in the preface to *A Treatise on the Astrolabe* as 'lewd compilator'. In the *Canterbury Tales* Chaucer also stresses his role as compiler when, in the *Miller's Prologue*, he claims that he must report the 'cherles tale' or 'elles falsen som of my mateere' (I, 3175). Manuscript evidence shows that at least some of his early readers perceived him as such. The colophon of the Ellesmere version of the *Canterbury Tales* reads: 'Heere is ended the book of the tales of Caunterbury, compiled by Geffrey Chaucer, of whos soule Jhesu Crist have mercy. Amen'.³⁹ As Minnis has shown, the *compilator* denied any personal authority and accepted responsibility only for arranging other men's statements. By contrast, an *auctor* was someone who bore full responsibility for the authoritative works he/she had written.⁴⁰ Apart from his indebtedness to the medieval compilers for his source-material and literary form, Chaucer's role as compiler permitted him to stage what Olson has called the 'fiction of orality' in a dialogism which gave voice to different points of view without the danger of meeting with censure. The tales of 'myrthe' that 'sownen into synne' (X, 1085) could thus share the same literary and material space with tales of 'moralitee and hoolynesse' (I, 3180) for the readers' instruction and entertainment. Chaucer's portrait in the *Regiment of Princes* served to authenticate Hoccleve's own work, which became 'a vehicle for the transmission not only of the image of the poet but also of the idea of his poetry and the concept of his tale of good counsel if not of his whole book'.⁴¹

In the *Tale of Melibee* the words 'fool' and 'folye'/'folie' occur mainly in connection with the concepts of prudence and wisdom, which are personified in the characters of Melibee's wife Prudence and his daughter Sophie, from the Greek *sophia* [wisdom]. The tale belongs to the genre of political writing known as the *specula principum* [mirrors of princes] used to instruct princes or powerful lords on aspects of good governance. Melibee's wrath, provoked by the mischief done to his wife and daughter in his absence by neighbouring lords, is appeased by Prudence's good counsels and wise discourses. In his anger and excessive sorrow he behaves 'lyk a fool', for, as his wife points out, 'it aperteneth nat to a wys man to maken swich a sorwe' (VII, 2170). According to Prudence's teachings, what makes a wise ruler is his ability to choose his counsellors and distinguish between the good and the bad ones; his willingness to change his mind if a decision proves to be wrong, for 'it is no folie to change conseil whan the thyng is chaunged, or elles whan the thyng semeth ootherweyes than it was biforn' (VII, 1064); his capacity to dissimulate his real thoughts as well as his 'folie' (intended here as anger); his haste in fleeing the counsels of fools because a fool 'kan noght conseille but after his owene lust and his affeccioun' (VII, 1172) and is quick to find faults in other people while refusing to acknowledge his own. Moreover, the wise ruler should neither be avaricious nor waste his goods 'folily'. Prudence displays a rich set of *auctoritates* to convince her husband that the bad counsellors' advice to go to war is nothing but a 'moevyng of folye' (VII, 1238). Engaging in battle with mightier or more powerful lords than oneself is 'woodnesse', and fighting weaker men is 'folie' (VII, 2670). The tale also introduces the theme of the rich and powerful lord who is punished by God for his great pride and his sins. Melibee's name is expounded by Prudence: it means the one who drinks the honey of 'sweete temporeel richesses, and delices and honours of this world' (VII, 2600), neglecting God's commands. The neighbours' wicked actions are thus presented as the natural consequence of, and just punishment for, Melibee's own sins. Prudence also advises her husband not to trust Fortune, for only 'greet fools' believe in its durability and ignore its power to cause the downfall and ruin of people regardless of their social and economic position. She quotes Solomon (Prov. 28: 14) in stating that rebuke is more useful than flattery, for the counsellor who 'repreveth or chideth a fool for his folye' is worthier than those courtiers who 'preyseth hym in his mysdoynge and laugheth at his folye' (VII, 1706–7). Melibee's anger is soothed and his foolish behaviour amended through his wife's good counsel and admonishments. The biblical contrast between *sapientia* and *insipientia* is thus transferred into a secular context, where its function is to teach rulers how to be prudent and wise.

Folly in the *Knight's Tale*

The words 'fool' and 'folye' also recur in the *Knight's Tale*, where they are used to indicate the melancholy lovers Arcite and Palamon, who are afflicted by *hereos*, a type of lovesickness which was considered to be the malady of the aristocracy.[42] According to Gerard of Berry, who was commenting on Constantinus Africanus's *Viaticum*, the leisurely and carefree lives of noblemen rendered them potential candidates for this disease of the brain.[43] In his *Glosule super Viaticum* (*c.*1236) Gerard describes *amor hereos* as a melancholic worry caused by obsessive musing over the object of desire and a malfunction of the estimative faculty triggered by excessive imagination. Unlike Constantinus, who believed that love was provoked by an imbalance in the four humours and the need to expel excess humour, Gerard identified the cause of the malady as the sight of a beautiful object or person. The patient's pathological overestimation of the beloved found a counterpart in the idealisation of the courtly lady and the service of love. Medical knowledge and theories concerning *hereos* were thus codified in treatises on the art of courtly love such as Andreas Capellanus's *De Amore* and filtered into vernacular courtly literature. Andreas famously defines love in terms which are similar to those of Gerard of Berry:

> Amor est passio quaedam innata procedens ex visione et immoderata cogitatione formae alterius sexus, ob quam aliquis super omnia cupit

alterius potiri amplexibus et omnia de utriusque voluntate in ipsius amplexu amoris praecepta compleri.[44] (I, 1:1)

As Wack has pointed out, both Andreas and Gerard localise passionate love in a moral or social elite and, in particular, in a masculine intellectual elite.[45] She has convincingly argued that lovesickness, and the cultural construct of 'noble love' the development of which it contributed to, evolved into a form of social behaviour among the aristocracy. Its function was to resolve psychological and social tensions by 'controlling a historically- and socially-conditioned experience of *eros* that was felt to threaten the normative hierarchy of gender and power'.[46]

In describing Arcite's sorrow Chaucer lists the conventional *signa amoris* of melancholic love: he can neither sleep, eat nor drink, his eyes are 'holwe and grisly to biholde' (I, 1363), his face is pale, he seeks solitude and cries at the sound of music, his voice and speech are unrecognisable. Besides the detailed account of the symptoms, which were widely used in courtly literature and which Chaucer probably found in his source (Boccaccio's *Teseida*), the poet also offers an accurate description of *amor hereos* in accordance with the prevailing medical views of the time:[47]

> [...] in his geere for al the world he ferde
> Nat oonly lik the loveris maladye
> Of Hereos, but rather lyk manye,
> Engendred of humour malencolik
> Biforen, in his celle fantastik. (I, 1372–76)

Since medical treatises examined melancholy as a form of *alienatio mentis*, and given the close resemblance between the symptoms of melancholic patients and those suffering from lovesickness, it is not surprising that *amor hereos* came to be associated with folly. The folly of love is a recurrent theme in medieval romance. In fact, most of the knights of the Round Table experience one or more episodes of *alienatio mentis* (melancholy or frenzy).[48] In the *Knight's Tale* Theseus offers a detached reflection on the folly of love. Seen from the perspective of old age, wisdom and authority, Arcite's and Palamon's love service, performed by Theseus himself in the past, is perceived as 'heigh folye':

> Now looketh, is nat that an heigh folye?
> Who may been a fool but if he love? (I, 1798–99)

> A man moot been a fool, or yong or oold
> I woot it by myself ful yore agon,
> For in my tyme a servant was I oon. (I, 1812–14)

The fool in Caxton's woodcut

The recurrence of the words 'fool' and 'folly' is less frequent in the other *Canterbury Tales*, and when they appear they are used in connection with one of the three types of folly exemplified in the *Parson's Tale*, the *Tale of Melibee* or the *Knight's Tale*. Yet these three tales offered a rich quarry of religious, medical and literary reflections on different forms of folly which Caxton may have drawn on if it was he who commissioned the insertion of a fool in the woodcut of the pilgrims at table. The printer's decision may have also been influenced by the fact that in fifteenth-century London certain inns were important cultural centres where innkeepers such as Harry Bailly were often figures from the entertainment world who acted as *animateurs*.[49] According to Welsford, the fool became an essential component of fifteenth-century social life. He was hired by corporations, kings and noblemen and was requested in taverns and brothels as well as pageants, processions and mysteries.[50] From the liminal position he occupied outside the walls of the city he gradually moved towards the centre of the stage of social life and became an instrument of social satire in the guise of the wise fool. As Foucault argued in his highly influential study, folly and fools seem to have obsessed Western imagination from the fifteenth century.[51] Within only ten years of Caxton's publication of his second edition of the *Canterbury Tales*, Sebastian Brant published his famous *Ship of Fools*, with its bitter criticism of corrupt morals.

In this context of profound interest in fools and folly it would be naïve to presume that Caxton was not aware of the implications the presence of the fool had for the group of pilgrims and for the *Canterbury Tales* as a whole. It would be just as naïve to believe that diligent readers such as the gentleman who rebuked Caxton for the discrepancies between the printer's 1476 edition and what the customer considered to be a better version would not have perceived the sexual and subversive connotations of the fool's presence. Moreover, even if the inclusion of the fool in the company of pilgrims was the result of the woodcutter's own interpretive intervention it remains a mystery how such an intervention might have escaped Caxton's notice.

Precedents for the fool

The literary and iconographic traditions reveal that the fool with coxcomb and ass's ears carried a rich set of connotations. As can be evinced from the historiated initials representing the jester in a courtly love scene, in the fifteenth century artists began to depict the fool in a courtly milieu where one of his functions was to emphasise the consuming folly of love and its excesses. An illustrative example of this tendency is the recurrent image of the fool in scenes of courtly love by Master E.S., a German engraver, goldsmith and printmaker who worked in the region of the Upper Rhine near Lake Constance in the second half of the fifteenth century. In one of his most popular engravings, known as the *Large Love Garden* (1465), two amorous couples seated at a richly garnished table are depicted in the background of a *hortus conclusus*. While one of the courtly couples is still engaged in pleasant 'daliaunce' over a cup of wine, the male partner in the second couple is fondling the lady's breast. In the foreground an elegantly dressed woman grabs at the jester's coat, uncovering his genitals. According to Moxey, in this exposing of his genitals to the spectator 'the fool seems literally to strip away the social convention of the "love garden" in order to assert that a sexual reality lies behind it'.[52]

The popularity of this engraving and the message it conveyed is testified by the watercolour copy made by the Housebook Master sometime after 1475.[53] The Housebook Master inserts into the picture another jester (with bubble and hood decorated with bells), who covers his eyes in order not to see the spectacle of exposed genitals, while a courtly lady encourages him to look by pointing at the uncovered space between the other fool's legs. The woman's gesture seems to reaffirm the widespread medieval idea that women were more subject to the sins of the flesh than men because of their natural frailty. The artist replaces the small well of Master E.S.'s engraving with a tall fountain whose prominent place in the composition of the image as a whole stresses the importance of water as a mirror-like element. The mirror, with its self-referential function and symbolism of narcissistic fascination with oneself, was often used to characterise the allegorical figure of *Luxuria*. The birds perched on the garden wall are also displaced by a peacock, whose presence draws attention to the vanity, pride and extravagance of the courtiers' behaviour and clothing. Both in the *Large Garden of Love* and in its later copy a poorly dressed young man (possibly a peasant) is depicted on the threshold of the garden's entrance. His liminal position suggests that he can look, but he cannot participate in the genteel dalliance of the courtly couples. Courtly love was a prerogative of the aristocratic elite from which other social classes were excluded.

That the theme of the folly of courtly love was ever-present in Master E.S.'s mind is testified by its recurrence throughout his work. In an earlier engraving, known as the *Small Love Garden* (*c*.1460), two courtly couples are depicted: the first is engaged in a passionate embrace whose lustful nature is emphasised by the man's hand, which caresses the woman's breast; the second couple, seated at the two opposite sides of a pond, are absorbed in conversation while listening to the sound of a fool's bagpipe. In medieval and early modern art the bagpipe was often used as a symbol of male genitalia, and it was usually associated with the lower classes of society.[54] So the depiction of a bagpipe in a courtly milieu as well as the bird perched on the lady's hand, which is reminiscent of the representation of the vice of Lechery, are pictorial signs which stress the lustful and beastly nature of

Figure 11.2   After the Master of the Housebook.
Design for a Quatrefoil with a Castle, Two Lovers, a Maiden Tempted by a
Fool, a Couple Seated by a Trough, and a Knight and His Lover Mounted on
a Horse (c.1475–1490), pen and black ink, 24.1 cm × 21.7 cm.
The John Paul Getty Museum, Los Angeles.

the encounter. In a later engraving known as *Luxuria and the fool* (c.1467),
the equation between folly, love and sin is carried to its extremes. Master
E.S. depicts the fool with his traditional ass's ears, coxcomb and tonsured
head in the company of *Luxuria*, whom he represents as a naked young
woman holding a mirror. The mirror reflects the fool's distorted features
instead of the woman's face in a symbolic equation of the folly of consuming
sexual desire with courtly love. The fifteenth-century success of the folly
of love theme is also testified to by a design for a stained-glass quatrefoil
(c.1475–90) attributed to an artist in the workshop of the Housebook Master
(Figure 11.2). The quatrefoil contains four courtly scenes: a castle on top of
a hill, a couple of young courtiers riding a horse, a courtly lady engaged in

caressing her lover near a mirror-like pond, and a fool who is depicted in the act of embracing a courtly lady in the middle of a winding road. The fool and his companion are silently observed from a distance by a traveller or a peasant whose bust and bag fastened to a stick can be distinguished in the background.[55] As in Master E.S.'s *Large Garden of Love*, the traveller is allowed to watch from the margins but not admitted to the centre of amorous courtly discourse. While I do not argue that these images are direct sources for Caxton's woodcut, I do suggest that they are based on the iconographic tradition of the late medieval fool whose presence provides a key to the kind of message being transmitted.

A reading of Caxton's woodcut

That the fool was perceived as an unsettling presence by at least one of the fifteenth-century readers of the 1483 edition of the *Canterbury Tales* may be suggested by the yellow colour applied to his costume in Oxford, St John's College, MS 266/b.2.21. Although, as Gage has shown, colour symbolism was 'fluid' and ambivalent in the Middle Ages, yellow often had negative connotations in medieval iconography, being associated with prostitutes, lepers, Jews, heretics and Judas.[56] Moreover, yellow and green were also employed to symbolise disorder and folly. This use is evident both in medieval heraldry, as can be evinced from Sagremor's and Tristan's coats of arms, and in the fourteenth- and fifteenth-century depictions of jesters' costumes and natural fools' tunics in the visual arts.[57] Was the fool in Caxton's woodcut perceived, then, as an element of disorder whose consuming folly had a significant impact on the way the text was consumed? I would answer in the affirmative. My contention is that the woodcut representing the group of pilgrims is a deliberate act of subversion in that it reaffirms the power of collective laughter, as well as the function of the fool as truth-teller, in a century in which collective laughter was regarded with suspicion by secular and ecclesiastical authorities alike.

As I have shown elsewhere, the fool's proximity to the figure of the courtly lady triggered a whole set of associations in connection with the theme of the folly of love discussed above.[58] Nevertheless, the medieval and early modern fool was not only a sinner plunged into the delights of earthly pleasures and forgetful of God's commands. He was also a teller of unspeakable truths who could make earnest out of game. That moral messages could be conveyed through laughter is well attested by the numerous collections of humorous *exempla* used by medieval preachers. Yet Chaucer also wrote tales that 'sownen into synne' (X, 1085) which he sometimes assigned to unruly storytellers. The scribes' and later editors' efforts to shape the poet's text through a textual layout which presented the 'Retraction' as the conclusion of the *Canterbury Tales*, not of the Parson's 'litel tretys' (X, 1080) on penitence and the Seven Deadly Sins, was part of an attempt to construct a moral *auctor* not subject to the consuming follies of the crowd who would populate Sebastian Brant's fifteenth-century ship of fools.[59] Whether inserted on Caxton's commission or not, the fool in the woodcut of the pilgrims at table contributes to opening up a new space of interpretation where the theme of folly subverts and sheds new light on the themes of wisdom and penitence exalted in the 'Retraction' and in the moral tales.

12

Anxieties at Table

Food and Drink in
Chaucer's Fabliaux Tales
and Heinrich Wittenwiler's *Der Ring*[1]

John Block Friedman

Eating, drinking and social behaviour at table and immediately after eating
are important sources of anxiety in medieval bourgeois and aristocratic
views of rustics and peasants, as they were very closely related to, and even
served as, a sign of class status.[2] Chaucer's *Canterbury Tales* shows this
clearly in its food-centred structure of a pilgrimage journey to Canterbury
with tales told going and coming, where the reward to the best teller is a
dinner. 'Churlish' behaviour is illustrated by several drunken pilgrims and
parvenu status by others. In Heinrich Wittenwiller's contemporary *Der
Ring*, much of the poem's action centres on a wedding feast and dance
following, which leads to lustful actions and brawling; the coarse behaviour
of the diners is contrasted with an ideal courtly style of dining and, by
implication, status.

   I should like to consider the two poets mentioned in the title to this
chapter, Geoffrey Chaucer and Heinrich Wittenwiler, from this perspective
of anxiety at table. In certain of the *Canterbury Tales* and in *Der Ring*
both poets are preoccupied with the anxieties of food and drink and their
relationship to the delicacies of class status. My concern here will be to
explore the way food- and drink-conveyed class anxieties are used as plot
devices to trigger dramatic action in *Der Ring* and in two of Chaucer's
best-known fabliaux, *The Miller's* and *The Reeve's Tales*.

   Admittedly, such a preoccupation with food, drink and status was
widespread in the late Middle Ages and, accordingly, there would be no
particular reason for examining it in these two poets rather than in others.
But there are so many striking similarities in their treatment of 'festive'

rustic or villager food and drink as to suggest that one poet knew the work of the other, and the last part of this chapter will explore briefly how the two writers may be related through possible knowledge of one another's work—a matter of 'intertextuality' defined by Erik Hertog in *Chaucer's Fabliaux as Analogues* (1991) as 'the fundamental and "structuring" presence of other texts, prior, contemporary or even posterior to the text one has before one's eyes'.[3]

One need only think here of the various conduct books which appeared about this time, such as the *Babees Book*, with detailed instruction for behaviour at table and the association of such behaviour with lower (churlish) or upper (*courtoise*) class status, to see as a class indicator this widespread anxiety of middle- and upper-class continental and English society over food and drink and the manner in which they should be consumed. Behavioural failures at table and uncontrolled appetites were associated with rustics and indeed served as revealing marks of a God-ordained rusticity for many middle- and upper-class writers and moralists. For it was largely by the ability to control eating habits and to consume 'correctly' that in the medieval imaginary the upper class is distinguished from the lower. Indeed, Norbert Elias suggests that the very process of training noble children in aristocratic households as pages at table shows how social control of food consumption is established, with the result that such social acts as eating, leaning and stretching at table, spitting, belching and farting are addressed in young persons' conduct literature in all the vernacular languages.[4] Some of these works in English, French and German, for example, specifically associate this control of eating with class differences, as in the late Middle English *Little Children's Little Book*: 'Bulk [belch] not, as a bean were in thy throat,/*As a carl that comes out of a cot*' (my emphasis).[5]

This anxiety centres largely on the consuming body, its intake and output. Though not speaking specifically of food intake, Peter Stallybrass and Allon White offer some useful observations about the inter-relatedness of the body and social class, such as that 'cultural categories of high and low social and aesthetic [...] of the physical body and geographic space, are never entirely separable [...] processes by which the low troubles the high' and 'transgressing the rules of hierarchy and order in any one of the domains can cause major consequences in the others'.[6]

Moreover, rustic bodies and their habits of consumption belong to the world of low culture well studied by Mikhail Bakhtin. A preoccupation with the eating and drinking behaviours of this low body leads to the 'grotesque realism' of low culture that we see in the work of the Netherlandish and German printmakers such as Israel von Meckenem and the various 'initial masters' such as BXG, where such bodies during and after eating and drinking are often 'excessive', bulging with rolls of flesh, as in Brueghel's peasants in 'The Wedding Feast' or the various kermis scenes of his contemporaries.[7] The jug-like rustic body with its orifices either emphasised or, if concealed, hidden in such a way as to draw attention to them, is diametrically opposed to the 'high' bodies we see in the courtly dining scenes of the *Très Riches Heures* of Jean de Berry, for example, which express high or official culture, the ideal values of that type of society being illustrated and exemplified in such scenes.[8] A number of such idealised eating scenes, in which the body is in harmony and control, expressing *courtoisie* while dining, are shown by C.M. Woolgar in his fascinating chapter 'Feasting and Fasting: Food and Taste in Europe in the Middle Ages'.[9] In the early modern period the contrast of *courtoisie* and the low body is much more apparent in Renaissance art, where bulging, lumpy, grotesquely featured and caricatured diners appear in Sebastian Brant's *Ship of Fools* (1494), with its illustrations by Dürer, and the dramatic work and *Schwänke* of Hans Sachs.[10]

During the period studied in the present chapter—roughly the last decade of the fourteenth and the first decade of the fifteenth centuries—eating and drinking were also ideologically related to social regulation and the proper political relationship between the classes. The lower classes were often criticised for excessive 'appetite', a voracious desire for the 'wrong' foods and excessive drink.[11] Many rural foods were associated with a 'golden age', when the lower classes were in a perfect balance with the upper and rustics desired to consume only modest quantities of wheat or bean bread, cheese and plain water. In later ages, the tastes for meat and wine are seen to show a reach beyond one's proper social station and to issue in, or be the cause of, social rebellion, such as the Peasants' Revolt of 1381. Thus, next to dress and speech as subjects for class examination, rustic voracity, and attendant drunkenness and quarrelsomeness following on strongly flavoured meals, was a stock topic presented for the amusement and entertainment of upper-class audiences as part of the 'obedient' or 'golden age' treatment of rustics.[12]

A good example of the unrebellious or 'unfestive' rustic obedient through 'proper' diet appears in the lyric 'Dit de Franc Gontier' of the French poet Philippe de Vitry (1291–1361). Franc Gontier illustrates the simplicity of well-ordered peasant life:

> Under the green leaves, on the soft turf besides a chattering brook with a clear spring near at hand, I found a rustic hut set up. Gontier and Dame Helen were dining there, on fresh cheese, milk, butter, [a dish made from cheese], cream, curds, apples, nuts, plums, pears, they had garlic and onions, and crushed shallots, on crusty black bread, with coarse salt to give them a thirst.[13] (My translation)

Such bucolic foods are associated with the socially obedient and well-ordered peasant of the golden age by Chaucer's contemporaries and great influences, Jean Froissart and John Gower. Froissart, in his Pastourelle 15, sees shepherds 'ordonner leur table ... Que sus n'avoit pieument ne vin/

Més pain et sel, aus et ongnons', while Gower in his *Miroir de l'Omme* notes that

> in olden days [peasants] were not accustomed to eat wheat bread; instead their bread was made of other grains or from beans. Likewise they drank only water. And they feasted on cheese and milk ... at that time the world was well ordered for people of their estate.[14]

Such exclusively vegetable foods were thought by the upper classes to be responsible for the oddities of rustic physiognomy and disposition. For example, Guillaume de Machaut's *Dit dou Lyon* speaks of 'gens de villages' with rustic names such as Robin and Marote, who eat milk, cheeses, cabbage, beans and turnips, and who perform ecstatic rural dances:

> Some say there were such that no painter, no mason, nor draughtsman, nor carver, nor writer, nor illuminator, nor sculptor in stone, nor artist working in wash—indeed even the subtle Pygmalion if he were there with all his tools—would know how to describe their strange countenances.[15] (My translation)

A somewhat similar explanation for the general condition of rusticity partly resulting from diet appears in a late fourteenth-century poem by the Lombard *jongleur* Matazano da Calignano, who (from a middle-class perspective) associates coarse vegetable foods with the actual conception of rustics, claiming that the first villein 'de quel malvaxio vento/nascé el vilan puzolento' [was born from the fart of an ass]. It is for this reason that villagers are by nature drawn to and should eat coarse brown bread or rye bread, beans and garlic.[16]

These rustic meals, especially if washed down with hard cider, wine and beer, frequently lead to uncourtly and instinctual behaviour during or after the meal, whether sexual or simply violent. Netherlandish and German kermis scenes, for example, often show festive behaviour with men and women drinking, embracing, even copulating, and men fighting. Other forms of instinctive behaviour could include excretion; again the immediacy of this was given as a typical rustic characteristic by middle- and upper-class observers. These kermis scenes, popular celebrations of a church's conse-cration or a saint's name day, first appear in German art and are extremely food-centred. They involve celebration in front of an inn with a prominent ale stake naming it, with much over-eating and drinking and sexual gesture or behaviour. The so-called 'nose' dance, a genital euphemism, also survives in later examples, and such scenes also contained a good deal of scatology associated with rustics. For example, the earliest kermis, that of Sebald Beham (1500–1550) at Mogeldörg, shows a peasant defecating at the edge of a bench; he and some vomiting revellers are associated with wandering pigs.[17]

I

The *Canterbury Tales* begins with all of the travellers coming by chance to the Tabard Inn in Southwark, whose naming and detailed description reminds us very much of the inns in Netherlandish and German kermis scenes just mentioned, as does the fact that the voyage is associated with a named local saint. The narrator is already established there and has the opportunity to describe events. As detailed portraits of each of the pilgrims are offered by this narrator in the *General Prologue*, he pays special attention to the eating behaviour of several of the travellers who are either of low or of shifting or ambiguous social status. Significantly, there is no comment made about food in relation to clearly and solidly upper-class characters such as the Knight and Squire. But when we get to the Prioress, some ten lines of her portrait are devoted to her eating habits, details of which are drawn, as has long been known, from the very courtesy books I have just mentioned.[18] Among comments on the other socially aspiring middle-class pilgrims, such as the Five Guildsmen, that on the Franklin's love of food and drink (he 'was Epicurus owene son', *General Prologue*, l. 336),[19] and on the fact that his trestle table was always erected and set for dining, are very important points in his character development. His bread and ale are of high quality, his own meat pies are always available; in all, some twelve lines of his portrait are devoted to his food and drink. The Five Guildsmen bring their own London cook, and his abilities with ale, cooking and baking are noted. The Shipman has stolen wine from merchants. The Summoner, a drunkard and thoroughly bad ecclesiastical character, is, interestingly, given a taste for peasant fare: 'Wel loved he garleek, oynons, and eek lekes' (*GP*, l. 633), foods associated with his inflamed and pimply face.

The portrait of Harry Bailly the Host also focuses on his relationship with food and drink: 'He served us with vitaille at the beste,/Strong was the wyn' (*GP*, ll. 749–50). The upwardly mobile Harry is suitable to be 'a marchal in an halle' (*GP*, l. 752), and he is large in size and even swears by wine or ale. Later, after the *Clerk's Tale*, he says he would rather have his wife hear this story than have a barrel of ale, a claim he makes again after listening to the *Tale of Melibee*. Upon hearing the *Physician's Tale* the Host says he has found it so sad that he fears he might have a heart attack unless he has a 'draughte of moyste and corny ale' (Introduction to *Pardoner's Tale*, l. 315) or can hear a cheerier tale.

Food and drink are even woven into the dramatic structure of the Tales, since drunken interruptions in the hierarchically ordered sequence of tellers by lower-class characters are common. No sooner has the Knight finished his tale than Harry (who has a strong sense of social hierarchy) calls upon the Monk to tell the next one. But the yeoman Miller, who through drink has lost, or perhaps never had, any sense of his ordained place in society, interrupts him:

> The Millere, that for dronken was al pale,
> So that unnethe upon his hors he sat,
> He nolde avalen neither hood ne hat,
> No abyde no man for his curteisie.
>
> (*Miller's Prologue*, ll. 3120–23)

The upwardly mobile Harry, recognising that he is drunk, tries to control him, identifying with him socially by calling him 'Robyn, my leeve brother' (*MP*, l. 3129). The Miller acknowledges that he is drunk on the ale of Southwark and will therefore tell a 'churls' tale of a carpenter, a thinly disguised 'occupational' attack on his fellow villager, the Reeve, whom he also calls 'Leve brother Osewold' (*MP*, l. 3151).

These two fabliau tales by the Miller and the Reeve help create a social universe; they are appropriately followed by that of the Cook, whom Harry Bailly accuses of evil-doing in his craft through images of mismanaged food—draining the blood out of meat pies to make them seem fresher, selling reheated pies, using rotten parsley on which geese have fed or which perhaps was cooked with geese in a kitchen full of flies. Though the Cook's tale never develops very far, it concerns a person like Harry Bailly, a 'hostileer' (*Cook's Prologue*, l. 4360).

As the Wife of Bath is finishing her Prologue she is again interrupted by two seemingly drunker pilgrims, the Friar and the Summoner, whose dislike for each other is based on their occupations, and who in their wrangles are compared to drunkards by Harry Bailly, perhaps with truth: 'Ye fare as folk that dronken ben of ale' (*Wife of Bath's Prologue*, l. 852). When the Summoner tells his tale of the Friar, the mendicant is quickly associated with class (the sick Thomas and his wife are villagers) and with gluttony and excess, as the Friar orders in French a meal with a capon, soft bread and a roasted pig's head while offering hypocritical attacks on gluttony. In the end the Friar's humiliation comes at the table of the lord of the village. The lord rewards his squire Jankyn's quick wit with the prize of a piece of cloth after Jankyn tells how to divide a fart thirteen ways. In a similar fashion, the Pardoner prepares to tell his tale of drunken greed and gluttony by himself eating and drinking: 'Here at this ale stake/I wol bothe drynke and eten of a cake' (Introduction to *Pardoner's Tale*, ll. 321–22).

In contrast to these villager fabliau tales of misused food and drink associated with the instinctual side of mankind, the sermon-like tale told by the Nun's Priest focuses at the opening on food, eating and drink, but of a different sort and with an altogether different point. He tells of a wonderful speaking rooster, Chauntecleer, and his hen, Pertelote, and Chauntecleer's dealings with a fox. The story is largely one about the sin of pride. But it is introduced—in a gibe at the upwardly mobile Prioress, her tastes in food and her parvenu table manners—by an unusually lengthy account of Chauntecleer's owner, a poor peasant widow who lives a moderate life with regard to food and drink. Indeed, so lengthy and detailed is this description that it displaces the beast fable it is supposedly introducing for a while and becomes an exemplum of restrained and unfestive peasant tastes in food and drink.[20]

The Widow represents the golden age of rusticity that we spoke of earlier in connection with Philippe de Vitry's lyric poem, where through diet and eating behaviour peasants exhibited their recognition of the proper order of society. In her combined sleeping and living area

> ... she eet ful many a sklendre meel.
> Of poynaunt sauce hir neded never a deel.
> No deyntee morsel passed thurgh hir throte;
> Hir diete was accordant to hir cote.
> Repleccioun ne made hir nevere sik;
> Attempre diete was al hir phisik ...
> No wyn ne drank she, neither whit ne reed;
> Hir bord was served moost with whit and blak –
> Milk and broun breed ...
>
> (Nun's Priest's Tale, ll. 2833–38, 2842–44)

It could be said, then, that at this crucial point of the Canterbury Tales the Widow serves as a contrastive exemplum against which the other eaters and drinkers can be measured.

One such element of contrast occurs in the Prologue to the Manciple's Tale. The Host begins to chide the Cook—a teller of a fabliau tale—for his drunken sleep while riding, and the Manciple joins in commenting on his drunken demeanour. The Cook falls off his horse, is hoisted up, and the Manciple in a final insult offers him more wine, which he eagerly drinks. The whole episode is an ironic and broadly comic commentary on the propensity of such socially low characters to drunken excess. It is clear, then, that even in the dramatic structure of the Canterbury Tales, with the head links indicating how the various characters relate to each other, anxieties of the table are pervasive and can serve a dramatic and narrative function which will now be examined in Chaucer's and Wittenwiler's works.

II

The food- and drink-centred moments so far noted in Chaucer among the characters most associated with fabliaux can also be seen in Heinrich Wittenwiler's Der Ring, an anti-peasant satire of 9699 lines.[21] Since Heinrich Wittenwiler's poem is probably less generally familiar than Chaucer's work, it may be useful to note that modern scholars believe that the author was a lawyer and administrator at the bishop's court of Constance with probable dates of activity of before 1387 to 1410. The ecclesiastical Council of

Constance (1414–18) made this city an important site for cultural inter-
change in the first quarter of the fifteenth century, and it is possible that it
was so a decade earlier. The precise civic status of Wittenwiler—whether
he was a member of the civic elite of the city (surviving documents refer to
him only as a lawyer) or an aristocrat—is not clear. The position he takes
towards those socially below him could fit either group. In many ways the
poem is like an extended conduct book, and indeed this purpose is stated
in the Prologue: 'Was man tuon und lassen schol' [what man should do
and what avoid].

Wittenwiler's poem exists only in a single copy now in the Meiningen
State Archives, Nr. 502, Hs. 29, a very plain and crudely illustrated
parchment codex of fifty-seven leaves in double columns (25.9 × 18.8 cm),
copied between 1390 and 1405; it could even be the author's holograph.
There is an opening miniature or drawing of a man holding the ring of the
title. Also on this page is an obscene drawing of a bearded hooded peasant
in dagged attire, with a belt pouch, embracing a woman while putting two
fingers of his right hand between her legs. There seems to be a system of
red marginal lines to direct the reader to moral truths and green ones for
silly or dishonest points.

References to gunpowder and bullets date it as contemporary with
Chaucer. These were in military use in Switzerland in 1386 in the Battle
of Sempach and are mentioned familiarly in Chaucer's *House of Fame* of
1380: 'as swifte as pelet out of gonne/Whan fyre is in the poudre ronne'
(ll. 637–38).[22] So too the *Ring*'s peasant council, in which aristocratic titles
are bestowed, and its mock epic battle may reflect Zuricher self-ennoblement
in 1385 and the Appenzell Peasant War of 1403–8. Thus, the poem was
probably composed at the same time as, or no more than several years later
than, the *Canterbury Tales*.

A seeming contemporary of Chaucer, Wittenwiler would find congenial
the Middle English poet's cultural milieu, and he shares a fondness for the
fabric and techniques of fabliaux. Moreover, both writers address audiences
of bourgeoisie and minor officials who look down on those socially below
them with respect to table manners, food choices and eating behaviour. A
hatred of peasants based largely on their dirtiness, lustful and quarrelsome
natures and coarse behaviour with regard to food, drink and excretion is
everywhere evident in *Der Ring*. The poem concerns the courtship and
marriage of a well-to-do peasant Bertschi Treifnas, or Snot-nose, to Metzli
Rüerenzumph, or Grab-the-cock, who live in the villages of Lappenhausen,
or Foolville, and Nissengen, or Quarrelerland, in the Black Forest, these
comic compound names being adapted from the German satirist poet
Neidhart. Their marriage, preceded by a peasant tournament, leads up to a
banquet and dance, a quarrel and then a combat between the villages, aided
by such supernatural allies as giants and dwarves. Some of these events are
familiar from the slightly later peasant wedding art of Pieter Brueghel and

in popular 'peasant brawl' poetry such as the Middle English *Tournament of Tottenham* (1400–1440) which often revolves around a quarrel after a wedding.[23]

Each episode leading up the wedding banquet is heightened by a witty, frequently obscene treatment of voracious peasant consumption, often compared with the 'measured' consumption of courtly persons. During the mock tournament which opens the poem we learn how the belly of Gunterfal the piper 'was seldom empty of turnips and barley' (Jones, Part 1, p. 14), and the poem's protagonist Bertchi Treifnas (in the midst of a mock aristocratic tournament to attract the attentions of his sweetheart Metzli) is suddenly and comically overcome by hunger and satisfies it like an animal: '"Bring me cheese and bread too, I'm almost dead of hunger." They quickly gave him some bread; Triefnas bit a piece off and thrust it whole into his gullet' (Jones, Part 1, p. 15). After a debacle in which Bertschi surprises his beloved while she is milking in the barn, he climbs on the roof of her house while Fritz the father and his family are sitting by the fire 'eating turnips' (Jones, Part 1, p. 20), falling through the chimney onto the hearth. He is revived with some of this turnip water and several farts in the face by the father.

Once much of the instinctive, rude, scatological and voracious behaviour typically attributed to peasants has been well illustrated, the narrative shifts focus to become a conduct book, especially the second part of Part 2 leading up to the wedding, where wise counsellors discuss proper modes of living. These villagers, in their more rational moments, are well aware of *courtoisie*. Indeed Lastersak, one of these village elders in the conduct sequence, says specifically:

I advise him [the theoretical young man like Bertschi] to go to court himself. There he will learn good breeding in many things ... people often say if one wishes to become a courtier, let him keep the peasants in mind; and whatever they do in their boorish way, let him do exactly the opposite, and thus he will become courtly and elegant ... I can tell Bertschi this. If he wishes to conduct himself in a well-bred way, he can learn to at his wedding. (Jones, Part 2, p. 65)

This lesson, alas, is unlearned. Structurally, the banquet occupies the centre of the poem, and it and its aftermath are the cause of the war between the Lappenhauseners and their neighbours that brings destruction to the region and death to the new bride. The banquet, dance and wedding night occupy the rest of Part 2 and lead to Part 3, which is entirely about the war that results from peasant bad behaviour.

The banqueting scene serves to illustrate middle- and upper-class views of the dietary habits of peasants and to affirm the courtly values of proper dining by ridiculing the behaviour of the Lappenhauseners and their bizarre tastes in food. This includes satire both of the tastes for 'low' food and drink such as the barley, oat and rye breads, pork-scrap-laced kraut, boiled eggs, milk and cider served at the banquet, and of high foods such as meat, especially the courtly varieties such as venison and fish. Wittenwiler's peasants eat white bread in a reprise of Chaucer's Prioress feeding her dogs on such bread. When the peasants eat flesh, it is either extremely fatty pork or a fish (recognised by the peasant Töreleina as an upper-class dish, l. 2905), which is swallowed whole. We have already remarked on the love of turnips in *Der Ring*, which were believed to bring on flatulence, of which there is a great deal in the poem. One peasant is named Gumpost after a dish prepared with turnip greens and fatty pork, a dish greedily eaten by the peasants at the wedding banquet, during which they quarrelsomely struggle with each other for these small bits of meat. Another peasant is named Schlinddenspek, or Swallow-Pork, while another is Hafensschlek, or Gulp-Oats.

As to the manners the peasants exhibit at table, one passage is representative. The diners, weak with hunger, begin with a soup and violate in every way the strictures placed on Bertschi for learning temperance at table:

> One of them was in such a hurry to eat that he almost scalded himself to death in his gullet. He ... struck the tureen with his fist so that the soup sloshed out on the ground along with the bread. Everyone said 'Before I perish thus of hunger, I would rather pick it up out of the dirt and eat it.' And no matter how well it was beshitted, not a bit of it remained. Believe me, that really happened! It was to their taste. (Jones, Part 2, p. 74)

The banquet continues with 'knives and sliced bread omitted', and a catalogue of peasant foods follows. The first course is 'apples, pears, nuts, and cheese' (Jones, Part 2, p. 75). The meat course is roast donkey, the animal having been mistakenly butchered instead of a cow, thought by one of the diners, Elsa, to be 'a noble venison' (Jones, Part 2, p. 76). This whole scene is contrasted with the proper manner of preparing to eat in an orderly way: 'according to court custom, [the towel] should have been held up between the basin and the clothes of anyone wishing to wash his hands' (Jones, Part 2, p. 75).

The banquet scene then shifts to drinking and the manner of doing it: 'if they had drunk more they would have come to blows'. Wine was, of course, the middle- and upper-class beverage, and water, apple or pear cider, or milk was appropriate to rustics. One peasant is called Rüherenmost, or Stir-Cider. As they drink the cider, in a reprise of the Prioress who 'ne wette hir fyngres in hir sauce depe' (*GP*, l. 129), 'one of the diners found something floating in it, which she pulled out with her bare hand' (Jones, Part 2, p. 76). It is at this point in the banquet that the quarrelsome guests order Bertschi to bring them wine and beer, and when the groom upbraids the servers they immediately attack him:

> [They] grabbed Bertschi and beat him till he fell. They pulled off his breeches and poured water into his arse ... They took him by his legs and beat his backside against a tree ... and gave him blows without number. (Jones, Part 2, p. 78)

This attack was enjoyed by the diners and considered the best course. Thus, Bertschi, who has throughout the poem wished to be spoken to in the polite rather than the familiar form of address, finds himself beaten for attempting to put on airs and impose some mannerly or courtly behaviour on the servers and wedding throng. Thereafter the dance gives way to lust and eventually to the violence which dominates the last part of the poem. When a peasant, Eisengrein, who loves one Gredul erotically scratches her palm, a disreputable gesture: 'the peasants' sport turned into disorder, according to their custom' (Jones, Part 2, p. 86).

III

Both Chaucer and Wittenwiler as writers were fascinated with the anxieties at table so common in this period. There is evidence, moreover, that these two poets were acquainted with each other's work; how this may have come about will occupy the remainder of this chapter.

One of the most obvious of the verbal echoes is that between Chaucer's *Merchant's Tale* and *Der Ring* in the topos regarding advice on marriage. When the aged knight January decides to marry he calls his wise counsellors Placebo and Justinus to him and they debate its advantages and disadvantages. This is a fairly lengthy introduction to a fabliau tale, and some of the images, such as that of a young bride being as malleable as wax, will appear later in dramatic form in the poem. In a similar but much lengthier scene, many of Bertschi's relatives gather to discuss marriage and its suitability for the young man. The women present strongly support marriage and some of the men oppose it with traditional complaints of exactly the sort made in Chaucer's tale; the pro-marriage figures, however, win. Metzli's father Fritz holds a similar marriage debate, and those attending agree to school Bertschi in proper conduct, get him to learn his Creed and so on, and Bertschi calls on various elders such as the Pharmacist to learn their lore. While such wisdom-of-marriage debates are not uncommon in medieval poetry (for example, one also appears in Deschamps' *Miroir de Mariage*), when combined with some of the other echoes and similarities, the marriage matter becomes a telling point for the intertextuality in which one writer serves as a source for another.

Chaucer's indebtedness to other writers and their echoes in his work—his use of them as direct sources or his use of similar themes—has long been a veritable industry in criticism. Scholars interested in this critical approach have even given us a terminology with which to investigate such borrowings. When Chaucer used the same story details or plot parallels as another contemporary or somewhat earlier medieval author, we can speak of direct sources, or, if the similarities are more general, of analogues. Older source and analogue studies have been largely hierarchical or stemmatic in character. Probably the best-known book of this type is that by Bryan and Dempster, *Sources and Analogues of Chaucer's Canterbury Tales.*[24]

If Chaucer and the other author are contemporaries or near contemporaries, but different languages and cultural contexts are involved, the stemmatic method of analysis is less effective. Obviously, if Chaucer names another writer as an influence, we might speak of that author as a 'source'. Yet naming or not naming can be an unreliable guide. For example, Chaucer makes demonstrable use of Boccaccio, Guillaume de Machaut and Jean Froissart, yet never mentions them by name. The term 'intertextuality,' for its avoidance of the stemmatic or 'ur'-text approach and its use of the structuring metaphor of weaving a narrative together from discrete strands, has much to commend it as a critical concept in examining Chaucer and Wittenwiler.

Some intertextual echoes and thematic parallels that seem to me significant, yet baffling in terms of origin, appear (besides the broad parallel in the marriage debate already mentioned) to occur in the two fabliau tales told by village narrators and in *Der Ring*. We have already mentioned the Miller's drunkenness, his intrusiveness and his lack of a sense of social hierarchy. His Tale ties many of these elements to food and drink, as does that of Oswald the Reeve in telling of a Trumpington Miller. One wonders whether Chaucer could have read Heinrich Wittenwiler's satiric anti-peasant Swiss German poem *Der Ring*, or whether Wittenwiler could have read or heard Chaucer's *Canterbury Tales*. Thus far, there has been little interest in considering these two poets together, and these questions remain unanswered. Among Chaucer scholars, Peter Beidler has briefly considered the matter, only to claim authoritatively that 'there is no evidence that Chaucer knew German, was familiar with German literature, or travelled in Germany'.[25]

Of the comic serenading of Metzli in *Der Ring* Beidler notes only that the *Ring* 'has one unimportant scene in which a woman presents her buttocks at a window for a kiss. The kiss is never delivered, however, and the events have no connection with the *Miller's Tale*' (p. 254). Accordingly, he believes that certain French, Flemish and Middle Dutch poems, especially *Heile van Beersele*, rather than any German work, were the sources for the *Reeve's* and *Miller's Tales*. And when Larry Benson and Theodore Andersson discussed *Der Ring* in connection with the *Miller's Tale*, they adduced as parallels only the suitors' serenades and the kissing of a bottom imagined as a face, also dismissing *Der Ring* as a source for Chaucer.[26]

Yet anyone reading the two poets together will hear echoes of character, theme and dramatic situation. To take the first of these, two of Chaucer's village girls who come to mind with regard to *Der Ring*'s rustic social milieu are Malyne in the *Reeve's Tale* and Alison in the *Miller's Tale*.[27] Though Wittenwiler's heroine Metzli—short, lame, ill kempt, and with breasts like lard sacks—is far more grotesque, she is similar to the former in physical coarseness and to the latter in youthful sexuality and exhibitionism. Bertschi is snobbish, dandified and sexually naïve. He affects aristocratic spurs, gores or pleats, and buttons on his clothes, and is angered when addressed in the familiar form or when his servants fail to live up to what he considers courtly and magnanimous feasting behaviour. He uses phrases from romances and *minnesang* in wooing Metzli and undergoes several humiliations in courting her. In these particulars he very much reminds us of Absolon, the Oxford parish clerk and dandy, in his lovesick pursuit of Alison.

There is the presence of a parodic dawn song in both poets. Aubades figure prominently. After a wedding night in which Metzli uses Krippen-kra's vaginal astringent and fish bladder full of blood to simulate virginity and violently resists her husband in order to pretend sexual innocence, the newly-weds are awakened, in a parody of a typical French or German illicit meeting of aristocratic lovers, by a dawn song, or aubade, sung by the 'watchman' on the rustic 'battlements': 'If one on lover's arms doth lie/He must get up, for time doth fly!/The sun her battle of the sky/Hath won with mighty power' (Jones, Part 3, p. 95).[28] This moment resembles the scene in Chaucer's *Reeve's Tale* when, after a night of love, Aleyn addresses Malyne in the language of the aubade: 'Fare weel, Malyne, sweete wight!/The day is come; I may no lenger byde' (ll. 4236–38). Thus, both parodic aubades (which are lacking in Beidler's proposed source for the *Reeve's Tale*) cap a night of sexual activity with strong overtones of deceit, violence and forcible intercourse. Admittedly, there are many aubades in medieval literature, from Provençal poetry onward, but the parodic use of this courtly motif and the verbal similarities are telling.

As noted earlier, Wittenwiler has the lovesick Bertschi go to Metzli's house and climb the roof while the family sits at the hearth; he falls through the chimney into the living quarters in front of them, emerging sooty 'like a monstrous devil' (Jones, Part 1, p. 20). In the *Miller's Tale* Chaucer uses a fall from a roof to cause the humiliation of an uxorious husband. John the carpenter, sleeping in his tub tied to the rafters of his house, hears Nicholas cry: 'Water!'—he has just been burnt on the bottom by a hot plough coulter after pretending to be Alison and farting through the window at Absolon. John cuts the rope of his tub, falling to the floor: 'And doun gooth al .../Upon the floor, and ther aswowne he lay .../... bothe pale and wan,/For with the fal he brosten hadde his arm' (ll. 3821, 3823, 3828–29). John is then injured as well as humiliated by the neighbours' knowledge of his plight.

These echoes and narrative parallels, however, are not as immediately connected with food and drink and the behaviour typically attributed to the excess consumption of villagers and rustics as other apparent borrowings in the work of the two poets. For both writers use the structural plot devices of class anxiety over food to move the action forward. We have already seen in Wittenwiler's work how peasant foods and the failure to maintain the decorum so necessary to the middle and upper classes lead ultimately to social destructiveness. Both of Chaucer's fabliau tales use food and drink in somewhat similar ways.

The action of the *Reeve's Tale* concerns food even at its opening, as two graduate students from Cambridge take the college grain to be ground by the Miller of Trumpington. This Miller and his wife are preoccupied with social status, and food and status are closely connected in the poem. The Miller, Symkin, has a wife who comes from a 'noble' family, as she is the illegitimate daughter of the town parson. Symkin is particularly proud of her because she was educated in a nunnery, a link to the *parvenu* Prioress's portrait. The wife is 'proud and peert as is a pye' (l. 3950), and Symkin is prepared to fight anyone who does not call her 'dame' (l. 3956). The wife, unnamed in the tale, is just as status-conscious as her husband:

> She was as digne as water in a dich,
> And ful of hoker and of bisemare.
> Hir thoughte that a lady sholde hire spare,
> What for her kynrede and hir nortelrie
> That she hadde lerned in the nonnerie.' (ll. 3964–68)

After the Miller cheats them of a large cake of their meal through the stratagem of releasing their horse to run wild after mares in the fens, the students return to the mill at nightfall, tired and hungry. One asks the Miller to 'get us som mete and drynke' (l. 4132) and Symkin sends his daughter into Trumpington to buy 'ale and breed' while the Miller's wife presumably 'rosted hem a goos' (l. 4137). This is food well above the typical villager fare, a point that is made by the discussion of the extremely tight quarters the Miller and his family share. The provision of a goose, a meal inappropriate to an ordinary miller, seems intended to rub in the students' humiliation and loss of grain at Symkin's hands.

When all have eaten this repast and drunk the ale they go to bed in the small room, the Miller exceptionally drunk—'Ful pale he was for dronken, and nat reed./He yexeth, and he speketh thurgh the nose' (ll. 4150–51)—and his wife likewise:

> As any jay she light was and jolyf,
> So was hir joly whistle wel ywet ...

> And whan that dronken al was in the crowke
> To bedde wente the doghter right anon ...
>
> This millere hath so wisely bibbed ale
> That as an hors he fnorteth in his sleep,
> Ne of hys tayl bihynde he took no keep.
>
> (ll. 4154–55, 4158–59, 4162–64)

The dinner and the drinking lead first to excess sexuality, as the two students make love to the wife and daughter, and then to violence. For Symkin is very concerned to preserve his daughter's chastity (for dynastic rather than moral reasons) and wishes, along with the girl's grandfather, the town priest, to ensure that she marry upward. When the Miller learns what the Cambridge clerk Aleyn has done to the girl, he is enraged at his vicarious loss of status: 'Who dorste to be so boold to disparage/My doghter, that is come of swich lynage?' (ll. 4271–72).

In similar fashion, the final action of the *Miller's Tale* is also motivated by drink and alludes to peasant foods, though with a far more scatological edge than the *Reeve's Tale* offers. John the carpenter, seeing his lodger Nicholas, a graduate student at Oxford, in a seeming trance, finally gains access to him. As part of his plan to increase the carpenter's natural foolishness, Nicholas says 'Fecche me drynke,/And after wol I speke in pryvetee/ Of certyn thing that toucheth me and thee' (ll. 3992–94). As with the *Reeve's Tale*, there is a slight delay and then John brings 'of mighty ale a large quart' (l. 3497).

Perhaps the high point, however, of these food- and drink-related anxieties lies in the matching serenades occasioned in Chaucer's poem by the revelations of the coming Flood made to the soon-tipsy John. Let us consider these serenades in greater detail. Both poems use parodic courtly serenades where extravagantly loud noise or secretive silence is emphasised and, in the *Miller's Tale*, a comically complex 'grooming' sequence which fastens on the mouth and on eating as an aspect of courtly delicacy, parodied in the figure of the Oxford dandy Absolon, who has dreamed all night that he has attended a feast not dissimilar to the *Ring's* banquet. When he learns that John the carpenter may be away from home he thinks to pay a nocturnal courting visit to Alison: 'My mouth hath iched al this longe day;/That is a signe of kissing atte leeste./Al nyght me mette eek I was at a feeste' (ll. 3682–84). As his preparations for the serenade develop, there are numerous references to food, eating and orality, some associated with class status. Absolon chews cardamom and licorice to make himself smell sweeter and places a sprig of a plant under his tongue. When he gets to the window of Alison's bedroom he uses food and spice images (honey-comb, cinnamon) and compares himself to a lamb that wishes to suckle.

Der Ring focuses on the noise of the village piper Gunterfei, and the *Miller's Tale* on the whispering quality of Absolon's voice and soft guitar: 'he syngeth in his voys gentil and small' (l. 3360) as he pays his night-time call on Alison. Bertschi, in the fashion of a courtly lover, attempts to serve and serenade Metzli:

> At night he regularly went out to her father's house. He tore the clay from the wall, his mind set on entering the door. How often he began to sing: 'I pine for you, I die for you.' He crept up to the window on the chance that he could see her there. He did this often and repeatedly.

For the last visit he arranges hired music with Gunterfei: 'The bagpipe resounded everywhere so that mountain and valley echoed' (Jones, Part 1, p. 18).

These moments in *Der Ring* remind us of the scene in the *Miller's Tale* under discussion. There is the build-up and travel to the scene: 'Absolon his gyterne hath ytake,/ ... /And forth he gooth, jolif and amorous,/Til he cam to the carpenters hous ...' (ll. 3353, 3355–56). Both poets emphasise the use of a small or low window, love-struck behaviour, night-time circumstances, sound, and fear of being seen by neighbours, Alison urging Absolon to be quick: 'Speed the faste,/Lest that oure neighebores thee espie' (ll. 3728–29). Absolon also uses elevated or courtly language and is quickly humiliated when he mistakes Alison's bottom for her face:

> 'Lemman, thy grace, and sweete bryd, thyn oore!' ...
> Dark was the nyght as pich, or as the cole,
> And at the window out she putte hir hole'
> (ll. 3726, 3731–32).

> As Absolon 'kiste hir naked ers' (l. 3734)

> Aback he stirte, and thoughte it was amys,
> Ful wel he wiste a woman hath no berd.
> He felt a thing al rough and long yherd ...' (ll. 3736–38)

Likewise Bertschi, confusing Metzli's bottom with her face, ironically congratulates himself on his good fortune in beholding his beloved's visage: 'They came to Metzli's house. She offered her arse at the window. Then Bertschi said right off: "Oh, fortunate am I that I have seen your shapely face! Lean toward me, dear Metzli, lean!"' (Jones, Part 1, p. 18). Neighbours angrily awakened by the noise interrupt what would then have transpired. This detailed face-fundament-genitalia confusion is more sharply focused later in *Der Ring*, when, in the post-wedding dance, one of the village girls, little Hüdel, 'got so hot she lifted up her kirtle in front; so they saw hers [genitalia] and many hearts were made glad. They all shouted, "She wants a man: she has a mouth with hair on it!"' (Jones, Part 2, p. 86). Like Nicholas when he offers his bottom to Absolon, Hüdel farts during this episode.

While the Middle Dutch *Heile*, one of Chaucer's mooted sources, has a developed scene of a man unknowingly kissing a bottom, it is a male, not a female, one, and there is no serenade by a lovesick suitor. Thus, for this key moment, Wittenwiler offers material which radically augments what we know of Chaucer's sources. It is, however, the medicinal 'cure' for love in each case, a 'cure' associated with scatological consumption, that achieves what scholars of intertextuality call 'near source' status. Bertschi and Absolon both suffer from *heroes*, or love sickness, and both are cured by a comic *remedium amoris*, a motif absent from Peter Beidler's claimed source *Heile van Beersele*. Deriving from Ovid's poem of that name, this topos, as Michael Calabrese and others have noted, offers the suitor an end to his passion by smelling the menstrual linen or chamber pot of his beloved and, realising her frailties, being instantly cured of love. Boccaccio's *Il Corbaccio* contains one of the best-known medieval examples.[29]

After the fall through the chimney, and fearful of the apparition of the love-struck, dazed and sooty Bertschi, the Rüerenzumphs flee the house, all but the father Fritz. Understanding the power of passion, he tries to revive Bertschi through turnip water and 'by farting three times in his face, and thus the lover was cured' (Jones, Part 1, p. 20). Absolon undergoes a similar cure after he realises he has kissed Alison's bottom: 'His hoote love was coold and al yqueynt;/For fro that tyme that he hadde kist her ers,/... he was heeled of his maladie' (ll. 3754–55, 3757). Absolon, a dandy and a fop, is also a snob, and his mis-'eating' adventure is particularly painful to him because it will become public knowledge and a cause of mockery and lowered status through the tattling of the university student Nicholas.

Given such similarities between the two poems, if Chaucer was unfamiliar with German poetry, as Beidler claims, what of the possibility that Wittenwiler could have heard or read Chaucer's work and been influenced by him? Since we know so little about this author, this is a difficult question to answer. His narrative's own sources in earlier Middle High German are familiar. He finds the comic village wedding, feast and peasant brawl in the fourteenth-century *Meier Betz* and *Metzen hochzit*. These poems, however, like the Middle Dutch *Heile*, lack the elements of serenade, misdirected kiss, lover on the roof, dawn song and curative farting.[30]

If my argument has been correct, numerous elements in the *Reeve's Tale* and in the *Miller's Tale* are not in the continental sources for these poems proposed by Beidler. Admittedly, some very detailed narrative features, such as the tubs in the rafters and the revenge by hot plough coulter that occur there, do not appear in *Der Ring*. Probably Chaucer combined several sources for his narrative. Indeed, Fred Biggs has recently made the revisionist argument that the author of *Heile van Beersele* obtained his material from Chaucer's tale and not the other way around. This, if true, would vitiate Beidler's claim for that poem as a source and would suggest instead rapid dissemination of literary motifs from Middle English to Northern European authors, a most interesting possibility indeed.[31]

In contrast to the stemmatic model, the metaphor of weaving, as is suggested in the very word 'intertextuality', is a useful one here. Chaucer 'wove' his fabliau tales from several sources, French, Middle Dutch, Flemish and possibly German, in order to construct his stories of rustic lovers and their relations to food and drink. He exhibited a well-known interest in continental poetry and nearly all his *Canterbury Tales* used pre-existing narratives, however much he himself changed them later. The 'intertextual' explanation, that Chaucer acquired these particular plot motifs from a single convenient source—the first two-thirds of Wittenwiler's very long poem—in order to 'weave' them into his two fabliaux, is somewhat more compelling than that which suggests that Wittenwiler somehow acquired these motifs from three different fabliau tales of Chaucer. That Chaucer exhibited no knowledge of German can be offset by the fact that once certain motifs, ideas or narrative elements are widely circulated they can be obtained through cultural hearsay as well as through direct reading, and in an age of memorisation such 'hearsay' may well be the explanation for the parallels I have adduced.

Whatever the exact relation between the Swiss German and the English poets, there is no denying that both writers participate in contemporaneous anxieties over status related to food and drink. In their long and highly incidental poems, or collections of tales, they use these anxieties not only for parodic purposes but as structural devices to move the action forward while mocking the concerns of rustics to appear better than they are through their use—or more often misuse—of food and drink.

13

Alongside St Margaret

The Childbirth Cult of Saints Quiricus and Julitta in Late Medieval English Manuscripts[1]

Mary Morse

In south-west England and Cornwall several parish churches carry dedications to SS Quiricus and Julitta, a martyred child and mother who emerged as childbirth protectors in the English manuscript traditions of affective piety. Compared to France, Spain and Italy, where church and village names frequently honour the pair, English dedications are rare, and no extant English parish records suggest the existence of a childbirth cult linked to the saints. Yet SS Quiricus and Julitta were invoked consistently against personal dangers such as fevers, fiends, battle and weather, and, most especially, for the protection of 'women in travail'. The context is a vernacular English prayer that appears in six late fifteenth-century English prayer rolls that may have functioned as birth girdles. Such birth girdle manuscripts with devotional texts and images replicate the intercessory power of an actual metal or fabric girdle associated with the Virgin Mary or other saints.

The evidence of what may be called 'consumer consumption', most particularly in the significant rubbing near or on the prayer's text and its accompanying cross iconography in the birth girdle rolls, implies that setting this prayer against the flesh of a woman's abdomen physically ensured eternal protection—in heaven if not on earth—for both mother and child. The prayer contains 'magical' elements found in other amuletic texts, but its avowedly Christian context encouraged monastic owners and scribes to regard the prayer as a legitimate devotional text. Even the future King Henry VIII signed his name to London, British Library, MS Additional 88929 when giving his lavishly illuminated roll containing the text to a servant.

Yet, despite this evidence for royal and monastic ownership or production of three of the birth girdles, the remaining rolls seemingly responded to a general market demand for easily portable manuscripts with prayers that could be packaged as a 'devotional double' for daily reading and specific protective needs.

SS Quiricus and Julitta in hagiographic texts and images

Both Quiricus, a three-year-old boy, and his mother Julitta, also known as Julitta of Tarsus, were martyred during the Diocletian persecutions of the early fourth century.[2] Their story, drawn from early martyrologies and popularised throughout Europe in Jacobus de Voragine's *Legenda Aurea*, was, however, pronounced false and heretical in the 494 *Decretum Gelasianum* once ascribed to Pope Gelasius. Their feast day was celebrated on 16 June on the continent and in England and still is celebrated on 15 July in the Orthodox church. The *Old English Martyrology* (*c.*850) includes their *passio* on the latter date, but its account is closer to the one in a ninth-century Coptic manuscript and differs considerably from the version in the *Legenda Aurea*.[3] They do not appear in the earliest Middle English vernacular collection of saints' lives, the thirteenth-century *South English Legendary*, but are present in the *Gilte Legende*, a 1438 redaction of the French *Légende Dorée*, as 'the lyff of Seint Quiryne'. William Caxton's *Golden Legende*, first printed in 1483, also follows the *Légende Dorée* in its account.[4] In the *Gilte Legende*, Julitta (Iulit, Iulyt), a widow of Iconium, sought refuge from persecution in Tarsus, but was discovered. Her terrified servants abandoned her, but Julitta bravely confronted the governor Alexander (Alisaundre) while holding her young son Quiricus (Quiryne) in her arms:

> [Alisaundre] constreined Iulit to do sacrifice, and she refused it atte alle, and thanne he [comaunded]ed that she shulde be bete withe rawe synues, and whanne the childe seigh his moder bete he wepte bitterly and cried pitously. The prouost toke the childe in his armes and vpon hys knees and wolde haue pleased the childe withe cussingges and withe faire wordes, and þe childe behelde his moder and hadd abhominacion of the prouostes cussinge and turned awaye his hede by gret despite and scratte hym in the visage and gaue a voyse acordinge to his moder as though he saide: 'I am cristen,' and continuelly he faught withe the prouost, and atte the laste he bote hym by the ere and raced it fro his hede. And thanne the prouost was [so] cursidly meued withe anger and withe payne that he [th]rewe the childe doune [the] degrees that the tender brayne was shedde. And whanne that Iulit seigh that her sone was goo before her to the kingdom of [God] she was glad and gaue thankyngges to God. And thanne it was

comaunded that Iulyt were flayne and thanne her body wasshe withe boylinge piche and after that to haue her hede smyte of.[5]

St Quiricus' role expands with the idea that God manifested himself within an innocent child who otherwise was too young to profess his faith:

And after þe tyme that he was a childe and witheoute speche, yet the holy goste was in hym. And whanne the prouoost asked hym who hadde taught hym so he saide: 'O thou prouost, I meruaile of thi folye. Sithe thou seest me so yonge a child whi enquerest thou of me who hathe taught me? Ner thi blind malice thou myght clerely see that the devine wisdom of God techithe me.' And whanne he was bete he cried: 'I am cristen,' and euer as he cried so he recouered more strength and more amonge his tormentes. And the iuge made dismembre the moder and the childe membre fro membre and comaunded that thei shulde be caste here and there to þat ende that thei shulde not be beried of cristen men. But for al that the aungel of oure Lorde God gadered hem togedre and thei were beried bi nyght of cristen men.[6]

Perhaps because he was just a year older than the male victims of Herod's massacre of the Holy Innocents, Quiricus' extraordinary faith resonated in a period where children often did not live past infancy. As with two other English male child martyrs, Little Hugh of Lincoln and William of Norwich, it is likely that the veneration of St Quiricus was also influenced by the late medieval crowning of the boy-bishop, a popular inversion of the liturgy for the Feast of the Holy Innocents, celebrated on 28 December in England and on the continent. An English charm for divination that requires writing on a child's thumb nail reveals the presumption that a child's innocence could augment a charm's power.[7]

Alban Butler's eighteenth-century *Lives of the Saints* adds even more detail to the legend, doubtless drawing from the florid early martyrologies condemned by pseudo-Gelasius.[8] Butler's Alexander required Julitta to identify herself by name, title and country (shades of Margery Kempe). Her reply, 'I am a Christian', forced an automatic death sentence. Specifically, she was to be stretched on the rack and 'scourged' until dead. The child Quiricus (Cyricus) 'kicked Alexander and scratched his face with his little nails'. After Alexander threw Cyricus down the stairs and heard Julitta praise God for her son's martyrdom, Julitta faced an even crueller death: to be ripped apart with hooks before beheading.[9] The sensations of 'stretching' and 'ripping' common to women in labour make Julitta's death sentence symbolically appropriate for a martyred mother who became a patron of childbirth in medieval England.[10]

Julitta's martyrdom embodies the expectation that medieval mothers would educate their children in the faith.[11] St Anne teaching the Virgin, a favourite iconographic motif in England and on the continent, offers the most obvious example. Other faithful mothers, notably St Monica, the mother of Augustine of Hippo, and St Helena, the mother of Constantine the Great, offered Christian models for their children, but both St Augustine and Constantine were adults at the time of their conversions. St Birgitta of Sweden, an enormously popular saint in late medieval England, was also a mother, and one of her children, Catherine, likewise achieved sainthood. But unlike SS Quiricus and Julitta, none of these mothers or their children died as martyrs. Despite Julitta's initial primacy in their joint martyrdom, English and continental devotional traditions assign primacy to Quiricus, sublimating Julitta to the role of an enabler for her juvenile son's martyrdom. She is not accorded the relative equality reserved for the Virgin Mary in the Middle Ages, although a medieval Spanish altarpiece suggests that she and Quiricus may have been perceived as typological stand-ins for the Virgin and Child.[12] Neither is she allowed the role of the *mater dolorosa*. Julitta does not mourn her son's martyrdom but exults in it, a late medieval exemplar for Salomona, the heroic mother of the seven Maccabee sons, martyred with them in 117 BC.[13]

English church dedications to SS Quiricus and Julitta

Except for Swaffham Prior near Cambridge, where double churches dedicated to St Mary and to St Cyriac and St Julitta share a small churchyard, and a few churches in Wales, including St Julitta's at Capel Curig, the churches and monasteries associated with one or both of the martyred pair are in Devon, Somerset, Gloucestershire and Cornwall.[14] Nicholas Orme's detailed survey of church and monastic dedications in Devon and Cornwall lists five in Cornwall—St Carrock, St Juliot, Lanteglos by Camelford, Luxulyan, and St Veep—and two in Devon—Newton St Cyres and South Pool.[15] The Tickenham church of St Quiricus and St Julietta is in Somerset. The churches of Stinchcombe and Stonehouse in Gloucestershire carry dedications to St Cyr. Known dedication dates suggest that the saints' cult, even if imported earlier, gained momentum in England during the mid-fourteenth century. In 1336 St Veep's high altar was dedicated to SS Cyricus and Julitta, the patron saints of the neighbouring Cluniac priory of St Carrock. Newton St Cyres in Devon dedicated its church to St Ciricii in the early fourteenth century, with the exact date unknown but no later than 1338; St Julitta was added in the nineteenth century.[16] Tickenham's church likewise cannot date its dedication exactly, but it also probably occurred in the fourteenth century.[17] In Luxulyan in south-east Cornwall yet another church was dedicated to SS Cyriac and Julitta by 1412. The church now dedicated to St Nicholas and St Cyriac in South Pool appears in 1459 episcopal registers as 'Sancti Ciriaci martyris'.[18]

The dedications to SS Quiricus and Julitta in the Norman churches of Swaffham Prior, Luxulyan, Tickenham and Newton St Cyres may reflect English crusaders' exposure to the martyred pair, something especially likely for those crusaders who followed Richard I to the Holy Land via Cyprus or those fighting near or for the Armenian kingdom of Cilicia, a Christian outpost that usually allied itself with the Frankish crusader kingdoms. Both English and Armenian chroniclers name Leon (Levon) the Great (or Magnificent) as one of Richard's staunch allies and a guest at his wedding to Berengaria of Navarre in 1191 in Limassol, Cyprus. In 1198 Levon was crowned as King Leon II at the church of the Holy Wisdom in Tarsus, the city that also was the site of the saints' martyrdom.[19] Leon received his crown with the approval of Pope Celestine, marking his kingdom as a Latin Christian empire. This distinction, together with the Frankish impression that the Cilician noble ranks were structured much like their own, and were thus equal to their aristocracy, meant that Cilician Armenia was now equal to, or perhaps even superior to, the remaining Latin states.[20] Earlier popes' concerns that the Armenians were heretical vanished. Leon's crown ensured that Cilician Armenia would remain a crusader stronghold until it fell to the Muslims in 1375. Pierpont Morgan MS 622, a 1348 *Synaxary* with half-length miniatures of SS Kyriakos and Julitta illuminated by Sargis Pidsak at Sis (f. 203[v]), indicates that their veneration in Cilicia continued into the late medieval period in the Latin-influenced but still Byzantine Armenian church.

The most compelling evidence for a crusader reinforcement or import of the saints' cult in south-west England lies in the three stone effigies on the north wall of the Tickenham church of St Quiricus and St Julietta (Figure 13.1). The church reveals its Norman architecture in its earliest part, a low arch between the nave and the chancel built about 1100. No church on this site is mentioned in the original Domesday survey of 1086, but Tickenham Court, adjacent to the church and a rural estate of the Anglo-Norman family that may have commissioned the effigies, is named.[21] The three stone effigies, assumed to be father-and-son crusader knights and the son's wife, date from the late twelfth and early thirteenth centuries. They probably honour a branch of the Berkeley family, whose first lord was Robert Fitz Harding, son of a Bristol merchant and a supporter of the Empress Maud and her son Henry II. Nicholas, a son of Robert, acquired the Tickenham estate through his marriage to Ala, whose family descended from Saxon aristocracy.[22] The first knight effigy, identified as Roger Fitz Nicholas de Tickenham (d. 1230), the grandson of the first Robert Fitz Harding and heir to Tickenham through his father Nicholas, wears crusader armour and clothing from Richard's reign. The second knight, wearing crusader armour from a later period, has been identified as Roger's son, Nicholas Fitz Roger (d. 1261), and the woman as Nicholas' first wife Wentlyan. The family apparently extended its patronage to the Tickenham church from its earliest ownership of Tickenham Court, and some of the

Figure 13.1   Three effigies that lie against the north wall of the parish church of St Quiricus and St Julietta at Tickenham probably relate to the Anglo-Norman family that rebuilt the church in the thirteenth century. The effigy pictured, third in the row, may represent Nicholas Fitz Roger (d. 1261). The other two effigies, of a woman and of a knight dressed in armour from the time of Richard I, may represent Nicholas' first wife, Wentlyan, and Nicholas' father, Roger Fitz Nicholas de Tickenham (d. 1230). Author's photo.

thirteenth-century parts of the building probably represent Nicholas Fitz Roger's additions to the church.[23]

Additional evidence supporting Anglo-Norman or Angevin crusaders as the most likely popularisers of SS Quiricus and Julitta in church dedications, and perhaps even in their childbirth cult, surfaces in Books of Hours owned by English noblewomen who either married into Norman families or were themselves of Norman descent. One of these, the Neville of Hornby Book of Hours (London, BL, Egerton MS 2781), commissioned c.1335 by Isabel Neville (née de Byron), the wife of Robert I de Neville of Hornby, contains both Anglo-Norman and Latin texts, including two Latin prayers to SS Quiricus and Julitta introduced with an Anglo-Norman rubric (f. 26ᵛ). The rubric, directed at women, instructs: 'If you are in any anguish or pain of childbirth say the following prayer or the antiphon and the verse in honour of God and of Saint Mary and of Saint Quiricus and Julitta and you will be quickly succoured'.[24]

In addition to the frontal altar painting at the Hermitage of Santa Yolita in Durro, other notable medieval continental images of the saints include the eighth-century frescoes in the Theodotus Chapel in the Church of Santa Maria Antiqua, Rome; a twelfth-century stained glass window in the south transept of Chartres Cathedral of Notre Dame; and a fifteenth-century stone carving above the door at the Eglise de St Cirgues la Loutre in France's Dordogne Valley.[25] No medieval images of SS Quiricus and

Julitta survive in English church art. The three predella panels depicting Julitta's trial and the saints' martyrdom that are part of the Gambier-Parry collection in London's Courtauld Institute Galleries are now attributed to the Italian painter Pietro di Borghese (formerly the Master of SS Quiricus and Julitta), and were probably part of the altarpiece commissioned for the Capannori church of Santi Quirico e Giulitta in 1448.[26] The only known English manuscript illumination depicts Julitta as a bearded man and Quiricus as a beardless youth in a historiated initial of the *sanctorale* of the Sherborne Missal (London, BL, Additional MS 74236, f. 462).[27] We can find more recent depictions in some of the English churches dedicated to them. At Tickenham, for example, nineteenth-century bas-relief sculptures of Julitta, Quiricus, Diocletian and the sword used to decapitate Julitta are carved into the church's tower. At Newton St Cyres the saints are depicted in a stained glass window completed in the twentieth century and also on the village sign.[28]

The English birth girdle tradition

Despite the lack of evidence for their association with childbirth in the parish records of churches dedicated to one or both saints, the vernacular Middle English prayer in six devotional manuscripts identified as birth girdles invokes and seeks, accompanied by one or more Latin orations, the pair's protection against various evils and personal dangers, with childbirth given special prominence. The most prominent English birth girdle relic was the Virgin's girdle owned by Westminster Abbey, probably the girdle referred to in the 1502 Privy Purse Expenses of Elizabeth of York, wife of Henry VII.[29] English abbeys at Bruton (Somerset), Dale (Derbyshire), Haltemprise (Yorkshire) and Bronholm (Norfolk) also each claimed a Virgin's girdle.[30]

Encircling the womb which bore Christ, the Virgin's girdle potently symbolised Christian redemption and salvation for the faithful. When Thomas doubts the Virgin's Assumption into heaven, because he did not see it occur, she sends him her girdle as proof. A woven cloth symbolising her girdle was the only prop noted in records of the Weavers' guild play, *Our Lady's Appearance to Thomas*, in the York Corpus Christi cycle.[31] In the play's text Mary explains to Thomas that her girdle is a 'token trewe'. She follows Thomas's gratitude with a promise that all those 'With pitevous playnte in perellis will pray me./If he synke or swete, in swelte or in swoune,/I schall sewe to my souerayne sone for to say me ... Be it manne in his mournyng,/Or womanne in childinge ...'. When Thomas shows the girdle to the other apostles, who, in an ironic turnabout, doubt that Thomas has seen Mary because he was not present at her death, they believe him and praise the girdle, welcoming it as the Virgin's gift and evidence of her maternal role in Christian salvation: 'Itt is welcome, i-wis, fro þat lady so light,/For hir wombe wolde scho wrappe with it and were it with wynne'.[32]

One Marian miracle in London, BL, Additional MS 37049 even mentions the girdle as part of the Virgin's Annunciation apparel. Appearing in a vision to a sick monk, the Virgin is 'cled in a blak cote, and abowte hyr a gyrdll ... And þan sche sayd ... "Þus was I anowrned when Gabriel schewed vnto me þe incarnacion of þe Son of God".' However, no extant English Miracle of the Virgin focuses exclusively upon the power of the Virgin's girdle.[33] Girdles associated with any saint assumed similar apotropaic powers. Canterbury Cathedral, for example, loaned a belt reputed to have belonged to St Anselm to women in labour, and other English monastic inventories mention girdles of St Aelred, St Bernard, St Francis and St Mary Magdalene.[34]

'Textual amulets', as Don C. Skemer describes them, 'exploit and enhance the magical efficacy of words' when worn by, or placed upon, a person.[35] Manuscript birth girdles, which attempted to convince their owners or borrowers that the manuscripts' texts and images possessed the same apotropaic powers as girdle relics, likewise belong to this category. London, Wellcome Historical Medical Library MS 632, the birth girdle which first prompted me to begin this study, offered both Christian solace and protection when the texts and images appearing upon the girdle's face were wrapped around a woman's belly or strategically placed against a woman's abdomen. Even if those aiding in childbirth could not read, as many midwives could not, the prayers and/or inscriptions written on the dorse of Wellcome MS 632 signified the correlation between a woman's pain in childbirth and Mary's grief at the Crucifixion.[36] Produced somewhere in England in the late fifteenth century, Wellcome MS 632 is narrow (10 cm), pieced together from four pieces of vellum, and long enough (332 cm) to wrap several times around a woman's waist. Its badly rubbed and fragile condition substantiates its use as a birth girdle. An incomplete Middle English inscription on the dorse of the roll offers the same protective powers as the Virgin's girdle. Its beginning reads: 'Thys parchement[?] ys oure lady seynt mary length / by vertu of thys holy length oure savyor Jhesu criste and of hys dere / mother oure lady seynte'.[37] Surprisingly, the legible texts on the face of Wellcome MS 632 do not invoke St Margaret, England's most popular childbirth saint and the primary subject of three extant French birth girdles.[38] Instead, in this English roll, as in the other five rolls included in this study, SS Quiricus and Julitta assume Margaret's traditional role as intercessors for childbirth protection.[39]

The English and Latin birth girdle prayers to SS Quiricus and Julitta[40]

Variants of the Middle English prayer invoking SS Quiricus and Julitta in Wellcome MS 632 also appear in five other manuscripts which may have been used as birth girdles: Yale Library, Beinecke MS 410; New York, Morgan Library, Glazier MS 39; London, British Library, MS Additional 88929 (formerly Durham, Ushaw College MS 29); London, British Library,

Rotulus Harley MS 43.A 14 and Rotulus Harley MS T.11.[41] The prayer also appears on a page in Oxford, Bodleian Library, Bodley MS 177, a miscellany that otherwise focuses on medicine, alchemy and astrology. One owner of the Carew-Poyntz Hours (Cambridge, Fitzwilliam Museum, MS 48) copied the Middle English prayer (f. 2ᵛ), but without the childbirth protection found in the other manuscripts.[42] Two early print fragments also contain versions of the vernacular prayer to SS Quiricus and Julitta, implying that even early English printers capitalised on the belief that reciting this prayer could deliver the saints' protection in childbirth.[43]

The English prayer to SS Quiricus and Julitta fits neatly into Eamon Duffy's devotional category of 'charms, pardons, and promises', prayers characterised by 'a robust interest in measurable results'.[44] Most of the Middle English prayers to SS Quiricus and Julitta begin with the formula: 'Thys crosse .xv tymes moten [measured] is þe lenght [sic] of our lorde ihesu criste', itself a measure that reconstructs the Crucifixion scene in a reader's mind. This mental visualisation relies upon an actual image of the cross, carefully drawn to a scale that could be multiplied either fifteen or twenty-one times to equal the traditional 6-foot 3-inch length of Christ's body.[45] The text represents an English variation on the Heavenly Letter, a protective prayer that an angel reportedly delivered to either Pope Leo or to Charlemagne for the emperor to carry into battle against the Saracens. The protections of the cross also appear in earlier prayers attributed to St Paul and St Peter. The Middle English 'length of the cross' prayer associated with SS Quiricus and Julitta might even conflate St Quiricus with the St Cyriacus who aided St Helena in her discovery of the True cross.[46]

The typical manuscript *mise-en-page* for the SS Quiricus and Julitta texts contains the Middle English prayer with its words wrapping around the image of an empty Tau cross. Just after the promise of protection in childbirth, the prayer invokes the saints' intercession and notes the petition's registration at St John Lateran in Rome, thus adding credibility and legitimacy to its promised protections.[47] A Latin suffrage to SS Quiricus and Julitta follows immediately after, usually announced with a rubric 'Anti*phon*' or 'Ora*cio*'. The suffrage does not allude to childbirth but elicits the saints' help in protecting the reader; in Rotulus Harley MS 43.A 14, for example, the generic 'michi famulo tuo' of the Latin suffrage in Glazier MS 39 is replaced with 'michi Will*el*mo famulo tuo'.[48] The different manuscript texts rearrange the prayer segments and feature distinct variations in their accompanying cross iconography, but all discussed here entreat a woman to place the cross and its prayer on her body during childbirth. The positions of the Middle English prayer, the Latin suffrage and the cross within the *mise-en-page* of each individual roll show their devotional relationship to other significant images and texts of English affective piety.

The English prayer to SS Quiricus and Julitta that Curt Bühler transcribes from BL, Rotulus Harley MS 43.A 14 presents a numerical list of the 'gret

Figure 13.2   The second membrane of Beinecke MS 410 features the Middle English prayer to SS Quiricus and Julitta. The empty Cross, with the text wrapped around it, characterizes the *mise-en-page* of the prayer in several of the birth girdle rolls. Photo: Beinecke MS 410, Beinecke Rare Book and Manuscript Library, Yale University.

giftis' that one will receive from bearing or looking upon the cross; the childbirth supplication is the eighth gift.[49] Neither the phrase 'gret giftis' nor a numerical list appears in the other English versions of the prayer, although this phrase and the list are sometimes associated with other amuletic images, such as the Side Wound or the Holy Nails. Because the prayer text in BL, MS Rotulus Harley 43.A 14 differs considerably from the other English prayers invoking the protection of SS Quiricus and Julitta, the prayer from Beinecke MS 410 (Figure 13.2) offers the most useful basis for comparison:

> Thys crosse .xv. tymes moten is þe lenght (*sic*) of our lorde ihesu criste
> & what day ye loke þeron or blysse ye þerwyth or bere it upon ye with
> deuocion þer shall no wykyd spyryt nor none enmyes haue pour to
> hurte ye slepyng nor wakyng. nor thu*n*dryng. nor lyghtnyng. wyndes
> nor wedirs on lande nor water nor wyth no wapen be slayne ne dye
> withoute confession and yf a woman haue this crosse on hyr when

she trauelith of chylde þe chy[l]de & she shall be departyd without peryll of dethe be the grace of god. Saynt Cyryace and saynt Iulite hys modyr desyryd thys petycyon of god and he graunted it them. As it is regystred in Rome at saynt Iohn latynes.[50]

Bühler's transcription of the Latin suffrage from BL, Rotulus Harley MS 43.A 14 bears reprinting below because only slight changes in wording and the insertion of a supplicant's name separate it from those in the other manuscripts:

Salue decus paruulorum, miles regis angelorum. O Cerice, cum beata Julitta. Christe & Maria nos saluet in hora mortis nostre. Amen.
    Preciosa est in conspectu Dei mors sanctorum eius.
    Deus qui gloriosis martiribus tuis Cerico & Julitte tribuisti dira nephandi iudicis tormenta superare tribue michi Willelmo famulo tuo humilitatem in virtute gloriose longitudinis tue et venerabilis crucis tue, preciosique corporis & sanguinis tui, & omnipotenciarum & virtutem per intercessionem sanctorum tuorum concede michi triumphum omnium inimicorum vt possum semper retinere constanciam per Christum Dominum nostrum Amen A.M.E.N.[51]

Yale University Library, Beinecke MS 410

Beinecke MS 410 is a wide (165 mm) and relatively short (1515 mm) late fifteenth-century prayer roll comprised of three parchment membranes sewn together. The scroll was originally owned or written by Thomas Bernake (Barnak) of Lincolnshire, presumably a monk. Thomas may be the patron in the white gown and blue robe of an Austin friar kneeling beneath the Instruments of the Passion in the first membrane.[52] At the end of the third membrane a sixteenth-century owner entitled it 'An Indulgence of Innocent VI c 1352', an attempt to connect the manuscript with the promise attributed to an unspecified Pope Innocent that daily worship of the Five Wounds of Christ will release devout men and women from seven parts of their penance in purgatory.[53] The thickness of its vellum, its saturated colour and iconographic motifs that blend continental and English illumination styles suggest an owner of some wealth.

    The first membrane contains two Instruments of the Passion miniatures. The first, set within a Gothic architectural frame, features a standing Christ, His right arm encircling the cross, centred among the Instruments. The second illumination, with the Veronica, the Sacred Heart superimposed upon the Three Holy Nails, the Crown of Thorns encircling the Heart, the Instruments of the Passion, and Christ's bleeding hands and feet floating in space, creates a highly textured visual reminder of Christ's agony. The third membrane, with a Salvator Mundi image of a naked Christ Child seated on a red cushion and a version of the prayers known as the Fifteen Oes, was probably added to the roll after the texts and miniatures on the first two membranes.[54]

The *mise-en-page* of the second membrane, with the English prayer invoking the aid of SS Quiricus and Julitta at its centre, is most applicable to this study. The membrane's first miniature portrays the kneeling monk-patron, followed by Innocent's indulgence for the prayer to the Wounds. This prayer to the Wounds, with its numerical list of just seven gifts, closely resembles the English prayer to Quiricus and Julitta in Rotulus Harley MS 43.A 14, but it neither includes protection in childbirth nor mentions the saints. A variant of the same prayer, invoking the protection of the Holy Nails and listing six gifts, appears in BL, MS Rotulus Harley MS T. 11. The second part of the prayer in Rotulus Harley MS T. 11, associated with the 'mesur of the blessyd [side] wounde', does contain the childbirth passage but without the intercession of Quiricus and Julitta. Yet another variant of this Beinecke prayer, invoking the length of the 'thre Nailis' sent to 'Kyng Charls', and listing seven gifts that do not include childbirth, surfaces in Glazier MS 39.[55]

The reader of the Beinecke manuscript then views a 17-mm long empty Tau cross, outlined in blue-black ink and filled in with brown. The Tau cross, originating in the sign that the Israelites painted on their lintels to protect their firstborn against God's tenth plague, became a popular Christian symbol for the Franciscans.[56] Most of the other rolls containing the English prayer also incorporate a Tau cross.[57] Pink and brown acanthus, with the occasional snail, bee or butterfly, border both sides of the membrane. The text of the English prayer to SS Quiricus (*Cyryace*) and Julitta (*Iulite*), inked in red, with one blue initial and two blue paraphs, begins beneath the cross-beam on the left, continues down the shaft, up again to the cross-beam and down the right side of the shaft. This pattern of wrapping, with the cross positioned vertically, likewise characterises the *mise-en-page* of several of the Quiricus and Julitta English prayer texts.[58]

The Latin oration that follows is nearly identical to the BL, Rotulus Harley MS 43.A 14 text, with Thomas' name (*Thome*) inserted into the suffrage to SS Quiricus (*Ciriaco*) and Julitta (*Iulitte*) where *Willemo* is inserted into the Harley roll: 'Deus qui gloriosis martiribus tuis Ciriaco et Iulitte tribuis Thome famulo tuo humilitatem et virtutatem ...'.[59] The insertion of men's names in the suffrage seems somewhat curious following a vernacular prayer that ends with specific protections for women in childbirth and their unborn children but may demonstrate that men, too, worried about the dangers of childbirth.[60] The death of a wife or an heir could lead to political or social upheaval, as King Henry VIII's preoccupation with begetting a male heir so famously illustrates. Ironically, Henry VIII gave away BL, MS Add. 88929, also known as 'Prince Henry's roll'.[61]

London, Wellcome Historical Medical Library MS 632

In comparison to the sophistication of the Beinecke MS miniatures and scribal hand, the mostly illegible English and Latin texts invoking SS Quiricus and Julitta on the face of Wellcome MS 632 are framed by two sets of crudely drawn images. Inked in black, a disproportionately large image of the Three Holy Nails appears immediately above the Middle English prayer to SS Quiricus (Ciryk) and Julitta (Julytte), which Moorat's catalogue entry describes as the 'Virtues of the Scroll'. The Latin oration follows the prayer. The Instruments of the Passion, inked in both red and black, flank a Tau cross placed below the Latin suffrage. The cross is empty except for an indeterminate shape (the Holy Ghost?) centred on the cross-beam, a red-inked heart representing the Sacred Heart in its approximate position on the shaft and an emblem of the Five Wounds, each wound represented with one drop of blood. Since so much of the English prayer is illegible, we cannot tell if it actually opens with the 'length of the cross' mnemonic or how closely the prayer follows the version in Beinecke MS 410. The child-birth passage in Wellcome MS 632 reads as follows:

> [...] yf a woman travail [wyth?]/chylde lay thys crosse on hyr wom/be and she shall be safe delyuerd wyth/oute perell and the childe shall haue/cristendome and the mother puri/ficacyon. [Ffor seynt Ciryk and seynt/julytte hys mother desyrd thes gyftes/of almyghty god and owre lorde/Jhesu criste graunted hyt unto them/and thys is regestred at rome at seynt/John lateranence in the pryncypall/ churche in Rome].[62]

The legible lines of the Latin suffrage that follows closely match those in Beinecke MS 410 and BL, Rotulus Harley MS 43.A 14.

A remarkably similar passage, yet not associated with SS Quiricus and Julitta, concludes the dorse prayer on the Wellcome birth girdle. The introductory rubric to the prayer ascribes its text to the Virgin Mary and identifies it as the Heavenly Letter:

> [...] hys dere mother owre blessyd lady seynt marye whych was wryttyn in letters of gold and send ffrome hevyn by an anngell to the pope Leo that tyme beying [?] at Rome and sayd to hym thys maner wyse: Who so beryth thys mesure [?] uppon hym wyth trewe fayth and good devocyon saying v pater nosters v aves and a credo in the worshypp of hym that thys mesure ys of he shall never be slayne in battel nor by no devyll be combryd [?] by day nor by nyght nor wyth thunder/ [...] nor wyth no [?] soden deth be smyttyn nor dye wythowte howsyll and shryft [?] nor byfore no juge wrongefuly dampned nor wyth no thevys be robbyd on see nor on lond nor perysshed wyth ffyer nor water nor blastys ne wyndys on water ne

on lond shal not grew hym nor of the pestylence dye. And yf he be in dedly synne he shal not dye theryn. And he shall encreace in worldly goods. And yf a woman travell wyth chylde gyrdes thys mesure abowte hyr wombe and she shall be safe delyvyrd wythowte parelle [peril?] and the chylde shall have crystendome and the mother puryfycatyon.[63]

Moorat's catalogue entry (p. 492) describes this prayer as the 'epitome of the very largely illegible passages in the main text [the Middle English prayer to SS Quiricus and Julitta] following the first Figure, in which are set out the Blessings and Protections given by the pious use of the Scroll'. Yet the rubbed images and illegible text on the face of the roll, especially in the area of the prayers invoking the intercession of Quiricus and Julitta, prove that women who used the roll to ensure safe delivery often must have placed this section against their bellies during labour.

Beneath the English prayer to SS Quiricus and Julitta on the face, Wellcome MS 632 contains three images inscribed with I.H.S., a variation on the usual I.H.C. of the Holy Monogram, an initial treatment of the Holy Name of Jesus, a meditation popularised by mystics such as Mechthild of Magdeburg, Richard Rolle and Walter Hilton.[64] The first of the three images places the monogram within a circle with text directing the birth girdle wearer to meditate upon the individual and aggregate drops of blood shed by Christ. A devotional verse, which Frances M.M. Comper describes as one of the 'abridgements and imitations of Richard Rolle's writings in BL MS Add 37049', follows the rubric:

[The nomber off the dropys of the/bloode off Jhesu all I wyll re/ herce[?] in generall v hundert thousand/ffor to tell] and also v thousand more shall/v hundert also greate and small/here bye the number off them all.[65]

The second Holy Monogram image in Wellcome MS 632, a flattened diamond shape with the I.H.S. in its middle, represents Christ's Side Wound, another iconographic motif associated with childbirth (Figure 13.3); the sites of the other Wounds, illustrated by two detached hands and two feet showering red droplets, float at the four corners of the diamond.[66] The same poem noted above, but this time placed below a vertical depiction of the Side Wound and detached hands and feet that bears a remarkable similarity to the image in Wellcome MS 632, also appears in Takamiya MS 56.[67] The third Holy Monogram is placed on an empty cross. The last drawing in Wellcome MS 632 is a diamond, probably intended as a simulation of the Wound, inscribed with 'Ecce Homo' and featuring a nearly erased standing Christ within it. The texts surrounding the images in Wellcome MS 632 alternate between English and Latin, but most are illegible.

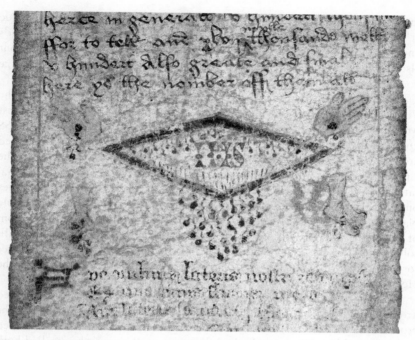

Figure 13.3   This representation of Christ's Side Wound, with the detached hands and feet at the corners of the diamond, appears in Wellcome MS 632. The Side Wound is often associated with childbirth in English devotional manuscripts. Photo: Wellcome MS 632, Wellcome Library, London.

New York, Morgan Library, Glazier MS 39

A canon at Coverham Abbey (Yorkshire) who names himself Percevall claims 'I dyd wryte' at the end of Glazier MS 39. The wide and very long (18.5 × 586.4 cm) roll consists of nine membranes; its eighteen vermilion and black images of saints and Passion iconography have been described as 'folk art' and are perhaps the work of Percevall himself.[68] The sides of the roll feature a running border with notched leaves wound together. The reader of the roll first encounters a large image of the Three Holy Nails bound by the Crown of Thorns. The opening prayer, placed just below the Nails, reminds the reader that 'Theis er the veray trew length of the thre Nailis of our Lorde Ihesu Criste to whame Pape Innocent sent this same length vn to Kyng Charls.' This pope–king pairing suggests that the roll was completed in or after 1484, the year when both Pope Innocent VIII and Charles VIII of France came to power.[69] A portrait of St Armel (Armagillus), a Breton saint, is associated with Henry VII, whose victory over Richard III marked the ascent of the Tudors in 1485.[70] Among others, images on the roll include St Sebastian, St Roche, St George, St Christopher, a Pietá, the Five Wounds and a Pelican in its piety. Glazier MS 39 is the only roll in this study that also includes an image of St Margaret, but its accompanying Latin suffrage does not mention protection in childbirth.

While the St Margaret image and devotion, as well as a prayer to the Virgin that designates its supplicant as 'Ego misera peccatrix', suggest women's usage, the most telling evidence lies in the segment with the SS Quiricus (Cerice) and Julitta (Julite) texts, the English prayer again wrapped around a Tau cross.[71] The cross, outlined in vermilion, is wreathed in the Crown of Thorns in vermilion and black and is inscribed with 'Maria' rather than the anticipated I.H.S. or I.H.C. of many Crucifixion scenes on its cross-beam. The cross is further distinguished with the Three Holy Nails in solid black (one at each end of the cross-beam and at the bottom of the shaft), the Heart near the middle of the shaft, and a second small, solid black Tau cross at the bottom. Unlike the artist who drew the images for Wellcome MS 632, the Glazier illuminator did not attempt to align the Heart or the third Nail with the position of Christ's body on the cross.

Even if the SS Quiricus and Julitta texts had not been not wrapped around the cross in Glazier MS 39, the inscription to the Virgin on the cross-beam connected Christ's sacrifice to the mother who bore, nurtured and mourned him. Women who laid this cross on their wombs recalled both Christ's physical agony and the Virgin's emotional agony, contemplation that led to the joy of Christ's forgiveness and mercy. Just so, a woman's physical pain in childbirth transformed itself into joy in her motherhood—and an heir for her husband. The red-inked Middle English prayer in Glazier MS 39 even includes the word 'joy' in the saints' promise at the end:

> And if a woman trawell of childe, take þis crose and lay it one hyr wome and she shalbe hastely be delyuerede with joy with-outen perell, the childe to haue Cristendom and þe moder purficacion of Haly Kirk. For Seynt Cerice and Seynt Julite, his moder, desired thes of almyghty Gode, the wich He grauntede þame. This is registrede at Rome in Seynt John Laternence.[72]

A black rubric, Antiphona, marks the beginning of the Latin suffrage in much the same form as it appears in Beinecke MS 410 and Rotulus Harley 43.A 14.

London, British Library, MS Additional 88929

Legend asserts that King Henry VIII wrapped BL, MS Add 88929 around his leg to relieve the pain of an ulcer,[73] but Henry's pre-1509 signature indicates that he was still Prince of Wales when he gave the roll to William

Thomas, his Groom of the Chamber. Perhaps he should have kept it. The first miniature in the 335.5 × 12 cm roll portrays an unknown bishop, perhaps the manuscript's commissioner. Its relatively narrow width allowed easy rolling for storage in a small box or bag, perhaps one like the French cylindrical case that has been preserved along with its birth girdle dedicated to St Margaret.[74] In the second illumination in BL, MS Add 88929, the English prayer to SS Quiricus and Julitta wraps around the outline of the crucified Christ hanging on a Tau cross, the only *mise-en-page* composition actually showing, rather than implying, Christ's physical body in correlation with the length of the cross.

In this segment of the roll, which Skemer identifies as 'the most clearly amuletic section', both the prayer and the subsequent Latin suffrage to SS Quiricus and Julitta are inscribed on scrolls unfurled by cherubic angels, creating an intricate scroll-within-a-scroll motif.[75] The script on each scroll is inked in a slightly different colour: reddish brown for the Middle English prayer and deeper brown for the Latin oration. The childbirth passage in the prayer appears at the bottom of the scroll-within-a-scroll on the reader's left: 'and if a woman be travell off childe ley this on her body and she shal be delyverd withowte parel the childe cristendom & the moder purificacyon. S. cire & hys moder S Julitt desired these petitions of our Lord ... [Sey this oracion]'. The instructional rubric then leads the reader's eye toward the right-hand scroll containing the Latin suffrage to the mother and child martyrs.[76]

A square-framed image of Christ's Side Wound as a mouth appears immediately below the angels' scrolls,[77] followed by a seemingly rare iconographic motif—the Three Holy Nails, entirely gold, with each nail broken to allow barely visible insertions of the Heart and the detached hands and feet; just as in Glazier MS 39, the nails are bound together with the Crown of Thorns. A Middle English text wrapped around the Holy Nails returns to the motif of the gifts seen in the Middle English prayer to SS Quiricus and Julitta in BL, Rotulus Harley MS 43.A 14, but this time with the prayer linked to the length of the nails rather than to the cross as an attribution to Pope Innocent IV.[78] The nails and their accompanying prayer are not rubbed, women in childbirth are not mentioned as recipients of any of the seven gifts, and SS Quiricus and Julitta are not invoked, suggesting that the compiler of the roll attempted to group the childbirth invocations in one place higher up on the scroll. A woman could then set this section of the roll on her abdomen and wrap the remainder around her waist.

London British Library Rotulus Harley MSS 43.A 14 and T. 11

BL, Rotulus Harley MS 43.A 14 contains only the Middle English prayer and the Latin suffrage. Both texts, inked in brown, wrap around a 13-cm long empty cross with the two cross-beams noted earlier. Although classified as a prayer roll, the 46-cm long roll, which is really no more than a sheet of parchment, is far too short to wrap around a woman's waist. The cross and prayers seem to have been pasted down on this piece of parchment, suggesting that the saints' cult was popular enough to inspire production of individual sheets containing only these prayers and the empty cross. The appearance of the page in Bodley MS 177 likewise suggests a pasted-down copy of the texts and cross image.

BL, Rotulus Harley MS T. 11 is known primarily for a set of illuminated seals that seem to offer apotropaic powers to the roll's owner. In addition to the often illegible English prayer to SS Quiricus and Julitta and the common Latin suffrage to the saints, the roll offers the protection of both the Side Wound and the Holy Nails. The Side Wound is depicted as a vertical lozenge, with layers of red and yellow; stylised red droplets spatter the edges of the lozenge. The prayer to the Side Wound incorporates both the now-familiar idea of a measure and the Charlemagne letter in its opening: 'This is the mesur of the blessyd wounde that oure Lord Ihesu Crist had in his right syde, the whiche an angell brought to Charlamayn, the nobyll emperour of Constrantyne, wyth-in a cofer of gold ...'.[79] The prayer to the Nails repeats the 'seven gifts' motif of the prayer attached to the Nails in BL, MS Add 88929, but without mention of SS Quiricus and Julitta or childbirth. BL, MS Rotulus Harley MS T. 11 also contains a list of forty-eight divine names, similar to the list entitled 'A prayer of the names of Christ' that often was added to printed Books of Hours for the English market. Wellcome MS 632 also seems to contain such a list, but it is mostly illegible.[80]

Oxford, Bodleian Library, Bodley MS 177

Bodley MS 177 may be the earliest manuscript containing the Middle English prayer to SS Quiricus and Julitta (f.61ᵛ). C.T. Onions concludes that the word 'dunder' for 'thunder' suggests that the prayer originated in the fourteenth century in south-west England, where most of the church dedications to the saints also occur.[81] In a manuscript otherwise dominated by medicine and magic, the *mise-en-page* of f. 61ᵛ, consisting only of the empty cross and prayers invoking the martyred pair, isolates itself from the dense, small hand that characterises the rest of the manuscript. Its simple Tau cross, measuring 11.5 cm from top to bottom, is drawn in brown and outlined in red. The English prayer, also inked in brown and underlined in red, begins with the familiar 'length of Christ' promise and then follows the wrapping pattern noted in Beinecke MS 410.[82] An empty space with faint tracings on the bottom right of the page suggests that another miniature may once have been inserted here or was intended for the page.

The Bodley prayer promises more benefits than the other versions of the English prayer, suggesting a closer relationship to the 'Deus Propicius Esto' sometimes attributed to St Peter.[83] Yet its promise of increased wealth for the wearer, 'encrese yt in worldely goodes' (a phrase which also appears in the prayer on the dorse of Wellcome MS 632), does not appear in these earlier prayers and indeed seems somewhat out of character in a devotional prayer that otherwise emphasises spiritual protection rather than temporal acquisition of power or riches. Onions provides a full transcription of the prayer, although Bühler disputes his dialect analysis in parts.[84]

The idea that SS Quiricus and Julitta have granted the protections listed above as a gift appears midway through the Bodley prayer ('desired thys gyft of god'), in contrast to its placement near the end of the prayer in Rotulus Harley MS 43.A 14 ('desirid þise graciouse gyftis of God'), Wellcome MS 632 ('desyryd thes gyfts of Almyghty god'), Beinecke MS 410 ('desyred thys petcyon of god') and Glazier MS 39 ('desired thes of almyghty Gode'). Like BL, MS Add 88929, Bodley MS 177 omits the registration of the petition at St John Lateran. It also omits any introductory rubric for the reader moving into the Latin suffrage to SS Quiricus and Julitta. As Bühler remarks, and as we have seen in the group of manuscripts containing these texts, Onions' contention that the Latin prayer was a collect 'composed specially for the occasion' is incorrect.[85]

The facing page (f. 62^{r}) contains a volvelle with cut-outs that reveal crude pictures or lettering when the user spins the circle. One turn reveals an a.m.e.n, the only overt Christian element in the revealed signs, while other turns stop at a male head, a female head, a gargoyle-like mask and a moon.[86] No obvious connection links the two facing pages, but either could function as a stand-alone page for amuletic or devotional use. The presence of the SS Quiricus and Julitta texts, especially, suggests that f. 61^{v} was intended as an apotropaic page-as-shield to place on a woman in labour.

The SS Quiricus and Julitta texts in the Wellcome MS 632 birth girdle, the five other rolls likely to have been used as birth girdles and Bodley MS 177 centralise the maternal bond, most particularly its initiation in childbirth, as a metaphor for the spiritual bonding of affective piety. A woman in labour not merely empathises with but enters into Christ's pain. Julitta's example teaches a woman to accept pain and possible death as the spiritual necessity for the beginning of her child's Christian life, just as Christ accepted pain and death to give eternal life to all women, men and children. And, just as the Virgin Mary's sorrow will be assuaged in her assumption and reunion with her Son in heaven, Julitta's heavenly reward and reunion with her son Quiricus awaits her. The Middle English prayer of SS Quiricus and Julitta offers all mothers and their children that same eternal joy.

Postscript

I have recently identified two other probable English birth girdles not included in this study. The first, which Rossell Hope Robbins refers to as an "Arma Christi" roll,[87] dates from the late fourteenth century. Most recently, Ann Eljenholm Nichols has identified the roll as the earliest in the manuscript tradition of the Middle English Passion poem, 'O Vernicle'.[88] Formerly owned by the now-closed Mount Alphonsus Monastery in Esopus, NY,[89] the roll is now catalogued as 'olim Esopus' (Redemptorist Archives of the Baltimore Province, Philadelphia). I especially thank the following: Rev. Matthew T. Allman for allowing me to view the roll while it was undergoing restoration; Minah Song, supervising conservator at the Center for Conservation of Art and Historic Artifacts (CCAHA), Philadelphia, for providing images and a description of the roll; Ann Eljenholm Nichols for sharing her knowledge of the roll with me (personal correspondence);[90] and Kathleen L. Scott for her dating of the borders and illuminations (personal correspondence). A variant of the Middle English prayer to SS Quiricus and Julitta (Cirice and Julitte) appears on the roll's dorse; a Tau cross, referred to in the prayer's opening as 'Þis syne', appears as a marginal decoration alongside the text. The Latin oration invoking the intercession of SS Quiricus and Julitta closes with red squares with white X-shaped crosses flanking the word 'tetragrammaton' and inserted between the letters A-g-l-a, both common magical elements which, although they sometimes appear elsewhere on the manuscript birth girdles, are not inserted into the English prayer to SS Quiricus and Julitta in my study group. With further analysis of the relationship between the SS Quiricus and Julitta prayers and the other texts on the roll, this roll may emerge as a significant forerunner in the English manuscript birth girdle tradition.

The other birth girdle contender, Takamiya MS 56, a mid-fifteenth-century prayer roll in Professor Toshiyuki Takamiya's private collection, contains neither English nor Latin texts connected to SS Quiricus and Julitta, but shares other textual and iconographic similarities to the English manuscript birth girdles (my study of Takamiya MS 56 is forthcoming). Takamiya connects the amuletic properties of his roll to Sir Gawain's acceptance of the Lady's magical girdle.[91]

14

Consuming the Text

Pulephilia in Fifteenth-Century French Debate Poetry[1]

Emma Cayley

The proverb or saying 'avoir/mettre la puce en l'oreille' (to have or put a flea in [some]one's ear) recurs frequently in fifteenth-century French debate poetry.[2] Pointing both to disquiet and to unsatisfied sexual desire, it figures the irresolution of the debate poem where it is most often found. Our expression further stands for the wider game of the text, deliberately perpetuated in order to prolong the painful pleasure of writing. Moreover, this 'expression grivoise' (suggestive expression) has a strong link with the notion of voice and of consumption within the text. The desire for all-consuming communion that it implies—both physical and verbal—hints at the 'presence in absence' that is the troubling lack at the heart of the debate (both lack of resolution and lack of the loved one). This leads us to ask how desire may be linked with voice, presence and absence in the text. The debate mode turns on the absence of, and longing for, the 'authentic' voice, paralleled by the absence of, and longing for, the love object. The debate form itself is, as Badel terms it, 'un dialogue en récit' (a dialogue in narrative): the literary dialogue mediates the voices of the 'acteurs' (actors) via the narrator figure.[3] We as readers are presented with the ghost of a performance (though it is unclear whether these poems were ever intended to be performed), reflected in the desire for presence/embodiment and intercourse/consumption that haunts the text.[4] The play of intercourse (physical and verbal) and consumption is one that underpins my discussion both of the debate poems themselves and of the material context in which they are situated. As the fleas ravage human flesh both actually and metaphorically (in the sense of gnawing desire), so the speakers long for a similar 'cannibalistic' union with their absent loved ones: to become one flesh. This is a desire that transcends the confines of each discrete debate poem, leaving each unresolved, and effectively unfinished. The longed-for union/

consumption never comes. This irresolution and ever-deferred promise of fulfilment, generating further writing, therefore operates too on the level of the manuscript. The late medieval debate poem does not stand alone, but interacts with a community of others, attempting to find resolution/fulfilment on a wider stage. Many of the medieval poems that I will discuss are most commonly copied together in large anthology or 'coterie' manuscripts,[5] promoting social bonds between the authors in what Jane Taylor has described as a 'fiction of intimacy'.[6] Thus while consumption/satisfaction (or the scratching of the itch) is not achieved on the level of the individual text, it may be better assuaged by the interactions of these debate texts within their material context.

Debate poetry of the fifteenth century in France plays extensively on the gender relationships and voices it constructs and mediates within its confines. The boundaries are often blurred so that we ask questions familiar from earlier lyric poetry.[7] Is it indeed the voices of female interlocutors that we are hearing through the text? Does voice, like the 'puce' (flea), exist in a gender-neutral space: the space of desire which is the absence at the heart of the text? In what follows, I begin to address these and other questions through an investigation of the voices of desire at work within the debate poem, and their longing for consumption. I demonstrate how these voices of desire speak through the 'puce' (flea) of the popular expression, and examine how, in their yearning for an ever-deferred act of consumption, the speakers themselves create the uncertainty and irresolution of the debate poem. After an account of the flea tradition in French literature I examine instances of the flea motif in its medieval material context, specifically highlighting patterns of transmission of these works and suggesting how consumption operates both at the level of the text itself and metaphorically across the manuscript transmission.

According to Marcel Françon, Giuseppe di Stefano, Rose Bidler and Claude Duneton, the origins of our 'expression grivoise' lie in the thirteenth or fourteenth centuries, where it signified the state of extreme anxiety and torment brought on by love: in other words, the state of sexual desire or arousal.[8] The motif of the flea later developed as a literary theme from the popularity of medieval and early modern songs about the wars between women and fleas and the debate of the woman and the flea. It was elaborated in texts well into the sixteenth and seventeenth centuries and beyond.[9] It is in its erotic context that it was predominantly used in the fifteenth-century debate poetry that is my focus here. The expression was occasionally divorced from this erotic context to signify unspecified torment and anguish. The modern French expression 'avoir/mettre la puce à l'oreille' has by and large lost its sexual meaning and come to signify something akin to 'suspecting something' or 'sowing the seed of doubt in someone's mind': a sense of disquiet, though not the torment indicated by the medieval phrase.[10] For Jean de la Fontaine or Rabelais, among a host

of other sixteenth- and seventeenth-century writers, the expression retained
its erotic origins:

> Elle ne dormit point durant toute la nuit,
> Ne fit que s'agiter, et mena tant de bruit,
> Que ni son père ni sa mere
> Ne purent fermer la paupière
> Un seul moment.
> Ce n'était pas grande merveille:
> Fille qui pense à son amant absent,
> Toute la nuit, dit-on, a la puce à l'oreille,
> Et ne dort que fort rarement.[11]

> She didn't sleep a wink all night/Just tossed about, and
> made such a fuss/That neither her mother nor father/
> Managed to get to sleep/At all./It was no great surprise
> though:/A girl who thinks about her absent lover/All night
> long is said to 'have a flea in her ear'/And only sleeps
> fitfully.[12]

La Fontaine here points to the original connection of the expression with
specifically female desire, though it is widely appropriated in the fifteenth
century as an expression of male desire in the absence of the lady. A
connection has long been made between the substantive 'oreille' (ear) and the
female genitalia through its comparison with the 'coquille' or 'coquillage'
(shell); we note the common modern designation of particular shellfish:
'oreilles-de-mer', 'oreilles-de-Vénus' (ears of the sea; ears of Venus: abalone).
In the context of our investigation into voice, desire and consumption in
the text, Jacques Derrida's interest in the deferral of interpretation implied
by the designation of 'l'oreille de l'autre' (the ear of the Other) may provide
an illuminating perspective. A parallel emerges between the notions of
the deferral of meaning (Derridean 'différance') and of satisfaction.[13] The
voice is received by the ear of the other, and is interpreted at the point of
reception rather than the point of origin. So both voice and desire require
the presence of the other (interlocutor/narrator/love object) for interpre-
tation/fulfilment. The promise of fulfilment, thus consumption, is at once
offered by the narrator/fellow interlocutor(s) of the debate and deferred
through the absence of the desired interlocutor/love object. The slippage
of meaning between the erotic and auditory receptive functions of 'oreille'
here provides a conceptual framework for my subsequent discussion of the
expression in our debates.

In her *Dictionnaire érotique* Rose Bidler points to the popular expressions attested in the fifteenth century in which 'oreille' is used respectively
as the male and female genitalia: 'faire dresser l'oreille/les oreilles' (to

be aroused, have an erection); 'en recevoir es oreilles' (to have sex [as a woman]). The former expression can be found in a number of debate poems of the fifteenth century. The following passage from the anonymous *Debat de la Damoiselle et de la Bourgeoise* (*The Debate of the Lady and the Woman*) employs the expression to indicate the state of arousal the narrator finds himself in upon waking, having spent the night, it is implied, in solitary sexual activity, inspired by the intense debate he has witnessed in a dream vision:

> Alors comme tout esblouÿ
> Tremblant [me] prins esmerveillier
> Et du debat plus riens n'ouÿ
> Si commamcé à m'esveiller[14]
> **Et à dressier mon oreillier[15]**
> Qui avoit lors beaucop affaire
> Et diz pour une nuyt veiller
> Que je releveroye l'istoire.[16]

> Then in a complete daze/Trembling with amazement/I
> heard nothing further of the debate/but began to get up and
> pricked up my ears/straightened my pillow? (see n. 15) which
> had witnessed a lot of action/And I swore that I would tell
> the story/of my sleepless night.

We come across the same expression in Guillaume Alexis's *Debat de l'omme mondain et du religieulx* (*The Debate of the Worldly Man and the Monk*), in which the Omme mondain enumerates the many delights of earthly existence and loves: 'Amours font drecer les oreilles' (Love makes us prick up our ears).[17] His stern interlocutor, Le religieulx, takes up the challenge and responds with a 'jeu de mots', implicitly suggesting that sexual pleasure is shortlived:

> Se tu as une joyeuseté
> Mondaine, qui te viengne à point,
> Tu auras cent picques de durté:
> Joy mondaine ne dure point (*DOMR*, 61–64).

> For every moment of pleasure/that you experience in this
> world,/You will feel a hundred hard and sharp pricks:/
> Earthly joy doesn't last.

It is surely not difficult to see in the 'cent picques de durté' the sharp pricks felt as the flea penetrates the fe/male body as well as the more obvious phallic analogy. Rabelais is one of the many French authors to employ the euphemisms 'oreille' and 'petit doigt' (little finger) to indicate the female genitalia and the phallus respectively. His *Tiers Livre* literalises the 'puce en l'oreille' metaphor. Panurge pierces his ear and suspends a black flea from a golden hoop: 'J'ay (respondit Panurge) la pusse en l'aureille. Je me veulx marier' (I have, replied Panurge, a flea in my ear: I want to get married).[18] 'Si l'oreille vous demange et vous le grattez de vostre petit doigt, qui a plus de plaisir et de bien?' (If your ear itches and you scratch it with your little finger, which of the two gets the greater pleasure and good?) asks Beroalde de Verville in the satirical *Le Moyen de parvenir* (*The Way to Succeed*) from 1610.[19]

The male protagonists of Alain Chartier's vastly popular *Debat Reveille Matin* (*The Debate of the Morning Wake Up Call*, c. 1423) and of the *Debat de l'omme mondain et du religieulx* attributed to Guillaume Alexis (c.1450) both cite the expression 'avoir puce en l'oreille' to express frustrated desire, and here it refers specifically to male desire. However, the male interlocutors of our poems are cast in a feminised role through their appropriation of the female 'oreille'. Thus not only are women's voices excluded from the debate, but the male interlocutors usurp female subject positions to console one another. Sexual desire is satisfied in intercourse of a different nature, between men. In the first of our quotations, the narrator uses the pronoun 'on' to suggest, I think, not a universal feeling, but one reserved for the 'nous' of this poem: the three male interlocutors and an implied male audience.

> *L'Acteur*
> Apres myenuyt **entre deux sommes,**
> Lors qu'Amours les amans **esveille,**
> En ce paÿs cy où nous sommes,
> Pensoye où lit, **ainsi qu'on vueille**
> **Quant on a la puce en l'oreille;**
> Si escoutay deux amoureux,
> Dont l'un à l'autre se conseille
> Du mal dont il est douloureux.[20]

> After midnight, in fitful sleep,/At the moment when Love wakes up lovers,/Here in this country where we find ourselves,/I was lying awake in my bed, thinking, as one does/When one 'has a flea in one's ear';/I overheard two lovers/One asking the other for advice/About the illness that tormented him.

Similarly, the Omme mondain of Alexis's debate uses the term to refer to male 'amans' (lovers), those ('ceulx') who serve a particular 'demoiselle' (young lady). Unusually here, the Omme mondain plays up the positive side of the flea-induced torment in his attempts to persuade his interlocutor of the pleasures of earthly love. As one might suspect, this is one expression that is very easy for Le religieulx to turn to his advantage:

> *Le mondain*
> Au regard de moy, je ne pense
> Fors à vestir robe nouvelle,
> Me trouver en feste, où l'en dance
> Pour servir quelque damoiselle;
> **Ceulx qui ont la puce en l'oreille**
> N'ont besoing que de joye et rire;
> Car vente, pleuve, gresle ou gelle,
> À cueur joyeulx rien ne peut nuyre (*DOMR*, 81–88).

> Well, me, I don't think much beyond/Buying new clothes/ And going to parties, where you jig about/And dance attention on some girl;/ Those who 'have a flea in their ear'/ Just laugh and enjoy themselves./It can blow a gale, hail or snow,/But nothing can harm a joyful heart.

The male lovers of these poems, and others like them, are assailed by Amours via the *domna* (courtly mistress) who takes on the role of 'puce'; they are feminised through their suffering and, it is implied, their penetration by 'puce'. In later sixteenth- and seventeenth-century literature, as we shall see, the male 'puce' breaks free of the 'oreille' of the expression, so to speak, and roams freely, uninvited, around his mistress's body and the text. Here, 'puce' and his wanderings become a sinister parody of classical man-to-beast metamorphosis and figure the author's (sub)conscious desire to rape his mistress. The literary 'puce' then appears to acquire a certain sexual ambivalence and indeterminacy, enabling it to take on both male and female identities, even as 'oreille' refuses an absolute sexual identity. 'Puce' enters both male and female bodies and leaves them tormented and unsatisfied.[21] In Chartier's debate this unfulfilled desire leads to sleeplessness and engagement in dialogue for both interlocutors; in Alexis's it is sublimated in religion. In both cases, whether cast as 'puce' or 'oreille', male desire and the male voice are foregrounded, in the absence both of the female voice and any indication of female desire.

European writers have long constructed a literary circus around the flea, drawing on such bloodthirsty and obscene avatars as the pseudo-Ovidian transformation poem the *Elegia de pulice* (*Elegy on the flea*), which was influential in the later Middle Ages and enjoyed vast popularity in the sixteenth and seventeenth centuries.[22] The poet-*pulex* of this short elegy leaves little to the imagination as he engages on his carnal assault of the female body, desiring transformation into his 'disagreeable' enemy:

And when you further fix your sharp hidden piercer into her side, the maid is driven to rise out of her deep sleep. And about the lap will you wander; there, to you, ways are open to other members [...] And meanwhile you have dared to broach even the passionate parts, and to taste the pleasures born in those places. May I perish if I do not desire to be immediately transformed into my enemy, so that the means will be open to my desires.[23]

From Nature's speech in the *Roman de la Rose*,[24] Deschamps, Charles d'Orléans, Villon,[25] Bruscambille,[26] Rabelais and Ronsard[27] to Estienne Pasquier and Catherine Des Roches,[28] to Marlowe's *Dr Faustus*[29] or John Donne's metaphysical *carpe diem* poem 'The Flea'[30] and the famous series of seventeenth-century Flea-Hunt paintings,[31] flea-ridden literature is more widespread than even I had anticipated. The ever-changing bug (a flea, fly, louse, bee, or sometimes a mosquito (*culex*)) awakens new passions in its successive literary hosts. This 'colonising parasite' becomes the subject of Ovidian transformation narratives of his own in which he is linked to a classical heritage of lovers who have literally given in to their bestial side (Leda's swan, Europa's bull, and so on). The flea motif in sixteenth- and seventeenth-century literature tends to associate the flea with the male lover, exploring and indeed viciously attacking the body of the helpless female, whom the lover-'puce' hopes to 'depuceler' (deflower): 'I am like to Ovid's flea; I can creep into every corner of a wench.'[32]

Male desire thus appropriates the flea in the early modern period, just as in the fourteenth and fifteenth centuries, in spite of the original semantic association of the expression 'avoir la puce en l'oreille' with female voices of desire, as I suggested. The painters of the subject took pleasure in the metaphor of paintbrush as *pulex*-phallus and, just as the writer's pen or the spectator's gaze, in exploring every corner of the 'wench'. As such, the flea is part of a proud upstanding classical and medieval tradition of literature about 'phallic' animals and pets belonging to or associated with women, such as Catullus' lament for Lesbia's dead sparrow, or Jean Lemaire de Belges' account of his lady's dead parrot in the *Épîtres de l'Amant vert*.[33] As Olson states in his article on Catherine Des Roches' transformations of the flea motif, 'the expression "puce à l'oreille" signifies both the passage of the flea and an irritability and disquiet associated with sexual arousal constructed as a discomfort to be relieved by phallic penetration'.[34] However, there are some rare exceptions, specifically Catherine Des Roches in her contribution to the well-known collaborative poetic collection *La puce de Madame Des Roches* (1583), initiated by Estienne Pasquier. Des Roches operates a reversal of the traditional male-on-female pattern of desire by establishing herself as both 'puce' and 'pucelle' (virgin), emphasising the gendered article 'la puce': 'Puce, quand vous estiez pucelle' (Flea, when you were a virgin). Word play on the substantives 'puce' and 'pucelle' ('puce'/'pucelle'/'pucelage' (virginity)/'depuceler') was frequent in the poetic flea tradition, as can be seen from Estienne Pasquier's challenge to Catherine:

> Tu [puce] la piques [et] elle craint, pour ne rien celer, que c'est la dépuceler, et bannir à jamais d'elle ce cruel nom de pucelle. [...] Pleust or à Dieu que je pusse seulement devenir Puce. [...] Et partant, Puce pucette, je veus, Puce pucelette, petite Puce, je veus adresser vers toy mes veus. [...] C'est que Madame par toy se puisse esveiller pour moy, que pour moy elle **s'esveille** et ayt la Puce en l'oreille.[35]

> You [flea] prick her [and] she is afraid, let's be honest, of your taking her virginity, and forever removing from her the cruel name of virgin. [...] I pray to God: if only I could be a flea. [...] And as I leave, Flea-girl, I want, Flea-maiden, little Flea, I want to address my wishes to you. [...] That my Lady should be aroused by you for me, that she should be **aroused** for me and have 'a flea in her ear'.

Note the use of the verb 'esveiller' here in its double sense, to arouse from sleep and to arouse sexually. The sleeplessness our interlocutors are subject to, frequently described using the verbs 'esveiller' or 'veiller', makes full use of this double meaning, as we observed earlier in the *Debat de la Damoiselle et de la Bourgeoise*.

I now turn again to two significant fifteenth-century debates: Alain Chartier's *Debat Reveille Matin* and Guillaume Alexis's *Debat de l'omme mondain et du religieulx*. These two debates embody notions of male desire and the endless deferral of the longed-for 'consumption' of the beloved that we find so commonly in fifteenth-century French debate poetry. Chartier's *Debat Reveille Matin* was almost as popular as his *La Belle Dame sans mercy* (*The Beautiful Lady who had no mercy*, 1424), with thirty-seven manuscripts recorded by Laidlaw.[36] This great popularity, as evidenced by the manuscript transmission, would no doubt surprise partisans of Hoffmann's 1942 classification of Chartier's work into the 'joyeuses escriptures' (joyful writings) and the serious poems. In his category of 'joyeuses escriptures' Hoffmann classifies both Chartier's *DRM* and his *LBDSM*.[37] Critics are now starting to agree on the Belle Dame's significance as a feminine and patriotic icon of autonomy and freedom, and have begun to look at the *DRM* in connection with the 'Querelle de la *Belle Dame sans mercy*' and the *LBDSM* itself.[38] The two poems, I suggest, are intimately connected, and were certainly often read against one another in the manuscript tradition, as we will also see with Chartier's *DRM* and Guillaume Alexis's *Debat de l'omme mondain*.[39] The *LBDSM* appears in thirty-four manuscripts with the *DRM*, and in fourteen it is copied directly after it, reinforcing the textual play between the poems by locating them together in the material space of play that is the codex.

The *DRM* derives its premise from a proverb recorded by Morawski: 'Ami pour aultre veille' (A friend stays up for another),[40] and seems ultimately to be more concerned with the ethical duty of loyalty to one's friends than with lovers' anecdotes. The narrator of Chartier's *DRM* is lying awake after midnight, 'entre deux sommes' (half-awake), awakened by thoughts of his lady, when he overhears a lover, Amoureux, trying to rouse a sleeper, Dormeur, in the same room: the two interlocutors of the debate. Here we have three 'sleepless knights': the clerkly would-be lover who records the debate, the Amoureux and the hapless Dormeur. The parallel implicit here, of course, is that of the sleepless night of love or love-making, which none of the three men is able to achieve. The male narrator remarks at the close of the *DRM* that he has written down the debate in order to become more friendly with Dormeur and Amoureux: 'Si mis en escript ce qu'ilz dirent/ Pour mieulx estre de leur butin' (I wrote down what they said/In order to be a part of their group, *DRM*, v. 365–66). This use of 'butin' is attested in the literature since at least 1350 as a currency of exchange (spoils), and points to the notion of a Kosofsky-esque traffic in women, but gives it a curious twist.[41] A further *Dictionnaire du Moyen Français* definition of 'butin', 'groupe de soldats constitué pour effectuer des prises de guerre selon une repartition fixée' (a group of soldiers responsible for the proper division of battle spoils), cites this couplet from Chartier's poem as one of its sources.[42] We could also see in 'butin' an indication of the pleasure the author will derive from his writing, both in terms of comfort from love's torments and in the admiration of the implied audience ('Et l'ont nommé ceulx qui ce virent/Le Debat Resveille Matin' (And those who saw it/Called it the *Debate of the Morning Wake Up Call*), v. 367–68).

Here, words are the currency of male exchange, and it is through male words and voices that women are to be won. However, women are never part of the 'butin' in the *Debat Reveille Matin*; what is won and played for by the 'impotent' knights is essentially male companionship and conversation as a substitute for action, love and a woman to keep one awake all night. Here being part of the 'butin' represents a displacement activity engaged in by those too cowardly, impotent or sleepy to go to love or war.

There is, to my mind at least, an eroticised transference that operates here between the longing for a hypothetical absent female and the relationship of the two interlocutors with one another and with the narrator, Kosofsky's notion of the homosocial bond. After all, the primary reason that the narrator and the Dormeur are 'éveillés', with the double sense of being kept up, is not the absence of the female, but the presence of the male. Again we see how female speakers are excluded from this debate, while men express and satisfy their desires via the 'oreille de l'autre':

«Ha Dieu!», dist l'Amoureux, «Beau sire,
Tel voulsist dormir qui sommeille

> Tel ploure qui bien voulsist rire,
> Et tel cuide dormir qui veille.
> Non pour tant Bonne Amour conseille
> Et bien souvent le dit on bien:
> Qu'un bon amy pour l'autre veille,
> Au gré d'aultruy non pas au sien» (*DRM*, v. 33–40).

> 'Indeed!', said the Lover, 'Dear Sir,/He who would rather
> sleep only dozes,/He who would rather laugh only cries,/
> And he lies awake who would rather fall asleep./And
> similarly Good Love advises/And it is often said/That one
> good friend stays up for another,/At another's whim and not
> his own.'

We find the same proverb in Alexis's *Debat de l'omme mondain*, this time deployed by the Omme mondain, who corresponds to Chartier's Amoureux figure in his evocation of the service one owes to one's friends:

> *Le mondain*
> J'ay intencïon d'acquerir
> De grans amis qu'il que le vueille
> Pour më aider et secourir:
> Ung bon amy pour l'autre veille (*DOMR*, v. 229–32).[43]

> I mean to acquire/good friends whatever you say/To help
> me and come to my defence:/One good friend stays up for
> another.

Here, though, Omme mondain's dour interlocutor, Le religieulx, rejects this service as belonging to a world which he has escaped, and which Omme mondain must now relinquish. In refusing to acknowledge the existence of sincere friendship or love in the world ('Il ne se fault fier qu'en Dieu', Put your trust in God alone, v. 240), Le religieulx enforces his role as Omme mondain's superior and his position outside the courtly game of love and the realm of Amours. Alexis's poem is very probably influenced by Chartier's *DRM*; the relationship of Omme mondain and Le religieulx is calqued on that of the Amoureux and Dormeur of Chartier's poem. Alexis's poem intensifies this relationship by removing the narrator figure from the equation so that we are left with a simple dialogue. Omme mondain and Le religieulx dominate the whole poem, each sticking largely to his own arguments: the joys versus the vanities of earthly life and loves, until a rapid and total *volte face* by Omme mondain, who goes from praising the joys of spring to the sudden realisation of his own mortality in the face of Le religieulx's deployment of standard *contemptus mundi* topoi:

> Amy, quand bien digereras
> Qu'il convient une foiz mourir,
> Toutes ses folies oublieras. (*DOMR*, v. 441–43)

> Friend, once you have fully digested/The fact that you only
> die once,/You will abandon all these foolish pursuits.

Like the Amoureux of Chartier's *DRM*, Omme mondain both trusts and
takes his friend's advice:

> Mon amy, ton parler me inspire,
> Et congnois que (tu) dis verité;
> Et desormais ne me vueil reduire:
> Crainte fait changer volonté. (*DOMR*, v. 453–56)

> My friend, your words have set me thinking,/And I
> recognise that you are telling the truth;/And so from now
> on there's no turning back:/Fear can make you change your
> mind.

I suggest that there is a strong thematic and linguistic connection
between the expressions 'un (bon) amy pour l'autre veille' (one [good] friend
stays up for another) and our 'puce en l'oreille', both of which we have seen
deployed in the *DRM* and the *DOMR* (*DRM*, v. 39, *DOMR*, v. 231; *DRM*,
v. 5, *DOMR*, v. 85). Both suggest the wakeful state in which lovers or friends
find themselves, tormented by exhaustion on the one hand and by desire
on the other. A slippage between the two expressions, between friends and
lovers, may lead us to read these friendships between male interlocutors
and narrators or 'amis' as erotically charged. As we have seen, the rhyming
pairs of 'oreille-veille/esveille', 'oreille-resveille' are frequent. Instances of
the expression 'puce en l'oreille' and other expressions connected with
'oreille' tend in the fifteenth century to signal awakening or insomnia of
some kind. This state of extreme wakefulness cannot be divorced from its
erotic context, as I have shown: from a desire for intercourse/consumption
both physical and verbal.

Talking the night away in the *DRM* seems a reasonable substitute for
action, but the suggestion of impotence surely lies not too far beneath the
surface. This sexual or amatory impotence and inability to communicate
with women is certainly linked in Chartier's work to the more specific
impotence and cowardice of the knight or chevalier in time of war.
Impotence in love, speech and war is a set of motifs that links our Amoureux
to the lacklustre Amant of Chartier's *LBDSM*. For the Amoureux and the
Dormeur, just as for the male narrators of the other debates under consideration here, a lady is merely a voiceless pawn in their homosocial exchange.

She is an excuse for male intercourse: an object but not a speaking subject of the debate. This is the 'traffic in women' of which Kosofsky Sedgwick speaks in her seminal work on the topic.[44] Here we see not so much René Girard's schematised erotic triangle but a male narrative triangle from which the female is forcibly excluded and absent: she has no narrative voice in the debate, and no specific identity. The men are all rivals for an illusory love, but, as Girard and Kosofsky Sedgwick would suggest, it is their own bonds that are reinforced by the debate: the elusive dames are symbolic property 'for the primary purpose of cementing the bonds of men with men'.[45]

An interesting parallel occurs here with a similar fifteenth-century amatory debate that stages the conversation between two ladies of the court, the *Debat de la Noire et de la Tannee* (*The Debate of the Black and Brown-dressed Ladies*), who are overheard by an eavesdropping male narrator.[46] We are told that the version of the debate we are reading is that mediated by the narrator's voice, who allegedly copied the ladies' speeches 'telles quelles' (word for word) from his hiding place, and then inserted them into his written version later. The words of the two primary speakers are reinterpreted by the narrator in his account of the debate, thereby calling into question the 'authenticity' of the female voices we are hearing. In spite of the narrator's description of the ladies' excellence as makers of poetry, we observe how he has usurped their authorial role as speakers of their own verse, undermining their position as speaking subjects within the debate. The simultaneous affirmation and undermining of the ladies' poetic talents and voices is figured in the poem by the motif of colour, and particularly by the colour and the flower violet. The narrator's insistence on the colour violet is felt in paratextual aspects of the debate's reception, too, with the ladies' violet trim and lining represented in miniatures from Paris, Rothschild 2798 and Paris, Bibliothèque nationale de France, fr. 25420, as well as the violets which appear in the border of the BnF miniature.[47] As Sylvia Huot argues in her article on the significance of the 'marguerite' or daisy in medieval French literature, the flower 'tends to replace' the lady as a prize for poetry or a love token given to the male poet-protagonist.[48] The emblematic use of the flower (rose, violet or daisy as a metaphor for love or for the love object in courtly literature) displaces the woman and her individual voice.[49] In the case of the *Noire et Tannee* it is the creative hand that displaces the women at the heart of the metaphor, as Jane Taylor has observed in the case of Guillaume de Lorris and Jean de Meun's *Rose*.[50] Rose always and emphatically remains a flower, in the same way that Rose and Violette, the two nominal protagonists of Jean Froissart's 1392 debate, the *Plaidoirie de la Rose et de la Violette* (*The Case of the Rose and the Violet*), remain silent and flowery.[51] De Lorris's and de Meun's Rose and Froissart's Rose and Violette are deprived of speaking subject status in the same way that Noire and Tannee have their 'libre arbitre' as poetic subjects and makers of text stolen from them by the male narrator who turns them into poetic objects in his own composition. My evocation of this debate between women demonstrates the extent to which the female voice is elided in debate poetry of this era. Even in instances where women are 'present' as characters within the text, then, their voices must remain elusive and absent.

Le Debat de l'omme mondain et du religieulx, written around 1450 and attributed to the well-known poet and prior Guillaume Alexis, takes as its theme the *contemptus mundi*. This is a theme it shares with the anonymous *Amant rendu cordelier à l'observance d'Amours* (*The Lover turned Friar through Love*, c. 1440),[52] a debate attached to the 'Querelle de la BDSM' and which *L'Omme mondain* follows closely. Both poems are steeped in the language of play and game—a language that often accompanies reflection on death or the *memento mori* in fifteenth-century poetry.[53]

The narrator of *L'Amant rendu cordelier*, lulled to sleep by the sound of a chambermaid singing, dreams that he is transported by a whirlwind (*ARC*, v. 11–12) to the forest of Desesperance (Despair). Amours, answering his call for help, leads him with the help of a shining arrow to a magnificent Chapelle where he encounters the sorrowing lover and observes the gradual process of the lover's conversion by the austere Damp Prieur (Father Prior/ Prayer, the double of Alexis's Le religieulx). Crucially, we again come across our 'puce en l'oreille', not once but twice. In the first instance Dangier, in the guise of the *pulex* ('puce'), asserts his protection of the 'pucelle's' 'oreille', while roused or aroused by thoughts of his own wanderings in that area:

> *Damp Prieur*
> – Raison est souvent endormie,
> Mais jamais Dangier **ne sommeille**
> **Ne ne dort heure ne demie;**
> **Tousjours a la puce en l'oreille,**
> Il court, il se trouve, il traveille,
> Pour guerroier jeunes et vieux;
> Il est bon mestier **qu'on y veille;**
> On ne demanderoit pas mieux (*ARC*, v. 345–52).

> Reason is often asleep,/But Danger never dozes/Nor sleeps
> even for a minute;/He always has 'a flea in his ear',/He runs
> around, he searches, he keeps going/Until he finds both
> young and old to menace;/You'd be well-advised to watch
> out for him;/You couldn't ask for anything else.

In the second, the passage of the flea is likened to a fever which can be healed only by the attentions and presence of his lady. This is a cure which the speakers of our debates desire, but never obtain, just as the debates themselves must remain inconclusive and open-ended. Desire here always implies the deferral of spoken/written judgement, and thus of verbal satisfaction:

> *Damp Prieur*
> La fievre si grant ne puet estre
> Que, se d'aventure la belle
> S'en vient de nuyt a la fenestre
> Voir le povre gallant, qui **veille**
> **Et qui a la puce en l'oreille,**
> Qu'il ne soit tost sur piés, guery
> D'un brin de girofle vermeille,
> S'elle luy jecte, tant soit marry (*ARC*, v. 729–36).

> Such a great fever doesn't exist/That, if by chance the beloved lady/One night came to the window/To look down on her poor servant, who was awake/With 'a flea in his ear',/He wouldn't get straight back on his feet, cured/By a twig of ripe clove/That she threw him, however tormented he had been.

David Hult suggests that in the first instance the expression is used more in its sense of disquiet, anxiety, and that in the second that it is deployed in an erotic context.[54] I would tend to think that both instances here employ the phrase in specifically erotic contexts.

L'Omme mondain is copied directly after *L'Amant rendu cordelier* in three of the seven extant manuscripts. These three (The Hague, Koninklijke Bibliotheek, 71 E 49, Paris, BnF, fr. 1642 and Vatican, Reg. Lat. 1720) are also attached to the 'Querelle de la *BDSM*'. The texts of *L'Omme mondain* in the Vatican and The Hague manuscripts are very similar, but the preponderance of scribal errors in the Vatican exemplar leads me to hypothesise that the Vatican *L'Omme mondain* is a copy of The Hague.[55] The texts collected in The Hague manuscript reinforce the notion of the dialogue of life and death, or more precisely of love and death. We find, in addition to our flea-ridden *Amant rendu cordelier* and *L'Omme mondain*, an abundance of texts with titles such as 'epitaph', 'miroir' or 'testament', and other didactic works such as Chartier's *Le Breviaire des nobles* (*The Breviary of Nobility*). *La Dance macabre des femmes* (*The Dance of Death of women*) follows *L'Omme mondain* here, and is copied with *La Dance macabre des femmes et des hommes* (*The Dance of Death of women and men*) in two other anthology manuscripts: Paris, BnF, nouv. acq. fr. 10032 and Paris, BnF, fr. 25434. Death in this context figures the ultimate silencing/satisfying of the voices of desire beyond the bounds of the text.

Our 'puce' continues to aggravate a number of different 'oreilles' in the material context of the reception of Chartier's and Alexis's poems with the 'Querelle de la *BDSM*' poems, from the *Amant rendu cordelier*, as we have seen, to the *Confession et Testament de l'amant trespassé de dueil* (*The Confession and Testament of the Lover who Died of Grief*),[56] and the *Inventaire de l'amant*,[57] or the vast printed lyric anthology of 1501, the *Jardin de Plaisance*.[58] Close study of the expression 'avoir la puce en l'oreille' has demonstrated how the ethics of courtly friendship are underwritten by the terms of erotic arousal and desire in late medieval poetry. Desire in our debates is the desire for intercourse—physical and verbal—with the object of desire. The deferred fulfilment of these desires generates text: so text is produced and 'consumed' by our interlocutors as a displacement activity. In many of the debate poems we have studied it is male desire that is ultimately satisfied through verbal intercourse with men in the absence of the female speaker. Where the female is present, her role as speaking subject is often elided by the male, who adopts a feminised position within the text. Gender difference in the 'puce'-'pucelle', poet-pulex dyads supposed by our erotic expression is confused and eroded. So the place of the 'puce' in the text is a gender-neutral space: one haunted by the spectres of textual desire. A slippage of meaning operates here between the erotic and auditory receptive functions of 'oreille', as we have seen. Through the 'oreille' of the text, as though across the permeable spaces of the trellis, we overhear the voice(s) of desire at the heart of the debate: voices perpetually debating an endlessly deferred conclusion in which they would finally be both sated and silenced.

Notes

1: *Anne Marie Lane* How can we Recognise 'Contemporary' Bookbindings of the Fifteenth and Early Sixteenth Centuries?

1   Mirjam M. Foot, *Studies in the History of Bookbinding* (Aldershot, 1993, repr. 1994) p. 1.

2   See further Anne Marie Lane, 'Notes on Libraries and Collections: Toppan Rare Books Library,' *JEBS* 11 (2008) pp. 283–8.

3   German and Dutch books with wooden boards and metal clasps can be seen on Toppan Library books into the nineteenth century. Toppan Library codices from Italy and France commonly appear bound in full vellum throughout the eighteenth century, as well as the more common half-bound form with vellum spine and corner supports with marbled and other paper covers.

4   See Richard J. Wolfe, *Marbled Paper: its History, Techniques, and Patterns, with Special Reference to the Relationship of Marbling to Bookbinding in Europe and the Western World* (Philadelphia PA, 1990); Linda Hohneke, 'Decorated Papers,' *Guild of Book Workers Journal* 37 (2002) pp. 2–13.

5   Three of the Renaissance printers who may have sold some books already bound were Sebastian Gryphius (Lyons), Peter Schoeffer (Mainz) and Thomas Berthelet (London). See Geoffrey Ashall Glaister, *Encyclopedia of the Book* (New Castle DE, 2001, 2nd edn) p. 207 ('Gryphius, Sebastien'); Lotte Hellinga, 'Peter Schoeffer and the Book-Trade in Mainz: Evidence for the Organization' in Dennis E. Rhodes (ed.) *Bookbindings and Other Bibliophily: Essays in Honour of Anthony Hobson* (Verona, 1994) pp. 131–83 (pp. 131–41, 161–64); Douglas C. McMurtrie, *The Book: the Story of Printing and Bookmaking* (New York, 1989) p. 543.

6   Philip Gaskell discusses this type of 'trade binding' in *A New Introduction to Bibliography* (New York and Oxford, 1972) pp. 146–47.

7   See the examples in J.A. Szirmai, *The Archaeology of Medieval Bookbinding* (Aldershot, 1999) p. 277 (n. 9), where he notes that Anton Koberger's editions of the Nuremberg Chronicle listed in his publisher's inventory were mostly unbound after several decades. Another example, from the Zutphen Library,

indicates that a time-lag from nine to forty-five years existed for some of their publications before binding.

8   'Contemporary' in Margaret Haller, *The Book Collector's Fact Book* (New York, 1976) p. 87.

9   'Contemporary' in John Carter, *ABC for Book Collectors* (New Castle DE, 1995, 7th edn) p. 73.

10 'Rebound' in Matt T. Roberts and Don Etherington, 'Bookbinding and the Conservation of Books: a Dictionary of Descriptive Terminology' <http://cool. conservation-us.org/don/toc/toc1.html> [accessed 11 November 2011].

11 'Bookplates' in Glaister, who cites Dürer as designer *c*.1503 for the collector Bilibald Pirckheimer and provides an illustration of a sixteenth-century woodcut bookplate (p. 64).

12 See Szirmai. See, too, Nicolas Pickwood, 'The Interpretation of Bookbinding Structure: an Examination of Sixteenth Century Bindings in the Ramey collection in the Pierpont Morgan Library' in Mirjam M. Foot (ed.) *Eloquent Witnesses: Bookbindings and Their History: a Volume of Essays Dedicated to the Memory of Dr. Phiroze Randeria* (London, 2004) pp. 127–70, 'Onward and Downward: how Binders Coped with the Printing Press before 1800' in Robin Myers (ed.) *A Millennium of the Book: Production, Design, and Illustration in Manuscript and Print, 900–1900* (New Castle DE, 1994) pp. 61–106.

13 Mirjam M. Foot, 'Bookbinding Research: Pitfalls, Possibilities and Needs' in Foot, *Eloquent Witnesses* pp. 13–29 (p. 24).

14 William Thomas, *Principal Rules of the Italian Grammer* (STC 24020, London, 1550), the only one of the eighty-eight books in this study printed in English (by Berthelet); Henry VIII, *Assertio Septem Sacramentorum* (dated 1523 on both title-page and colophon, but without publisher or place of publication—there is no 1523 edition listed in STC).

15 A printed book from Zaragoza; a small Spanish manuscript from San Martin; a large choir book from Burgos; a smaller choir book (exact provenance unknown).

16 Two books printed in Cologne, four in Nuremburg (one by Albrecht Dürer, two by Anton Koberger, his godfather, and the fourth by Johann vom Berg and Ulrich Newber).

17 All six printed in Basel (one by Froben).

18 Of the twelve printed books one was printed in Strasburg, four in Lyons (one by Sebastien Gryphius and three volumes of Plato by his former apprentice Jean de Tournes) and seven in Paris (one by Kerver, one by Simon de Colines, one by his step-son Robert Estienne, one by Josse Bade [Jodocus Badius [Ascensius]], father-in-law of Estienne, and one by Jean Petit, leader of the Parisian booktrade who helped set up Badius, who was formerly of Lyon). The single manuscript is simply catalogued as 'French'.

19 Of the rest, seven were printed in Florence (four by Giunta), two in Rome and one each in Bologna, Naples, Milan and Brescia. The three manuscripts are simply catalogued as 'from Italy.'

20 Florence Edler de Roover, 'New Facets on the Financing and Marketing of Early Printed Books' *Bulletin of the Business Historical Society* (1953) pp. 222–30.

21 Mirjam M. Foot, *The History of Bookbinding as a Mirror of Society* (London, 1998) Plate 2 illustrates 'An English panel-stamped binding by John Reynes, *c*.1520' on a book printed in Venice in 1518.

22 E. Ph. Goldschmidt, *Gothic & Renaissance Bookbindings, Exemplified and Illustrated from the Author's Collection*, 2 vols (Nieuwkoop, 1967) I, 24.

23 It takes a very trained eye to determine a specific geographical provenance (see Goldschmidt).

24 For a close-up photograph that compares the skin textures of sheep, pig and calf, see Szirmai p. 227 (fig. 9.34). For descriptions of skins used in bindings, see the following entries in Roberts and Etherington: 'calfskin', 'goatskin', 'morocco', 'parchment', 'pigskin', 'sheepskin', 'tawing' and 'vellum'; when no other attribution is given, these entries have been used in the discussion below.

25 For pigskin, see Jane Greenfield, *ABC of Bookbinding* (New Castle DE and New York, 1998) pp. 95, 97; for sheepskin, see the 'reddish-brown sheepskin' of a Romanesque binding on a Parisian book from 1150 in Leila Avrin, *Scribes, Script and Books: the Book Arts from Antiquity to the Renaissance* (Chicago IL, 1991) p. 313 (plate 271); for deerskin, see Glaister pp. 131–32; for doeskin (the favourite binding of Thomas Berthelet, the early-sixteenth-century royal binder in England), see Avrin pp. 314 (plate 273, a mid-fifteeenth-century girdle-book from Germany with a doeskin binding) and 319.

26 Glaister attributes the substitution of fibrous boards for wooden ones to Aldus Manutius ('Boards') and dates their use in England from the early sixteenth century ('Pasteboards') (pp. 51, 368). Anthony Hobson, *Humanists and Bookbinders: the Origins and Diffusion of the Humanistic Bookbinding 1459–1559, with a Census of Historiated Plaquette and Medallion Bindings of the Renaissance* (Cambridge, 1989), notes that pasteboards became common in Europe after 1470, having orginated in Bologna, Milan and Padua in the mid-fifteenth century; the first Western gilt-tooled binding on pasteboards was on a 1471 Paduan book. Hobson also details the earlier history, noting the dominance of pasteboards in Islamic books from very early medieval times, when only occasionally used in Europe (Appendix 1, 'The Use of Pasteboard in Binding' pp. 252–54).

27 Pigskin was used extensively in Germany from *c*.1550 to *c*.1640, usually on books with wooden boards. The Toppan Library has such a book, with its typical clasps and rolled-tool decoration, but printed in Leipzig at the late date of 1756.

28 Roberts and Etherington ('limp binding') note that limp vellum was used for blank books as early as the fourteenth century, that it was produced in large numbers in the sixteenth and seventeenth centuries, and that it then declined until revived by the private presses of the late nineteenth century.

29 Szirmai (p. 225) refers to 'reversed wool sheep of the whittawed or oil-tanned variety' imitating and replacing chamois; one or both of these books might be 'reversed sheepskin' but it is too difficult to tell.

30 Morocco, the best-known goatskin, was imported into and produced by the Moors in Spain at least as early as the eleventh century but was not used in the rest of Europe until the mid- to late-fifteenth century in Italy, and was not common in Northern Europe until the sixteenth century.

31 Glaister ('Pasteboards') notes that some boards were made of pulped paper shavings; although known as pasteboards, pulpboard is a more accurate term (p. 368). Greenfield ('Pulpboard') describes it as a paper product pulp used instead of sheets of paper pasted together as with pasteboard (p. 55).

32 See Eike Barbara Durrfeld, 'Toward a Historiography of Book Fastenings and Book Furniture,' in Ezra Greenspan and Jonathan Rose (eds) *Book History* (University Park PA, 2000) pp. 305–13. Durrfeld uses the term 'furniture' to refer to all the elements put on the books to protect them: bosses, edge guards,

corner pieces and centre pieces, as does *Binding Terms: a Thesaurus for Use in Rare Book and Special Collections Cataloging* (Chicago IL, 1988), published by the Association of College and Research Libraries (ACRL) and compiled by the Standards Committee of the Rare Books and Manuscripts Section, p. 11 (but with no separate entries for 'fastenings', 'furnishings' or 'fittings').

33 Avrin p. 312.

34 '[T]he heyday of the recycling of leaves and other fragments of older books occurred in the sixteenth century', Michael Olmert, *The Smithsonian Book of Books* (Washington DC, 1992) p. 289. Olmert (p. 288) illustrates a Renaissance choir-book manuscript used as a complete cover for a 1481 book.

35 Printed by Johann vom Berg and Ulrich Newber (see Note 17 above).

36 Roberts and Etherington ('rolls') note that these tools (in both intaglio and relief) were first used in Germany *c*.1460 and were common by the second decade of the sixteenth century. The average length of the run was five to six inches.

37 Roberts and Etherington ('panel-stamp') note that they were used in Antwerp in the thirteenth century, throughout the Netherlands in the fourteenth century, in Cologne before 1460, in Paris before 1500 and in England *c*.1480–90. After 1550 they were used only in Germany and the Netherlands.

38 Roberts and Etherington ('bookbinding') note that gold tooling was used by Islamic binders by the thirteenth century; its use *c*.1470 in northern Italy, probably Venice (with influence of Near Eastern designs and delicacy of workmanship), influenced the rest of Europe (especially France) by the mid-sixteenth century. The earliest use in England was in 1519 but it was not common until 1530, when introduced by Thomas Berthelet (Avrin p. 319).

39 See Note 18.

40 In reference to future research, Mirjam M. Foot has stated that 'more work should be devoted to the simple, plain, run-of-the-mill trade bindings that have so far managed to escape both the restorer's knife and the attention of most historians' ('Bookbinding Research' p. 27).

41 <http://www.bl.uk/catalogues/bookbindings/> [accessed 11 November 2011].

42 For example, Durrfeld (p. 310) illustrates three books in a Dutch painted portrait from 1519; *Incunabula from the Court Library at Donaueschingen*, Sotheby's (London, 1994) illustrates two books with bosses on them from a 1497 book (p. 35).

43 'Repairing and restoration' in Carter p. 182.

2: *Matti Peikola* Guidelines for Consumption: Scribal Ruling Patterns and Designing the *Mise-en page* in Later Medieval England

1 I wish to acknowledge the support of the Academy of Finland for this essay (decision numbers 130638, 136404, 141022).

2 Albert Derolez, *Codicologie des manuscrits en écriture humanistique sur parchemin* (Turnhout, 1984), and *The Palaeography of Gothic Manuscript Books: From the Twelfth to the Early Sixteenth Century* (Cambridge, 2003) pp. 34–39; Léon Gilissen, 'Un élément codicologique trop peu exploité: la réglure' *Scriptorium* 23 (1969) pp. 150–62; Denis Muzerelle, 'Pour décrire les schémas de réglure: Une méthode de notation symbolique applicable aux manuscrits latins (et autres)' *Quinio* 1 (1999) pp. 123–70. Important for the methodology of studying ruling patterns, see also James Douglas Farquhar, 'The Manuscript as a Book' in Sandra Hindman and James Douglas Farquhar,

Pen to Press: Illustrated Manuscripts and Printed Books in the First Century of Printing (College Park and Baltimore MD, 1977) pp. 11–99 (pp. 41–54).

3 Derolez, *Palaeography* p. 37.

4 *The Digital Scriptorium* <http://www.scriptorium.columbia.edu/> [accessed 14 March 2010]; *Rylands Medieval Collection* <http://www.library.manchester.ac. uk/eresources/imagecollections/university/medieval/> [accessed 14 March 2010]

5 Muzerelle; see also Matti Peikola, 'Aspects of *mise-en-page* in Manuscripts of the *Wycliffite Bible*' in Graham D. Caie and Denis Renevey (eds) *Medieval Texts in Context* (London, 2008) pp. 28–67 (p. 64). The coding system provides an accurate method for recording information on ruling patterns in Western manuscripts of the Gothic period and for referring to them unambiguously.

6 For these terms applied to ruling, see Farquhar p. 53.

7 See further Derolez, *Palaeography* pp. 37–39; M.B. Parkes, 'Layout and Presen-tation of the Text' in Nigel Morgan and Rodney M. Thomson (eds) *The Cambridge History of the Book in Britain II: 1100–1400* (Cambridge, 2008) pp. 55–74; Rodney M. Thomson, Nigel Morgan, Michael Gullick and Nicholas Hadgraft, 'Technology of Production of the Manuscript Book' in Morgan and Thomson (eds) pp. 75–109 (p. 80); Raymond Clemens and Timothy Graham, *Introduction to Manuscript Studies* (Ithaca NY, 2007) p. 16.

8 For aesthetic aspects of ruling and layout, see Derolez, *Paleography* pp. 37–38; Albert Derolez, 'Observations on the Aesthetics of the Gothic Manuscript' *Scriptorium* 50 (1996) pp. 3–12; Thomson *et al.* p. 80.

9 See, for example, Manchester, JRUL, MS English 87, f. 29^v.

10 The remuneration of medieval scribes is discussed, for example, by John Scattergood, *Manuscripts and Ghosts: Essays on the Transmission of Medieval and Early Renaissance Literature* (Dublin, 2006) pp. 67–68. Scattergood's examples include the scribe William Ebesham charging for his copying of texts for the 'Grete Boke' of Sir John Paston (London, BL, MS Lansdowne 285) and the account of the anonymous scribe of a manuscript of English poems of Charles of Orleans (London, BL, MS Harley 682). Ebesham charged for the number of leaves and quires he had copied, whereas the scribe of MS Harley 682 calculated the payment on the basis of the number of lines. See also M.B. Parkes, *Their Hands Before Our Eyes: A Closer Look at Scribes* (Aldershot, 2008) pp. 48–49; Joanne Filippone Overty, 'The Cost of Doing Scribal Business: Prices of Manuscript Books in England, 1300–1483' *Book History* 11 (2008) pp. 1–32.

11 For a list of standard production features in early manuscripts of the *Confessio*, see Derek Pearsall, 'The Manuscripts and Illustrations of Gower's Works' in Siân Echard (ed.) *A Companion to Gower* (Cambridge, 2004) pp. 73–97 (p. 80).

12 Derek Pearsall, 'The Organisation of the Latin Apparatus in Gower's *Confessio Amantis*: The Scribes and Their Problems', in Takami Matsuda, Richard A. Linenthal and John Scahill (eds) *The Medieval Book and the Modern Collector: Essays in Honour of Toshiyuki Takamiya* (Cambridge and Tokyo, 2004) pp. 99–112.

13 Later manuscripts of the *Confessio* with a simplified ruling pattern include Oxford, Bodleian Library, MSS Bodley 294, Laud misc. 609, Lyell 31; Glasgow University Library, MS Hunter 7; New York, The Morgan Library & Museum, MS M.126.

14 Glossed manuscripts of the Wycliffite Bible ruled with patterns using double vertical bounding lines and single vertical lines in either or both margins include CUL, MS Mm.2.15 (*c.*1410–1420) (for a description of the manuscript

see Mary Dove, *The First English Bible: The Text and Context of the Wycliffite Versions* (Cambridge, 2007) pp. 241–42); London, BL, MS Cotton Claudius E.II (*c.*1410, Dove pp. 245–46); London, BL, MS Harley 5017 and MS Royal 1.C.ix (both *c.*1400–1410, originally two volumes of a single three-volume Bible, Dove pp. 248–50); London, BL, MS Lansdowne 454 (*c.*1420, Dove p. 292); Oxford, Lincoln College, MS Latin 119 (*c.*1410, Dove pp. 262–63). The same features occur in at least two copies of the Wycliffite *Glossed Gospels*: London, BL, MS Additional 41175 and Oxford, Bodleian Library, MS Bodley 243. See also Peikola, 'Aspects' pp. 42–43. For types of glosses in manuscripts of the Wycliffite Bible and their scribal treatment, see Dove pp. 152–72.

15 For features of ruling in manuscripts of the Wycliffite Bible, see Peikola, 'Aspects' pp. 36–44. The study was based on a smaller sample of the manuscripts than the present one.

16 Fifty-six surviving manuscripts of the *Pore Caitif* are listed by Valerie M. Lagorio and Michael G. Sargent, 'English Mystical Writings' in *A Manual of the Writings in Middle English*: IX (New Haven CT, 1993) pp. 3049–137, 3405–71 (p. 3470). Two of these are post-medieval transcriptions. An addition to the list (Durham University Library, MS Additional 754) is reported by Ralph Hanna III, *IMEP Handlist XII: Manuscripts in Smaller Bodleian Collections* (Cambridge, 1997) p. 9. A list of the fourteen constituent tracts of the *Pore Caitif* is provided, for example, by Sister M. Teresa Brady, 'Lollard Interpolations and Omissions in Manuscripts of *The Pore Caitif*' in Michael G. Sargent (ed.) *De Cella in Seculum: Religious and Secular Life and Devotion in Late Medieval England* (Cambridge, 1989) pp. 183–203 (p. 185).

17 *A1*: CUL, MSS Ff.5.45, Ff.6.34, Ff.6.55, Ii.6.40; Cambridge, Trinity College, MS B.14.53; Cambridge MA, Harvard University, Houghton Library, MS Eng 701; London, BL, MSS Additional 30897, Harley 953, Harley 1197, Harley 2322; London, Lambeth Palace, MSS 484, 541; Oxford, Bodleian Library, MSS Additional B.66, Bodley 3, Bodley 423 (Section B), Lyell 29, Rawlinson c. 209, Rawlinson c. 882. *A2*: London, BL, MS Harley 1706 (Section 1); Oxford, Bodleian Library, MS Ashmole 1286. *B1*: London, BL, MS Harley 2335; New York Public Library, MS MA 068. *C1*: CUL, MS Hh.1.12; London, BL, MS Stowe 38; Manchester, JRUL, MS English 412; Oxford, Bodleian Library, MSS Rawlinson c. 699, Douce 288, Douce 322. *D1*: Oxford, Bodleian Library, MS Lyell 29.

18 Jeremy J. Smith, 'Dialect and Standardisation in the Waseda Manuscript of Nicholas Love's *Mirror of the Blessed Life of Jesus Christ*' in Shoichi Oguro, Richard Beadle and Michael G. Sargent (eds) *Nicholas Love at Waseda: Proceedings of the International Conference 20–22 July 1995* (Cambridge, 1997) pp. 129–41. See also Peikola, 'Aspects' p. 51.

19 Cf. Derolez, 'Observations' p. 6, who points out that in the fifteenth century '[c]omplicated ruling patterns ... are replaced by less elaborate, simple and standardized types, which generally have only single or double horizontal through-lines at the top and at the bottom of the writing area'.

20 For the incipient standardisation of the written language in the Wycliffite Bible, including earlier scholarship on this topic, see Matti Peikola, 'The Wycliffite Bible and "Central Midland Standard": Assessing the Manuscript Evidence' *Nordic Journal of English Studies* 2 (2003) pp. 29–51. For the standardisation of layout in the Wycliffite Bible, see the discussion and further references in Peikola, 'Aspects' pp. 31, 51. Standardised aspects of production in the *Pore Caitif* are discussed by Vincent Gillespie, 'Vernacular Books of Religion' in

Jeremy Griffiths and Derek Pearsall (eds) *Book Production and Publishing in Britain, 1375–1475* (Cambridge, 1989) pp. 317–44 (p. 332); Kalpen Trivedi, 'The *Pore Caitif*: Lectio through Compilatio. Some Manuscript Contexts' *Mediaevalia* 21 (2001) pp. 129–52.

21 Gillespie p. 332; for examples of such manuscripts, including MS Lyell 29, see Gillespie p. 343.

22 For the presence of two hands in MS Lyell 29, see Hanna, *IMEP* p. 18. The ruling pattern on ff. 67^v–69^v is 1-1/0/1-0/(J). Prickings in the margins suggest that the first scribe ruled the text lines as well in addition to the bounding lines but erased them after copying the text. Unlike the bounding lines, which are ruled in ink, the text lines are likely to have been ruled in lead or crayon.

23 1-1/0/2-0/J.

24 Cambridge, Trinity College, MS B.10.7; London, BL, MSS Harley 272, Harley 1212, Lansdowne 455, Royal 1.A.x; London, Lambeth Palace, MSS 532, 1150–51; Manchester, JRUL, MSS English 77, English 78; New York, American Bible Society, MS B.3.66; New York, The Morgan Library & Museum, MS M.362; New York Public Library, MSS MA 065, MA 066; Oxford, Bodleian Library, MSS Bodley 665, Bodley 979, Douce 265, Laud misc. 388, Lyell 26, Rawlinson c. 237–238; Philadelphia, Pennsylvania University, MS Codex 201; Berkeley, University of California, MS 13.

25 For an example of how the demand to write more densely makes a scribe change his ruling method see Rolf H. Bremmer Jr., 'Footprints of Monastic Instruction: A Latin Psalter with Interverbal Old Frisian Glosses' in Sarah Larratt Keefer and Rolf H. Bremmer Jr. (eds) *Signs on the Edge: Space, Text and Margin in Medieval Manuscripts* (Paris, 2007) pp. 203–33 (p. 215). Constraints of the copying space for scribes are discussed by Matti Peikola, 'Copying Space, Length of Entries, and Textual Transmission in Middle English Tables of Lessons' in Jacob Thaisen and Hanna Rutkowska (eds) *Scribes, Printers, and the Accidentals of Their Texts* (Frankfurt am Main, 2011) pp. 107–24.

26 For the use of borders and border elements in the later medieval period in English and Continental manuscripts see respectively Kathleen L. Scott, *Dated & Datable English Manuscript Borders c.1395–1499* (London, 2002) pp. 7–16 and Farquhar pp. 72–77.

27 See Peikola, 'Aspects' pp. 36–37.

28 The average for the *Pore Caitif* is based on sixteen of the twenty manuscripts ruled in Type A for which the measurement of the writing area was available to me.

29 Single-column manuscripts of the *Mirror* in which the width of the writing area exceeds 120 mm include Cambridge, Trinity College, MS B.2.18, MS B.15.32; CUL, MS Ll.iv.3; Oxford, Bodleian Library, MS e Musaeo 35; San Marino CA, Huntington Library, MSS HM 149, HM 1339; New Haven CT, Beinecke Rare Book & Manuscript Library, MS 535.

30 Oxford, Bodleian Library, MS Bodley 634.

31 See Parkes, 'Layout' p. 55 and the earlier studies by N.R. Ker cited there.

32 Cf. the twelfth-century example discussed by N.R. Ker, *Books, Collectors, and Libraries: Studies in the Medieval Heritage* (London, 1985) p. 85, where a professional scribe's motive to copy a single-column exemplar of a biblical commentary in double columns seems to have been his perception of the single-column layout as 'old fashioned'.

33 Trivedi p. 133.

34 Parkes, 'Layout' p. 55. See also Farquhar pp. 45–46.

35 For the layout of Latin Bibles, see e.g. Parkes, 'Layout' p. 55; Christopher de Hamel, *The Book: A History of the Bible* (London, 2001) pp. 114–19.

36 The size of the Breviary is characterised as follows by Christopher de Hamel, *A History of Illuminated Manuscripts* (London, 1994, 2nd edn) pp. 213–14: 'In medieval England a Breviary was generally called a "portiforium", a book which a priest carried outdoors ("portat foras"), the term reflecting its convenience of size'. Double-column Breviaries of English origin for which images are available through *The Digital Scriptorium* include Austin, University of Texas, Harry Ransom Humanities Research Center, MS HRC leaf A35 (s. xv); Columbia, University of Missouri, Ellis Library, MSS Fragmenta Manuscripta 106 (s. xiii/xiv), Fragmenta Manuscripta 165 (s. xv^{in}, ruled in Type A2 in ink), Fragmenta Manuscripta 169 (s. xv^1, A2, ink), Fragmenta Manuscripta 170 (s. xv^1, A2, ink), Fragmenta Manuscripta 171 (s. xiv/xv, A2, ink); New York, Columbia University, Rare Book and Manuscript Library MS Med/Ren Frag. 052 (s. xiv); San Marino CA, Huntington Library, MS HM 57341 (s. xiv/xv). De Hamel, *The Book* p. 180, notes the resemblance between the type of script used in Wycliffite Bible manuscripts and Breviaries/Books of Hours.

37 See Matti Peikola, '"First is writen a clause of the bigynnynge therof …": The Table of Lections in Manuscripts of the Wycliffite Bible' *Boletín Millares Carlo* 24–25 (2005–2006) pp. 343–78; Dove pp. 58–67; Matti Peikola, 'The Sanctorale, Thomas of Woodstock's English Bible, and the Orthodox Appropriation of Wycliffite Tables of Lessons' in Mishtooni Bose and J. Patrick Hornbeck II (eds) *Wycliffite Controversies* (Turnhout, 2011) pp. 153–74.

38 Derolez, *Palaeography* p. 37. See also Derolez, 'Observations' p. 5, where liturgical manuscripts are mentioned as an exception to the general trend.

39 Of the forty-one manuscripts, twenty-four are written in Textualis; two manuscripts contain both Textualis and cursive hands.

40 Michael G. Sargent (ed.) *Nicholas Love: The Mirror of the Blessed Life of Jesus Christ: A Reading Text* (Exeter, 2004) pp. xxxiii–xxxiv lists sixty-one extant manuscript copies for the text, including several fragments. My ruling data are based on thirty-four copies; among this sample, twenty-four manuscripts are ruled in single-column patterns.

41 For the anti-Wycliffite use of the *Mirror*, see, for example, Sargent pp. xv–xxi.

42 N.R. Ker and A.J. Piper, *Medieval Manuscripts in British Libraries*, 5 vols (Oxford, 1969–2002).

43 The exceptions comprise Ker and Piper I, 425 (*Scale of Perfection*, s. xv^1); III, 413–14 (*Prick of Conscience*, s. xiv/xv), 415–16 (Nicholas Love's *Mirror*, s. xv med.), 416 (Nicholas Love's *Mirror*, s. xv med.). Single-column manuscripts of Middle English catechetical/devotional texts include Ker and Piper I, 46 (*Handlyng Synne*, s. xv in.), 289 (*Prick of Conscience* etc., s. xiv/xv), 290–91 (*Pilgrimage of Human Life*, s. xv med.), 418 (extracts from *Scale of Perfection*, s. xvi in.), 422–24 (theological treatises in English, s. xv^1); II, 11–12 (*Mirror of Our Lady*, s. xv ex.), 416 (*Prick of Conscience*, s. xiv/xv), 925 (Nicholas Love's *Mirror* etc., s. xv med.); III, 17 (Nicholas Love's *Mirror*, s. xv^1), 67 (*Prick of Conscience* etc., s. xiv/xv), 67–70 (*Prick of Conscience* etc., s. xv^1), 116 (*Prick of Conscience* etc., s. xv in.), 124–25 (*Dives and Pauper*, s. xv^2), 125 (*Prick of Conscience*, s. xiv^2), 309–10 (*Chastising of God's Children* etc., s. xv^2), 330–31 (*Fervor amoris* etc., s. xv^1), 343–44 (Nicholas Love's *Mirror* etc., s. xv med.), 402–03 (*Prick of Conscience* etc., s. xv in.), 426 (Nicholas Love's *Mirror*, s. xv

in.), 521–22 (theological treatises, s. xv med.), 523–24 ('A pistle of sent Jerom' etc., s. xv[1]); IV, 138 (*Cloud of Unknowing* etc., s. xvi in.), 166 (*Oon of Foure*, s. xv in.), 237–39 (catechetical texts, s. xv med.), 403 (*Scale of Perfection*, s. xvi[1]), 422–23 (*Life of St Katherine* etc., s. xv med.), 637–39 (Richard Rolle etc., s. xv med.), 740–41 (catechetical texts, s. xv med.).

44 Scribal practices of adapting texts into compilations are discussed, for example, by Elizabeth Dutton, 'Textual Disunities and Ambiguities of *mise-en-page* in the Manuscripts Containing *Book to a Mother*' *JEBS* 6 (2003) pp. 149–59.

45 The development of the table of contents in Middle English religious miscellanea is discussed by Gillespie pp. 328–31. For the paratextual function of tables of contents in medieval manuscripts (as a type of calendar), see Matti Peikola, 'Instructional Aspects of the Calendar in Later Medieval England, with Special Reference to the John Rylands University Library MS English 80' in Matti Peikola, Janne Skaffari and Sanna-Kaisa Tanskanen (eds) *Instructional Writing in English: Studies in Honour of Risto Hiltunen* (Amsterdam, 2009) pp. 83–104 (pp. 85–87).

46 For MS Douce 322 see A.I. Doyle, 'Books Connected with the Vere Family and Barking Abbey' *Transactions of the Essex Archaeological Society* 25 (1958) pp. 222–43; Gillespie p. 330; Ralph Hanna, 'Middle English Books and Middle English Literary History' *Modern Philology* 102 (2004) pp. 157–78 (pp. 176–78); Margaret Connolly, 'Mapping Manuscripts and Readers of *Contemplations of the Dread and Love of God*' in Margaret Connolly and Linne R. Mooney (eds) *Design and Distribution of Late Medieval Manuscripts in England* (York, 2008) pp. 261–78 (p. 268).

47 For MS Trinity R.3.21, see, for example, Kathleen L. Scott, *Later Gothic Manuscripts 1390–1490* (London, 1996) I, 465–66 (images), II, 337–39 (description); Connolly pp. 268–69.

48 The inscription recording its donation to Dartford has been printed by Laureen Braswell, *IMEP Handlist IV: A Handlist of Douce Manuscripts containing Middle English Prose in the Bodleian Library, Oxford* (Cambridge, 1987) p. 84.

49 Doyle, 'Books'; Gillespie p. 330.

50 For a detailed description of the manuscript, with a focus on Sections B and C, see John Ayto and Alexandra Barratt (eds) *Aelred of Rievaulx's De Institutione Inclusarum* (London, 1984) pp. xix–xxvi. Nicole R. Rice, 'Profitable Devotions: Bodley 423, Guildhall MS 7114, and a Sixteenth-Century London Pewterer' *JEBS* 10 (2007) pp. 175–83 discusses the thematic contents of the two Sections vis-à-vis the owners of the manuscript in the early sixteenth century.

51 For Dodesham's *oeuvre*, see A.I. Doyle, 'Stephen Dodesham of Witham and Sheen' in P.R. Robinson and Rivkah Zim (eds) *Of the Making of Books: Medieval Manuscripts, Their Scribes and Readers. Essays Presented to M.B. Parkes* (Aldershot, 1997) pp. 94–115.

52 Ayto and Barratt pp. xxi–xxvi.

53 Ayto and Barratt pp. xxii–xxiv.

54 Doyle, 'Stephen Dodesham'.

55 I have not personally inspected MSS Hunter 77, 258 and 259; detailed descriptions of these manuscripts, including their ruling technique, are available online through the University of Glasgow Special Collections website at <http://special. lib.gla.ac.uk/manuscripts/> [accessed 14 March 2010]. Now separate, MSS Hunter 258 and 259 were originally parts of the same codex (Doyle, 'Stephen Dodesham' p. 103). For ruling techniques used in medieval manuscripts, see, for

example, Derolez, *Palaeography* pp. 34–35; Barbara A. Shailor, *The Medieval Book* (Toronto, 1991) pp. 13–18; Clemens and Graham pp. 16–17.

56 Ayto and Barratt p. xx.

57 For details of the change in decoration, see Ayto and Barratt pp. xix–xx.

58 Ayto and Barratt p. xx.

59 Peikola, 'Aspects' p. 44.

60 The five patterns are 1. 1-1-11/0/3-3-3/JJ: Manchester, Chetham's Library, MS Mun.A.2.160; Manchester, JRUL, MS English 79; Princeton University, MS Scheide 13 (pattern b); 2. 1-1-11/0/2-2-2/JJ: York Minster, MS XVI.O.1; Orlando FL, Van Kampen MS 639; 3. 1-1/0-0/2-2-2/J: Cambridge, St John's College, MS E.18 (pattern a); 4. 1-1-11/0/2-3-2/JJ: London, BL, MS Egerton 1171; 5. 1-1-11/0/1-3-1/JJ; Princeton University, MS Scheide 13 (pattern a). I have not as yet had the chance to analyse in detail the scribal hands and decoration of these manuscripts, so the question of possibly shared production networks between some of them must remain open for the time being.

61 Examples of Bibles ruled with a double or triple horizontal line in the middle of the page include London, BL, MS Royal 1.B.x (s. xiii); New Haven CT, Beinecke Rare Book & Manuscript Library, MSS 81 (s. xiii^2), 82 (s. xiii med.), 83 (s. xiv in.), 455 (ca 1250), 604 (s. xiii$^{2/4}$); New York, Columbia University, Rare Book and Manuscript Library, Western MS 85 (s. xiii$^{2/4}$); Oxford, Bodleian Library, MS Auct D.3.6. (s. xiv in.); San Marino CA, Huntington Library, MS HM 1073 (s. xiii^2). For biblical commentaries ruled in this way, see, for example, London and Oslo, The Schøyen Collection, MS 258 (Peter Lombard's *Great Gloss* on the Psalms, ca 1200) (see de Hamel, *The Book* pp. 114–15); New Haven CT, Beinecke Rare Book & Manuscript Library, MSS 322 (Jerome, Rabanus Maurus, etc, s. xiii$^{3/4}$, pattern a) and Marston 216 (Nicolaus de Torriaco, s. xiii$^{2/4}$), and the following manuscripts from Paris, Bibliothèque de l'Arsenal illustrated in Muzerelle, 'Pour décrire': Figures 18 (MS 170, Origenes: *Homiliae in Testamentum Vetus*, s. xii), 25 (MS 15, *Concordantiae Bibliorum sacrorum*, s. xiii), 32 (MS 139, *Biblia sacra ... cum glossa*, s. xiii), 33 (MS 147, *Epistolae Pauli apostoli cum glossa*, s. xiii), 34 (MS 180, *Evangelia Lucae et Ioannis cum glossa*, s. xiii). The element also occurs in the Latin gospel harmony of Clement of Llanthony (*Unum ex quattuor*) in London, BL, MS Royal 3.A.x (s. xiii).

62 Psalters ruled with this element include Cambridge MA, Harvard University, Houghton Library, MS Typ 0311 (France s. xiii$^{2/4}$); New Haven CT, Beinecke Rare Book & Manuscript Library, MSS 220 (England, s. xiv in., pattern a), 417 (East Anglia, ca 1325).

63 Derolez, *Palaeography* p. 38.

64 Matthew 16, for example, begins in the following way: 'Et accesserunt ad eum pharisei & saducei. temptantes eum ¶ And þe farisees & þe saducees ...' (Manchester, Chetham's Library, MS Mun.A.2.160, f. 30^v). The whole manuscript is digitally available in the *Rylands Medieval Collection*.

3: *Kate Maxwell* The Order of the Lays in the 'Odd' Machaut Manuscript BnF, fr. 9221 (E)

1 Lay 14 (E11). All citations from Machaut's lays are taken from the forthcoming digital edition 'Je chante ung chant: An Archive of Late-Medieval French Lyrics' <http://www.jechante.ex.ac.uk/archive/> [accessed 15 November 2011], which forms part of the AHRC-funded project 'Citation and Allusion in the

Ars Nova French Chanson and Motet: Memory, Tradition, and Innovation' led by Yolanda Plumley at the University of Exeter. Machaut's lays are edited by Benjamin Albritton, and his editions of these works will soon be incorporated on the existing digital repository of lyrics. I thank Dr Albritton for generously sharing these texts with me in advance of publication. The lay numbers correspond to the numeration in that edition, with the number in brackets referring to their position in E's music section. Unless otherwise stated, all translations are my own, although considerable thanks are owed to Dr Peter Davies for his invaluable assistance.

2   Citation and translation from Benjamin L. Albritton, 'Citation and Allusion in the Lays of Guillaume de Machaut' (unpublished doctoral thesis, University of Washington, 2009) pp. 1–2. Thanks are due once again to Dr Albritton, who shared his dissertation with me.

3   David Fallows, 'Lai' in *Grove Music Online* [accessed via *Oxford Music Online* 14 July 2011] <http://www.oxfordmusiconline.com/subscriber/article/grove/music/15841>.

4   For the most comprehensive treatment of the history of the lay with relation to Guillaume de Machaut, see Armand Machabey, *Guillaume de Machault 130?–1377: La Vie et l'Oeuvre Musical*, 2 vols (Paris, 1955) I, 98–130.

5   Paul Imbs (ed.) *Le Livre du Voir Dit* (Paris, 1999) lettre 22 (de la dame).

6   For a recent book-length study which considers Machaut's oeuvre with music at the centre, see Elizabeth Eva Leach, *Guillaume de Machaut: Secretary, Poet, Musician* (Ithaca NY and London, 2011).

7   There are six extant single-author manuscripts which appear to contain all Machaut's musical and poetical works available to their compilers (here listed with sigla): Paris, Bibliothèque nationale de France, fr. 1586 (C, *c*.1350); private collection of E.J. and J.E. Ferrel, currently housed in Cambridge, Parker Library, without shelfmark (Vg, *c*.1370); Paris, BnF, fr. 1585 (B, *c*.1370); Paris, BnF, fr. 1584 (A, *c*.1370); Paris, BnF, fr. 9221 (E, *c*.1390); Paris, BnF, fr. 22545–6 (F–G, *c*.1390: a single manuscript currently bound in two volumes). A further manuscript, which may well have also once been of this design, will not be considered in this discussion owing to its fragmentary nature: Aberystwyth, National Library of Wales, 5010 C (W, *c*.1355). All the above mentioned manuscripts owned by the BnF have been digitised and can be viewed through Gallica <www.gallica.bnf.fr>; the Ferrel-Voguë codex (Vg) can be viewed through the Digital Image Archive of Medieval Music <http://www.diamm.ac.uk/index.html> [all accessed 4 March 2013]. For more information and evidence of dates of compilation see François Avril, *Manuscript Painting at the Court of France* trans. Ursule Molinaro and Bruce Benderson (London, 1978) pp. 26–27 and 'Les Manuscrits enluminés de Guillaume de Machaut: essai de chronologie' in *Guillaume de Machaut: Colloque—Table Ronde Organisé par l'Université de Reims Reims, 19–22 Avril 1978* (Paris, 1982) pp. 117–33. Avril's studies form the basis of the seminal work and starting-point for Machaut studies: Lawrence Earp, *Guillaume de Machaut: A Guide to Research* (New York and London, 1995).

8   There is not space here to delve deeply into the question of Machaut's 'supervision' (or not) of these codices, since it is a question which continues to be debated in modern scholarship: see in particular Leach; Margaret Bent, 'Some Criteria for Establishing Relationships Between Sources of Late-Medieval Polyphony' in Iain Fenlon (ed.) *Music in Medieval and Early Modern Europe:*

Patronage, Sources and Texts (Cambridge, 1981) pp. 295–317, 'The Machaut Manuscripts Vg, B, and E' *Musica Disciplina* 37 (1983) pp. 53–82; Lawrence Earp, 'Scribal Practice, Manuscript Production and the Transmission of Music in Late Medieval France: The Manuscripts of Guillaume de Machaut' (unpublished doctoral thesis, Princeton University, 1983), 'Machaut's Role in the Production of Manuscripts of his Works' *Journal of the American Musicological Society* 42 (1989) pp. 461–503, *Guillaume de Machaut: A Guide to Research*; Elizabeth A. Keitel, 'The Musical Manuscripts of Guillaume de Machaut', *Early Music* 5 (1977) pp. 469–72; Domenic Leo, 'Authorial Presence in the Illuminated Machaut Manuscripts' (unpublished doctoral thesis, New York University Institute of Fine Arts, 2005); Kate Maxwell, 'Guillaume de Machaut and the *mise en page* of Medieval French Sung Verse' (unpublished doctoral thesis, University of Glasgow, 2009); Sarah Jane Williams, 'An Author's Role in Fourteenth-Century Book Production: Guillaume de Machaut's "livre où je mets toutes mes choses"' *Romania* 90 (1969) pp. 433–54. It is always worth bearing in mind that, ultimately, such a question is of course unanswerable with certainty.

9   The single most complete codicological analysis of the manuscripts remains Earp, 'Scribal Practice', much of which is collected in his later work, *Guillaume de Machaut*.

10 For recent discussions of the layout of the *Voir Dit*, see Maxwell (chapter 5); Deborah McGrady, *Controlling Readers: Guillaume de Machaut and his Late-Medieval Audience* (Toronto, 2006) pp. 77–87.

11 Earp, 'Scribal Practice' p. 122.

12 For the significance of the fifteenth-century use of this term (previously reserved for the writers of antiquity) to relate to Machaut, see Kevin Brownlee, *Poetic Identity in Guillaume de Machaut* (Madison WI, 1984) pp. 7–9.

13 R. Barton Palmer has edited and translated both of Machaut's judgment poems: *Guillaume de Machaut: The Judgment of the King of Bohemia (Le Jugement dou Roy de Behaigne)* (New York and London, 1984), *Guillaume de Machaut: The Judgment of the King of Navarre* (New York and London, 1988). Whether or not the *Navarre* actually 'reverses' the decision of the *Behaigne* is itself a matter of debate and, ultimately, opinion. For the most recent overview of the arguments, see Leach, pp. 164–76, and Emma Cayley, 'Machaut and Debate Poetry', in *A Companion to Guillaume de Machaut—An Interdisciplinary Approach to the Master* (Leiden, 2012) pp. 103–18.

14 For a recent analysis of the music of the lays and its internal and external relationships, see Albritton, 'Citation and Allusion'. See also Earp's analysis of the notational practices in the lay section of E in 'Scribal practice' pp. 309–26.

15 Earp, 'Scribal Practice' p. 325, incorrectly states that this lay is not in E, and incorrectly lists this lay as being set to music in E (*Guillaume de Machaut*, p. 341). Here Earp also notes Schrade's confusion regarding this lay and 'Qui bien aimme', which, like 'Malgré Fortune', is entitled the 'Lay de plour'. The positioning of 'Malgré Fortune' in E is fascinating, and I intend to undertake a thorough analysis of it in the future. Here, it suffices to point out that on f. 210ʳ of E the *Voir Dit* finishes midway through the second column under the final letter. In the remaining space in this column is the rubric 'Explicit le livre du Voir Dit' [Here ends the book of the True Tale]. The next column (still below the letter) opens with the rubric 'Le lay de plour', and 'Malgré Fortune' begins. It continues on the verso, finishing at the end of the first column of f. 211ʳ with the rubric 'Cy fine le lay de plour' [Here ends the lay de plour]. The next column

on this folio transmits a *unicum* (in the 'complete-works' manuscripts) rondeau, 'Doulz cuers gentilz', before the boxed rubric (in the centre of the writing area) 'Explicit le voir dit' [Here ends the True Tale]. The addition of these two lyric items to the *Voir Dit* is unusual and intriguing. The only other manuscript to contain the rondeau is the anthology manuscript Philadelphia, University of Pennsylvania Libraries MS 902 (formerly Fr. 15, and known by the siglum Pa). Earp believes parts of this manuscript, including this rondeau, to have been copied directly from E (*Guillaume de Machaut* pp. 115–18).

16 For a comparative analysis of the two lays entitled 'Le Lay de Plour', see Isabelle Bétemps, 'Les Lais de plour: Guillaume de Machaut et Oton de Granson' in Jacqueline Cerquiglini-Toulet and Nigel Wilkins (eds) *Guillaume de Machaut 1300–2000: Actes du Colloque de la Sorbonne 28–29 septembre 2000* (Paris, 2002) pp. 95–106.

17 The summaries from C are based on the analysis of Sylvia Huot, *From Song to Book* (Ithaca NY and London, 1987) pp. 263–70. A fuller description of the miniatures in A and F–G can be found in Earp, *Guillaume de Machaut* pp. 186–87.

18 'Vesci l'ordenence que G. de Machau vuet qu'il ait en son livre' [Here is the order that G. de Machaut wants his book to have]. The index to A has been discussed in relation to the lays by Earp, 'Scribal Practice' pp. 62–65 and Maxwell pp. 40–41.

19 Uri Smilansky and Yolanda Plumley have uncovered the patron as Aubert de Puychalin, a member of the minor nobility with a formidable reputation for his lavish lifestyle. The discovery was presented in a paper, 'Early Ownership of Machaut Manuscripts, or Sex, Drugs and High-End Art Music in the late 14th century', at the Royal Musicological Association Medieval and Renaissance Music conference, University of Nottingham, 8–11 July 2012.

20 Earp, *Guillaume de Machaut* p. 84.

21 McGrady p. 132 considers the music section in E to be privileged in comparison to its placement in the other 'complete-works' manuscripts: 'MS E presents a new ordering of Machaut's works that reserves a central role for musical compositions. Instead of relegating the music to a final section in the manuscript, MS E locates the various lais, motets, *rondeaux*, *ballades*, *virelais*, and even Machaut's Mass at the heart of the compendium.' Leach p. 120, n. 91, disagrees explicitly with McGrady's concept of 'relegation': 'I view music to be at the "heart" (albeit not the codicological center) of Machaut's enterprise.'

22 The title also, perhaps, alludes to the mirror-like structure of the motets in the 'complete-works' manuscripts, with the exception of E, as analysed by Thomas Brown, 'Another *Mirror of Lovers?*—Order, Structure and Allusion in Machaut's Motets' *Plainsong and Medieval Music* 10 (2001) pp. 121–33.

23 Maxwell p. 94.

24 Huot p. 265.

25 Huot p. 263; the miniature is reproduced on p. 264. See also the discussion in Maxwell pp. 94–95.

26 Huot p. 263.

27 The considerable evidence for this is given in Earp, 'Scribal Practice' p. 120, n. 224. It has been pointed out, however, that ownership is not the same as patronage (McGrady pp. 84–85). Nevertheless, it is my view that, from the evidence presented here, this manuscript was produced with the royal house of France in mind.

28 Armand Strubel (ed.), *Le Roman de la Rose* (Paris, 1992).

29 Huot p. 266 (n. 21).

30 It is worth noting that E is considered such an unreliable source that the attribution of the two *unica* lays to Machaut has been questioned (Earp, *Guillaume de Machaut* p. 357, 'Scribal Practice' pp. 310–26). Earp notes, however, that Bent ('The Machaut Manuscripts' pp. 72–73) supports the attribution to Machaut.

31 McGrady p. 83.

4: *Sonja Drimmer* Picturing the King or Picturing the Saint: Two Miniature Programmes for John Lydgate's *Lives of Saints Edmund and Fremund*

1 This chapter originated in my MA Dissertation for the University of York (2004). I am grateful to Professor Richard Marks and Professor Tony Edwards for their advice, guidance and support.

2 On Lydgate's aptitude for producing this effect in his hagiographies see Karen A. Winstead, 'Lydgate's Lives of Saints Edmund and Alban: Martyrdom and *Prudent Pollicie*' *Mediaevalia* 17 (1994) pp. 221–41.

3 The most comprehensive art historical survey of hagiographies to date is Cynthia Hahn's *Portrayed on the Heart: Narrative Effect in Pictorial Lives of Saints from the Tenth through the Thirteenth Century* (Berkeley CA, 2001). See also Barbara Abou-El-Haj, *The Medieval Cult of Saints: Formations and Transformations* (Binghamton NY, 1994).

4 Quoted from the manuscript facsimile: A.S.G. Edwards (ed.) *Life of Saint Edmund, King and Martyr: A Facsimile* (London, 2004) p. 8. For a full description of the manuscript, see Kathleen L. Scott, *Later Gothic Manuscripts 1390–1490* (London, 1996) II, no. 78. The manuscript has been fully digitised and made accessible to the public via the British Library's Digitised Manuscripts website: <http://www.bl.uk/manuscripts/>.

5 For a full description of this manuscript, see Scott, *Later Gothic Manuscripts* II, no. 112. A nearly identical manuscript to YT is housed in Arundel Castle and is described at length in Kathleen L. Scott, 'Lydgate's "Lives of Saints Edmund and Fremund": A Newly Located Manuscript in Arundel Castle' *Viator* 13 (1982) pp. 335–66. Select images from this manuscript have been digitised and made accessible to the public via the British Library's catalogue of illuminated manuscripts: <http://www.bl.uk/catalogues/illuminatedmanuscripts/>.

6 Michael C. Seymour, 'Some Lydgate Manuscripts: *Lives of Saints Edmund and Fremund* and *Danse Macabre*' *Edinburgh Bibliographical Society Transactions* 5 (1983–85) pp. 10–21 (p. 160).

7 Scott, 'Lydgate's "Lives of Saints Edmund and Fremund"' p. 360. I have not had an opportunity to examine the Arundel Castle manuscript.

8 I make this argument against previous assessments of the triviality of pictorial variation in fifteenth-century manuscripts, whether due to a predominant commercial interest or a presumption of the illustrator's partial illiteracy or ignorance. See Lesley Lawton, 'The Illustration of Late Medieval Secular Texts with Special Reference to Lydgate's "Troy Book"' in Derek Pearsall (ed.) *Manuscripts and Readers in Fifteenth-Century England* (Cambridge, 1983) pp. 41–69; Kathleen L. Scott, 'Caveat lector: Ownership and Standardization in the Illustration of Fifteenth-Century English Manuscripts' *English Manuscript Studies 1100–1700* 1 (1989) pp. 19–63.

9 While the civil disturbances in fourteenth-century Bury are well known, less

frequently discussed are the events of the fifteenth century, which witnessed the rise of Bury's burgher class and their intense competition with the abbey for control of the region. See Robert S. Gottfried, *Bury St. Edmunds and the Urban Crisis: 1290–1539* (Princeton NJ, 1982).

10 The poem has recently been re-edited: Anthony Bale and A.S.G. Edwards (eds) *John Lydgate's Lives of Ss Edmund & Fremund and the Extra Miracles of St Edmund: Edited from British Library MS Harley 2278 and Bodleian Library MS Ashmole 46* (Heidelberg, 2009). Previously it was only available in an 1881 edition with German notes: C. Horstmann, 'The Lives of Saints Edmund and Fremund', *Altenglische Legenden: neue Folge mit Einleitung und Anmerkungen* (Heilbronn, 1881) pp. 376–445, and an unpublished doctoral dissertation: James Miller, 'John Lydgate's Saint Edmund and Saint Fremund: An Annotated Edition' (Harvard University, 1967).

11 After a long period of relative disdain and neglect, there has been a surge of interest in Lydgate and his poetry in both monographs and collected essays. Of note are: Lisa H. Cooper and Andrea Denny-Brown (eds) *Lydgate Matters: Poetry and Material Culture in the Fifteenth Century* (New York, 2008); Larry Scanlon and James Simpson (eds) *John Lydgate: Poetry, Culture, and Lancastrian England* (Notre Dame IN, 2006); Maura Nolan, *John Lydgate and the Making of Public Culture* (Cambridge, 2005); Derek Pearsall, *John Lydgate (1371–1449): A Bio-bibliography* (Victoria BC, 1997).

12 A fuller account of the commission and Henry's visit to Bury can be found in Edwards's introduction to the *Life* (pp. 1–3). It is possible, as he suggests, that the commission actually succeeded Henry's visit. Nicholas Rogers and Michael Seymour have surmised, independently, that it was likely to have been composed at some point between 1434 and 1439. See Seymour p. 10 and Nicholas Rogers, 'The Bury Artists of Harley 2278 and the Origins of Topographical Awareness in English Art' in Antonia Gransden (ed.) *Bury St Edmunds: Medieval Art, Architecture, Archaeology and Economy* (London, 1998) pp. 219–27 (pp. 215, 224).

13 All quotations and line-references, except where otherwise noted, are from Bale and Edwards.

14 Edwards, *The Life* p. 1.

15 For the early history of the abbey and its rise to prominence see Barbara Abou-el-Haj, 'Bury St Edmunds Abbey Between 1070 and 1124: A History of Property, Privilege, and Monastic Art Production' *Art History* 6 (1983) pp. 1–29, and Antonia Gransden, *A History of the Abbey of Bury St Edmunds, 1182–1256: Samson of Tottington to Edmund of Walpole* (Woodbridge, 2007). See also Rodney M. Thomson (ed.), *The Archives of the Abbey of Bury St Edmunds* (Woodbridge, 1980), and Antonia Gransden (ed.), *Bury St Edmunds: Medieval Art, Architecture, Archaeology, and Economy*, The British Archaeological Association Conference Transactions 20 (Leeds, 1998).

16 For an exhaustive study of Henry VI see Ralph Griffiths, *The Reign of King Henry VI: The Exercise of Royal Authority, 1422–1461* (Stroud, 1998, 2nd edn).

17 William Curteys (abbot 1429–1446) had a reputation as an ardent defender of the abbey's rights, demonstrated, significantly, in his 'prowess as an administrator' and the fact that 'from [his] reign no fewer than 15 archival books survive' (Thomson p. 34). See also Walter F. Schirmer, *John Lydgate; A Study in the Culture of the XVth Century*, trans. Ann E. Keep (Berkeley CA, 1961) chapter 2.

18 For a summary and transcription of letters between Henry V and Abbot Excetre of Bury, as well as the relevant acts and statutes issued at Westminster, see

William Abel Pantin (ed.), *Documents Illustrating the Activities of the General and Provincial Chapters of the English Black Monks, 1215–1540* (London, 1933) II, 104–16. See also Ernest Fraser Jacob, *The Fifteenth Century, 1399–1485* (Oxford, 1961) pp. 196–98.

19 See G. Loomis, 'The Growth of the St. Edmund Legend' *Harvard Studies and Notes in Philology and Literature* 14 (1932) pp. 83–113, and J.I. Miller, 'Literature to History: Exploring a Medieval Saint's Legend and its Context' in *Literature and History: University of Tulsa Department of English Monograph*, Series 9 (1970) pp. 59–72. Edwards provides a summary of these in *The Life* pp. 6–7, as does Anthony Bale (ed.), *St Edmund, King and Martyr: Changing Images of a Medieval Saint* (York, 2009) pp. 1–6.

20 Cited in Loomis p. 83. My translation, with thanks to the editors of this volume for their revisions.

21 J.I. Miller p. 62.

22 J.I. Miller p. 65.

23 Edwards, *The Life* p. 8.

24 Edwards, *The Life* pp. 66–67.

25 Interpreting this doubling more broadly, Somerset writes, 'Lydgate's narrative creates a dynastic succession that is not patrilineal (for nephews succeed, rather than sons); it is not even linear (for the dead return to intervene in succeeding events, and the poem begins in and repeatedly reminds us of the present). It is founded instead on the martyric furthering of God's will' (Fiona Somerset, '"Hard is with seyntis for to make affray": Lydgate the "Poet-Propagandist" as Hagiographer' in Scanlon and Simpson (eds) pp. 258–78 (p. 266)).

26 Derek Pearsall, *John Lydgate* (London, 1970) p. 169. See also Linne R. Mooney, 'Lydgate's "Kings of England" and Another Verse Chronicle of the Kings' *Viator* 20 (1989) pp. 255–89.

27 Somerset p. 261.

28 Recently, Anthony Edwards and Fiona Somerset have published studies on the political nature of the *Lives*: A.S.G. Edwards, 'John Lydgate's Lives of Ss Edmund and Fremund: Politics, Hagiography and Literature' in Anthony Bale (ed.) *St Edmund, King and Martyr: Changing Images of a Medieval Saint* (York, 2009) pp. 133–44; Somerset, '"Hard is with seyntis for to make affray"'. See also Lee Patterson, 'Making Identities in Fifteenth-Century England: Henry V and John Lydgate' in Jeffrey Cox and Larry J. Reynolds (eds) *New Historical Literary Study: Essays on Reproducing Texts, Representing History* (Princeton NJ, 1993) pp. 69–107, and Paul Strohm, 'Hoccleve, Lydgate and the Lancastrian Court' in David Wallace (ed.) *The Cambridge History of Medieval English Literature* (Cambridge, 1999) pp. 640–61.

29 Alain Renoir and David C. Benson, 'John Lydgate' in Albert E. Hartung (ed.) *A Manual of the Writings in Middle English 1050–1500* (New Haven CT, 1980) VI, 1832.

30 Lydgate's support for Henry is most emphatically stated in the closing prayer to the poem, which beseeches the protection of St Edmund, with the refrain that he should safeguard Henry VI, "thenherytour off Inglond and France" (III. 1464, 1472, 1480, 1488, 1496, 1504, 1512, 1520).

31 John Lowden, 'The Royal/Imperial Book and the Image or Self-Image of the Medieval Ruler' in Anne J. Duggan (ed.) *Kings and Kingship in Medieval Europe* (London, 1993) pp. 213–40 (p. 240).

32 This conclusion is further supported by the location of the second standard

(f. 3ᵛ) after a blank recto and facing the text that describes it. The text, in its use of deictics, is, in fact, inseparable from the image it describes, e.g. 'This other standard' (General Prol. 49).

33 Edwards notes the anomalous nature of the first gathering (of six folios, as opposed to the standard eight throughout the remainder of the manuscript, excepting the last quire), suggesting that 'it may have been a late addition to the manuscript ... added in the final stages in the manuscript's preparation' (*The Life* p. 13).

34 Victor Stoichita, *The Self-Aware Image: An Insight into Early Modern Meta-Painting* (Cambridge, 1996) p. 55. I am grateful to Elizabeth Perkins for this reference. On the semiotics of frame, see Meyer Schapiro's classic essay 'On Some Problems in the Semiotics of Visual Art: Field and Vehicle in Image-Signs' *Semiotica* 1 (1969) pp. 223–42. See also Derrida's discussion of the frame as establishing the image as image, different from presence, in *The Truth in Painting* (Chicago IL, 1978) pp. 11–12, 21–23, 31–32, 38–41, etc.

35 Every other miniature in the manuscript, with the exception of the second frontispiece, is bound by a pink-and-mauve frame.

36 On the use of propaganda to assert Henry's legitimacy see J.H. Rowe, 'King Henry VI's Claim to France in Picture and Poem' *The Library* series 4, 13 (1932) pp. 77–88, and J.W. McKenna, 'Henry VI of England and the Dual Monarchy: Aspects of Royal Political Propaganda' *Journal of the Warburg and Courtauld Institutes* 28 (1965) pp. 145–62.

37 'Henry VI's Triumphal Entry into London, 21 Feb., 1432', ll. 405–11, in Henry Noble MacCracken (ed.) *The Minor Poems of John Lydgate* (London, 1934).

38 Discussed by Rowe (p. 78). Lydgate was commissioned by the Earl of Warwick to translate this poem. See 'The Title and Pedigree of Henry VI' in MacCracken pp. 613–22.

39 McKenna, 'Henry VI of England and the Dual Monarchy' pp. 145–51.

40 Jacques Lacan, 'The Mirror Stage as Formative of the *I* Function as Revealed in Psychoanalytic Experience' in Bruce Fink (trans.) *Écrits* (New York, 2006) pp. 75–81 (p. 78).

41 Augustine, *Enarratio in Psalmum 103*, in J.-P. Migne (ed.) *Patrologia Latina* 37 (Paris, 1845), col. 1338. See also Ritamary Bradley, 'Backgrounds of the Title *Speculum* in Mediaeval Literature' *Speculum* 29 (1954) pp. 100–15, and Herbert Grabes, *The Mutable Glass: Mirror-imagery in Titles and Texts of the Middle Ages and English Renaissance*, trans. Gordon Collier (New York, 1982).

42 See J.W. McKenna, 'Piety and Propaganda: The Cult of King Henry VI' in Beryl Rowland (ed.) *Chaucer and Middle English Studies in Honour of Rossell Hope Robbins* (Kent OH, 1974) pp. 72–88. Richard Marks's essay on representations of Henry VI shows how widespread this cult was in the later fifteenth- and early-sixteenth centuries: 'Images of Henry VI' in Jenny Stratford (ed.) *The Lancastrian Court* (Donington, 2003) pp. 111–24.

43 Based on stylistic similarities with manuscripts affiliated with the Abbey, Scott claims Bury St Edmunds as its place of origin (*Later Gothic Manuscripts*, II, no. 112). Because several references to Henry in the manuscript have been replaced with the name of Edward IV the manuscript must have a *terminus post quem* of 1461. Moreover, owing to the fire that devastated the Abbey in 1465 it is unlikely to have been produced after that date. That Henry's name remains in earlier parts of the manuscript suggests to me a date early in Edward's reign, perhaps even straddling Henry's deposition and his accession.

44 A reader's note on f. 107^r, which I discuss in further detail below, records one owner of the book as Margaret Fitzwalter (d. 1496), the second wife of Sir John Ratcliffe of Attleborough. Margaret was raised in the north of France and relocated to England only upon her marriage to Ratcliffe in 1476. She is thus likely to have received the manuscript from a member of John's family, most probably his mother Elizabeth Fitzwalter, who herself came from a family with deep roots in Essex, and thus potentially strong links to Bury Abbey. Other details regarding her biography support this conclusion. See *ODNB* [accessed 14 January 2012]: Ian Arthurson, 'Ratcliffe, John, sixth Baron Fitzwalter (1452–1496)'; Christopher Starr, 'Fitzwalter family (*per. 1200–c.1500*)'; see too 'Elizabeth FitzWalter' in *The Complete Peerage of England, Scotland, Ireland, Great Britain, and the United Kingdom* (London, 1926), V, 484–86.

45 Both this manuscript and the Arundel Castle manuscript, its 'almost identical twin' (Scott, *Later Gothic Manuscripts*, II, 308), were joined by a number of other copies of the *Lives*, all produced by the same scribe (Scott, 'Lydgate's 'Lives of Saints Edmund and Fremund'' pp. 335–36)—ample support for the conclusion that they were produced as part of, or comprising, a raft of speculative copies for the local market. For evidence of speculative manuscript production in England see Linne R. Mooney and Lister Matheson, 'The Beryn Scribe and his Texts: Evidence for Multiple-Copy Production of Manuscripts in Fifteenth-Century England' *The Library*, 7th series, 4 (2003) pp. 347–70.

46 I. 646–89 have been excised. These lines recount the initial preparations for Edmund's departure to East England, and his father's sadness at his impending absence.

47 Seymour p. 10. Anthony Bale has recently reviewed the nature of these stanzas, concluding that they are, at least in part, genuine Lydgate productions, though not produced at the same time: 'St Edmund in Fifteenth-Century London: The Lydgatian *Miracles of St Edmund*' in Bale (ed.) pp. 145–61.

48 The final lines of the *General Prologue* (73–80 and two stanzas of Latin prayer) have been excised. These verses guarantee two hundred days' pardon to anyone who recites the included prayer to St Edmund.

49 Scott discusses briefly the relationship between Harley 2278 and YT 47 ('Lydgate's "Lives of Saints Edmund and Fremund"' pp. 357–60). A sixteenth-century inscription in Harley, 'Audelay baron' (f. 119^v), places the manuscript in the hands of John Touchet (d. 1559), eighth Baron of Audley. James Carley, *The Libraries of Henry VIII* (London, 2000) p. xlvii, postulates that Harley was a gift from Touchet to the king in appreciation for the restoration of his titles *c.*1512. In the years between Touchet's acquisition of the volume and its donation to Henry VIII it escaped the royal collection and may have served as a direct model for YT, whose place of production is almost certainly Bury. See my catalogue entry for this manuscript in: Scot McKendrick, Kathleen Doyle and John Lowden (eds), *Royal Manuscripts: The Genius of Illumination* (London, 2011), no. 30.

50 Many of those images from Harley not selected for illustration in YT are those which expand a given episode into two or three pictorial moments. In a decision driven, perhaps, by economy, the YT producers provided only one illustration for any given episode. For example, three miniatures in Harley illustrate Edmund's departure for, journey to and arrival in East Anglia (ff 26^r, 27^r, 27^v), whereas the YT artist collapsed departure and journey into a single miniature (f. 26^r).

51 Scott, 'Lydgate's "Lives of Saints Edmund and Fremund"' pp. 358–59.

52 A number of illustrations from Harley not included in this manuscript support this conclusion. For example, YT omits the Harleian illustration that accompanies the episode in which Bishop Kunbertus proves Edmund's legitimacy before a doubtful crowd of his prospective subjects (f. 29^v). Even more significantly, the climax of Edmund's legend, before his martyrdom, is the inner conflict he experiences between his duty to his people and his duty to God (II. 512–611). Harley illustrates this episode with images of Edmund consulting his bishop, foreswearing violence by laying down his sword before an altar; replying to the messenger of Hinguar, his enemy, and then kneeling in surrender to Hinguar (ff. 54^r, 55^v, 56^v, 58^r). YT is pictorially silent on every one of these episodes, skipping from Edmund's earlier battle with Hinguar (f. 54^r) to his capture and assault by Hinguar's soldiers (f. 60^v).

53 Hans Belting, *Bild-Anthropologie: Entwürfe für eine Bildwissenschaft* (Munich, 2001) pp. 115–42.

54 The phrase was coined by Robert Scribner in his 'Popular Piety and Modes of Visual Perception in Late-Medieval and Reformation Germany' *Journal of Religious History* 15 (1989) pp. 448–69. See also the seminal work by David Freedberg, *The Power of Images: Studies in the History and Theory of Response* (Chicago IL, 1989) pp. 27–40.

55 Leslie Ross, *Text, Image, Message: Saints in Medieval Manuscript Illustrations* (Westport CT, 1994) has observed that '[i]n preserving the memory of ... an Abbey's saintly founder, the libellus itself often assumed the role of a precious relic' (p. 42). See also Seeta Chaganti, *The Medieval Poetics of the Reliquary: Enshrinement, Inscription, Performance* (New York, 2008).

56 Images of St Edmund enthroned with devotees at his side include Oxford, Bodleian Library, MS Ashmole 46, f. 1^r and London, British Library, MS Harley 1766, f. 5^r.

57 If I am correct that this manuscript was produced as a speculative venture (see above), it would make sense that a space next to Edmund was left empty: either, as I argue here, it was meant for the reader/viewer to envision himself, or herself, occupying, or it was intended to be painted over with a donor portrait.

58 On Becket's shrine, see Stephen Lamia, 'The Cross and the Crown, the Tomb and the Shrine: Decoration and Accommodation for England's Premier Saints' in Stephen Lamia and Elizabeth Valdez del Álamo (eds) *Decorations for the Holy Dead: Visual Embellishments on Tombs and Shrines of Saints* (Turnhout, 2002) pp. 39–56.

59 One other image is soiled (apparently accidentally), and has succumbed to subsequent flaking (f. 12^r). There are also heavy annotations to this manuscript, mostly executed by the antiquarian John Stowe. See A.S.G. Edwards and J.I. Miller, 'John Stowe and Lydgate's *St. Edmund*' *Notes and Queries* 228 (1973) pp. 355–69, and Alexandra Gillespie, 'The Later Lives of St Edmund: John Lydgate to John Stow' in Bale (ed.) pp. 163–85.

60 This sort of tactile engagement was apparently widespread enough (and presumably censured enough) to prompt a defence from Reginald Pecock, who wrote (*c*.1455) that it 'ought not to be scorned or rebuked', asking, 'Why, in like manner, may not the more love and good affection be engendered towards God or a saint by touch?' (quoted from James Hall, 'Desire and Disgust: Touching Artworks from 1500 to 1800' in Robert Maniura and Rupert Shepherd (eds) *Presence: The Inherence of the Prototype within Images and Other Objects* (Aldershot, 2006) pp. 145–60 (pp. 147–48).

61 On f. 49ᵛ the archers are rubbed. On f. 51ʳ the soldier threatening Edmund with a sword has been scratched and smudged, and on f. 51ᵛ (Edmund's martyrdom) the face of the soldier who raises his sword over Edmund's head has been rubbed. This last folio even has a significant tear on the upper margin.

62 Rogers pp. 235–36.

63 On late medieval iconography of book presentation, see Eric Inglis, 'A Book in the Hand: Some Late Medieval Accounts of Manuscript Presentations' *Journal of the Early Book Society* 5 (2002) pp. 57–97, and Dhira B. Mahoney, 'Courtly Presentation and Authorial Self-Fashioning: Frontispiece Miniatures in Late Medieval French and English Manuscripts' *Mediaevalia* 21 (1996) pp. 97–160.

64 Jean-Paul Sartre, 'Official Portraits' in Anne P. Jones (trans.) and Maurice Natanson (ed.) *Essays in Phenomenology* (The Hague, 1966) pp. 157–58.

65 The distinction between kneeling with one knee and kneeling with two is addressed in several contemporary texts. In *Dives and Pauper*, Pauper explains that 'to God men shuldyn knelyn wyt bothe knees in tokene þat in hym is al oure principal helpe, but to man only wyt þe to [one] knee' (*Dives and Pauper*, Priscilla Heath Barnum (ed.), EETS 275 (1976), I, part 1, 106). J.A. Burrow discusses this and several other texts that address kneeling in: *Gestures and Looks in Medieval Narrative* (Cambridge, 2002) pp. 19–25.

66 For literature on the blue nimbus see Robert Nelson, 'A Thirteenth-Century Byzantine Miniature in the Vatican Library' *Gesta* 20 (1981) pp. 213–22 (p. 221, n. 14).

67 Cynthia Hahn, '*Peregrinatio et natio*: The Illustrated Life of Edmund, King and Martyr' *Gesta* 30 (1991) pp. 119–39 (p. 123).

5: *Yvonne Rode* Sixty-three Gallons of Books: Shipping Books to London in the Late Middle Ages

1 Dennis Rhodes, 'Don Fernando Colón and His London Book Purchases, June 1552' in his *Studies in Early European Printing and Book Collecting* (London, 1983) pp. 163–80. For a recent discussion, see David Rundle, 'English books and the continent' in Alexandra Gillespie and Daniel Wakelin (eds) *The Production of Books in England 1350–1500* (Cambridge, 2011) pp. 276–91 *passim*.

2 By 1480 London controlled almost 61% of the country's overseas trade by value, increasing to 80% by 1540. See Maryanne Kowaleski, 'Port Towns: England and Wales 1300–1540' in Peter Clark (ed.) *The Cambridge Urban History of Britain,* 3 vols (Cambridge, 2000) I, 467–94 (pp. 477–78 and table 19.1). Details of the accounts are not specified in Peter Ramsey, 'Overseas Trade in the Reign of Henry VII: The Evidence of Customs Accounts' *Economic History Review* 6 (1953) pp. 179–81; Henry Cobb, '"Books of Rates" and the London Customs, 1507–1558' *The Guildhall Miscellany* 4 (1971) pp. 1–13, p. 2. See too Caroline M. Barron, *London in the Later Middle Ages: Government and People 1200–1500* (Oxford, 2004) pp. 84–117 and figs 5.2, 5.10 and 5.12. (Barron examined petty customs, customs on wool, cloth and wine). London handled 65.4% of alien trade 1478–82, although this accounted for only 37.1% of total London overseas trade at that time. See too Kowaleski pp. 481–83; Ramsey p. 180; Olive Coleman, 'The Collectors of Customs in London under Richard II' in A.E.J. Hollaender and William Kellaway (eds) *Studies in London History Presented to Philip Edmund Jones* (London, 1969) pp. 181–94 (p. 185).

3 James Raven, *The Business of Books: Booksellers and the English Book Trade*

(New Haven CT, 2007) pp. 30–31. For a discussion of the regulations affecting aliens and trade see Howard W. Winger, 'Regulations Relating to the Book Trade in London from 1337 to 1586' *Library Quarterly* 26 (1965) pp. 157–95 and A.W. Reed, 'The Regulation of the Book Trade before the Proclamation of 1538' *Transactions of the Bibliographical Society* 15 (1917) pp. 157–84.

4   Raven pp. 9, 54. Consumer demand for goods such as spices, jewels and books was also higher in London than in provincial towns, and those living outside London would frequently purchase luxury goods there, either in person or via an agent. See Barron pp. 46, 69 and Christopher Dyer, 'The Consumer and the Market in the Later Middle Ages' *Economic History Review* 42 (1989) pp. 305–27 (pp. 308–9, 320, 325).

5   In Southampton eight consignments of books have been found, two in published accounts: D.B. Quinn (ed.) *The Port Books or Local Customs Accounts of Southampton for the Reign of Edward IV*, 2 vols, Publications of the South-ampton Record Society 37, 38 (Southampton, 1938) II, 247 (22 Dec. 1480, f. 6ʳ) and Thomas B. James (ed.) *The Port Book of Southampton*, 2 vols, Southampton Records Series 32, 33 (Southampton, 1990), I (weeks 1–26) (23 Dec. 1509). C. Paul Christianson has found imports of books through Southampton in 1494/5 (six cargoes), 1502 and 1504 ('The Rise of London's Book-Trade' in Lotte Hellinga and J.B. Trapp (eds) *The Cambridge History of the Book in Britain III: 1400–1557* (hereafter *CHBB III*) (Cambridge, 1999) pp. 128–47 (pp. 141–42); he lists only the account for 1502/5, E122/209/2 (15–17 Henry VIII). Other accounts examined include Quinn vol. II; James vol. II; Henry Cobb (ed.), *The Local Port Book of Southampton for 1439–40*, Southampton Records Series 5 (Southampton, 1961); Olive Coleman (ed.), *The Brokerage Book of Southampton, 1443–44*, 2 vols, Southampton Record Series 4, 6 (Southampton, 1960–61). Coleman notes that many of the luxury goods entering Southampton were immediately brought to London, with Italians accounting for over 80% of goods sent to London. See Olive Coleman, 'Trade and Prosperity in the Fifteenth Century: Some Aspects of the Trade of South-ampton' *Economic History Review* 16 (1963) pp. 9–22 (p. 12). For the port of Bristol Dr Evan Jones of the University of Bristol has transcribed and made available several customs accounts; of the three falling within the scope of this paper, two have a single consignment of primers each: four dozen in 1517/18 (E122/21/2) and three dozen in 1525/6 (E122/21/5). See Evan Jones, 'Bristol "Particular" Customs Account, 1503/04' in *ROSE Repository of Scholarly EPrints* <http://rose.bris.ac.uk/handle/1983/1296> [accessed 3 February 2012], 'Bristol "Particular" Customs Account, 1518/17 [*sic*]' in *ROSE* <http://rose. bris.ac.uk/handle/1983/1297> [accessed 3 February 2012], 'Bristol "Particular" Customs Account, 1525/26' in *ROSE* <http://rose.bris.ac.uk/handle/1983/1298> [accessed 3 February 2012].

6   Lotte Hellinga, 'Importation of Books Printed on the Continent into England and Scotland before c1520' in Sandra Hindman (ed.) *Printing the Written Word: The Social History of Books Circa 1450–1520* (Ithaca NY, 1991) pp. 205–24; Nicholas Barker, 'The Importation of Books into England, 1460–1526' in Herbert G. Göpfert (ed.) *Beiträge zur Geschichte des Buchwesens im Konfesionellen Zeitalter* (Wiesbaden, 1985) pp. 251–66; Margaret Lane Ford, 'Importation of Printed Books into England and Scotland' in *CHBB III*, pp. 179–201.

7   C.M. Meale, '"... Alle the Bokes that I have of Latyn, Englisch, and Frensch": Laywomen and their Books in Late Medieval England' in C.M. Meale (ed.)

Women and Literature in Britain: 1150–1500 (Cambridge, 1996) pp. 128–58. See too Barker pp. 251–66, and Alan Piper and Meryl Foster, 'Evidence of the Oxford Book Trade, about 1300' *Viator* 20 (1989) pp. 155–60.

8   Henry Robert Plomer, 'The Importation of Books into England in the Fifteenth and Sixteenth Centuries: An Examination of some Customs Rolls' *The Library* series 4, 4 (1923) pp. 146–50; this is expanded on in Henry Robert Plomer, 'The Importation of Low Country and French Books into England, 1480 and 1502–3' *The Library* series 4, 9 (1928/9) pp. 165–68. Plomer examined The National Archives (hereafter TNA, then Public Record Office (PRO)), E122/194/24 (1480/1); E122/78/9 (1490/1); E122/79/5 (1494/5); E122/80/2 (1502/3).

9   Paul Needham, 'The Customs Rolls as Documents for the Printed-Book Trade in England' in *CHBB III* pp. 148–63.

10 Julian Roberts, 'Importing Books for Oxford, 1500–1640' in James Carley and Colin G.C. Tite (eds) *Books and Collectors, 1200–1700: Essays Presented to Andrew Watson* (London, 1997) pp. 322–24. Roberts examined TNA E122/81/9 (1520/1); TNA E122/80/2 (1502/4); TNA E122/86/6 (1534/5); TNA E122/86/8 (1556/7).

11 N.J.M. Kerling, 'Caxton and the Trade in Printed Books' *Book Collector* 4 (1955) pp. 190–99. The earliest mention of printed books in the London customs accounts found so far is 30 December 1477 (TNA E122/194/22). Membrane number not cited.

12 Kerling p. 193.

13 N.S.B. Gras, *The Early English Customs System: A Documentary Study of the Institutional and Economic History of the Customs from the Thirteenth to the Sixteenth Century* (Cambridge MA, 1918) pp. 59–77. See too Henry Cobb, 'Local Port Customs Accounts Prior to 1550' *Journal of the Society of Archivists* 1 (1959) pp. 213–24.

14 Cobb, 'Books of Rates' p. 1.

15 The national system was in place as early as the thirteenth century, with local customs existing possibly in the eighth century. See Gras p. 14; Cobb, 'Local Port Customs' p. 214. The summary accounts are in TNA E356 class.

16 Gras pp. 96, 142; H.S. Cobb (ed.), *The Overseas Trade of London Exchequer Customs Accounts, 1480–81*, London Record Society Publications 27 (London, 1990) pp. xxii–xxvi. Gras refers to the controller's account as a 'poor duplicate' of the collector's account, although the controller's account can be used if the collector's account does not survive. See Cobb, *Overseas Trade* p. xxvi. Both the collector's and controller's accounts would be sent to the Exchequer where they would be compared against each other.

17 Gras pp. 94–99, 130; Cobb, 'Local Port Customs' p. 214; Cobb, *Overseas Trade* p. xiii.

18 See Cobb, 'Books of Rates' p. 2, and 'Local Port Customs' pp. 222–23; Needham, 'Customs Rolls' p. 154. For Hanse privileges, see T.H. Lloyd, *England and the German Hanse, 1157–1611: A Study of their Trade and Commercial Diplomacy* (Cambridge, 1991) pp. 17, 34, 57, 61–62, 204). Poundage was paid by everyone, while petty customs was paid by denizens, aliens and Hanseatic merchants, although individuals, groups (primarily Hanse merchants) or entire towns could be exempt or given special privileges.

19 For a complete picture of the London overseas trade all of these accounts (wool customs; petty customs and cloth customs; tunnage and poundage) would be needed for a given year, but not all the accounts survive. Paul Needham

estimates that only 30% of petty customs (which would include book imports) survive between the years 1475 and 1554, while Henry Cobb established that there is no single year from 1461 to 1509 where all three accounts survive. See Needham, 'Customs Rolls' pp. 155–56; Cobb, *Overseas Trade* pp. xiii–xiv.

20 See Appendix A for the list of accounts examined. Using the National Archives database, I compiled a list of all extant petty customs and tunnage and poundage accounts from 1450 to 1540. Out of eighty-one extant accounts, only twenty-nine are ten membranes/folios or longer (i.e. may contain a full year of data). All the accounts examined for this paper were eighteen membranes or longer (27.6% of accounts ten membranes or longer).

21 TNA E 122/80/3 m.11.

22 As large sections of the 1456/7 account are damaged it is not possible to state conclusively that there are no book imports recorded in that account. I transcribed all cargoes from digital photographs of the originals. Dr Maryanne Kowaleski photographed the import section of seven accounts (1457/8, 1471/2; 1480/1, 1490/1; 1507/8, 1512/3 and 1534/5); I photographed the accounts for 1514/5, 1520/1 and 1537/8. To this group I added the print account for 1480/1 in Cobb, *Overseas Trade*. For a full description of the accounts see Appendix A. I would like to thank Dr Maryanne Kowaleski for allowing me to use her photographs for this project, Dr Heather Wolfe at the Folger Institute for help in transcribing some difficult entries and Dr Kowaleski and Dr Mary Erler at Fordham University for their helpful comments on earlier versions of this paper.

23 TNA E122/203/4 (1457/8) and TNA E122/194/19 (1471–3). See Kerling p. 191, who examined London accounts from 1460 to 1492.

24 Kate Harris, 'Patrons, Buyers and Owners: The Evidence for Ownership and the Rôle of Book Owners in Book Production and the Book Trade' in Jeremy Griffiths and Derek Pearsall (eds) *Book Production and Publishing in Britain, 1375–1475* (Cambridge, 1989) pp. 163–99 (p. 182).

25 The 1457/8 and 1520/1 accounts are for tunnage and poundage; all the remaining accounts examined are petty customs, which only aliens were liable to pay. See Needham, 'Customs Rolls' p. 154.

26 Lloyd p. 204.

27 Barbara C. Halporn (ed.) *The Correspondence of Johann Amerbach: Early Printing in Its Social Context* (Ann Arbor MI, 2000) n. 174; also nn. 175–80.

28 Both Henry VIII and Henry V (of France) impressed merchant ships during times of war, further curtailing trade. See Clifford S.L. Davies, 'Henry VIII and Henry V: The Wars in France' in John L. Watts (ed.) *The End of the Middle Ages? England in the Fifteenth and Sixteenth Centuries* (Thrupp, 1998) pp. 235–62 (p. 245).

29 Needham, 'Customs Rolls' pp. 157–58.

30 The pipe was half a tun and the hogshead a quarter tun. See R.D. O'Connor, *The Weights and Measures of England* (London, 1987) pp. 151, 171; Ronald Edward Zupko, *Revolution in Measurement: Western European Weights and Measures since the Age of Science* (Philadelphia PA, 1990) Appendix 2. There is a single occurrence of a *dolium*, or tun, in 1507/8 (TNA E122/ 80/5, m.8). This contained a mixed cargo containing *libris impressis* and 'other'. See Ronald Edward Zupko, *A Dictionary of Weights and Measures for the British Isles: The Middle Ages to the Twentieth Century* (Philadelphia PA, 1985), 'Dolium', at pp. 110–11.

31 Halporn nn. 207–9.

32 Halporn nn. 155, 160, 174, 175.

33 Halporn n. 184.

34 Halporn nn. 181, 253.

35 Halporn nn. 253.

36 O'Connor p. 363.

37 Zupko, *Dictionary of Weights*, 'Fatt', at p. 134. His example equating the fatt with half a maund is from the eighteenth century (Zupko, *Revolution* pp. 300, 306). In contrast, he says that the French cognate of fatt (vat) was of undetermined size (Ronald Edward Zupko, 'Vat' in *French Weights and Measures before the Revolution: A Dictionary of Provincial and Local Units* (Bloomington IN, 1978) p. 180).

38 Needham, 'Customs Rolls' p. 160.

39 A.F. Sutton and Livier Visser-Fuchs (eds) *The Book of Privileges of the Merchant Adventurers of England, 1296–1483* (Oxford, 2009) 3b §6. One instance is for a 'iiij cornerd maunde or fatte'.

40 Zupko, *Dictionary of Weights*, 'Maund', 'Hamper', at pp. 243–44, 8. Sutton and Visser-Fuchs, in their Glossary, also define maunds as baskets made of wicker with handles.

41 Zupko, *French Weights*, 'Fargot', at p. 68.

42 A *livre* is, very roughly, 16 oz. See Zupko, *French Weights*, 'Livre', at pp. 97–100. Zupko, *Dictionary of Weights*, 'Truss', at pp. 421–22; O'Connor p. 332. Sutton and Visser-Fuchs, in their Glossary, define truss and fardle as the same thing.

43 Halporn n. 174. There are no books shipped in bales in the accounts I examined. See also n. 260: 'I am of a mind to have the works transported here to Nuremberg in bales and save the cost of the barrels since the barrels you have sent previously are so bad.'

44 Zupko, *Dictionary of Weights*, 'Chest', at pp. 89–90. He says that the case and coffer are equivalent to the chest. See Zupko, *Dictionary of Weights*, 'Case', 'Coffer', at pp. 75–76, 94.

45 Needham, 'Customs Rolls' p. 160. This is in general agreement with Needham, who finds the basket, maund and vat become standard shipping units for books in the 1540s with the basket falling out of favour in the 1550s.

46 Graham Pollard, 'The English Market for Printed Books' *Publishing History* 4 (1978) pp. 7–48 (pp. 19–20). He also credits the decrease in the number of general merchants involved in the book trade to the registration of copyright, although non-members of the Stationers' Company were able to purchase publishing rights.

47 For example, TNA E122/80/8, m.13 and m.6 (paper); 81/8, m.30[d] (paper); m.21 (paper) and m.23[d] ('bordes' and 'bordes for bokes').

48 Needham, 'Customs Rolls' p. 159. Since the primer cargoes found here include items such as spectacles, combs, caps and beads, it seems likely that these books are that type of merchandise.

49 Casks were containers made through a labour-intensive process, while baskets were cheaply and quickly made of de-barked willow reeds that had been soaked in water and woven. See Ken Kilby, *Coopers and Coopering* (Princes Risborough, 2004) pp. 5, 7–20; Paul Ronald, *The Basketmakers' Company: A History of the Worshipful Company of Basketmakers of the City of London* (London, 1978) pp. 81, 125.

50 Cobb, *Overseas Trade* n. 23 (29 volumes), n. 174 (96 volumes). However, it may be that the chest is a bad example, as there is no standard size to this container.

51 Mary C. Erler, 'The Maner of Lyue Well and the Coming of English in François Regnault's Primers of the 1520s and 1530s' The Library series 6, 6 (1984) pp. 229–43 (p. 230) and 'Devotional Literature' in CHBB III pp. 495–525 (pp. 503–4). See too Eamon Duffy, Marking the Hours: English People and Their Prayers 1240–1570 (New Haven CT, 2006) pp. 136–37.

52 Erler, 'Lyue Well' p. 230 and 'Devotional Literature' pp. 503–4; Duffy, Marking the Hours pp. 136–43. See also E. Gordon Duff, 'Regnault (François)' in A Century of the English Book Trade (London, 1948) pp. 133–34.

53 Regnault must be the merchant identified as 'Francisci Reynold'.

54 Duffy, Marking the Hours p. 138.

55 TNA E 122/82/8, m.5.

56 Plomer, 'Low Country' p. 165.

57 TNA E 122/80/3 m.3^d.

58 TNA E 122/80/5, m.8.

59 TNA E 122/80/5, m.2.

60 TNA E 122/80/5, m.8.

61 TNA E 122/81/18, m.26^d.

62 TNA E 122/81/18, m.10.

63 Pollard stated that there is 'as yet' no evidence that books were imported already bound, although he thought it was certainly possible. See Pollard, 'English Market' p. 15 and 'The Early Constitution of the Stationers' Company' The Library series 4, 18 (1937) pp. 1–38 (p. 27).

64 25 Henry VIII, c15. (15 Jan. 1534) in James Gairdner (ed.) Letters and Papers, Foreign and Domestic, Henry VIII, VII (London, 1883) pp. 23–24 (repr. in CHBB III pp. 609–10 (Appendix).

65 Howard Winger (p. 169) believes that this regulation has more to do with keeping an eye on incoming texts than benefiting local book artisans, as the unbound sheets would be sent in bulk to wholesalers instead of being dispersed to numerous retailers, making them easier to control.

66 In 1483 an Act preventing alien merchants from selling retail and alien craftsmen from employing foreign apprentices ended with the proviso that it excluded those involved in the book trade (writers, limners, binders and printers). See I Richard III, c.9 in The Statutes of the Realm, 1377–1504 III (London, 1900) (repr. in CHBB III p. 608 (Appendix). See also Winger, 'Regulations' p. 164.

67 Winger, 'Regulations' p. 176. Regnault is not listed as importing bound books in 1534/5.

68 TNA E 122/81/18, m.10.

69 Needham, 'Customs Rolls' p. 159; Raven p. 5. These primers were considered chapmen's-ware: low-profit but high-volume and sold with other cheap goods such as ribbons and assorted pills and medicine; Needham and Raven consider this type of primer, valued by the dozen or gross, to fall outside the traditional book trade. This may explain why Regnault's works are not described as primers in the customs accounts.

70 TNA E122/82/8, m.2; m.5 and m.17^d respectively.

71 STC 15924. Printed in Paris by Nicholas Higman for Birckman and Regnault.

72 F. Madan, 'Day-Book of John Dorne, Bookseller in Oxford, A.D. 1520' Collectanea 1st series (Oxford, 1885) pp. 71–181.

73 Madan nn. 718, 913. In contrast, a missale sarum rowan paruum ligatum by an unnamed printer could be had for only 1s. 8d. (Madan n. 335). William Jackson believes that, since John Dorne was an alien bookseller, the bulk of his stock

would have been imported books (William A. Jackson, 'A London Booksellers Ledger of 1535' *Colophon* new series l (1936) pp. 498–509 (p. 498)). Dorne's list includes native printers such as John Rastell (Madan nn. 609, 1056). See Duff, 'Rastell (John)' in *Century of the English Book Trade* p. 129. Noting printers' names in booksellers accounts seems to be unusual. See Jackson pp. 498–509; Leslie Mahin Oliver, 'A Bookseller's Account Book, 1545' *Harvard Library Bulletin* 16 (1968) pp. 139–55; E. Gordon Duff, 'A Bookseller's Accounts, *c.*1510' *The Library* series 2, 8 (1907) pp. 256–66.

74 The 1507 rate book (*Book of Rates*) contained 300 items, while 790 were listed in the 1545 book (*The Rate of the Custome House both Inwarde and Outwarde*). See Cobb, 'Books of Rates' p. 11; Needham, 'Customs Rolls' pp. 159–60.

75 Was 1 in Appendix A   Cobb, *Overseas Trade*, pp. xxiii–xxvi.

6: *Anna Lewis* 'But solid food is for the mature, who ... have their senses trained to discern good and evil': John Colop's Book and the Spiritual Diet of the Discerning Lay Londoner

1 Bernard of Clairvaux, *On the Song of Songs*, trans. Kilian Walsh, 4 vols (Kalamazoo MI, 1976) II, 175–76 (sermon 36).

2 Colop was employed by John Carpenter, Common Clerk of London and executor of Mayor Richard Whittington's will, to help in the administration of the will's bequests. Colop was also a co-founder of a pious fraternity that maintained a chapel and a hospital for nine needy men. The fraternity had links to Syon Abbey, and fellow members included John Somerset, physician to Henry VI and Chancellor of the Exchequer, and Reginald Pecock. See A.I. Doyle, 'A Survey of the Origins and Circulation of Theological Writings in English in the 14th, 15th and Early 16th Centuries, with Special Consideration to the Part of the Clergy Therein' (unpublished doctoral thesis, University of Cambridge, 1953) II, pp. 211–12; Wendy Scase, 'Reginald Pecock, John Carpenter and John Colop's "Common-Profit" Books: Aspects of Book Ownership and Circulation in Fifteenth-Century London' *Medium Aevum*, 61 (1992) pp. 261–74.

3 A.I. Doyle, 'The European Circulation of Three Latin Spiritual Texts' in A.J. Minnis (ed.) *Latin and Vernacular: Studies in Late-Medieval Texts and Manuscripts* (Cambridge, 1989) pp. 129–46 (p. 133). The texts composed of biblical translation and commentary have been taken from the Lollard Glossed Gospels, books of authoritative commentary—without any independent comment—on the four gospels. On the Glossed Gospels see Anne Hudson, *The Premature Reformation* (Oxford, 1998) pp. 248–59.

4 Bernard p. 177.

5 John Cassian, *Conferences,* trans. Colm Luibheid (Mahwah NJ, 2002) p. 64.

6 Robert E. Lerner, *The Heresy of the Free Spirit in the Later Middle Ages* (Berkeley CA, 1972) p. 221.

7 Lerner p. 128.

8 Lerner p. 45.

9 Lerner pp. 182–99.

10 Kathryn Kerby-Fulton, *Books under Suspicion: Censorship and Tolerance of Revelatory Writing in Late Medieval England* (Notre Dame IN, 2006) pp. 260–71.

11 See Kerby-Fulton pp. 261, 309–11.

12   Rosalynn Voaden, *God's Words, Women's Voices: The Discernment of Spirits in the Writings of Late-Medieval Women Visionaries* (York, 1999) p. 57.

13   Vincent Gillespie, 'The Haunted Text: Reflections in The Mirrour to Deuote Peple' in J. Mann and M. Nolan (eds) *The Text in the Community: Essays on Medieval Works, Manuscripts, Authors and Readers* (Notre Dame IN, 2006) pp. 129–72 (pp. 131, 135).

14   Gillespie, 'The Haunted Text' pp. 135–36.

15   Reginald Pecock, *Reginald Peacock's Book of Faith: A Fifteenth Century Theological Tractate*, ed. J.L. Morison (London, 1909) p. 110.

16   Reginald Pecock, *The Repressor of Over Much Blaming of the Clergy*, ed. C. Babington, 2 vols (London, 1860) I, 67–68.

17   Margery Kempe offers a contemporary example of the way 'singuleer holynes' creates resentment and bitterness among others in the community.

18   The gender of the novice is not made clear and the entire use of the form of personal letter may be only a literary convention (see Phyllis Hodgson (ed.), *Deonise Hid Divinite and Other Treatises on Contemplative Prayer Related to The Cloud of Unknowing*, EETS OS 231 (London, 1955) p. xxxvii). However, as several of the comments made by the author imply that he has in mind the context of a monastic brotherhood, I have used the male pronoun in the discussion of the text given here.

19   The text is described by Doyle, 'The European Circulation' pp. 133–38.

20   Kerby-Fulton; Marleen Cré, *Vernacular Mysticism in the Charterhouse: A Study of London, British Library, MS Additional 37790* (Turnhout, 2006).

21   Kerby-Fulton p. 295; Cré p. 97.

22   Kerby-Fulton p. 295.

23   Kerby-Fulton p. 290.

24   Kerby-Fulton p. 295.

25   Cré p. 97.

26   Reginald Pecock, *The Reule of Crysten Religioun*, ed. William Cabell Greet (London, 1927) p. 16.

27   Pecock, *Reule* pp. 87–99.

28   Pecock, *Reule* pp. 18–19; Pecock, *Book of Faith* p. 120.

29   Pecock, *Reule* p. 365.

30   See Doyle, 'A Survey'; Scase; Gillespie, 'The Haunted Text' pp. 131–37 and 'Walter Hilton at Syon Abbey', in James Hogg (ed.) *Stand up to Godwards: Essays in Mystical and Monastic Theology in Honour of the Reverend John Clark on his Sixty-Fifth Birthday*, Analecta Cartusiana 204 (Salzburg, 2002) pp. 40–50.

31   Mary Erler, *Women, Reading, and Piety in Late Medieval England* (Cambridge, 2002) p. 71.

32   For example, London, BL, MS Harley 993, a common-profit book made from the goods of Robert Holland, passed through the hands of an attorney of the bishop of London and a priest before ending up in the hands of a nun of Syon Abbey. Another, Oxford, Bodleian Library, MS Douce 25, seems to have entered a London house of Franciscan nuns where it remained into the sixteenth century. See Doyle, 'A Survey' II, 212, and Scase.

33   Gillespie, 'Walter Hilton at Syon' p. 41.

34   Erler, *Women, Reading* p. 137.

7: *Anne F. Sutton*   The Acquisition and Disposal of Books for Worship and Pleasure by Mercers of London in the Later Middle Ages

1   A.F. Sutton, 'Fifteenth-century Mercers and the Written Word: Mercers and their Scribes and Scriveners' in J. Boffey and V. Davis (eds) *Recording Medieval Lives* (Donington, 2009) pp. 42–58.

2   A list of all surviving mercers' books known to her was made by K.L. Scott, *The Mirroure of the Worlde. MS Bodley 283 (England c.1470–1480). The Physical Composition, Decoration and Illustration*, The Roxburghe Club (Oxford, 1980) p. 9, nn. 1–4, used with profit by A.F. Sutton, *The Mercery of London: Trade, Goods and People 1130–1578* (Aldershot, 2005) p. 168. A correction must be made to this list: the John Brown who owned the book of hours, Philadelphia Free Library, Widener 3, depicting him and his wife at a mass of St Gregory, was the John Brown of Stamford not the London mercer (see R. Marks and P. Williamson (eds), *Gothic Art for England 1400–1547* (London, 2003) p. 278 (cat. 140).

3   C.W. Brockwell, *Bishop Reginald Pecock and the Lancastrian Church* (Lewiston NY and Queenstown ONT, 1985) p. 21.

4   Wendy Scase, 'Reginald Pecock' in M.C. Seymour (ed.) *English Writers of the Late Middle Ages* III, nos 7–11 (Aldershot, 1996) pp. 86–91 (esp. p. 89).

5   M. Aston, 'Devotional Literacy' in M. Aston, *Lollards and Reformers. Images and Literacy in Late Medieval England* (1984) pp. 127–33; Sutton, *Mercery* pp. 164–66.

6   Sutton, *Mercery* pp. 181–82.

7   See in this volume Anna Lewis's discussion of Colop and 'common profit' books.

8   John Killum was an apprentice and servant of Nicholas Brembre (P. Nightingale, *A Medieval Mercantile Community. The Grocers' Company and the Politics and Trade of London 1000–1485* (London and New Haven CT, 1995) p. 322). He entered a bond for another grocer in 1387 and was trading in Bruges, Middelburg and Calais in the 1380s to 1390s (A.H. Thomas and P.E. Jones (eds), *Calendar of Plea and Memoranda Rolls ... of the City of London* (hereafter CPMR), 6 vols (Cambridge, 1926–61) III, 127–28; *Calendar of Close Rolls* (hereafter CCR) ... *Richard II*, 6 vols (London, 1914–27) VI, 204). He attended Grocers' elections (1398–1408) (J.A. Kingdon, *Facsimile of First Volume of MS Archives of the Worshipful Company of Grocers of the City of London, AD 1345–1463*, 2 vols (London, 1886) I, 76, 85, 89, 94, 103). In April 1414 he and others bailed a Laurence de Platea from the Fleet (CCR ... *Henry V*, 2 vols, I, 146). Killum's will shows him as a parishioner of St Stephen Walbrook but requests burial in Holy Trinity Aldgate; he mentioned kindred but no other Killums; his executors were Colop, William Michell [grocer], John Sudbury and his kinsman Thomas Page; his overseer was Robert Chichele, alderman (1402–26) and rebuilder of St Stephen's; he had associations in Essex, as did Martin Kelom, and in Suffolk (The National Archives (hereafter TNA) PROB 11/2B, ff. 36ᵛ–37ᵛ, proved 4 April 1416). For the fact that Sudbury knew John Carpenter and received one of his books, see M. Erler, *Women, Reading, and Piety in Late Medieval England* (Cambridge, 2002) pp. 64, 173 (n. 77). For Martin see below.

9   W. Scase, 'Reginald Pecock, John Carpenter and John Colop's "Common-profit" Books: Aspects of Book Ownership and Circulation in Fifteenth-century London' *Medium Aevum* 61 (1992) pp. 261–74 (esp. pp. 261–62 for Colop and Killum).

10 M.G. Sargent, 'Walter Hilton's *Scale of Perfection*: the London Manuscript Group Reconsidered' *Medium Aevum* 52 (1983) pp. 205–6, and Scase, 'Reginald Pecock' pp. 262–65 (for the extension of the concept to libraries), 265–70 (for Pecock's involvement).

11 For William Bury, see Guildhall Library (hereafter GL) MS 9171/3, f. 107 (proved 1423); R. Smith, 'The Library at Guildhall in the Fifteenth and Sixteenth Centuries, Part I: to 1425' and 'Part II. Inter-chapter: William Bury, John White and William Grove' *Guildhall Miscellany* no. 1 (1952) pp. 2–9, *Guildhall Miscellany* no. 6 (1956) pp. 2–6.

12 Haxey inscribed in a book in the church of Haxey, Lincs., the names of the relatives he wished prayed for; he supervised and paid a stationer for the binding of the twenty quires that made up the Mercers' new book of ordinances 1436–37; he funded a pilgrimage to St James Compostella and left small sums to the Holy Sepulchre and the Hospital of St Thomas, Rome (GL MS 9171/5, f. 305, proved 27 January 1461; Sutton, *Mercery* p. 180).

13 Roger Merssh, clerk and mercer, left his library and other property to Sherington's chantry at St Paul's (R.R. Sharpe (ed.) *Calendar of Wills Proved and Enrolled in the Court of Husting, London, A.D. 1258–A.D. 1688* (hereafter *CWH*), 2 vols (London, 1889–90) II, 539–40, dated 1457, enrolled 1459). Sherington had been a royal clerk and, as a prebendary of St Paul's (1440–49), overhauled the cathedral's library and records; his executors included Thomas Lisieux, Merssh (once keeper of the rolls of the duchy of Lancaster) and Nicholas Sturgeon, uncle of Joan Sturgeon, the wife of Thomas Frowyk (see below) (D. Keene, A. Burns, and A. Saint (eds), *St Paul's. The Cathedral Church of London 604–2004* (New Haven CT and London, 2004) pp. 415–17).

14 Sutton, *Mercery* pp. 167–68. For Whittington's Bible, see below and nn. 18, 19; for Roos, see below nn. 85, 90–91.

15 For some matters of debate, see Wendy Scase, *Piers Plowman and the New Anticlericalism* (Cambridge, 1989) *passim*; Aston pp. 100–33.

16 C.M. Barron, 'Richard Whittington: the man behind the myth' in A.E.J. Hollaender and W. Kellaway (eds) *Studies in London History Presented to P.E. Jones* (1969) pp. 213–15, and 'William Langland: A London poet' in B. Hanawalt (ed.) *Chaucer's England: Literature in Historical Context* (Minneapolis MN, 1992) pp. 95–96; Sutton, *Mercery* pp. 163–64.

17 Cok added a short extract from the poem to a collection of pious texts in Cambridge, Gonville and Caius MS 669[X]/646 and also added (and signed) a text on the Paternoster (A.I. Doyle, 'More Light on John Shirley' *Medium Aevum* 30 (1961) pp. 98–99, and 'Remarks on surviving copies of *Piers Plowman*' in G. Kratzmann and J. Simpson (eds) *Medieval English Religious and Ethical Literature. Essays in Honour of G.H. Russell* (Cambridge, 1986) p. 45.

18 In 1463 Cok, in his sixty-ninth year and at the request of John Wakering in the forty-second year of his mastership, added to the Bible a summary catalogue (*quod Johannes Cok*) which he finished in 1464, adding in that year a further glossary of difficult words (*Valete quia mors kapit me de medio. Orate pro anima scriptoris.*). See H. Butzmann, *Katalog der Herzog August Bibliothek Wolfenbüttel: Die mittelalterlichen Handschriften der Gruppen Extravagantes, Novi und Novissimi* (Frankfurt am Main, 1972) pp. 9–21: 25.1 Extravagantes, esp. ff. 489[r], 493[v], 498[r]–99[v], 501[r]. The present author is most grateful to the library at Wolfenbüttel for access to this book.

19 N. Moore, *The History of St Bartholomew's Hospital*, 2 vols (London, 1918) II, 14–15, citing Cok's note about the recovery in the Hospital's Cartulary (f. 63); for Cok, see Moore II, 1–44, and N.J.M. Kerling (ed.) *The Cartulary of St Bartholomew's Hospital. A Calendar* (London, 1973) pp. 2–3, 8.

20 A.F. Sutton, 'The Hospital of St Thomas of Acre of London: The Search for Patronage, Liturgical Improvement and a School, under Master John Neel, 1420–63' in C. Burgess and M. Heale (eds) *The Late Medieval English College and Its Context* (Woodbridge, 2008) pp. 218–26; Scase, 'Reginald Pecok' pp. 93–95, 98–99, 101 (n. 191).

21 Original wills have not been checked to see if the calendar missed books, but on the whole it seems that *CWH* includes most (but not necessarily minor bequests such as primers). Second wills of one person have not been counted, and those with duplicate Prerogative Court of Canterbury wills have been placed in that court.

22 Picot: *CWH* I, pp. 233–34, and A.F. Sutton, 'The *Tumbling Bear* and Its Patrons: A Venue for the London Puy and Mercery' in J. Boffey and P. King (eds) *London and Europe in the Later Middle Ages* (London, 1995) pp. 85–110 (esp. pp. 102–7).

23 For the psalter see n. 61 below (Elizabeth Burley (Burlee)). For further figures on books in wills of this court, see R. Wood, 'A Fourteenth-century London Owner of *Piers Plowman*' *Medium Aevum* 53 (1984) p. 85.

24 Between 1400 and 1499, of the 227 PCC and Commissary Court of London (CC) wills of mercers and their widows and a daughter, only 39 (17%) refer to 75 books (counting a plural such as 'all' as one), which gives them a third of a book each.

25 Worstead: *CWH* II, 114–15. He was MP in 1366: A.B. Beaven, *The Aldermen of London*, 2 vols (London, 1908, 1913) I, 267.

26 Berney: *CWH* II, pp. 205–6. He was alderman (1368–69) but declined to be mayor, owned manors in Norfolk and wrote his will in Norwich where he was buried: W. Rye, *History of the Parish of Hellesdon in the City of Norwich*, Rye Monographs of Norwich Hamlets 3 (Norwich, 1917) pp. 151–52, 156. Norton: A.B. Emden, *A Biographical Register of the University of Cambridge to 1500* (hereafter *BRUC*) (Cambridge, 1963) p. 428.

27 Bury: see n. 52 below. Frowyk: n. 49 below. Wells: GL MS 9171/4, f. 19v (proved 1439). See A.F. Sutton, 'London Mercers from Suffolk c. 1200 to 1570: Benefactors, Pirates and Merchant Adventurers, parts 1 and 2' *Proceedings of the Suffolk Institute of Archaeology and History* 42 (2009–10) part 1 p. 7 (Bury), part 2 p. 163 (Wells).

28 Davy: PROB 11/4, ff. 28^v–29 (proved 1456); *CWH* II, p. 548, which does not refer to his primer, for which see n. 52 below. Frowyk: n. 49 below.

29 BL Arundel MS 109, cited by Scott, *Mirroure* p. 9 n. 1. For the fifth missal of John Sibille, see n. 40 below. Melreth: n. 95 below.

30 Sutton, *Mercery* p. 171.

31 Tenacre: n. 58 below. Denton: PROB 11/3, f. 129^{r-v} (proved 1432).

32 Woodcock: PROB 11/2A, ff. 133^v–37^v, esp. f. 133^v (proved January 1409); *CWH* II, pp. 397–98.

33 Sonningwell: GL MS 9171/1, f. 456^v (proved 1400); J.S. Roskell, L. Clark and C. Rawcliffe (eds), *The House of Commons 1386–1421*, 4 vols (Stroud, 1992) (*sub* Sunningwell).

34 Berby: PROB 11/5, ff. 172–74 (proved 1468).

35 Weston: PROB 11/17, f. 242 (written by himself and proved 6 February 1515).

36 Dunton: PROB 11/4, ff. 147ᵛ–49 (proved 1460). Kent: PROB 11/5, ff. 205–06ᵛ
    (proved 1469). Kent was a long-term ally of the Mercers and Adventurers;
    for his many books A.B. Emden, *A Biographical Register of the University
    of Oxford to 1500* (hereafter *BRUO*) 3 vols (Oxford, 1957–59) II, 1037–39;
    Sutton, *Mercery passim*. A surviving *Canterbury Tales* (Cambridge, Fitzwilliam
    Museum, McClean 181) was once in Kent's hands (J. Boffey and C. Meale,
    'Selecting the Text: Rawlinson C.86 and some other Books for London
    Readers' in F. Riddy (ed.) *Regionalism in Late Medieval Manuscripts and Texts*
    (Cambridge, 1991) p. 165 (n. 76).

37 West: PROB 11/18, f. 259ᵛ (proved 18 Sept. 1518).

38 Madour: *CWH* I, p. 583. I am most grateful for the advice of Nigel Morgan on
    the books for divine service.

39 Hellesdon: PROB 11/1, ff. 3ᵛ–4ᵛ (proved 26 April 1384). He was alderman
    1377–84: Rye pp. 114, 151–54.

40 Sibille: PROB 11/2A, f. 2ʳ⁻ᵛ (proved 1400).

41 Sonningwell: n. 33 above.

42 Marchford: PROB 11/2B, ff. 3, 8ʳ⁻ᵛ, 21 (foliation confused) (proved 1413).

43 Bally: PROB 11/2B, f. 89ᵛ (proved 23 December 1417). For Isabel, see A.F. Sutton,
    'Two Dozen and More Silkwomen of Fifteenth-century London' *The Ricardian*
    16 (2006) pp. 49–50.

44 Tickhill: PROB 11/2B, f. 127ʳ⁻ᵛ (proved 1419); Sutton *Mercery passim*. He was
    warden in 1409 and is not to be confused with the Thomas Tickhill who married
    the daughter of William Melreth (Sutton, *Mercery* pp. 249 (n. 50), 305, 556).

45 Estfeld: Lambeth Palace, Register Stafford, ff. 139–41ᵛ (repeated *CWH* II,
    pp. 509–11); Sutton, *Mercery* pp. 531–33. No will survives for Trees.

46 Katherine Rich: nn. 92, 93 below. Stokton: PROB 11/4, ff. 71ᵛ–75 (proved 1473);
    both sons *d.v.p.* Stokton's inventory, PROB 2/6, contains only debts. John
    Sutton: PROB 11/6 (esp. f. 284ᵛ).

47 Shore: PROB 11/10, ff. 77ᵛ–78ᵛ (in full in A.F. Sutton, 'William Shore,
    Merchant of London and Derby' *Derbyshire Archaeological Journal* 106 (1986)
    pp. 135–36). Thwaites: Dean and Chapter of Canterbury, Register F, ff. 185ᵛ–86
    (*sede vacante* will, proved 15 August 1503); *CWH* II, p. 621. His will shows he
    had books when he died but many had no doubt been seized by the king in 1495.
    For a discussion of the books commissioned by him now in the Royal Library,
    see J. Backhouse, 'Founders of the Royal Library: Edward IV and Henry VII
    as Collectors of Illuminated Manuscripts' in D. Williams (ed.) *England in the
    Fifteenth Century* (Woodbridge, 1987) pp. 23–41 (pp. 30, 34–35, 36–38).

48 See G.R. Owst, 'Some Books and Book-owners of Fifteenth-century St Albans'
    Transactions of St Albans and Hertfordshire Archaeological Society [no
    vol. number] (1929) p. 180, and Aston pp. 122–25.

49 Henry Frowyk: will proved 8 March 1460; Isabel Frowyk: PROB 11/5, ff. 73–74
    (proved 1465). For the text of both wills, see W.G. Davis, *The Ancestry of Mary
    Isaac* (Portland ME, 1955) pp. 236–39 (altar p. 234); pp. 240–41.

50 Wells: n. 27 above.

51 Syff: PROB 11/6, ff. 180–82 (proved 1476); A.F. Sutton, 'The Women of
    the Mercery: Wives, Widows and Maidens' in M. Davies and A. Prescott
    (eds) *London and the Kingdom. Essays in Honour of Caroline M. Barron*
    (Donington, 2008) p. 171.

52 Davy: n. 28. Wise: GL MS 9171/7, f. 14 (proved 18 February 1485); A.F. Sutton,

'Alice Claver d. 1489' in C.M. Barron and A.F. Sutton (eds) *Medieval London Widows 1300–1500* (London, 1994) p. 141 (n. 42).

53 Kirkby: PROB 11/5, ff. 53ᵛ–54 (proved 1 February 1465): the only hint at his status in his brief will is that Alderman Ralph Verney was an executor. Chatterley: GL MS 9171/6, f. 345ᵛ (proved 1483).

54 Sutton: PROB 11/6, ff. 282ᵛ–86ᵛ (proved 27 Oct. 1479); for his portiforium, see n. 46 above.

55 Hugh Brown: PROB 11/13, ff. 223ᵛ–24ᵛ, esp. f. 224ᵛ (proved 7 November 1503). He also paid for a 'table' for the Virgin's altar at Crutched Friars as well as vestments and altar furnishings.

56 Ripon: PROB 11/7, f. 104ʳ⁻ᵛ (made 1485, no probate).

57 Compare the 'great 'platt that has a pagent of Jesse be for *beatus vir* whyche I gave to my sayd godson more than iij yeres past but I desired to occupye hyt whyche I heve', left by the mercer Richard Golofer, who died in 1518 at the age of 83, to his godson, Richard Lee. For books he mentions only 'an Inventory' written in his own hand kept for him by his cousin Lee, one of several documents the old man had prepared in connection with the disposal of his estate. His son-in-law and executor was John Brown, a painter–stainer, who perhaps had some connection with the 'platt'. Golofer: GL MS 9171/9, f. 81ʳ⁻ᵛ (proved 10 March 1518).

58 Tenacre: PROB 11/10, ff. 119ᵛ–21; A.F. Sutton, 'Caxton was a Mercer' in N. Rogers (ed.) *England in the Fifteenth Century* (Stamford, 1994) p. 147. Colyns: C.M. Meale, 'Wynkyn de Worde's Setting Copy for *Ipomydon' Studies in Bibliography* 35 (1982) pp. 156–71, and 'The Compiler at Work: John Colyns and BL, MS Harley 2252' in D. Pearsall (ed.) *Manuscripts and Readers in Fifteenth-Century England: The Literary Implications of Manuscript Study* (Cambridge, 1983) pp. 82–103, and 'London, BL, Harley MS 2252: John Colyns' "Boke": Structure and Content' *English Manuscript Studies 1100–1700* 15 (2011).

59 Alwyn: PROB 11/15, ff. 9–12; A.F. Sutton, *A Merchant Family of Coventry, London and Calais: the Tates, c. 1450–1515* (London, 1998) pp. 5–7.

60 Carvile: PROB 11/14, f. 211ʳ⁻ᵛ (proved 10 March 1506). He was buried at St Benet Holme, Norfolk, leaving it many religious mementos; his nephew, John Carvile, was his sole executor. Compton: PROB 11/25, f. 269 (proved 4 May 1536).

61 Hellesdon: n. 39 above. Burley (Burlee): GL MS 9051/1, f. 9ʳ⁻ᵛ (proved 13 October 1403); D. Keene, *The Summary Report on the Walbrook Study*, Economic and Social Research Council (London, 1987) Appendix: Property Histories 118/15 (p. 44), 132/16 and 17 (pp. 58, 62).

62 Erler, *Women, Reading* p. 60. Whatley was an MP and well connected (Roskell *et al.* (eds) IV, 825–26; *CWH* II, p. 458).

63 Thake: GL MS 9171/3, f. 82ᵛ (proved 9 July 1421).

64 Cressy: PROB 11/3, f. 9ᵛ (proved 9 February 1423). His son, Thomas, appears to have become a mercer, but his admission is not recorded (Sutton, *Mercery* pp. 145, 246 n. 37, 556).

65 Thomas Aleyn: GL MS 9171/3, f. 508 (proved 1438). Margery Aleyn: GL MS 9171/4, ff. 81–82 (proved 11 April 1442).

66 Isabel Fleet: GL MS 9171/5, f. 190ʳ⁻ᵛ (proved 1455). Pikton: PROB 11/14, f. 229ᵛ–30 (proved 22 April 1505). Margaret Pikton: PROB 11/21, ff. 280–81 (proved 18 July 1525). See A.F. Sutton, 'The Shopfloor of the London Mercery

Trade, c. 1200–c. 1500: The Marginalisation of the Artisan, the Itinerant Mercer and the Shopholder' *Nottingham Medieval Studies* 45 (2001) pp. 43–45.

67 John Donne the elder: PROB 11/7, ff. 9–11ᵛ (proved 16 December 1480). Donne's interest in books and education is complemented by his provision in the will of £100 to young friars 'to comfort and chere him to his boke and lernyng' and support for young scholars of the universities to encourage them to become preachers. See Sutton, *Mercery passim*). Mustell: PROB 11/7, ff. 144–44 (proved 14 February 1486).

68 Maud Muschamp: PROB 11/11, ff. 163ᵛ–64ᵛ (proved 14 May 1498). Thomas Muschamp: PROB 11/6, ff. 104ᵛ–6 (proved 6 May 1473). See Sutton, *Mercery passim*. London, BL Harley MS 1807, a collection of legal texts, was acquired by them or their son in 1471 (A.F. Sutton, 'Alice Domenyk-Markby-Shipley-Portaleyn' *The Ricardian* 20 (2010) p. 60).

69 Also Ferre and Ferrys: TNA C 1/61/500 (dateable to 1480–83).

70 Stile, PROB 11/14, ff. 292ᵛ–94, esp. ff. 293ᵛ, 294; proved 17 October 1505; he forbade his children's portion being put out to earn interest so that they should not be supported by usury. Sutton, 'Caxton was a Mercer' pp. 140–46, and Sutton, *Mercery* p. 168. I am grateful to Dr Nigel Ramsay for Overton's position.

71 William Pratte: PROB 11/7, f. 192ʳ⁻ᵛ (proved 1486). Alice Pratte: PROB 11/8, f. 391ʳ⁻ᵛ; (proved 1491). See Sutton, 'Caxton was a Mercer' pp. 140–46.

72 Anne Bonyfaunt: PROB 11/11, f. 134 (proved 12 March 1498). Roger Bonyfaunt: PROB 11/10, ff. 122ᵛ–23 (proved 7 November 1494). See Sutton, *Mercery passim*.

73 Trussbut ('Trussebus'): PROB 11/3, ff. 211–12ᵛ (proved 11 December 1439).

74 Burton: GL MS 9171/5, ff. 303–4 (proved 13 December 1460). The book is now Oxford, Bodleian Library, Douce MS 372/392 (inscription f. 163ᵛ). See Sutton, 'Alice Claver' pp. 131–34.

75 Glasier: PROB 11/15, f. 236ᵛ–37 (proved 27 July 1507).

76 Bromwell: PROB 11/27, f. 13–14ᵛ (written 1536, proved 23 February 1537). Bromwell's wife was Jane Dormer, sister of Sir Robert Dormer; for his Froissart see below.

77 For the ordinances see Sutton, *Mercery* pp. 515–19. In 1401 the sisters, Joan and Agnes, had a remainder of the estate of John Cumberton after John's son, James, their father, William Cumberton, and their brother, John (*CCR ... Henry IV*, 5 vols, I, 399–400). By this date Joan was Martin's wife. Martin referred to Robert Comberton as his benefactor (GL MS 9171/3, f. 291).

78 Sutton, *Mercery* pp. 95–113.

79 *CCR Henry V*, I, 106, 117; *CPMR* IV, 46, 145–46.

80 D. Keene and V. Harding, *Historical Gazetteer of London before the Great Fire*, I *Cheapside* (Cambridge, 1987) pp. 418–19 (105/2). For her bequest to Whatley, see Erler, *Women, Reading* ch. 2 (esp. pp. 60–62 and n. 58). In 1411 Whatley and Roos acted as feoffees for the Mercers' Crown seld (*Calendar of Patent Rolls* (hereafter *CPR*) ... *Henry IV*, 4 vols, IV, 274); C.P. Christianson, *Memorials of the Book Trade in Medieval London* (Woodbridge, 1987) p. 6 (nn. 10, 15).

81 Erler, *Women, Reading* p. 65

82 *CPMR* IV, 217; P. Morant, *History and Antiquities of Essex*, 2 vols (London, 1768) II, 62. The manor descended to Anne's son, Humphrey Stafford, 1st duke of Buckingham.

83 Kelom: GL MS 9171/3, ff. 290–91 (no probate date, but probably 1431 by its placing in the register). In 1434 William Kyrkton, mercer, and his wife Joan,

daughter of Martin Kelom mercer, quitclaimed Margaret the widow and her fellow executors, *CPMR* IV, 273, and see *CPR* ... *Henry VI*, 6 vols, III, 4. Margaret Kelom: GL MS 9171/3, f. 395ᵛ: she left her tenement in Ashburton, inherited on her mother's death, to her son, John Covyn; her executors included John Sturgeon, mercer.

84 J.G. Richter, 'Education and Association: The Bureaucrat in the Reign of Henry VI' *Journal of Medieval History* 12 (1986) p. 96; *CPR* ... *Henry VI*, V, 301; *CCR* ... *Henry VI*, 6 vols, VI, 338; A.F. Sutton, 'A Community in St Bartholomew's Close' (forthcoming).

85 Mercers' Company, Wardens' Accounts 1348, 1391–1464, f. 8 (Richard Roos), f. 8ᵛ (Thomas Roos).

86 Sutton, 'London Mercers from Suffolk' part 2 pp. 162–463.

87 Wood, 'A Fourteenth-century London Owner' pp. 83–89 (esp. pp. 83–85).

88 *CPR* ... *Henry IV*, IV, 274; Barron, 'Richard Whittington' pp. 222–23, 233; Sutton, *Mercery* p. 556.

89 *Letter Book I* pp. 112, 193. The young Thomas Roos died in 1412 in the same parish of St Alphage as his uncle Thomas, referring to his father Richard as buried in Drayton church (no county); he made his uncle Thomas Roos and his step-father his executors (Archdeaconry Court GL MS 9051/1, ff. 10ᵛ–11). Wood ('A Fourteenth-century London Owner ' pp. 85–86) appears to conflate the two Thomas Rooses. For Davy see nn. 28, 52 above.

90 Only the fact of apprenticeship is recorded in the Mercers' Warden's Accounts and there is no issue date; given the tenour of Thomas's will, the indentures may have been cancelled. Gerebray may have died 1442 when he made a gift of his goods and chattels (*CPMR* V, 167).

91 GL MS 9171/3, ff. 369–70 (in 3 parts, proved 11 January 1434). He placed money in trust to support Elena and her children (Bernard, Florence, a boy, and Dionisia), but it was not to go to Roger; his other executor was John Knight, draper. He was to be buried in St Alpage with his wife Alice but was now living in St Mary Aldermanbury, where John 'Stodey' was parish clerk; the land in Beverley was bought from a Thomas Yole.

92 Richard Rich: PROB 11/5, ff. 32ᵛ–35ᵛ (proved 16 August 1464). Urswick's inventory listed a Froissart, *Speculum Sancti Edmundi* (in French), Mandeville's *Travels, Dialogue of the Holy Ghost* (in French), statutes of the 'custumage' (i.e. the English customs), and a *Canterbury Tales* (F.W. Steer, 'A Medieval Household. The Urswick Inventory' *Essex Review* 63 (1954) pp. 4–20, esp. p. 12). For the Rich family, see B.H. Putnam, *Early Treatises on the Practice of the Justices of the Peace in the Fifteenth and Sixteenth Century* (Oxford, 1924) pp. 120–21, 129, and C.L. Kingsford (ed.) *The Stonor Letters and Papers*, 2 vols, Camden Society 3rd ser. 29 (London, 1919) I, xxvi–viii. The Riches' son, John, left his wife a large estate of 1,200 marks (PROB 11/4, f. 108, proved 4 November 1458). The sole surviving son, Thomas, executor of both his parents, married Elizabeth Croke, member of another wealthy London aldermanic family, and died 1471 (PROB 11/6, f. 147ʳ⁻ᵛ, only proved 4 Oct 1475, the burden falling on Robert Love). Complexities were caused by his widow's remarriages to John Fenne, who died in 1474 (PROB 11/6, ff. 125ᵛ–26), and then Sir William Stonor (see A. Hanham, 'The Stonors and Thomas Betson: Some Neglected Evidence' *The Ricardian* 15 (2005) pp. 33–52).

93 Katherine Rich: GL MS 9171/6, ff. 47–48 (proved 18 August 1469); for her great portuous, see above. See Sutton, 'Women of the Mercery' pp. 164–65.

94 C.M. Meale, "'... Alle the Bokes that I haue of Latyn, Englisch, and Frensch":
    Laywomen and their Books in Late Medieval England' in C.M. Meale (ed.)
    Women and Literature in Britain, 1150–1500 (Cambridge, 1991) p. 132; Sutton,
    'Women of the Mercery' pp. 160–62.

95 Melreth: PROB 11/3, ff. 257–58ᵛ (no probate date). For his missal, BL Arundel
    MS 109 (his image f. 161ᵛ), see Scott, *Mirroure* p. 9 (n. 1). For Beatrice's will,
    see H. Jenkinson and G.H. Fowler (eds) 'Some Bedfordshire Wills at Lambeth
    and Lincoln', *The Publications of the Bedfordshire Record Society* 14 (1931)
    pp. 123–25. 'Merce and gramerce' is probably to be identified as Henry of
    Lancaster's *Le Livre de Seyntes Medicines*, with thanks to Catherine Batt for
    this identification.

96 See also C.M. Meale, '*The Libelle of Englyshe Polycye* and Mercantile Literary
    Culture in Late-Medieval London' in Boffey and King (eds) pp. 198–202. Brown:
    PROB 11/13, ff. 223ᵛ–24ᵛ, esp. f. 224ᵛ (proved 7 November 1503). Bromwell:
    PROB 11/27, f. 13–14ᵛ (proved 23 February 1537). See above for his *Vitas
    Patrum*.

97 A.F. Sutton and L. Visser-Fuchs, *Richard III's Books* (Stroud, 1997) pp. 156–57,
    168–69, 182–84. For Caxton's complaint see N.F. Blake, *Caxtons' Own Prose*
    (London, 1973) pp. 132–33 (86b).

98 Frowyk: PROB 11/7, ff. 137ᵛ–38ᵛ (proved 10 November 1485). For all that
    follows, see A.F. Sutton and L. Visser-Fuchs, 'The Making of a Minor London
    Chronicle in the Household of Sir Thomas Frowyk (died 1485)' *The Ricardian*
    10 (1994–96) pp. 86–103, pp. 198–99; the pedigree should read: Margaret,
    wife of Thomas Tuddenham, was heiress to the de Refham fortune, and their
    daughter, Margaret, was the next heiress (Keene and Harding, *Historical
    Gazetteer*, 105/12).

99 Meale, '*Libelle*' esp. pp. 217–18; Sutton, *Mercery* pp. 236–37.

100 Scrayningham: PROB 11/5, f. 183ᵛ (proved 2 July 1468). Thirland not identified.

101 Illustrated in Sutton and Visser-Fuchs, *Richard III's Books* p. 255 (n. 65, fig. 77).
    Purde was admitted 1467, but no will survives.

102 Sutton, 'Caxton was a Mercer' p. 118.

103 E. Armstrong, 'English Purchases of Printed Books from the Continent
    1465–1526' *English Historical Review* 94 (1979) pp. 268–90.

104 *Pace* Sutton, *Mercery* p. 269, who momentarily confused this with the
    Polychronicon!

105 See G. Bone, 'Extant Manuscripts Printed from by W. de Worde with Notes
    on the Owner, Roger Thorney' *The Library* series 4, 12 (1932) pp. 284–306;
    A.F. Sutton and L. Visser-Fuchs (eds) *The Book of Privileges of the Merchant
    Adventurers 1296–1484* (London, 2009) App. 2; Sutton, *A Merchant Family* ch.
    2, esp. pp. 22–27, and p. 16 (the poem); A.S.G. Edwards and C.M. Meale, 'The
    Marketing of Printed Books in Late Medieval England' *The Library* series 6,
    15 (1993) pp. 123–24; Meale, '*Libelle*' pp. 204–6; A.S.G. Edwards, 'Continental
    Influences on London Printings and Reading in the Fifteenth and Sixteenth
    Centuries' in Boffey and King (eds) pp. 230–56.

106 Thorney was the first owner of Cambridge, Trinity College, MSS R.3.19
    (probably) and R.3.21 (certainly), in which he wrote his name, joined by that
    of William Middleton (a mercer?) who married Thorney's widow. See Bone,
    esp. pp. 301–4; N.F. Blake, *William Caxton: England's First Publisher* (London,
    1976) pp. 88–90; Scott, *Mirroure* pp. 9 (n. 1), 25, 32–33; Boffey and Meale
    pp. 147–48; Sutton and Visser-Fuchs, *Richard III's Books* p. 207.

107 C.J.F. Slootmans, *Paas-en Koudemarkten te Bergen op Zoom, 1365–1565* (Tilburg, 1985) p. 821. He founded a chantry at Jesus College, Cambridge, whose master was brother of his second wife (Bone pp. 299–302). Thorney: GL MS 9171/9, ff. 13–14 (proved January 1517).

108 C. Burgess (ed.) *The Pre-Reformation Records of All Saints, Bristol: Part I,* Bristol Record Society 46 (1995) pp. xvii–xviii; Sutton, 'Alice Claver' p. 135, *Mercery* pp. 229, 279, 303, 'Women of the Mercery' pp. 169–70. For the manuscript, see C.W. Dutschke and R.H. Rouse, *Guide to the Medieval and Renaissance Manuscripts in the Huntington Library,* 2 vols (San Marino CA, 1989) II, 247–51.

109 Cambridge, Magdalene College, Pepys MS 2006, a collection of several texts in which he is called 'Fetypace' (Boffey and Meale p. 164 (n. 74); Scott, *Mirroure* p. 9 (n. 1); Meale, '*Libelle*' p. 188 (n. 20)).

110 Oxford Bodleian Library, Rawlinson MS D 82, was part of a now-dismembered miscellany, including some Gower, which 'seems to have been early in the possession of John Keme, mercer and alderman of London (d. 1528)' who inscribed his name f. 14 (K. Harris, 'John Gower's *Confessio Amantis*: the Virtues of Bad Texts' in Pearsall (ed.) pp. 27–40 (p. 30)).

111 R. Thomson, *Descriptive Catalogue of Manuscripts at Corpus Christi College Oxford* (Cambridge, 2011).

112 Crisp: PROB 11/24, ff. 90–91 (written 12 December 1531, proved 14 March 1532). Crisps had been mercers since 1409: Thomas's father may be the Richard admitted in 1451, and his brother was admitted in 1513. A Crisp married the mercer William Merland (PROB 11/22, ff. 43ᵛ–44 proved 21 April 1526) who remembered his brothers-in-law, Hugh, Richard and Thomas Crisp. See Sutton, *Mercery* pp. 386, 558.

113 In the interests of completeness other manuscripts which have been associated with mercers are as follows, but none is entirely convincing: (1) BL, Harley MS 565 has been associated with (a) Richard Myton mercer, in fact more correctly *de civitate londoniensis mercatorem*: that is, a merchant (f. 101), but no Richard Myton is recorded as a mercer; and with (b) the mercer family of Lock (*iste liber constat walterus luck,* f. 125ᵛ), but no Walter Lock/Luck was ever a mercer, and the Lock family usually spelled their name 'Lok' and associated themselves with locks, not luck; and (c) with the mercer family of Alen or Aleyn, a Johannes Alyn being named (f. 125ᵛ). John Aleyn, however spelt, was a common name, and Sir John Alen, alderman, was the most famous of this name (d. 1546) (Boffey and Meale pp. 163–64 (n. 71)). (2) Harvard University Library, MS f. Engl. 752. Thomas Valens, who was appointed common meter by the Mercers in 1480 when the current officer fell ill, has been suggested as the marker of this copy of Lydgate's *Troy Book* (Meale, '*Libelle*' p. 188 (n. 23)). Valens or Valance may be another spelling of Thomas Fallows, admitted as a mercer in 1462 and fallen on hard times, as was usual with appointees to this post. (3) New York, Morgan Library, MS Bühler 5, a copy of Harding's Chronicle, has inscribed in it the name of William Statham, citizen of 'Towne', along with several other persons definitely of London. Of the two William Stathams admitted to the Mercers, the one admitted in 1476 is the most likely as regards the date of the handwriting (Meale, '*Libelle*' pp. 199–200). (Dr Meale kindly estimated the date of the hand; the word 'Towne' remains a problem.)

8: *Martha W. Driver*   'By Me Elysabeth Pykeryng': Women and Book Production in the Early Tudor Period

1   Some of this essay is drawn from Martha Driver, 'Women Printers and the Page, 1477–1541', *Gutenberg-Jahrbuch* (1998) pp. 139–53. Roberta Krueger kindly read a version of this talk at the meeting of the Modern Language Association in December 2009 when I was too ill to do so.

2   David Herlihy, *Opera Muliebria: Women and Work in Medieval Europe* (New York, 1990) p. 186.

3   Short biographies of printers appear, along with a cursory list of the books they printed, in *STC* III. Yolande Bonhomme is listed under her husband, Kerver (p. 97). For more on Yolande Bonhomme, see Beatrice Hibbard Beech, 'Yolande Bonhomme: A Renaissance Printer' *Medieval Prosopography* 6 (1983) pp. 79–100, and 'Women Printers in Paris in the Sixteenth Century' *Medieval Prosopography* 10 (1989) pp. 78, 82; Susan V. Lenky, 'Printer's Wives in the Age of Humanism' *Gutenberg-Jahrbuch* (1975) pp. 331–37 (pp. 334–35). See also E. Gordon Duff, *A Century of the English Book Trade* (London, 1948) p. 16. Birckman, the London stationer with a shop in St Paul's Churchyard, employed many French printers; his partner was apparently his wife's brother (Duff, *English Book Trade* p. 14). *STC* numbers are cited in the notes that follow for books examined at first hand in the order they are mentioned in the text.

4   *STC* 6832.31, the sole extant copy of the dictionary, is in Dublin Public Library. Biographical information is supplied in *STC* III, 27, and Duff, *English Book Trade* p. 17. See also Axel Erdmann, *My Gracious Silence: Women in the Mirror of Sixteenth-Century Printing in Western Europe* (Lucerne, 1999) pp. 139–40; he includes a helpful, though not comprehensive, list of women printers, 'Women in the Printing Business' (pp. 227–53).

5   For example, *STC* 15956, a Sarum Hours, 32mo in 8s, printed by Yolande Bonhomme for F. Byckman 1527, and *STC* 15836, a two-volume Sarum Breviary in 8vo printed 1555 for 1554 by Madeleine Boursette.

6   Duff, *English Book Trade* p. 140.

7   *STC* 2825, with emendations by George Joye, is the third edition of William Tyndale's New Testament (the first published in Cologne in 1525, the second in Worms *c.*1526), printed by Catherine van Ruremund in 1534; *STC* 2827, printed in 1535. A few examples of false colophons and other misleading attributions will suffice: *STC* 14826, *George Joye Confuteth Winchesters False Articles*, purportedly printed in 'Wesill in Cliefe lande' but actually in Antwerp by Catherine van Ruremund; *STC* 17798, Philip Melanchthon, *A Very Godly Defense*, translated by 'Lewis beuchame' (Joye) and printed in 'Lipse' by 'U. Hoff', a pseudonym for Catherine; *STC* 21804, James Sawtry (another pseudonym for Joye), *The Defence of Mariage of Preistes: Agenst Steuen Gardiner*, purportedly printed in 'Auryk' by 'J. Troost' but actually in Antwerp and by Catherine again; *STC* 14556, *Our sauior Iesus Christ hath not ouercharged his chirche with many ceremonies*, probably by Joye and said to have been printed in 'Zijrik' but actually in Antwerp by Catherine, here nameless.

8   *STC* 2372.4, *STC* 1280.

9   Stacey Gee, 'The Printers, Stationers and Bookbinders of York Before 1557' *Transactions of the Cambridge Bibliographical Society* 12, 1 (2000) pp. 27–54 (p. 41), and 'The Coming of Print to York *c.* 1490–1550' in Peter C.G. Isaac

and Barry McKay (eds) *The Mighty Engine: the Printing Press and Its Impact* (New Castle DE, 2000) pp. 79–88 (p. 83).

10 Duff, *English Book Trade* pp. 121, 132; *STC* III, 143. Barbara Kreps, 'Elizabeth Pickering: The First Woman to Print Law Books in England and Relations within the Community of Tudor London's Printers and Lawyers' *Renaissance Quarterly* 56 (2003) pp. 1053–88.

11 Francis Hamill, 'Some Unconventional Women before 1800: Printers, Booksellers, Collectors' *Papers of the Bibliographical Society of America* 49 (1955) pp. 300–14 (p. 305); Duff, *English Book Trade* p. 121. Copies of Pickering's law books examined in the Huntington Library and Harvard Law School include *Abregement of the Statutes Made in the .xxxii. Yere of the Reygne of Kyng Henry the Eyght* (London: by me Elysabeth late wyfe to Robert Redman dwellyng at the sygne of the George nexte to saynt Dunstones church, 1541?; *STC* 9543); George Ferrers, trans., *The Great Charter Called in Latyn Magna Carta* (London: by Elisabeth wydow of Robert Redman dwellyng at the sygne of the George next to saynte Dunstones churche, c. 1541; *STC* 9275); *The Maner of Kepynge a Courte Baron and a Lete with Diuers Fourmes of Entreis, Playntes, Processes, Presentments & Other Matters Determinable There* (London: per me Elisabeth Pykerynge viduam nuper vxoram spectabilis viri Roberti Redmani, n.d.; *STC* 7716); *In This Boke Is Conteyned the Offyce of Shyreffes, Bailliffes of Liberties, Escheatours, Constables and Coroners, & Sheweth What Euery One of Them May Do by Virtue of Theyr Offices, Drawen out of Bokes of the Comon Lawe & of the Statutes* (London: by me Elysabeth Pykerynge wydo to Robert Redman dwellynge at the sygne of the Gorge nexte to saynt Dunstones Churche, n.d.; *STC* 10985).

12 *STC* 18219, *STC* 9543.

13 *STC* 9275 reprints Redman's earlier edition, *STC* 9272.

14 *STC* 10970.

15 *STC* 7716.

16 *STC* 10985.

17 *STC* 9543.

18 Kreps pp. 1065–66.

19 In addition to reprinting the same titles published by Elizabeth Pickering, William Middleton used the same type and ornaments. Close comparison of Pickering's and Middleton's copies of *The Maner of Kepynge a Courte Baron*, for example, shows that Middleton used the same border on the title page and the same woodcut of the British royal arms on its verso. The Magna Carta editions printed by Pickering and Middleton also employ the same page layout, woodcuts and ornaments.

20 Kreps p. 1081.

21 Kreps (p. 1061) points out that the majority of Pickering's previous biographers omitted to mention Pickering's marriages to two men named Cholmeley, instead combining them into one husband.

22 Kreps pp. 1061–62.

23 Peter W.M. Blayney, *The Stationers' Company before the Charter, 1403–1557* (London, 2003) p. 41. Kreps (p. 1064) cites H.J. Byrom, 'Richard Tottel—His Life and Work' *The Library*, series 4, 8 (1928) pp. 199–232 (p. 202), who explains that, after Middleton was fined and imprisoned in 1543, 'he borrowed 170 pounds from William Cholmeley which he seems never to have repaid'.

24 Blayney p. 51.

9: *Shayne Husbands*   The Roxburghe Club: Consumption, Obsession and the Passion for Print

1   For a fascinating examination of the anxieties and pressures facing Britain during this period, see Ben Wilson, *Decency and Disorder: The Age of Cant 1789–1837* (London, 2007).

2   He had attempted to claim the Barony of Chandos although it appears that he had little or no connection to the family that had previously held the title but was in fact descended from a different family of the same name but lower social standing. Eventually, after a long period of humiliating failure, he was created a baronet in his own right in 1814. See *ODNB* [accessed 18 January 2012]: K.A. Manley, 'Brydges, Sir (Samuel) Egerton, first baronet, styled thirteenth Baron Chandos (1762–1837)'.

3   Edward Edwards' amusing description of Dibdin's works is that 'his well-known books have had the curious fortune to keep their price without keeping their reputation. They are lustily abused, and eagerly bought' (*Libraries and Founders of Libraries* (London, 1864) p. 418).

4   The founder members were Earl Spencer, Earl Gower, Sir Mark Masterman Sykes, Sir Samuel Egerton Brydges, William Bentham, William Bolland, John Dent, Rev. Thomas Frognall Dibdin, Francis Freeling, George Freeling, Joseph Haslewood, Richard Heber, Rev. Thomas Heber, George Isted, Robert Lang, John Delafield Phelps, Edward Utterson, Roger Wilbraham, the Duke of Devonshire, the Marquess of Blandford, Viscount Morpeth, James Markland, Thomas Ponton and Peregrine Towneley. At the first anniversary a further seven joined: Viscount Althorp, James Boswell, Rev. William Holwell Carr, Rev. James Dodd, Rev. Henry Drury, Edward Littledale and Joseph Littledale. This brought the club up to its full number of thirty-one. See *Roxburghe Club: List of Members 1812–1991, List of Books 1814–1990* (Otley, 1991) (unpaginated); for the same information, see <http://www.roxburgheclub.org.uk/> [accessed 18 January 2012].

5   Edward Edwards, *Memoirs of Libraries*, 2 vols (London, 1859) II, 136.

6   Edwards, *Libraries and Founders* pp. 440–41.

7   To discuss the manuscript interests of the Roxburghe members is too large a subject to tackle here, but as an example of the type of manuscript item that found favour among their collections one only has to look at the auction catalogue of the sale held after the death of John Dent, in which, having described one item, *Liber Regalis*, as 'one of the most curious, authentic and important manuscripts relating to the coronation of the Kings and Queens of England which exists', the catalogue goes on to say: 'It is quite surprising that it should be found in a private collection' (*Catalogue of the Second Portion of the Splendid, Curious, and Extensive Library of the Late John Dent, Esq., F.R.S. and F.S.A.* (London, 1827) p. 85).

8   Earl Spencer's library, for example, contained 'no less than fourteen block-books, comprising three editions of the *Ars Moriendi*, three of the *Speculum Humanae Salvationis*, two of the *Apocalypsis S. Johannis*, together with copies of the *Biblia Pauperum*, *Ars Memorandi*, *Historia Virginis ex Cantico Canticorum*, *Wie die fünfzehen zaichen kimen vor dem hingsten tag*, the *Enndchrist*, and *Mirabilia Romae*.' See William Younger Fletcher, *English Book Collectors* (London, 1902) p. 308.

9   T.F. Dibdin, *Reminiscences of a Literary Life*, 2 vols (London, 1836) I, 375 (also

mentioned by Joseph Haslewood in the manuscript of *The Roxburghe Revels*, a journal of meetings which is now held in the Roxburghe Club Archive).

10 John Ferriar, *The Bibliomania: an epistle to Richard Heber, Esq.* (London, 1809).

11 T.F. Dibdin, *Bibliomania; or, Book-madness; Containing Some Account of the History, Symptoms and Cure of this Fatal Disease, in an Epistle Addressed to Richard Heber, Esq.* (London, 1809).

12 T.F. Dibdin, *Bibliomania; or Book-Madness: A Bibliographical Romance in Six Parts* (London, 1811).

13 Dibdin, *Bibliomania* (1811) p. 4.

14 Jane Campbell, *The Retrospective Review (1820–1828) and the Revival of Seventeenth-Century Poetry* (Waterloo Ontario, 1972) p. 5.

15 J.M., letter, *The Gentleman's Magazine* (September 1813) pp. 211–12.

16 The Right Honorable Lorde Henry earle of Surrey, *Certaine Bokes of Virgiles Aenaeis, Turned into English Meter* (1557), reprinted by William Bolland for the Roxburghe Club (1814).

17 Harrison Ross Steeves, *Learned societies and English Literary Scholarship* (New York, 1913) p. 109.

18 'The value of [*Havelock the Dane*] as a contribution to English literature has been attested by the extensive critical examination it has received, and by its being reprinted for sale. And this, by the way, suggests a practical answer to those who complain of the arrangement, essential to the club system, of limiting the number of the impression of each volume. There is, in the general case, no copyright in the book, and it is free to any one who thinks the public at large will buy it, to reprint it, and supply the market' (John Hill Burton, 'The Book Hunter's Club', *Blackwood's Edinburgh Magazine* 90 (October 1861) p. 448).

19 John Gower, *Balades and other Poems*. 'Printed from the original MS. in the Library of the Marquess of Stafford, at Trentham. With an Introduction by Lord Gower' (*Roxburghe Club*).

20 David Matthews, *The Making of Middle English, 1765–1910* (Minneapolis MN, 1999) pp. 85–109; Alice Chandler, *A Dream of Order* (London, 1971).

21 J.K., letter, *The Gentleman's Magazine* (December 1813) p. 544.

22 Michael Edward Robinson has also noted the extremity of reaction provoked by the Roxburghe Club in their early days, although he attributes it to different motives, seeing it as a reaction to the perceived effeminacy of the bibliophile ('Ornamental Gentlemen: Literary Curiosities and Queer Romanticisms' (unpublished doctoral thesis, University of Southern California, 2010), published online at <http://digitallibrary.usc.edu/assetserver/controller/item/etd-Robinson–3496.pdf> [accessed 18 January 2012].

23 Sir Samuel Egerton Brydges, 'On Bibliomania', *Theatrical Inquisitor, or Monthly Mirror* 14, 81 (April 1819) p. 277.

24 John Hill Burton, *The Book Hunter etc ... with Additional Notes by Richard Grant White* (New York, 1863) p. 285.

25 John Martin, *A Bibliographical Catalogue of Books Privately Printed* (London, 1834) p. 379.

26 Will Ransom, *Private Presses and their Books* (New York, 1929) p. 29. Ransom describes these publications as being 'under the editorial direction of Sir Egerton Brydges and most of them were his own writings'.

27 Sir Samuel Egerton Brydges, *A Catalogue of All the Works Printed at the Private*

Press at Lee Priory in Kent: from its Commencement in July 1813, Till Its Termination in Jan. 1823. [With a Ms. Letter from Geneva by Sir E. Brydges, Dated March 29, 1824, Respecting the Difficulty of Transmitting Books to England] (1824) <http://www.presscom.co.uk/leepriory1.html> [accessed 18 January 2012].

28 *Roxburghe Club.*

29 T.F. Dibdin, *The Bibliographical Decameron; or, Ten days Pleasant Discourse upon Illuminated Manuscripts, and Subjects connected with Early Engraving, Typography, and Bibliography*, 3 vols (London, 1817) III, 454.

30 Ransom p. 207; Martin pp. 349, 357.

31 Dibdin, *Bibliographical Decameron* III, 454.

32 *Roxburghe Club*; John Payne Collier, 'Lady Pecunia, or the Praise of Money' in *Bibliographical and Critical Account of the Rarest Books in the English Language, Alphabetically Arranged*, 2 vols (London, 1865) I, 58–62.

33 'The products of the press amounted to 'about forty distinct publications, from the most recondite treatises to rare old chap ballads besides a multitude of scarce tractates and leaflets bearing on history, social economy, philosophy &c, the number and titles of which it is almost impossible now to trace' (Robert Howie Smith, *The Poetical Works of Sir Alexander Boswell* (Glasgow, 1871) p. xxxiii).

34 *ODNB* [accessed 18 January 2012]: Arthur Sherbo, 'Utterson, Edward Vernon (*bap.* 1777, *d.* 1856)'.

35 John Payne Collier, 'Reprints of Early English Poetry', *Notes and Queries* series 2:I (1) (1856) pp. 6–7.

36 Ransom p. 213

37 *ODNB* [accessed 18 January 2012]: Reavley Gair, 'Rowlands, Samuel (*fl.* 1598–1628)'. The works were *The Knave of Harts. Haile Fellow well met* (of which fifteen copies were printed and distributed to friends, no. 6 being James Heywood's copy); *The Knave of Clubbs* (fifteen copies); *More Knaves yet? The knaves of Spades and Diamonds* (sixteen copies); *The Night-Raven* (sixteen copies); *Looke to it: for, Ile stabbe ye* (fifteen copies) *and The melancholie Knight* (sixteen copies).

38 *ODNB* [accessed 18 January 2012]: Gary Taylor, 'Middleton, Thomas (*bap.* 1580, *d.* 1627)'.

39 David Matthews (p. 90) highlights this crossover of influences inside and outside the Club when he writes: 'Between 1812 and the late 1830s, [the Roxburghe and Bannatyne Clubs] were responsible for almost the entirety of Middle English production. The Roxburghe was alone in the field until 1823, and even when a publication came from elsewhere, it was typically done by someone who was a member of the Club.'

40 'The volume was bought at the sale by Mr. Thorpe for 40l. and by him offered, through me, to the purchase of the Roxburghe Club. Of course, no gentleman would think of putting his hand into his pocket with a view, as it might have been said, of hushing up any strictures advanced upon SUCH an association. The characters and rank in life of the members placed them far above it.' (Dibdin, *Reminiscences* I, 426).

41 *ODNB* [accessed 18 January 2012]: Alan Bell, 'Haslewood, Joseph (1769–1833)'.

42 Cathleen Hayhurst Wheat, 'Joseph Haslewood and the Roxburghe Club', *The Huntington Library Quarterly* 11 (1947) pp. 37–49.

43 Letter from Joseph Haslewood to an unknown recipient contained in a scrapbook (Roxburghe Club Archive).

44 'The Roxburghe Revels, MS', *The Athenaeum* (4 January 1834), based on information from Haslewood's journal (see n. 9 above).

45 T.F. Dibdin and James Maidment (Edinburgh, 1837).

46 'Sale of the Library of Joseph Haslewood Esq.', *The Gentleman's Magazine* (March 1834) pp. 286–8.

47 Edwards, *Libraries and Founders* p. 419

48 Burton, *The Book Hunter* p. 270

49 As H.R. Steeves expressed it, 'The club prided itself upon exclusiveness, but an exclusiveness which belonged to the nature of its hobby, rather than to aristocratic preferences' (*Learned Societies and English literary scholarship in Great Britain and the United States* (New York, 1913) p. 102).

50 For this and the following quotation, see Burton, *The Book Hunter* p. 270.

51 Dibdin, *Reminiscences* (London, 1836) I, 429.

52 T.F. Dibdin, *The Library Companion; or, the Young Man's Guide, and the Old Man's Comfort, in the Choice of a Library* (London, 1824).

53 '*The Library Companion; or, the Young Man's Guide, and the Old Man's Comfort, in the Choice of a Library*' *Quarterly Review* 32 (1825) p. 152.

54 'The value of such a series (apart from all typographic considerations) as materials of literary history and as aids to textual criticism is obvious enough. Even those wise critics who are wont to say: "Do not talk to us about 'rare' books, but about good books" may be pleased to comprehend that such a series represents so many precious manuscripts, most of which have perished' (Edwards, *Libraries and Founders* p. 435).

55 Frederick Adolphus Ebert, *A General Bibliographical Dictionary* (Oxford, 1838) III, 1258.

56 David Matthews notes: 'Where the Roxburghe Club did attempt some fidelity to a fifteenth-century model for its books, the Scottish clubs recreated their texts more in terms of what the nineteenth century thought was "medieval"' (Matthews p. 94).

57 JPC in a review of vol. III of Dibdin's *Typographical Antiquities; or the History of Printing in England, Scotland and Ireland* (London, 1816) in *The Critical Review, or, Annals of Literature* series 4:IV (1816) p. 246. For the identification, see Arthur Freeman and Janet Ing Freeman, *John Payne Collier: Scholarship and Forgery in the Nineteenth Century* (New Haven CT, 2004) p. 69.

58 Edwards, *Libraries and Founders* p. 424.

59 One of the 'crimes' of Joseph Haslewood recounted in the *Athenaeum* article was phrased thus: 'How he contrived to become one of the number, is, to us, a mystery which possibly Dr. Dibdin could explain, for we do not think that at the sale of the library of the Duke of Roxburghe, in 1812, his purchases were sufficient in number or value to warrant his filling so prominent a station' (Anon., 'The Roxburghe Revels, MS.' *The Athenaeum* (4 January 1834)).

10: *Carrie Griffin*   Reconsidering the Recipe: Materiality, Narrative and Text in Later Medieval Instructional Manuscripts and Collections

1 My research is generously supported by the IRC Government of Ireland CARA Postdoctoral Mobility Fellowship Scheme.

2 The doyennes of studies on medieval culinary recipes are C.B. Hieatt and S. Butler; see in particular their *Curye on Inglysch: English Culinary Manuscripts of the Fourteenth Century (including the Forme of Cury)* (Oxford,

1985). Important work on culinary and other recipe texts and contexts includes: R. Carroll, 'Vague Language in the Medieval Recipes of the *Forme of Cury*' in Matti Peikola, Janne Skaffari and Sanna-Kaisa Tanskanen (eds) *Instructional Writing in English: Studies in Honour of Risto Hiltunen* (Amsterdam, 2009) pp. 55–82 and 'Middle English Recipes: Evolution of a Text-Type' in Irma Taavitsainen and Päivi Pahta (eds) *Medical and Scientific Writing in Medieval and Early Modern English* (Cambridge, 2004) pp. 174–91; T. Hunt, *Popular Medicine in Thirteenth-Century England: Introduction and Texts* (Cambridge, 1990); G. Keiser, 'Verse Introductions to Middle English Medical Treatises' *English Studies* 84 (2004) pp. 301–17; J. Stannard, 'Medieval Herbals and Their Development' *Clio Medica* 9 (1974) pp. 23–33; I. Taavitsainen, 'Middle English recipes: Genre characteristics, text type features and underlying traditions of writing' *Journal of Historical Pragmatics* 2 (2001) pp. 85–113.

3 K.A. Rand Schmidt, '*The Index of Middle English Prose* and Late Medieval English Recipes' *English Studies* 75 (1994) pp. 423–29 (p. 423). (Further page references to her arguments are incorporated in the text.)

4 H. Hargreaves, 'Some Problems in Indexing Middle English Recipes' in A.S.G. Edwards and D. Pearsall (eds) *Middle English Prose: Essays on Bibliographical Problems* (New York, 1981) pp. 91–113.

5 Taavitsainen, p. 106.

6 Rand Schmidt (pp. 423–24) notes that, according to *IMEP* guidelines, 'a distinction is to be made between collections of recipes and individual ones. Collections are to be indexed by transcribing at least fifty words, including the first ten or twelve of each of the first three recipes. One should then transcribe the lines which conclude the collection, giving some indication of the approximate number of recipes in the collection, as well as their subject matter, i.e. whether they are medical, culinary, or general.'

7 George R. Keiser, *A Manual of Writings in Middle English, 1050–1500, Vol. 10: Works of Science and Information* (New Haven CT, 1998).

8 George Keiser, 'Scientific, Medical and Utilitarian Prose' in A.S.G. Edwards (ed.) *A Companion to Middle English Prose* (Cambridge, 2004) pp. 231–47 (p. 242).

9 Taavitsainen p. 86.

10 D. Edmar (ed) 'A Middle English Leech-book: MS Wellcome 405' (unpubl. Lic. Phil. thesis, University of Stockholm, 1967) pp. 43–44.

11 M. Görlach, 'Text-types and language history: the cookery recipe' in M. Risanen, O. Ihalainen, T. Nevalaieren and I. Taavitsainen (eds) *History of Englishes* (Berlin, 1992) p. 756; Taavitsainen p. 86.

12 Ben Jonson, *The New Inn*, M. Hattaway (ed.) (Manchester, 2001).

13 T.W. Machan, *Textual Criticism and Middle English Texts* (Charlottesville VA, 1994) p. 7.

14 Keiser, *Manual* p. 3598.

15 Carroll, 'Vague Language' p. 57.

16 Carroll, 'Vague Language' p. 57.

17 Taavitsainen (p. 88) distinguishes between text-type and genre: genre refers to groupings made on the basis of external features and functions of texts, whereas text types are defined according to the internal linguistic features of texts.

18 This tendency to see recipes as 'units' rather than as short 'texts' seems to be common practice in work on medieval recipes: the *Forme of Cury*, for example, is considered a single work, even though it is actually assembled of 200 or more

individual recipes. Recent work carries this practice forward; for example, Carroll, in her work on *Directions for Laces*, analyses what she terms the 'small units of which the text is composed, showing them to share the linguistic and discoursal features of medieval recipes' (Ruth Carroll, 'Recipes for Laces: An example of a Middle English discourse colony' in R. Hiltunen and J. Skaffari (eds) *Discourse Perspectives on English* (Amsterdam, 2003) p. 138). Carroll, moreover, employs the work of discourse analyst Michael Hoey, who uses the term 'discourse colony' to describe texts composed of smaller units, not all of which are present in all versions. According to Hoey, the difference between a text composed of continuous prose and a text such as a recipe book is like the difference between a mammal and a beehive, a mammal being composed of parts which cannot be reordered or removed, and a beehive 'being made up of many independent units, which are not interconnected in a physical sense' (Michael Hoey, *Textual Interaction: An Introduction to Written Discourse Analysis* (London, 2001) p. 74, cited in Carroll, 'Recipes for Laces' p. 150). These treatments and definitions apparently resist defining smaller units as text and see them as relevant in the context of the collective only.

19 Machan p. 5.
20 Taavitsainen p. 89.
21 Terence Scully, *The Art of Cookery in the Middle Ages* (Woodbridge, 1995) p. 5.
22 Scully p. 9; Carroll, 'Vague Language' p. 58.
23 For a study of this manuscript see Elaine M. Miller, '"In Hoote Somere": A Fifteenth-Century Medical Manuscript' (unpublished doctoral thesis, University of Princeton, 1978); for the contents according to *IMEP*, see Linne R. Mooney, *The Index of Middle English Prose, Handlist XI: Manuscripts in the Library of Trinity College Cambridge* (Cambridge, 1995).
24 Linne R. Mooney, 'Practical Didactical Works in Middle English: Edition and Analysis of the Class of Short Middle English Works Containing Useful Information' (unpublished doctoral thesis, University of Toronto, 1981) p. 483.
25 Taavitsainen p. 93.
26 E. Miller p. xvii.
27 Approximately 40% of the recipes in this collection are in verse (E. Miller p. xvi).
28 See G. Keiser, 'Verse Introductions to Middle English Medical Treatises' *English Studies* 84 (2003) pp. 301–7. Indeed, recipes composed in verse, particularly culinary, persisted until the nineteenth century, and even today some enthusiasts like to transmit recipes as poetry. Moreover, it is not at all uncommon to find verse prologues to medical treatises, where they serve either as ornament or with a more practical function.
29 J. Boffey and A.S.G. Edwards, *A New Index of Middle English Verse* (London, 2005), no. 1496.3.
30 Keiser, *Manual* pp. 3643, 3824.
31 Keiser, *Manual* p. 3643. See M. Young's recent study of this manuscript, 'The Web of Knowledge in a Medieval "Medical" Manuscript: An Examination of Two Representative Examples from British Library MS Royal 17.A.iii' (unpublished MA thesis, University College Cork, 2009).
32 Taavitsainen p. 93.
33 The manuscript is not in Shirley's autograph but its three translated texts are attributed to him and his name appears in the colophons.

34 Spiller argues that the 'recognisably modern version of the recipe-book first appeared in in the late seventeenth century'; moreover, she points out that Renaissance cookbooks developed in opposition to the medieval dietary text and were 'fundamentally distinct from health' (Elizabeth Spiller, 'Recipes for Knowledge: Maker's Knowledge Traditions, Paracelsian Recipes, and the Invention of the Cookbook, 1600–1660' in J. Fitzpatrick (ed.) *Renaissance Food from Rabelais to Shakespeare: Culinary Readings and Culinary Histories* (Aldershot, 2010) p. 55).

35 Taavitsainen p. 91.

11: *Anamaria Gellert*   Fools, 'Folye' and Caxton's Woodcut of the Pilgrims at Table

1 I would like to thank Martha Driver for her comments and suggestions concerning the figure of the fool in Caxton's woodcut, and I acknowledge my debt to the methodological approach in M. Driver, *The Image in Print: Book Illustration in Late Medieval England and its Sources* (London, 2004), where she argues for a radically new understanding of early printed book illustration and discusses woodcuts as a means of reconstructing social history and reading habits and as a force of social and political change. I am also grateful to St John's College Library, Oxford, and to the J. Paul Getty Museum for allowing me to reproduce the images which appear in this chapter.

2 See D. McKenzie, *Bibliography and the Sociology of Texts* (Cambridge, 1999).

3 M. Schapiro, *Words and Pictures: On the Literal and the Symbolic in the Illustration of a Text* (The Hague and Paris, 1973) pp. 12–13.

4 *The General Prologue*, ll. 747–50, quoted from the BL copy of Caxton's second edition (1483) of the *Canterbury Tales* (STC 5083). Other quotations from Chaucer's works are from L.D. Benson (ed.) *The Riverside Chaucer* (Oxford and New York, 1988).

5 E. Hodnett, *English Woodcuts 1480–1535* (Oxford, 1973) p. 3.

6 From a formal and stylistic point of view, one possible iconographic source for Caxton's woodcuts of the single pilgrims may be the 'Oxford fragments' (Manchester, John Rylands University Library, MS English 63 and Philadelphia, Rosenbach Library, MS 1084/2). This codex, of which only thirteen leaves survive, contains outline drawings in which each pilgrim is depicted on horseback against a coloured ground and placed behind a plain framing line within the text column. See D.R. Carlson, 'Woodcut Illustrations of the *Canterbury Tales*, 1483–1602' *The Library* series 6, 19 (1997) pp. 25–67.

7 See Peter Weidhaas, *A History of the Frankfurt Book Fair* (Frankfurt, 2003; repr. Toronto, 2007).

8 This *Sammelband* is discussed by A. Gillespie, *Print Culture and the Medieval Author: Chaucer, Lydgate and Their Books* (Oxford, 2006) pp. 77–88, and A.S.G. Edwards, 'Decorated Caxtons' in M. Davies (ed.) *Incunabula: Studies in Fifteenth-Century Printed Books Presented to Lotte Hellinga* (London, 1999) pp. 493–506. See also Ralph Hanna, *A Descriptive Catalogue of the Western Medieval Manuscripts of St John's College Oxford* (Oxford, 2002) pp. 329–31.

9 Edwards, 'Decorated Caxtons' p. 505.

10 A. Oizumi (ed.), *Complete Concordance to the Works of Geoffrey Chaucer*, 10 vols (Hildesheim, 1991) I, 618, 622, 623.

11 A fifth type may be added: the saint fool whose prototype is Christ. Saint Paul's first letter to the Corinthians had laid the basis for a dialectic relationship

between folly (*stultitia*) and wisdom (*sapientia*). The wisdom of the world is foolishness in God's sight, and that which is deemed foolish to God is wiser than men's wisdom: 'ubi sapiens ubi scriba ubi conquisitor huius saeculi nonne stultam fecit Deus sapientiam huius mundi' [Where [is] the wise? Where [is] the scribe? Where [is] the disputer of this world? Hath not God made foolish the wisdom of this world?] (1 Cor. 1:20); 'quia quod stultum est Dei sapientius est hominibus et quod infirmum est Dei fortius est hominibus' [For the foolishness of God is wiser than men; and the weakness of God is stronger than men] (1 Cor. 1:25). Quotations are from the Latin Vulgate and the English translations from the Douay-Rheims Bible. In his *Summa Theologiae* Aquinas argues that, just as there is an evil or worldly wisdom and a divine wisdom, there is *stultitia bona* [good foolishnesss] which is opposed to the *sapientia saeculi* [wisdom of the world], and *stultitia mala* [bad foolishness] (II^a–IIae q. 46 a. 1 ad 2).

12 See J. Fritz, *Le discours du fou au Moyen Age (XIIe–XIIIe siècles): Étude comparée des discours littéraire, médical, juridique et théologique de la folie* (Paris, 1992).

13 Quotations from *Summa Theologiae* are from S. Thomae de Aquino, *Opera Omnia*, <http://www.corpusthomisticum.org/iopera.html#OM> [accessed 20 September 2010].

14 Fritz p. 7.

15 See D.J. Gifford, 'Iconographical Notes Toward the Definition of the Medieval Fool' *Journal of the Warburg and Courtauld Institutes* 37 (1974) pp. 336–42.

16 Some examples are Oxford, Bodleian Library, MSS Canon. Liturg. 378, f. 59^v; Canon. Bibl. Lat. 58, f. 219^r; Douce 50, f. 169^r; Douce 118, f. 60^v.

17 Fritz p. 18.

18 M. Foucault, *History of Madness* (Paris, 1961, repr. London, 2006) p. 11.

19 Although the fool's homelessness and vagrancy often placed him in the category of vagabonds, peregrination was not always perceived in a negative key. The biblical idea that the Christian person was a stranger (*alienus*) on earth, a *peregrinus* or *homo viator* on his way to his heavenly abode, promoted by Saint Augustine in *De Civitate Dei*, greatly influenced the medieval view of man's historical destiny and contributed to developing a genuinely hospitable attitude towards pilgrims. See G.B. Ladner, '*Homo Viator*: Medieval Ideas on Alienation and Order' *Speculum* 42 (1967) pp. 233–59.

20 N. Guglielmi, *Il medioevo degli ultimi* (Rome, 2001) pp. 38–39.

21 V.A. Kolve, *Telling Images: Chaucer and the Imagery of Narrative II* (Stanford CA, 2009) p. 225.

22 Kolve p. 225.

23 Feathers were associated with folly because of their pneumatic component: they are filled with air, just like the fool's head. However, the use of feathers in the depiction of Folly may also suggest a partial transformation from human being into beast. In the medieval Irish poem *Buile Suibhne*, composed sometime during the ninth or the tenth century, Suibhne's folly is accompanied by his physical transformation into a human–bird whose body is covered with feathers.

24 A fool with long dishevelled hair and club appears, however, among the cycle of Vices and Virtues on a bas-relief in the cathedrals of Notre-Dame in Chartres and Paris (*c.*1194–1230).

25 In the *Psychomachia* Prudentius describes the battle of the virtues (*Pudicitia*, *Patientia*, *Mens Humilis* or *Spes*, *Sobrietas*, *Ratio* or *Operatio*) and vices (*Superbia*, *Libido*, *Ira*, *Luxuria*, *Avaritia*) in the form of an epic poem. Gregory

the Great mentions seven deadly sins to which seven principal vices correspond: vain-glory, envy, anger, melancholy, avarice, gluttony and lust (*Moralia in Job*, xxxi, 87). Each deadly sin is described as having an army of its own engaged in the battle for man's soul.

26 See A. Katzenellenbogen, *Allegories of Vices and Virtues in Medieval Art: From Early Christian Times to the Thirteenth Century* (Toronto, 1989).

27 D.P. Lackey, 'A New Geography of the Human Soul' *The Journal of Ethics* 3–4 (2005) p. 551.

28 Lackey p. 568.

29 Some examples are Oxford, Bodleian Library, MSS Douce 366 (*c.*1300), f. 22^r; Douce 131 (*c.*1340), f. 43^r; Canon. Liturg. 286 (early fifteenth century), f. 28^r.

30 Laharie has argued that the function of the court fool had a counterpart in the popular *festa stultorum*, in which hierarchies were temporarily reversed and unpleasant truths were expressed through laughter without any serious threat to the established system (M. Laharie, *La folie au moyen age: XIe–XIIIe siècles* (Paris, 1991)). See, too, Bakhtin's concept of carnival laughter in M. Bakhtin, *Rabelais and His World* (Moscow 1965; repr. Bloomington IN, 1984) and Aaron Gurevich's critical analysis of Bakhtin's theory of carnival, 'Bakhtin and His Theory of Carnival' in J. Bremmer and H. Roodenburg (eds) *A Cultural History of Humour: From Antiquity to the Present Day* (Cambridge, 1997) pp. 54–60. Gurevich has pointed out that the opposition between popular culture and serious official culture was not as sharp as Bakhtin had posited, since in the Middle Ages seriousness and humour were linked as part of the same worldview.

31 The fool of the initial 'D(ixit)' was sometimes represented as king Saul in the act of committing suicide. See, for example, Paris, BnF, MS Lat. 11930 (*c.*1220), f. 136^r.

32 The biblical prototype of the 'mad sinner', which played an important role in shaping the medieval concept of folly as sin, was Nebuchadnezzar. Though no actual metamorphosis takes place, he is condemned to live and behave like a beast, an exemplary punishment which leads to his purgation and eventual redemption. The medieval concept of folly as sin is extensively discussed in P.B.R. Doob, *Nebuchadnezzar's Children: Conventions of Madness in Middle English Literature* (New Haven CT and London, 1974).

33 In Cambridge, University Library, MS Gg.4.27, the *Parson's Tale* is illustrated with the pairs of Vices and Virtues. The following miniatures have survived: 'Inuidia' and 'Charite' (f. 416^r), 'Glotenye' and 'Abstinence' (f. 432^r), 'Lecherye' and 'Chastite' (f. 433^r). Lechery is depicted as a fashionable, richly dressed woman seated on a goat, holding a bird on her right hand and grabbing one of the goat's horns with the left. A chain and clasp are hanging from her right wrist, symbolising the *vinculum amoris* [chain of love]. For a useful analysis of the symbolism used in the representation of *Luxuria* in medieval art, see E. Kosmer, 'The "noyous humoure of lecherie"' *The Art Bulletin* 57 (1975) pp. 1–8. See also R. Tuve, 'Notes on the Virtues and Vices' *Journal of the Warburg and Courtauld Institutes* 26 (1963) pp. 264–303, and 27 (1964) pp. 42–72.

34 The same scene is re-elaborated in the initial 'D(ixit)' from a fifteenth-century English Psalter (*c.*1405–15), Turin, Bibl. Naz. Universitaria di Torino, MS I. 1. 9, f. 16^r. Here, the sexual act is explicitly represented: the lover does not content himself with an embrace, but his hand, after having slipped up the courtly woman's dress, rests undisturbed between her thighs.

35 The author portrait of the Ellesmere manuscript is thoroughly discussed in

A.T. Gaylord, 'Portrait of a Poet' in M. Stevens and D. Woodward (eds), *The Ellesmere Chaucer: Essays in Interpretation* (San Marino CA, 1995) pp. 121–42. Gaylord has argued (p. 133) that, since there was no pictorial tradition of lifelikeness in the depiction of vernacular secular authors, it is highly probable that the portrait does not reproduce any of Chaucer's actual physical features. Yet Hoccleve's claim that the miniature in the *Regiment of Princes* was a life-like portrait of Chaucer would hardly have found consensus among his readers, most of whom must have still remembered the poet within only ten years of his death, unless it contained some truth in it. See, too, A. Patterson, '"The Human face Divine": Identity and the Portrait from Locke to Chaucer' in S. McKee (ed.) *Crossing Boundaries: Issues of Cultural and Individual Identity in the Middle Ages and the Renaissance* (Turnhout, 1999) pp. 155–86, and M.C. Olson, 'Marginal Portraits and the Fiction of Orality: The Ellesmere Manuscript' in J. Rosenblum and W.K. Finley (eds) *Chaucer Illustrated: Five Hundred Years of Canterbury Tales in Pictures* (New Castle DE and London, 2003) pp. 1–35.

36 Quoted from Thomas Hoccleve, *The Regiment of Princes* (London, BL, MS Harley 4866 (*c.*1411), f. 88^r).

37 Olson p. 22.

38 W.J.B. Crotch, *The Prologues and Epilogues of William Caxton* (London, 1956) p. 90.

39 The term 'compiler' also appears in the headings of manuscripts such as London, BL, MS Harley 1758 and Cambridge, Fitzwilliam Museum, MS Fitzwilliam McClean 181.

40 A. Minnis, *Medieval Theory of Authorship: Scholastic Literary Attitudes in the Later Middle Ages* (London, 1984) pp. 190–210.

41 Gaylord p. 128.

42 See J.L. Lowes's classic study of the meanings and uses of the term *hereos* in medical treatises, as well as in medieval and Renaissance literature: 'The Loveres Maladye of *Hereos*' *Modern Philology* 11 (1914) pp. 491–546. Among more recent contributions, see P. Boitani, '"O viva morte": amore, malinconia e l'io diviso' in *Il tragico e il sublime nella letteratura medievale* (Bologna, 1992) pp. 93–116; E. Giaccherini, *Orfeo in Albione: Tradizione colta e tradizione popolare nella letteratura inglese medievale* (Pisa, 2002), in particular pp. 129–50; S. D'Agata D'Ottavi, 'Melancholy and Dreams in Chaucer's *Troilus and Criseyde*' in G. Iamartino, M.L. Maggioni and R. Facchinetti (eds) *Thou Sittest at Another Boke ...: English Studies in Honour of Domenico Pezzini* (Milan, 2008) pp. 209–21.

43 The *Viaticum peregrinantis* was an adaptation of a tenth-century medical handbook written by the Arabic physician Ibn al-Jazzar. It was divided into seven sections arranged by maladies affecting the body *a capite ad calcem* [from the head to the heel]. The twentieth chapter of the first book, which deals with diseases of the head, contains a chapter on the malady of passionate love.

44 'Love is a certain suffering born within, proceeding from the sight and immoderate cogitation on a form of the opposite sex, on account of which one desires above all things to enjoy the embraces of another and by mutual wish to fulfil all the precepts of love in the embrace of the other.' (trans. M.F. Wack, *Lovesickness in the Middle Ages: The Viaticum and Its Commentaries* (Philadelphia PA, 1990) p. 62.

45 Wack p. 62.

46 Wack pp. 147–48.

47 For an overview of the most influential medieval medical theories, see N.G. Siraisi, *Medieval and Early Renaissance Medicine* (Chicago IL, 1990).

48 See Fritz's analysis of the theme of folly in medieval romances and *chansons de geste* (pp. 241–74). See also Laharie pp. 145–52.

49 P. Burke, *Popular Culture in Early Modern Europe* (London, 1978) p. 110.

50 E. Welsford, *The Fool: His Social and Literary History* (London, 1935) p. 121.

51 Foucault p. 14.

52 K. Moxey, 'Master E.S. and the Folly of Love' *Simiolus* 3–4 (1980) p. 131.

53 The Master of the Housebook is named after a well-known manuscript, the *Medieval Housebook*, created in South Germany *c*.1475. This richly decorated volume contains pen-and-ink and watercolour drawings which illustrate different aspects of life at court: images of weapons, allegories of the planets, tournament and hunting scenes, landscapes and castles, coats of arms. For a bibliographical description of the manuscript, see W. Wolfegg, *Venus and Mars: The World of the Medieval Housebook* (Munich, 1998).

54 See D. Stephens, 'History at the Margins: Bagpipers in Medieval Manuscripts' *History Today* 19 (1989) pp. 42–48. See also M. Jones, 'Folklore Motifs in Late Medieval Art I: Proverbial Follies and Impossibilities' *Folklore* 2 (1989) pp. 201–17, and E.A. Block, 'Chaucer's Millers and Their Bagpipes' *Speculum* 29 (1954) pp. 239–43.

55 Since the design has been damaged in the process of transmission, only the traveller's bust and his bag fastened to a stick are visible in the background. The section containing his head seems to have been torn off.

56 J. Gage, *Colour and Culture: Practice and Meaning from Antiquity to Abstraction* (London, 1993) p. 83. For examples of the negative connotations of yellow in the visual arts, see R. Mellinkoff, *Outcasts: Signs of Otherness in Northern European Art of the Late Middle Ages* (Berkeley CA, 1993). In Giotto's representation of the betrayal scene in the Scrovegni Chapel, Judas's mantle and tunic are yellow.

57 See M. Pastoureau, 'Formes et couleurs du désordre: le jaune avec le vert' *Médiévales* 4 (1983) pp. 62–73.

58 A. Gellert, '"Abit ne makith neithir monk ne frere": Text and Pictorial Paratext in the *Prioress's Tale*' *Textus* 22 (2009) pp. 339–64.

59 The 'Retraction' appears after the *Parson's Tale* in all manuscripts that contain the complete tale. The phrase 'litel tretys' has usually been interpreted as referring to the *Parson's Tale* and not to the *Canterbury Tales* as a whole. Owen has suggested that Chaucer may have intended what is known as the *Parson's Tale* as an independent treatise on penitence, with the Retraction as a fitting conclusion. See C. Owen, 'What the Manuscripts Tell Us About the Parson's Tale' *Medium Aevum* 63 (1994) pp. 239–49.

12: *John Block Friedman* Anxieties at Table: Food and Drink in Chaucer's Fabliaux Tales and Heinrich Wittenwiler's *Der Ring*

1 I am very grateful to Kathrin Giogoli of the Free University of Berlin for aid with the sources of Wittenwiler's *Der Ring* and points of translation. Paul Freedman contributed as well from his extensive knowledge of medieval food and drink. Cynthia Rottenborn of the Kent State University Salem Library was, as always, most helpful in finding me books and articles. I am grateful to the librarians of

The Ohio State University Library for obtaining for me rare books used in the preparation of this chapter.

2 Good general surveys of food from a cultural perspective in the Middle Ages are: Allen J. Greico, 'Food and Social Class in Medieval and Renaissance Italy' in Jean-Louis Flandrin and Massimo Montanari (eds) *Food: A Culinary History from Antiquity to the Present* (New York, 1999) pp. 302–12; Bruno Laurioux, *Une histoire culinaire du Moyen Age* (Paris, 2005); Sidney W. Mintz, *Tasting Food, Tasting Freedom: Excursions into Eating, Culture, and the Past* (Boston MA, 1996); Martha Carlin and Joel Rosenthal (eds) *Food and Eating in Medieval Europe* (London and Rio Grande OH, 1998); Bridget Ann Henisch, *Fast and Feast: Food in Medieval Society* (University Park PA, 1976); D. Menjot (ed.), *Manger et boire au Moyen Age. Actes du Colloque de Nice (15–17 Octobre 1982)*, 2 vols (Paris, 1984); and C.M. Woolgar, Dale Serjeantson, Tony Waldron (eds) *Food in Medieval England: Diet and Nutrition* (Oxford, 2006).

3 Erik Hertog, *Chaucer's Fabliaux as Analogues* (Leuven, 1991) pp. 105–30.

4 Norbert Elias, *The Civilizing Process: The History of Manners*, trans. Edmund Jephcott (New York, 1978) p. 130.

5 F.J. Furnivall (ed.) *The Babees Book: Medieval Manners for the Young* (Colchester, 1923) pp. 17–18. See generally Kathleen Ashley and Robert L.A. Clark (eds), *Medieval Conduct* (Minneapolis MN, 2001).

6 Peter Stallybrass and Allon White, *The Politics and Poetics of Transgression* (Ithaca NY, 1986) pp. 2–3.

7 A kermis is a popular celebration of the consecration of a saint's name day.

8 M.M. Bakhtin, *Rabelais and His World* (Moscow 1965; repr. Bloomington IN, 1984) and *Dialogic Imagination: Four Essays*, ed. and trans. M. Wehrle (Cambridge MA, 1981).

9 Paul Freedman (ed.) *Food, The History of Taste* (Berkeley CA, 2007) pp. 163–95.

10 An excellent and accessible Dutch Realist example of the 'courteous' table with diners of the proper class appears in Freedman, *Food* p. 204. See generally Malcolm Jones, *The Secret Middle Ages: Discovering the Real Medieval World* (Stroud, 2002).

11 See Paul Freedman, *Images of the Medieval Peasant* (Stanford CA, 1999) pp. 149–50.

12 See Freedman, *Images* ch. 9: 'Pious and Exemplary Peasants'.

13 For a critical edition of this poem see A. Piaget, 'Chapel des fleurs de lis par Philippe de Vitry' *Romania* 27 (1898) pp. 55–92.

14 See Rob Roy McGregor Jr. (ed.) *The Lyric Poems of Jean Froissart: A Critical Edition* (Chapel Hill NC, 1975) p. 181 and John Gower, *Mirour de l'Omme*, trans. William Burton Wilson (East Lansing MI, 1992) p. 347.

15 Ernest Hoepffner (ed.), *Oeuvres de Guillaume de Machaut* (Paris, 1908, repr. New York, 1965), 2.212–14, ll. 1523–86.

16 Gianfranco Contini (ed.), *Poeti del Duecento*, 2 vols (Milan, 1960) I, 789–801.

17 For some examples, discussion and bibliography, see John Block Friedman, *Brueghel's Heavy Dancers: Transgressive Clothing, Class, and Culture in the Late Middle Ages* (Syracuse NY, 2010) pp. 4–7.

18 The Monk's gluttonous taste for fat swans is itemised (this forms part of the typical satire on monks for excess in eating) and the Friar is well acquainted with food dealers and considers them superior to the unfortunate parishioners, but these points are not particularly class-related, rather forming part of anti-clerical and anti-mendicant satire.

19 All quotations from Chaucer's poetry are from Larry D. Benson (ed.) *The Riverside Chaucer* (Boston MA, 1987).

20 For the widow as *exemplum*, see John Block Friedman, 'The Nun's Priest's Tale: The Preacher and the Mermaid's Song' *The Chaucer Review* 7 (1972) pp. 250–66.

21 The bibliography for the *Ring* is very large and the works often of uneven quality. I give here the studies I found most generally useful. For an excellent overview in English, see Albrecht Classen, 'Heinrich Wittenwiler (before 1387–circa 1414?)' in James Hardin and Max Reinhart (eds) *German Writers of the Renaissance and Reformation 1280–1580* (Detroit MI, Washington DC and London, 1997) pp. 326–31. The standard edition is Edmund Wiessner (ed.) *Heinrich Wittenwilers Ring, nach der Meiniger Handschrift* (Darmstadt, 1964) and his commentary on the work, *Kommentar zu Heinrich Wittenwilers Ring* (Darmstadt, 1974). A newer edition is that of Rolf Bräuer *et al.* (eds) *Heinrich Wittenwiler, Der Ring: In Abbildung der Meininger Handschrift* (Göppingen, 1991). Recent critical books include Jürgen Belitz, *Studien zur Parodie in Heinrich Wittenwilers 'Ring'* (Göppingen, 1978); Ulrich Gaier, *Satire, Studien zu Neidhart, Wittenwiler, Brant und zur satirischen Schreibart* (Tübingen, 1967); John Michael Clifton-Everest, 'Wittenwiler's Marriage Debate' *Modern Language Notes* 90 (1975) pp. 629–42; Christa Wolf-Cross, *Magister ludens: Der Erzähler in Heinrich Wittenwilers 'Ring'* (Chapel Hill NC, 1984); Charles G. Fehrenbach, *Marriage in Wittenwiler's Ring* (Washington DC, 1941); Hermine Joldersma, 'Modern Parodic Theory and Heinrich Wittenwiler's *Der Ring*' in Clive Thomson (ed.) *Essays on Parody* (Toronto, 1986) pp. 48–59; Bernward Plate, *Heinrich Wittenwiler, Ertäge der Forshung* (Darmstadt, 1977); Elisabeth de Kadt, '"er ist ein gpaur in meinem muot, Der unrecht lept und läppisch tuot": Zur Bauernsatire in Heinrich Wittenwilers *Ring*' *Daphnis* 15 (1986) pp. 1–29; Birgit Knühl, *Die Komik in Heinrich Wittenwilers 'Ring' im Vergleich zu den Fastnachtspielen des 15. Jahrhunderts* (Göppingen, 1981); Rolf Mueller, 'On the Medieval Satiric Fictions of Neidhart and Wittenwiler: Fools for Their Theme: Let Satire Be Their Song' in Winder McConnell (ed.) *In hôhem prîse. A Festschrift in Honor of Ernst S. Dick* (Göppingen, 1989) pp. 295–305; Ortrun Riha, *Die Forschung zu Heinrich Wittenwilers Ring 1851–1988* (Würtzburg, 1990) and 'Die Forschung zu Heinrich Wittenwilers *Ring* 1988–1998' in Dorothea Klein *et al.* (eds) *Vom Mittelalter zur Neuzeit: Festschrift für Horst Brunnen* (Weisbaden, 2000) pp. 423–30; Christoph Gruchot, *Heinrich Wittenwilers 'Ring': Konzept und Konstruktion eines Lehrbuches* (Göppingen, 1988); George Fenwick Jones, 'Heinrich Wittenwiler—Nobleman or Burgher' *Monatshefte* 45 (1953) pp. 67–69; 'Late Medieval "Realism" as exemplified in Heinrich Wittenwiler's *Ring*' in Sheema A. Buehne *et al.* (eds) *Helen Adolf Festschrift* (New York, 1968) pp. 86–98; George Fenwick Jones (trans.), *Wittenwiler's Ring and the Anonymous Scots Poet, Colkelbie Sow: Two Comic-Didactic Works from the Fifteenth Century* (Chapel Hill NC, 1956). See, most recently, Friedman, *Brueghel's Heavy Dancers* pp. 258–73. All quotations from *The Ring* will be drawn from Jones' translation.

22 On gunpowder, see John Norris, *Early Gunpowder Artillery 1300–1600* (Ramsbury, 2003).

23 On this genre of poetry, see Allen H. Maclaine, *The Christis Kirk Tradition and Scots Poetry of Folk Festivity* (Glasgow, 1996).

24 W.F. Bryan and Germaine Dempster (eds) *Sources and Analogues of Chaucer's*

Canterbury Tales (London, 1958) pp. 106–23, rev. by Robert M. Correale and Mary Hamel (eds) *Sources and Analogues of the Canterbury Tales*, 2 vols (Cambridge, 2002; Woodbridge, 2005).

25 Peter Beidler, 'The *Miller's Tale* and its Analogues' in Correale and Hamel (eds) II, 254. For his study, 'The *Reeve's Tale*', see I, 23–26.

26 Larry D. Benson and Theodore M. Andersson (eds), *The Literary Context of Chaucer's Fabliaux: Texts and Translations* (Indianapolis IN and New York, 1971) pp. 40–45. A translation of lines 1282–1386, the analogue to the Misdirected Kiss, appears in this work.

27 See John Block Friedman, 'A Reading of Chaucer's *Reeve's Tale*' *The Chaucer Review* 2 (1967) pp. 9–18, and *Brueghel's Heavy Dancers* pp. 183–96.

28 See, too, Elizabeth Lienert, 'Das Tagelied in Wittenwilers 'Ring'' *Jahrbuch der Oswald von Wolkenstein-Gesellschaft* 8 (1994–95) pp. 109–24.

29 See Michael Calabrese, 'The Lover's Cure in Ovid's *Remedia Amoris* and Chaucer's *Miller's Tale*' *English Language Notes* 31 (1994) pp. 413–18.

30 For these earlier sources for, and analogues to, *Der Ring*, see Helga Schüppert (ed.) 'Der Bauer in der deutschen Literatur des Spätmittelalters—Topik und Realitätsbezug' in Heinrich Appelt (ed.) *Bauerliche Sachkultur des Spätmittelalters: Internationaler Kongress Krems an der Donau 21.bis 24. September, 1982* (Vienna, 1984) pp. 146–71. See, too, Don Patrick Savell, '"Meier Betz" and "Metzen Hochzit" as Examples of Peasant Satire in the Late Middle Ages' (unpubl. MA thesis, University of Maryland, 1968). The peasant-wedding literary genre seems to have been well established by about 1300, and Wittenwiler seems to have used only 'Metzen Hochzit' as a source (and then only 672 lines of it), according to Edmund Wiessner, 'Der Gedicht von der Bauernhochzeit' *Zeitschrift für Deutsche Archiv* 50 (1908) pp. 245–79.

31 Frederick W. Biggs, 'The *Miller's Tale* and *Heile van Beersele*' *Review of English Studies* 56 (2005) pp. 497–523.

13: *Mary Morse*   Alongside St Margaret: The Childbirth Cult of Saints Quiricus and Julitta in Late Medieval English Manuscripts

1 For encouragement and assistance in this paper, I thank Laurel Broughton, Emma Cayley, Brian Donaghey, Martha Driver, John Friedman, Joseph Gwara, Philippa Hardman, Laura Hodges, Derek Pearsall, Sue Powell, Candace Robb, Kathleen Scott, Barbara Shailor, Don Skemer, Robert Swanson and Toshiyuki Takamiya. I also acknowledge and thank the British Academy and the Huntington Library for awarding me a 2006 Huntington Library–British Academy grant to support my on-site study of manuscripts owned by UK libraries.

2 Quiricus appears as Cerice, Cerico, Cire, Ciriaco, Cirice, Circus, Cyr, Cyrce, Cyriac, Cyryace and Quiryne, among other variations, in the English manuscripts and church dedications discussed here. Julitta is the most common name for his mother, but she may be referred to as Iulit, Iulitta, Iulitte, Julietta, Julitt or Julytte. In French names Quiricus is usually Cyr, Cirque or Cirgues; the cathedral of SS Cyr and Julitte at Nevers is dedicated to the pair. I refer to Quiricus and Julitta in all introductory material but use the pertinent variations when describing the respective churches and texts related to them.

3 Jonathan Good, *The Cult of St. George in Medieval England* (Woodbridge, Suffolk, 2009) pp. 25–26; George Herzfeld (ed.) *An Old English Martyrology*,

EETS OS 116 (Oxford, 1900) pp. 120–23; Elinor M. Husselman, 'The Martyrdom of Cyriacus and Julitta in Coptic' *Journal of the American Research Center in Egypt* 4 (1965) pp. 79–86 (pp. 80–81).

4 Caxton concurrently printed two 1483 editions of the *Golden Legende* (STC 24873–74), both containing the same information (sig. z3^{r-v}).

5 Richard Hamer with Vida Russell (eds), *Gilte Legende*, 2 vols, EETS OS 327, 328 (Oxford, 2006), I, 370, ll. 7–23. I thank Vida Russell for alerting me to the inclusion of these saints in the *Gilte Legende*.

6 Hamer with Russell (eds) I, 370–71, ll. 26–38.

7 Nicholas Orme, *Medieval Children* (New Haven CT, 2003) pp. 188–89; Patricia Healy Wasyliw, *Martyrdom, Murder, and Magic: Child Saints and Their Cults in Medieval Europe* (New York, 2008) pp. 44–48; Cameron Louis (ed.) *The Commonplace Book of Robert Reynes of Acle: An Edition of Tanner MS 407* (New York, 1980) pp. 169–70 (n. 29), 386–87.

8 For the earliest Latin sources, see *Acta sanctorum*, XXIV: *Iunii tomus quartus* (Paris, 1867) pp. 13–31.

9 Alban Butler, *Lives of the Saints*, eds Herbert Thurston and Donald Attwater, 2 vols (London, 1956, 2nd edn) I, 552–54.

10 Mary Morse, 'Seeing and Hearing: Margery Kempe and the *mise-en-page*', *Studia Mystica* 20 (1999) pp. 15–42 (pp. 24–25).

11 Kathryn A. Smith, *Art, Identity and Devotion in Fourteenth Century England: Three Women and Their Books of Hours* (Toronto, 2003) p. 256.

12 This mid-twelfth-century altar painting from the Chapel of Sant Quirc at the Hermitage of Santa Yolita in Durro (Lleida) is now in the Museu Nacional d'Art de Catalunya in Barcelona (Index of Christian Art, Princeton University, Princeton NJ, system no. 000066915). (The Index is electronically accessible by institutional or individual subscription at <http://ica.princeton.edu/index.php>. Three additional copies of the Index are available to researchers at Dumbarton Oaks Research Library and Collection of Harvard University, Washington DC; Getty Research Center, Los Angeles; and Rijksuniversiteit, Utrecht.) In the central section the portrayal of the seated Julitta, who holds a front-facing Quiricus in her arms, is so closely modelled on the Enthroned Madonna iconography that 'only the adjacent inscriptions naming the saints prevent their erroneous identification' (Metropolitan Museum of Art, *The Art of Medieval Spain, A.D. 500–1200* (New York, 1993) p. 170.

13 I thank E. Ann Matter for suggesting this comparison. Lois Drewer specifically addresses the maternal influences of Salomona and Julitta in 'Saints and Their Families in Byzantine Art' *Deltion tes Christianikes Archaiologikes Hetaireias* 16 (1991–1992) pp. 259–70 (pp. 260–62).

14 Swaffham Prior owes its Norman origins to knights of Alan of Brittany, who also received the manor and double churches of Fulbourn from William the Conqueror in 1080 (Simon Cotton, 'Church Dedications' in Carola Hicks (ed.) *Cambridgeshire Churches* (Stamford, 1997) pp. 209–15 (pp. 212–13)). Originally known as Curig's Chapel, St Julitta's is located in Capel Curig (Conway) in Snowdonia. Parts of the church date from the thirteenth century. It was deconsecrated in the 1970s and is now owned by the Friends of St Julitta. The dedications to Curig in some of these Welsh churches may represent a conflation of a sixth-century Welsh bishop Curig with the child martyr Quiricus (Cyriacus). Besides Capel Curig (dedicated to Cyriacus and Julitta), the most likely Welsh churches connected with either or both Quiricus or Julitta are at

Llangurig (Curig), Eglwys Fair a Churig (Curig), Llanid (Julitta and Cyriacus), Llanilid (Julitta) and Llanelidan (Julitta). Scholars connect the dedication of St Curig's Porthkerry only to the bishop Curig. Two place-names in Scotland, Ceres (Fife) and St Cyrus (Kincardineshire) also may be associated with Quiricus (Cyric). See S. Baring-Gould and John Fisher, *The Lives of the British Saints: The Saints of Wales, Cornwall and Such Irish Saints as Have Dedications in Britain*, 2 vols (London, 1907; repr. Whitefish MT, 2005) II, 198–99; James Murray MacKinley, *Ecclesiastical Place-Names of Scotland: Influence of the Pre-Reformation Church on Scottish Place-Names* (Edinburgh, 1904) p. 20.

15 Nicholas Orme, *English Church Dedications with a Survey of Cornwall and Devon* (Exeter, 1996) pp. 36, 39–40, 73, 88, 95, 99, 122, 186, 202–3, 237, 239.

16 Orme, *English Church Dedications* pp. 39–40, 73, 88, 99, 122, 186, 202–3.

17 For information on Tickenham, see Charles Andrew, *St Quiricus and St Julietta, Tickenham: A Short Guide to the History of this Ancient Parish Church*, rev. Bridget Wheeler (2005). I am indebted to the Rev. Preb. Alastair Wheeler, rector of St Cuthbert Wells (rector of St Quiricus and St Julietta, Tickenham from 1997 to 2010), and his wife Bridget (Bid) Wheeler, whose father wrote the pamphlet which she revised. Bid and Alistair Wheeler welcomed me as a guest into their home, shared their considerable knowledge of Tickenham parish with me, and provided me with several key references on the church's history. In addition I wish to thank the following: William (Bill) Holt, churchwarden at the parish church of St Cyr & St Julitta in Newton St Cyres, who spent several hours answering my questions about the architecture and history of the church; Susannah Morse and Jeremy Uecker, who gathered local information and photographed the parish churches of St Cyriac & St Julitta at Luxulyan, St Ciricus and St Julitta at St Veep, St Julitta in Lanteglos and St Julitta's in Capel Curig; and Stephen Morse, who travelled with me, photographed several churches and created detailed location maps for me.

18 For descriptions of some of the other churches in England dedicated to SS Quiricus and Julitta see Frances Arnold-Forster, *Studies in Church Dedications, or England's Patron Saints*, 2 vols (London, 1899) I, 170–72. For probable locations of monasteries associated with SS Quiricus and Julitta, see Nicholas Orme, *The Saints of Cornwall* (Oxford, 2000) pp. 101–2, 154, and Sam Turner, *Making a Christian Landscape: The Countryside in Early Medieval Cornwall, Devon and Wessex* (Exeter, 2006) p. 161.

19 M. Chahin, *The Kingdom of Armenia: A History*, 2nd edn (Richmond, 2001) pp. 244–47.

20 Charles A. Frazee, 'The Christian Church in Cilician Armenia: Its Relations with Rome and Constantinople to 1198' *Church History* 45 (1976) pp. 166–84 (pp. 171, 183).

21 Andrew pp. 2, 4.

22 Andrew p. 9, and R.B. Patterson, 'Robert Fitz Harding of Bristol: Portrait of an Early Angevin Burgess Baron Patrician and His Family's Urban Involvement' *Haskins Society Journal* 1 (1989) pp. 109–22 (pp. 116, 122).

23 Denys Forrest, *The Making of a Manor: The Story of Tickenham Court* (Bradford-on-Avon, 1975) pp. 7–8.

24 On Isabel's ownership and dating of the manuscript, see Smith, *Art, Identity and Devotion* pp. 32–36. Smith also provides this translation and the original rubric in French: 'Si vous estes es ascun anguisse ou travaille d'enfaunt dites

cest orisoun e(n)s(e)want ou l'antenie et le verset en l'onour de dieu et de sei(n) t[e] marie et de seinte [*sic*] cirice et julicte et vous serrez tost eydé' (p. 256).

25   On the Theodotus Chapel see Lesley Jessop, 'Pictorial Cycles of Non-Biblical Saints: The Seventh- and Eighth-Century Mural Cycles in Rome and Contexts for their Use' *Papers of the British School in Rome* 67 (1999) pp. 233–79 (pp. 236–55), and Chartres Cathedral (Index of Christian Art, system no. 000076487). Information on the Église de St. Cirgues la Loutre is my own research with assistance from Stephen Morse, and Chuck and Judyth Babst.

26   Maria Teresa Filieri, 'Proposte per il Maestro dei Santi Quirico e Giulitta' *Arte Cristiana* 83 (1995) pp. 267–74 (pp. 270, 272 n. 2).

27   Kathleen L. Scott, *Later Gothic Manuscripts 1390–1490*, 2 vols (London, 1996) II, 50 ('p. 462' *sic*). In personal conversations both Laura Hodges, a specialist in medieval costume, and Don C. Skemer, manuscript curator at the Princeton Rare Books Library, regard Julitta's beard as a likely illuminator's 'mistake'. I thank Dr Kathleen Doyle, Curator of Illuminated Manuscripts at the British Library, for providing me with a copy of this image.

28   Joseph Brychmore, *Collections for a Parochial History of Tickenham* (Bristol, 1895) pp. 28–29; see too *The Parish Church of St Cyr & St Julitta Newton St Cyres Exeter* (no publication details, unpaginated).

29   Nicholas Harris Nicolas (ed.), *Privy Purse Expenses of Elizabeth of York: Wardrobe Accounts of Edward the Fourth* (London, 1830; repr. New York, 1972) p. 78. This expenditure was first discussed by Walter J. Dilling in 'Girdles: Their Origin and Development, Particularly with Regard to their Use as Charms in Medicine, Marriage, and Midwifery' *Caledonian Medical Journal* 9 (1912–14) pp. 337–57, 403–25 (p. 421).

30   Other references to girdle relics appear in Thomas Wright (ed.) *Three Chapters of Letters Relating to the Suppression of the Monasteries*, Camden Society OS 26 (London, 1843) pp. 58–59; Eamon Duffy, *The Stripping of the Altars: Traditional Religion in England, c.1400–c.1580* (New Haven CT, 1992) pp. 384–85; Orme, *Medieval Children* pp. 16–18. For an overview of textual amulets used in birthing in medieval Europe, especially in France, see Don C. Skemer, *Binding Words: Textual Amulets in the Middle Ages* (University Park PA, 2006) pp. 236–78 (chap. 5). I am grateful to Dr Brian Donaghey for the Bronholm reference.

31   Alan D. Justice, 'Trade Symbolism in the York Cycle' *Theatre Journal* 31 (1979) pp. 47–58 (p. 49).

32   The Wefferes [Weavers]: *The Appearance of Our Lady to Thomas*, XLVI in L. Toulmin Smith (ed.), *York Mystery Plays* (Oxford, 1885; repr. London, 1963) pp. 480–90 (p. 486, 1. 13.167, ll. 15.188–93; p. 489, ll. 22.275–76).

33   Brant Lee Doty, 'An Edition of British Museum Manuscript Additional 37049: A Religious Miscellany' (unpublished doctoral thesis, Michigan State University, 1969) pp. 177–78. In personal correspondence, Laurel Broughton, who is preparing an edition of Cambridge, Sidney Sussex College MS 95 (one of England's major collections of Miracles of the Virgin), mentions an excision of several pages with the possibility that any miracles associated with the Virgin's girdle might have been removed from manuscripts during the Reformation.

34   Orme, *Medieval Children* p. 16. While most sources identify the Bruton girdle as a Virgin's girdle, Duffy associates it with St Mary Magdalene (*Stripping of the Altars* p. 384).

35   Skemer, *Binding Words* p. 1.

36 Medieval commentators such as Rupert of Deutz specifically linked Mary's grief at her Son's death to a woman's labour in childbirth. See Karma Lochrie, *Margery Kempe and Translations of the Flesh* (Philadelphia PA, 1991) p. 180.

37 Transcription from S.A.J. Moorat, *Catalogue of Western Manuscripts on Medicine and Science in the Wellcome Historical Medical Library*, 2 vols (London, 1962) I, 492–93. I correct Moorat's transcription as recommended by Curt F. Bühler, 'Prayers and Charms in Certain Middle English Scrolls' *Speculum* 39 (1964) pp. 270–78 (p. 272 n. 19).

38 See, for example, Katherine L. French's description of a pearl frontlet bequeathed to 'garnish the [St Margaret] image … at every feast' at St Margaret's, Westminster (*The Good Women of the Parish: Gender and Religion After the Black Death* (Philadelphia PA, 2008) p. 118). John Mirk notes that St Margaret's feast is 'a lyght haly-day' but that there are some who 'haue suche love to hure þat he wyl faston hur evon' (Susan Powell (ed.), *John Mirk's Festial*, 2 vols, EETS OS 334, 335 (Oxford, 2009, 2011) I, sermon 48/3–5). The mystic Margery Kempe worshipped at St Margaret's in King's Lynn, and Gail McMurray Gibson suggests that 'Margery the self-styled saint was especially a self-styled Saint Margaret' (*The Theater of Devotion: East Anglian Drama and Society in the Late Middle Ages* (Chicago IL, 1989) p. 64). See, too, Morse pp. 23, 25–26.

39 Skemer, *Binding Words* pp. 239–41, 266.

40 The French birth girdles are not considered here. They are: London, Wellcome Historical Medical Library MSS 804 and possibly 804A (Moorat, *Catalogue of Western MSS*, I, 1472–74); New York, Morgan Library, MSS 779 and 1092 (Skemer, *Binding Words* pp. 245–47; see also 'Amulet Rolls and Female Devotion in the Late Middle Ages' *Scriptorium* 55 (2001) pp. 197–227 (pp. 202 n. 632, 204).

41 Bühler is more interested in textual comparisons than in the specific significance of SS Quiricus and Julitta, but his comparative study includes Rotulus Harley MSS 43.A.14 and T. 11, Glazier MS 39, and Wellcome MS 632. In *Binding Words*, Skemer describes Wellcome MS 632 (pp. 259–60; see, too, 'Amulet' p. 202 n. 16), Beinecke MS 410 (p. 262), Glazier MS 39 (pp. 262–63), and especially BL Additional MS 88929 (pp. 264–67). John Block Friedman describes Glazier MS 39 in detail but does not mention the SS Quiricus and Julitta texts (*Northern English Books, Owners, and Makers in the Late Middle Ages* (Syracuse NY, 1995) pp. 167–70, 181, 197).

42 See C.T. Onions, 'A Devotion to the Cross Written in the South-west of England' *Modern Language Review* 13 (1918) pp. 228–30. Scholars now believe that the Carew-Poyntz Hours was commissioned for a female in the family of Sir John Carew (d. 1363), and signatures show that it was owned in the fifteenth century by women in the Poyntz family (Eamon Duffy, *Marking the Hours: English People & their Prayers 1240–1570* (New Haven CT, 2006) p. 44 pl. 33). Latin prayers to the saints, usually those that commonly appear with the English prayer, are also found in several devotional manuscripts, including London, BL, MS Additional 37787 (also known as 'A Worcestershire Miscellany'), f. 92, and Cambridge, Fitzwilliam Museum, MS 49 (a Book of Hours), f. 11ᵛ. Princeton University Library, MS Kane 21 (Nicholas Love's *The Mirror of the Blessed Life of Jesus Christ*) contains a Latin variant of the English prayer on f. 1ᵛ (for a transcription, see Skemer, *Binding Words* p. 152 n. 70). London, BL, MS Sloane 783B, a medical miscellany, contains Latin suffrages to Quiricus and Julitta (especially to Quiricus) that do not refer to childbirth and that differ

considerably from the Latin orations to the pair in this group of birth girdle manuscripts.

43 Joseph J. Gwara and I discovered this connection after I presented an earlier version of this paper at the Early Book Society conference celebrated in the present volume. Gwara and I examine two printed texts, STC 14547.5 (London, BL, MS. Harley 5919) and STC 14077c.64 (Cambridge MA, Harvard University, Houghton Library) and provide a transcription of these texts and relevant texts in MS Sloane 783B in Joseph J. Gwara and Mary Morse, 'A Birth Girdle Printed by Wynkyn de Worde' *The Library* series 7, 13 (2012) pp. 33–62 (pp. 59–62).

44 *Marking the Hours* p. 64.

45 Onions p. 229; Bühler pp. 273–74; Duffy, *Stripping of the Altars* p. 275.

46 On the Charlemagne letter, see Duffy, *Stripping of the Altars* pp. 273–75 and *Marking the Hours* pp. 76–77; Skemer, *Binding Words* pp. 96–99. On the protections of the cross see Duffy, *Stripping of the Altars* p. 273; Nicholas Orme, 'Two Early Prayer-Books from North Devon' *Devon and Cornwall Notes and Queries* 36 (1991) pp. 345–50 (p. 349). On the saints' possible connection to the finding of the True Cross, see Smith, *Art, Identity and Devotion*, p. 289 n. 17.

47 This marketing strategy was used by many English churches, which exploited 'branded pardons' to sell their 'transferred' indulgences (the Boston guild of Our Lady, for example, issued Lateran indulgences in England). See R.N. Swanson, *Indulgences in Late Medieval England: Passports to Paradise?* (Cambridge, 2007) pp. 54–55. St John Lateran also possessed a famous relic of Christ's measure (see Louis Gougaud, 'La prière dite de Charlemagne et les pièces apocryphes apparentées' *Revue d'histoire ecclésiastique* 20 (1924) pp. 211–38 (p. 222)).

48 Skemer suggests that 'the text, which is not gender-specific ("michi famulo tuo") could have been used devotionally and amuletically for the benefit of family and household' (*Binding Words* p. 263). The name 'Elizabeth' is inserted into roughly the same place in a version of the Latin suffrage (f. 11ᵛ) in Fitzwilliam MS 49, a fifteenth-century Book of Hours from western England, but Elizabeth is not otherwise identified as an owner (Montague R. James, *A Descriptive Catalogue of the Manuscripts in the Fitzwilliam Museum* (Cambridge, 1895) pp. 121–23).

49 Bühler p. 274 (the 'woman in travail' passage reads: 'The viijth is yf a woman be in trauell of childe [...]').

50 Transcription in Gwara and Morse p. 47.

51 Bühler pp. 274–75.

52 Barbara A. Shailor, *Catalogue of Medieval and Renaissance Manuscripts in the Beinecke Rare Book and Manuscript Library Yale University*, 2 vols (Binghamton NY, 1987) II, 308–11.

53 See Shailor, *Catalogue* pp. 308–11. Innocent VI was pope in Avignon 1352–62. Popes named Innocent frequently appear in manuscripts that also contain the texts related to SS Quiricus and Julitta or in manuscripts with similar prayers. Bühler (pp. 272 n. 15, 277 n. 48) notes that Innocent II (1130–43) may have 'authenticated the relic of the "holy nails" belonging to the Viennese court' and is invoked in a prayer to Christ's Side Wound in the 1527 *Sarum Horae*, but he concludes that Innocent VIII (1484–92) is intended (as in BL Rotulus Harley MS T. 11), rather than Innocent VI. Similar references to 'Pope Innocent' occur in prayers to the Holy Nails in BL MS Add. 88929 and Glazier MS 39.

54 Shailor, *Catalogue* pp. 308–11.

55 Bühler p. 277.

56 Skemer, *Binding Words* pp. 176–77.

57 In BL MS Rotulus Harley 43.A 14, the shaft is crossed with two beams.

58 An early print exception is discussed in Gwara and Morse pp. 46, 51.

59 BL Rotulus Harley MS 43.A 14 does not contain any other evidence for ownership.

60 French, *Good Women of the Parish* p. 136.

61 The manuscript (then Durham, Ushaw College, MS 29 but subsequently acquired by the British Library) was displayed in the 2009 'Henry VIII: Man and Monarch' exhibition and in the 2011–12 'Royal Manuscripts: The Genius of Illumination' exhibition, both at the British Library. I thank Dr Andrea Clarke, Curator of Early Modern Historical Manuscripts, for providing me with images to study while the manuscript was unavailable. For a description and images see Scot McKendrick, Kathleen Doyle and John Lowden, *Royal Manuscripts: The Genius of Illumination* (London, 2011) pp. 186–87.

62 Bracketed ellipses in the first part of this transcription indicate illegibility; bracketed words indicate questionable spellings. The bracketed final sentence represents Moorat's incomplete transcription of the prayer (p. 492). I thank Stefania Signorello, conservator at the Wellcome Trust, for making it possible for me to recheck my earlier transcriptions of the legible texts in Wellcome MS 632.

63 Transcription from Moorat (p. 492).

64 See Duffy, *Stripping of the Altars* p. 45; Kathleen L. Scott, 'The Illustration and Decoration of Manuscripts of Nicholas Love's *Mirror*', in Shoichi Ogura, Richard Beadle and Michael Sargent (eds) *Nicholas Love at Waseda: Proceedings of the International Conference 20–22 July 1995* (Cambridge, 1997) pp. 61–86 (p. 67); Rosemary Woolf, *The English Religious Lyric in the Middle Ages* (Oxford, 1968) pp. 172–79; Morse pp. 20–23.

65 Frances M.M. Comper, *The Life and Lyrics of Richard Rolle as Gathered from Contemporary Manuscripts* (London and New York, 1928; repr. New York, 1969) pp. 315, 318. Other manuscript witnesses include: Oxford, Bodleian Library, Tanner MS 407 (*The Commonplace Book of Robert Reynes of Acle*), f. 10ᵛ; Oxford, Bodleian Library, Douce MS 1, ff. 70ᵛ–71; Oxford, Trinity College, MS R.3.21, f. 278ᵛ; BL MS Add. 37049; for other variants see Julia Boffey and A.S.G. Edwards, *A New Index of Middle English Verse* (London, 2005), no. 3443 (hereafter *NIMEV*); Linne Mooney, David Mosser, and Elizabeth Sopolova, eds, *DIMEV: An Open Access, Digital Edition of the Index of Middle English Verse*, no. 5425 (hereafter *DIMEV*) at <http://www.cddc.vt.edu/host/imev> [accessed 15 August 2012].

66 On the Side Wound's association with women and childbirth specifically, see Skemer, *Binding Words* p. 249, and Flora Lewis, 'The Wound in Christ's Side and the Instruments of the Passion: Gendered Experience and Response' in Jane H.M. Taylor and Lesley Smith (eds) *Women and the Book: Assessing the Visual Evidence* (Toronto, 1996) pp. 204–29; for a more general discussion on the cult of the Wounds, see Duffy, *Stripping of the Altars* pp. 244–47.

67 This particular Side Wound iconography seems rare, with these two the only manuscript witnesses that I have found. For the verse in Takamiya MS 56 (not in *NIMEV* or *DIMEV*) see Christopher de Hamel in his description of the manuscript in *Catalogue of Western Manuscripts and Miniatures* (London:

Sotheby Parke Bernet & Co., 24 June 1980), lot 73 (cited in Toshiyuki Takamiya, 'Gawain's Green Girdle as a Medieval Talisman' in Richard Beadle and Toshiyuki Takamiya (eds) *Chaucer to Shakespeare: Essays in Honor of Shinsuke Ando* (Woodbridge, 1992) pp. 75–79 (p. 77 n. 7)). I thank Kathleen L. Scott for sharing her knowledge of Wounds iconography, especially depictions of the detached hands and feet.

68   John Plummer, *The Glazier Collection of Illuminated Manuscripts* (New York, 1968) p. 38; see, too, Friedman, *Northern English Books* p. 167.

69   Bühler p. 277 n. 48 for transcription; see, too, William Legge, 'A Decorated Mediæval Roll of Prayers' *The Reliquary and Illustrated Archaeologist* 10 (1904) pp. 99–112 (p. 100).

70   Friedman, *Northern English Books* p. 167.

71   Legge p. 102. Utilising the prayer to SS Quiricus and Julitta as evidence, Carole Rawcliffe discusses the possible use of Glazier MS 39 as a birth girdle in *Medicine and Society in Later Medieval England* (London, 1995) pp. 96–98.

72   Transcription from Bühler p. 275.

73   I owe this anecdote to the late Alistair MacGregor, curator of manuscripts at Ushaw College, Durham.

74   McKendrick, *Royal Manuscripts* p. 186; Skemer, *Binding Words* pp. 264 n. 62, 264–66. The case for this roll, as described in the Sotheby's sale catalogue, is 'of cuir-ciselé, gilded and coloured, beautifully preserved and more-or-less exactly datable [the roll is dated 1491] ... technique localisable to France' (*Collection of Otto Schäfer, II: Parisian Books*, Sotheby's Sale LN5385, London, 27 June 1995, lot 192).

75   Skemer, *Binding Words* p. 264.

76   Transcription of the first part of the passage from Edward Charlton, 'A Roll of Prayers Formerly Belonging to Henry VIII When Prince' *Archæologia æliana: or, Miscellaneous Tracts Relating to Antiquity* 2 (1858) pp. 41–45 (pp. 43–44). Brackets indicate my transcription of the rubric. Skemer transcribes 'cristendom' as 'cristendin' (*Binding Words* p. 265).

77   Julian of Norwich evokes related iconography in her analogy of a mother's breast and Christ's Side Wound in *Revelations of Divine Love*: 'The mother can lay the child tenderly to her breast, but our tender mother Jesus, he can familiarly lead us into his blessed breast through his sweet open side ...' (*Julian of Norwich: Revelations of Divine Love*, trans. Elizabeth Spearing (New York, 1998) p. 141 (Long Text 60)).

78   For a fourteenth-century French book of hours with an indulgence of Innocent IV, see Skemer, *Binding Words* p. 266 n. 64.

79   Transcribed by W. Sparrow Simpson, 'On a Magical Roll Preserved in the British Museum' *Journal of the British Archaeological Association* 48 (1892) pp. 38–54 (p. 51). Bühler notes this transcription (p. 272 n. 18) and provides a transcription of the prayer to the Nails (p. 277). See, too, Kathryn M. Rudy, 'Kissing Images, Unfurling Rolls, Measuring Wounds, Sewing Badges and Carrying Talismans: Considering Some Harley Manuscripts through the Physical Rituals They Reveal' *eBritish Library Journal* Article 5 pp. 1–56 (pp. 42–51) at <http://www.bl.uk/eblj/index.html> [accessed 6 February 2012].

80   On the 'names of Christ' and the list's relationship to the Charlemagne legend see Duffy, *Stripping of the Altars* pp. 274–76, and Skemer, *Binding Words* pp. 112–15. The few names often found in the lists that can be determined in Wellcome MS 632 include *elayson, te[t]ragrammaton, ego sum, [et] oo,*

pater, agnus and *ovis*. All except *elayson* commonly appear in lists of divine names in early English print sources. Although the appearance of *elayson* on Wellcome MS 632 is unusual among English sources, *Eleison* appears between *Otheos* and *Eloy* as the fourth divine name in 'the standard list of divine names' in a thirteenth-century French amuletic roll for women (Skemer pp. 241–42). For another list of divine names in BL Rotulus Harley T. 11 see Skemer p. 263. Also see Gwara and Morse pp. 39–40, 52.

81 Onions p. 228; see too Bühler p. 275.

82 Onions terms the red underlining an 'error' (p. 229).

83 Duffy, *Stripping of the Altars* pp. 269–70; Orme, 'Prayer-books' p. 349.

84 Onions pp. 228–29; Bühler pp. 275–76.

85 Onions p. 228; Bühler p. 271.

86 For a description of the page see Ann E. Nichols, Michael T. Orr, Kathleen L. Scott and Lynda Dennison (eds), *An Index of Images in English Manuscripts from the Time of Chaucer to Henry VIII. c.1380–c.1509: The Bodleian Library, Oxford: I: MSS Additional—Digby* (Turnhout, 2002) pp. 53–54.

87 Rossell Hope Robbins, 'The "Arma Christi" Rolls', *Modern Language Review* 34 (1939) pp. 415–21, p. 415 n. 1.

88 Ann E. Nichols, '"O Vernicle": Illustrations of an Arma Christi Poem' in Marlene Villalobos Hennessy (ed.) *Tributes to Kathleen L. Scott: English Medieval Manuscripts: Readers, Makers and Illuminators* (Turnhout, 2009) pp. 139–69 (pp. 142, 167).

89 Seymour de Ricci, *Census of Medieval and Renaissance Manuscripts in the United States and Canada*, 2 vols (New York, 1935–1940) II, 1222.

90 I am grateful to Ann E. Nichols for alerting me to yet another appearance of the Middle English and Latin prayers to SS Quiricus and Julitta in CUL, MS Ii.6.43 (f. 20ᵛ), a religious miscellany containing Latin and English texts, c.1425 (personal correspondence).

91 See Takamiya, 'Gawain's Green Girdle' pp. 75–79. For a brief description of Takamiya MS 56, see T. Takamiya, 'A Handlist of Western Medieval Manuscripts in the Takamiya Collection' in James H. Marrow, Richard A. Linenthal and William Noel (eds) *The Medieval Book: Glosses from Friends & Colleagues of Christopher de Hamel* (Houten, 2010) pp. 421–40 (p. 431).

14: *Emma Cayley* Consuming the Text: Pulephilia in Fifteenth-Century French Debate Poetry

1 With grateful thanks to *Cahiers de recherches médiévales et humanistes/ Journal of Medieval and Humanistic Studies* for permission to use material from my article, '"Avoir puce en l'oreille": Voices of Desire in Alain Chartier's *Debat Reveille Matin* and Guillaume Alexis' *Le Debat de l'omme mondain et du religieulx*', *CRMH* 22 (2011) pp. 43–57. This chapter is a refocused and expanded version of that article.

2 The modern English and French idioms differ in that the English expression, 'a flea in one's ear', refers to a 'sharp rebuke or reproof' (*OED flea*, n. 4a), whereas the French expression refers to a sense of disquiet or suspicion. The connotations of sexual discomfort are absent from the modern English expression, as from the modern French.

3 For the mediation of voice in the debate poem, see P.-Y. Badel, 'Le Débat' in D. Poirion (ed.) *Grundriss der romanischen Literaturen des Mittelalters* VIII:1

(Heidelberg, 1988) pp. 95–110 (p. 97) and E. Cayley, *Debate and Dialogue: Alain Chartier in his Cultural Context* (Oxford, 2006) pp. 6–7.

4   Not least in the multiple voices of 'dead' authorities who return to 'haunt' the text, as Helen Swift has observed with her theory of 'spectropoetics' via Jacques Derrida's notion of 'spectropolitics': see H.J. Swift, *Gender, Writing, and Performance : Men Defending Women in Late Medieval France (1440–1538)* (Oxford, 2008) esp. pp. 33–38.

5   Jane Taylor adopts Arthur M. Marotti's term in her discussion of the social dynamics of late-medieval anthology manuscripts, see J.H.M. Taylor, *The Making of Poetry: Late-Medieval Poetic Anthologies* (Turnhout, 2007), p. 9; A.M. Marotti, *John Donne, Coterie Poet* (Madison WI, 1986) pp. 44–82.

6   Taylor p. 154.

7   On questions of voice in earlier lyric poetry, see esp. S. Kay, *Subjectivity in Troubadour Poetry* (Cambridge, 1990).

8   M. Françon, 'Un Motif de la poésie amoureuse au XVIe siècle' *PMLA* 56 (1941) pp. 307–36; G. di Stefano, *Dictionnaire des locutions en moyen français* (Montreal, 1991); R. Bidler, *Dictionnaire érotique* (Montreal, 2002) pp. 530–31; C. Duneton, *La puce à l'oreille: anthologie des expressions populaires avec leur origine* (Paris, 1990) pp. 58–64.

9   For the development of the flea motif in French literature, see Françon; for discussion of late medieval French and German literature which stages debate trials between women and fleas, see Swift pp. 227–29. Patrizia Bettella looks at the Italian tradition and bodily infestation in *The Ugly Woman: Transgressive Aesthetic Models in Italian Poetry from the Middle Ages to the Baroque* (Toronto, 2005) pp. 159–63.

10 In 1907 Georges Feydeau's farce 'La Puce à l'oreille' uses the expression in its modern French sense, evoking suspicion and disquiet; however, here too there is a sexual element, since the context is the wife's suspicion of her husband's infidelity. There was a 1968 French/American film adaptation, *A Flea in Her Ear*, directed by Jacques Charon with a screenplay by John Mortimer, starring Rex Harrison, Rosemary Harris and Louis Jourdan, as well as a more recent French TV film (1997) directed by Yves di Tullio, starring Jean-Paul Belmondo and Cristiana Réali. See Georges Feydeau *La Puce à l'oreille : Pièce en trois actes* (Paris, 1968).

11 Jean de la Fontaine: *Le Rossignol, contes et nouvelles en vers par Monsieur de La Fontaine* (Amsterdam, 1709); see an online version at <http://www. micheloud.com/FXM/Lafontaine/Rossignol.htm> [accessed 30 November 2011].

12 All translations from the French are mine unless otherwise stated.

13 See J. Derrida, C. Lévesque and C.V. McDonald (eds) *L'oreille de l'autre: otobiographies, transferts, traductions. Textes et débats avec Jacques Derrida* (Montreal, 1982) and J. Derrida, 'L'Oreille de Heidegger : Philopolémologie (Geschlecht IV)' in *Politiques de l'amitié* (Paris, 1994) pp. 343–419.

14 The verb 'esveillier' (to awake) here may of course also be read with its erotic sense of arousal.

15 This line is problematic: while it closely resembles the erotic expression 'faire dresser les oreilles' (to have an erection/be aroused), the scribe has used the word 'oreillier' (pillow), perhaps in error, or as a sanitisation of the passage.

16 *Debat de la Damoiselle et de la Bourgeoise*, ll. 641–48. For an edition of this debate, see Emma Cayley, *Sleepless Knights and Wanton Women, Volume*

1: The Debate Poems (Tempe AZ, forthcoming); for further discussion see, too, Emma Cayley, '"Le chapperon tousjours dure": The Language of Ageing Desire in the *Debat de la damoiselle et de la bourgeoise* and *Debat du viel et du jeune*' in Rebecca Dixon (ed.) *Essays in Later Medieval French Literature: The Legacy of Jane H.M. Taylor* (Manchester, 2010) pp. 71–87. As noted in this article (p. 81), two of the seven manuscripts of this debate substitute the line 'Si commençay à moy/me habiller' (I began to get dressed) for '(Si) commamcé à m'esveiller' (I began to wake up), suggesting the narrator's hasty dressing following a sexual encounter.

17 Guillaume Alexis, *Debat de l'omme mondain et du religieulx* (hereafter *DOMR*), l. 56. All references are to my forthcoming edition and English translation (Cayley, *Sleepless Knights*). Subsequent references to *DOMR* will be incorporated in the text.

18 François Rabelais: P. Michel (ed.), *Le Tiers Livre* (Paris, 1966) pp. 142–48.

19 See B. de Verville, *Le Moyen de parvenir* (Paris, 1896). Further medieval and early modern expressions from Bidler's *Dictionnaire érotique* include 'secouer les pulces a une femme' (to have sex with a woman) and 'je le trouverois mieux dans un lict qu'une pulce' (I would rather find *her* in my bed than a flea, i.e. to find a woman desirable).

20 Alain Chartier, *Debat Reveille Matin* (hereafter *DRM*) ll. 1–8. All references are to my forthcoming edition and English translation (Cayley, *Sleepless Knights*). Subsequent references to *DRM* will be incorporated in the text.

21 I am grateful to Jane Gilbert for her illuminating suggestion of the 'puce' as gender-neutral 'part-object' in a Žižekian sense (via Melanie Klein and Lacan's 'objet petit a') at the British Branch conference of the International Courtly Literature Society, Cambridge, April 2009. See S. Žižek, *Organs without Bodies: On Deleuze and Consequences* (London and New York, 2003).

22 See Françon for the flea motif in European and Arabic literature.

23 *Elegia de pulice* in N.E. Le Maire (ed.), *Poetae Latini Minores*, 8 vols (Paris, 1767–1832) VII, 275–78. The English translation is by H.D. Brumble in 'John Donne's "The Flea": Some Implications of the Encyclopedic and Poetic Flea Traditions' *Critical Quarterly* 15 (1973) pp. 147–54.

24 Thanks to Jonathan Morton for the reference here: Nature describes a world where animals have the power to reason, explaining that men would be helpless to resist them. See Guillaume de Lorris and Jean de Meun: Armand Strubel (ed.) *Le Roman de la rose* (Paris, 1992) ll. 17845–48.

25 See Di Stefano for instances of the expression in Deschamps, Charles d'Orléans and François Villon.

26 Thanks to Hugh Roberts for the reference to *Des puces*, a delightful argument between two fleas in Bruscambille's *Les Nouvelles et plaisantes imagintations de Bruscambille* [...] (Paris, 1613).

27 *Folastrie* VI (1553), 'Que pleust à Dieu que je peusse/Pour un soir devenir puce', also the sonnet 'Ha, Seigneur dieu, que de graces écloses', in P. Laumonier (ed.), *Oeuvres complètes*, 20 vols (Paris, 1914–75) V, 38, 110, and *Les Amours* XX (1552), 'Je vouldroy bien richement jaunissant' in M. Bensimon and J.L. Martin (eds), *Les Amours* (Paris, 1981) p. 67.

28 For Estienne Pasquier's and Catherine Des Roches' poetic contributions to a literary contest staged around the motif of the flea, see Estienne Pasquier and Catherine Des Roches, *La Puce de Madame Des Roches, qui est un recueil de divers poèmes Grecs, Latins et François. Composez pars plusieurs doctes*

personnages aux Grands Jours tenus à Poitiers l'an MDLXXIX (Paris, Pour Abel l'Angelier, 1582).

29 See Christopher Marlowe: J. O'Connor (ed.), *Dr Faustus* (Harlow, 2003).

30 See John Donne: A.J. Smith (ed.), *The Complete English Poems* (New York, 1986).

31 See Barry Wind, 'Close Encounters of the Baroque Kind: Amatory Paintings by Terbrugghen, Baburen and La Tour' *Studies in Iconography* 4 (1978) pp. 115–22 and J.F. Moffitt, 'La Femme à la puce: The Textual Background of Seventeenth-Century Painted Flea-Hunts' *Gazette des Beaux-Arts* 110 (1987) pp. 99–103.

32 Quoted from Marlowe's personification of *Pride* in *Dr Faustus*, ll. 110–11, Act II, Scene III.

33 See Gaius Valerius Catullus: P. Green (ed. and trans.), *The Poems of Catullus: A Bilingual Edition* (Berkeley CA, 2007), and A. Armstrong, 'Is This an Ex-Parrot? The Printed Afterlife of Jean Lemaire de Belges' *Épîtres de l'Amant vert*' *Journal de la Renaissance* 5 (2007) pp. 323–36.

34 Todd P. Olson, 'La Femme à la Puce et la Puce à l'oreille: Catherine Des Roches and the Poetics of Sexual Resistance in Sixteenth-Century French Poetry' *Journal of Medieval and Early Modern Studies* 32 (2002) pp. 327–42 (p. 337). See also C. Yandell, 'Of Lice and Women: Rhetoric and Gender in *La puce de Madame Des Roches*' *Journal of Medieval and Renaissance Studies* 20 (1990) pp. 123–35.

35 Pasquier and Des Roches, *La Puce de Madame Des Roches* pp. 20–22.

36 I make it thirty-eight manuscripts, as opposed to forty-four, for the *Belle Dame sans mercy* (hereafter *LBDSM*), thirty-four of which belong to the *Belle Dame* tradition (in thirty-seven of these the *DRM* appears with the *LBDSM*). The additional manuscript is Turin, Bibl. Naz. Univ., L. IV. 3 (ff. 64–68) unfortunately destroyed in a fire in 1904. For details of the manuscript tradition and an edition, see J.C. Laidlaw (ed.) *The Poetical Works of Alain Chartier* (Cambridge, 1974) pp. 305–6, and David F. Hult and Joan E. McRae (eds) *Le Cycle de la Belle Dame sans mercy* (Paris, 2003) pp. 439–71, as well as Cayley, *Sleepless Knights*.

37 See E.J. Hoffman, *Alain Chartier, His Works and Reputation* (Geneva, 1975) pp. 39–43.

38 See Cayley, *Debate and Dialogue* pp. 110–21 and Emma Cayley and A. Kinch (eds), *Chartier in Europe* (Cambridge, 2008).

39 Cayley, *Debate and Dialogue* pp. 129–33.

40 See J. Morawski, *Proverbes français antérieurs au XVᵉ siècle* (Paris, 1925) no. 81.

41 See E. Kosofsky Sedgwick, *Between Men: English Literature and Male Homosocial Desire* (New York, 1985).

42 See the online *Dictionnaire du Moyen Français 1330–1500*, version 2010 (ATILF—CNRS & Nancy Université) at <http://www.atilf.fr/dmf/> [accessed 30 November 2011].

43 This proverb is the premise for Chartier's *DRM* (l. 39); see Cayley, *Debate and Dialogue* pp. 129–31.

44 Kosofsky Sedgwick pp. 16, 18, 25 and *passim*.

45 Kosofsky Sedgwick p. 26; see also R. Girard, Y. Freccero (trans.) *Deceit, Desire, and the Novel: Self and Other in Literary Structure* (Baltimore MD, 1972); Lacan's discussion of the triangulation of the gaze: J. Lacan, *Les Quatre*

Concepts fondamentaux de la psychanalyse : le séminaire XI (Paris, 1990); and Simon Gaunt's reading of Lacan in S. Gaunt, *Love and Death in Medieval French and Occitan Courtly Literature* (Oxford, 2006) pp. 182–83.

46 See Cayley, *Sleepless Knights* (forthcoming) and E. Cayley, 'Debate after Alain Chartier: Authority and Materiality in the *Debat de la Noire et de la Tannee*' in Jean-Claude Mühlethaler and Jean-Yves Tilliette (eds) *Mythes à la cour, mythes pour la cour* (Geneva, 2010) pp. 311–21. See also Olivier Delsaux (ed.), *Je meurs de soif empres le puys. Le debat de la noire et de la tannée* (Louvain-la-Neuve, 2006), and his articles on the *Noire et tannee*: 'Du debat à l'esbat. Le debat de la noire et de la tannée: une définition en jeu' *Cahiers Moyen Âge-Renaissance 1: Jugement par esbatement* (2006) pp. 105–18; '*(D)ebat* pour recueil en noir majeur. La supériorité du ms.-recueil sur le ms. d'auteur pour l'approche d'un texte poétique en moyen français' in T. Van Hemelryck and C. Thiry (eds) *Le recueil au Moyen Âge. La fin du Moyen Âge* (Turnhout, 2010) pp. 101–11; '*Le Debat de la noire et de la tannee*. À la recherche d'un signalement' (forthcoming in *Romania*).

47 There are three manuscript witnesses: Paris, BnF, fr. 25420 (ff. 1–21); Paris, BnF, Rothschild 2798 (ff. 1–22); Chantilly, Musée Condé, 685 (ff. 123–38ᵛ). The Chantilly manuscript does not have any illustration and is a compilation manuscript; Paris, BnF, fr. 25420 is monotextual.

48 See S. Huot, 'The Daisy and the Laurel: Myths of Desire and Creativity in the Poetry of Jean Froissart' *Yale French Studies* 80 (1991) pp. 240–51, esp. pp. 246–47.

49 For an account of the cult of the 'marguerite', exemplified in the poetry of Machaut, Froissart, Deschamps and Chaucer, see Huot, 'The Daisy and the Laurel' p. 246.

50 See J.H.M. Taylor, 'Embodying the Rose: An Intertextual Reading of Alain Chartier's *La Belle Dame Sans Mercy*' in B.K. Altmann and C.W. Carroll (eds) *The Court Reconvenes: Courtly Literature Across the Disciplines* (Cambridge, 2003) pp. 325–43.

51 See Jean Froissart: A. Fourrier (ed.), *Plaidoirie de la Rose et de la Violette, 'Dits' et 'Débats'* (Geneva, 1979).

52 A. de Montaiglon (ed.) *L'Amant rendu cordelier a l'observance d'amours* (hereafter *ARC*) (Paris, 1881). Subsequent references to *ARC* will be incorporated in the text. This poem was attributed to Martial d'Auvergne by Lenglet-Dufresnoy in the 1731 Amsterdam edition of the *Arrêts d'amours*, and subsequently by A. de Montaiglon and W. Söderhjelm, *Anteckningar om Martial d'Auvergne och hans Kärleksdommar* (Helsingfors, 1889), but see A. Piaget's discussion: '*La Belle Dame sans merci* et ses imitations' *Romania* 34 (1905) pp. 416–23. The claim for authorship based solely on the similarities of expression of *arrêt* XXXVII and *ARC* is doubtful given that Martial d'Auvergne is probably not the author of the *Arrêts*, and given the common reservoir of images drawn on by poets of the *LBDSM* cycle.

53 On death in medieval French poetry see J.H.M. Taylor, *Dies Illa: Death in the Middle Ages* (Liverpool, 1984) and Gaunt.

54 See Hult and McRae p. 441.

55 For further discussion of these manuscripts and their relationship, see E. Cayley, 'Polyphonie et dialogisme: espaces ludiques dans le recueil manuscrit à la fin du moyen âge. Le cas de trois recueils poétiques du quinzième siècle' in Van Hemelryck and Thiry pp. 47–60.

56 Pierre de Hauteville: R.M. Bidler (ed.), *La Confession et testament de l'amant trespassé de deuil* (Montreal, 1982) l. 1009.

57 R.M. Bidler (ed.) 'Complainte de l'amant trespassé de deuil, et l'inventaire des biens demourez du deces de l'amant trespassé de deuil' *Le Moyen Français* 18 (1986) pp. 11–104, l. 311.

58 E. Droz and A. Piaget (eds in facsimile), *Jardin de plaisance et fleur de rethorique*, 2 vols (Paris, 1910–25) I, 233.

Bibliography

Abou-el-Haj, Barbara, 'Bury St Edmunds Abbey Between 1070 and 1124: A History of Property, Privilege, and Monastic Art Production' *Art History* 6 (1983) pp. 1–29.

Abou-El-Haj, Barbara, *The Medieval Cult of Saints: Formations and Transformations* (Binghamton NY, 1994).

Albritton, Benjamin L., 'Citation and Allusion in the Lays of Guillaume de Machaut' (unpublished doctoral thesis, University of Washington, 2009).

Andrew, Charles, *St Quiricus and St Julietta, Tickenham: A Short Guide to the History of this Ancient Parish Church*, rev. Bridget Wheeler (2005).

Anon., 'The Roxburghe Revels, MS.' *The Athenaeum* (4 January 1834).

Armstrong, A., 'Is This an Ex-Parrot? The Printed Afterlife of Jean Lemaire de Belges' Épîtres de l'Amant vert' *Journal de la Renaissance* 5 (2007) pp. 323–36.

Armstrong, E., 'English Purchases of Printed Books from the Continent 1465–1526' *English Historical Review* 94 (1979) pp. 268–90.

Arnold-Forster, Frances, *Studies in Church Dedications, or England's Patron Saints*, 2 vols (London, 1899).

Arthurson, Ian, 'Ratcliffe, John, sixth Baron Fitzwalter (1452–1496)' *ODNB*.

Ashley, Kathleen and Robert L.A. Clark (eds), *Medieval Conduct* (Minneapolis MN, 2001).

Association of College and Research Libraries, *Binding Terms: a Thesaurus for Use in Rare Book and Special Collections Cataloging* (Chicago IL, 1988).

Aston, M.,'Devotional Literacy' in her *Lollards and Reformers. Images and Literacy in Late Medieval England* (London, 1984) pp. 101–33.

Avril, François, *Manuscript Painting at the Court of France*, trans. Ursule Molinaro and Bruce Benderson (London, 1978).

Avril, François, 'Les Manuscrits enluminés de Guillaume de Machaut: essai de chronologie' in *Guillaume de Machaut: Colloque – Table Ronde Organisé par l'Université de Reims Reims, 19–22 Avril 1978* (Paris, 1982) pp. 117–33.

Avrin, Leila, *Scribes, Script and Books: the Book Arts from Antiquity to the Renaissance* (Chicago IL, 1991).

Ayto, John and Alexandra Barratt (eds) *Aelred of Rievaulx's De Institutione Inclusarum* (London, 1984).

Backhouse, J., 'Founders of the Royal Library: Edward IV and Henry VII as Collectors of Illuminated Manuscripts' in D. Williams (ed.) *England in the Fifteenth Century* (Woodbridge, 1987) pp. 23–41.

Badel, P.-Y., 'Le Débat' in D. Poirion (ed.) *Grundriss der romanischen Literaturen des Mittelalters* VIII:1 (Heidelberg, 1988) pp. 95–110.

Bakhtin, M.M., *Rabelais and His World* (Moscow 1965; repr. Bloomington IN, 1984).

Bakhtin, M.M., *Dialogic Imagination: Four Essays*, ed. and trans. M. Wehrle (Cambridge MA, 1981).

Bale, Anthony (ed.), *St Edmund, King and Martyr: Changing Images of a Medieval Saint* (York, 2009).

Bale, Anthony, 'St Edmund in Fifteenth-Century London: The Lydgatian Miracles of St Edmund' in Anthony Bale (ed.) *St Edmund, King and Martyr: Changing Images of a Medieval Saint* (York, 2009) pp. 145–61.

Bale, Anthony and A.S.G. Edwards (eds), *John Lydgate's Lives of Ss Edmund & Fremund and the Extra Miracles of St Edmund: Edited from British Library MS Harley 2278 and Bodleian Library MS Ashmole 46* (Heidelberg, 2009).

Baring-Gould, S. and John Fisher, *The Lives of the British Saints: The Saints of Wales, Cornwall and Such Irish Saints as Have Dedications in Britain*, 2 vols (London, 1907; repr. Whitefish MT, 2005).

Barker, Nicholas, 'The Importation of Books into England, 1460–1526' in Herbert G. Göpfert (ed.) *Beiträge zur Geschichte des Buchwesens im Konfesionellen Zeitalter* (Wiesbaden, 1985) pp. 251–66.

Barron, C.M., 'Richard Whittington: the man behind the myth' in A.E.J. Hollaender and W. Kellaway (eds) *Studies in London History Presented to P.E. Jones* (1969) pp. 213–15.

Barron, C.M., 'William Langland: A London poet' in B. Hanawalt (ed.) *Chaucer's England: Literature in Historical Context* (Minneapolis MN, 1992) pp. 95–6.

Barron, C.M., *London in the Later Middle Ages: Government and People 1200–1500* (Oxford, 2004).

Beaven, A.B., *The Aldermen of London*, 2 vols (London, 1908, 1913).

Beech, Beatrice Hibbard, 'Yolande Bonhomme: A Renaissance Printer' *Medieval Prosopography* 6 (1983) pp. 79–100.

Beech, Beatrice Hibbard, 'Women Printers in Paris in the Sixteenth Century' *Medieval Prosopography* 10 (1989) pp. 75–93.

Beidler, Peter, 'The Miller's Tale and its Analogues' in Robert M. Correale and Mary Hamel (eds) *Sources and Analogues of the Canterbury Tales*, 2 vols (Cambridge, 2002; Woodbridge, 2005) II, 249–65.

Belitz, Jürgen, *Studien zur Parodie in Heinrich Wittenwilers 'Ring'* (Göppingen, 1978).

Bell, Alan, 'Haslewood, Joseph (1769–1833)' *ODNB*.

Belting, Hans, *Bild-Anthropologie: Entwürfe für eine Bildwissenschaft* (Munich, 2001).

Bensimon, M. and J.L. Martin (eds), *Les Amours* (Paris, 1981).

Benson, Larry D. (ed.), *The Riverside Chaucer* (Boston MA, 1987).

Benson, Larry D. and Theodore M. Andersson (eds), *The Literary Context of Chaucer's Fabliaux: Texts and Translations* (Indianapolis IN and New York, 1971).

Bent, Margaret, 'Some Criteria for Establishing Relationships Between Sources of Late-Medieval Polyphony' in Iain Fenlon (ed.) *Music in Medieval and Early Modern Europe: Patronage, Sources and Texts* (Cambridge, 1981) pp. 295–317.

Bent, Margaret, 'The Machaut Manuscripts Vg, B, and E' *Musica Disciplina* 37 (1983) pp. 53–82.

Bernard of Clairvaux, *On the Song of Songs*, trans. Kilian Walsh, 4 vols (Kalamazoo MI, 1976).

Bétemps, Isabelle, 'Les Lais de plour: Guillaume de Machaut et Oton de Granson' in Jacqueline Cerquiglini-Toulet and Nigel Wilkins (eds) *Guillaume de Machaut 1300–2000: Actes du Colloque de la Sorbonne 28–29 septembre 2000* (Paris, 2002) pp. 95–106.

Bettella, Patrizia, *The Ugly Woman: Transgressive Aesthetic Models in Italian Poetry from the Middle Ages to the Baroque* (Toronto, 2005).

Bidler, R.M., *Dictionnaire érotique* (Montreal, 2002).

Bidler, R.M. (ed.), *La Confession et testament de l'amant trespassé de deuil* (Montreal, 1982).

Bidler, R.M. (ed.), 'Complainte de l'amant trespassé de deuil, et l'inventaire des biens demourez du deces de l'amant trespassé de deuil' *Le Moyen Français* 18 (1986) pp. 11–104.

Biggs, Frederick W., '*The Miller's Tale* and *Heile van Beersele*' *Review of English Studies* 56 (2005) pp. 497–523.

Blake, N.F., *Caxton's Own Prose* (London, 1973).

Blake, N.F., *William Caxton: England's First Publisher* (London, 1976).

Blayney, Peter W.M., *The Stationers' Company before the Charter, 1403–1557* (London, 2003).

Block, E.A., 'Chaucer's Millers and Their Bagpipes' *Speculum* 29 (1954) pp. 239–43.

Boffey, J. and A.S.G. Edwards, *A New Index of Middle English Verse* (London, 2005).

Boffey, J. and C. Meale, 'Selecting the Text: Rawlinson C.86 and some other Books for London Readers' in F. Riddy (ed.) *Regionalism in Late Medieval Manuscripts and Texts* (Cambridge, 1991) p. 143–69.

Boitani, P., '"O viva morte": amore, malinconia e l'io diviso' in *Il tragico e il sublime nella letteratura medievale* (Bologna, 1992) pp. 93–116.

Bone, G., 'Extant Manuscripts Printed from by W. de Worde with Notes on the Owner, Roger Thorney' *The Library* series 4, 12 (1932) pp. 284–306.

Bradley, Ritamary, 'Backgrounds of the Title Speculum in Mediaeval Literature' *Speculum* 29 (1954) pp. 100–15.

Brady, Sister M. Teresa, 'Lollard Interpolations and Omissions in Manuscripts of *The Pore Caitif*' in Michael G. Sargent (ed.) *De Cella in Seculum: Religious and Secular Life and Devotion in Late Medieval England* (Cambridge, 1989) pp. 183–203.

Braswell, Laureen, *IMEP Handlist IV: A Handlist of Douce Manuscripts containing Middle English Prose in the Bodleian Library, Oxford* (Cambridge, 1987).

Bräuer, Rolf *et al.* (eds), *Heinrich Wittenwiler, Der Ring: In Abbildung der Meininger Handschrift* (Göppingen, 1991).

Bremmer Jr., Rolf H., 'Footprints of Monastic Instruction: A Latin Psalter with Interverbal Old Frisian Glosses' in Sarah Larratt Keefer and Rolf H. Bremmer Jr. (eds) *Signs on the Edge: Space, Text and Margin in Medieval Manuscripts* (Paris, 2007) pp. 203–33.

British Library, 'Bindings at the British Library,' <http://prodigi.bl.uk/bindings/>.

Brockwell, C.W., *Bishop Reginald Pecock and the Lancastrian Church* (Lewiston NY and Queenstown ONT, 1985).

Brown, Thomas, 'Another *Mirror of Lovers*? – Order, Structure and Allusion in Machaut's Motets' *Plainsong and Medieval Music* 10 (2001) pp. 121–33.

Brownlee, Kevin, *Poetic Identity in Guillaume de Machaut* (Madison WI, 1984).

Brumble, H.D., 'John Donne's "The Flea": Some Implications of the Encyclopedic and Poetic Flea Traditions' *Critical Quarterly* 15 (1973) pp. 147–54.

Bryan, W.F. and Germaine Dempster (eds), *Sources and Analogues of Chaucer's Canterbury Tales* (London, 1958), rev. by Robert M. Correale and Mary Hamel (eds) *Sources and Analogues of the Canterbury Tales*, 2 vols (Cambridge, 2002; Woodbridge, 2005).

Brychmore, Joseph, *Collections for a Parochial History of Tickenham* (Bristol, 1895).

Brydges, Sir Samuel Egerton, 'On Bibliomania', *Theatrical Inquisitor, or Monthly Mirror* 14, 81 (April 1819) pp. 277–79.

Brydges, Sir Samuel Egerton, *A Catalogue of All the Works Printed at the Private Press at Lee Priory in Kent: from its Commencement in July 1813, Till Its Termination in Jan. 1823. [With a Ms. Letter from Geneva by Sir E. Brydges, Dated March 29, 1824, Respecting the Difficulty of Transmitting Books to England]* (1824) <http://www.presscom.co.uk/leepriory1.html>.

Bühler, Curt, 'Prayers and Charms in Certain Middle English Scrolls', *Speculum* 39 (1964) pp. 270–78.

Burgess, C. (ed.), *The Pre-Reformation Records of All Saints, Bristol: Part I*, Bristol Record Society 46 (1995).

Burke, P., *Popular Culture in Early Modern Europe* (London, 1978) p. 110.

Burrow, J.A., *Gestures and Looks in Medieval Narrative* (Cambridge, 2002).

Burton, John Hill, 'The Book Hunter's Club', *Blackwood's Edinburgh Magazine* 90 (October 1861).

Burton, John Hill, *The Book Hunter etc ... with Additional Notes by Richard Grant White* (London, 1863).

Butler, Alban, *Lives of the Saints*, eds Herbert Thurston and Donald Attwater, 2 vols (London, 1956, 2nd edn).

Butzmann, H., *Kataloge der Herzog August Bibliothek Wolfenbüttel: Die mittelalterlichen Handschriften der Gruppen Extravagantes, Novi und Novissimi* (Frankfurt am Main, 1972).

Byrom, H.J., 'Richard Tottel – His Life and Work' *The Library*, series 4, 8 (1928) pp. 199–232.

Calabrese, Michael, 'The Lover's Cure in Ovid's *Remedia Amoris* and Chaucer's *Miller's Tale*' *English Language Notes* 31 (1994) pp. 413–18.

Calendar of Close Rolls.

Campbell, Jane, *The Retrospective Review (1820–1828) and the Revival of Seventeenth-Century Poetry* (Waterloo ONT, 1972).

Carley, James, *The Libraries of Henry VIII* (London, 2000).

Carlin, Martha and Joel Rosenthal (eds), *Food and Eating in Medieval Europe* (London and Rio Grande OH, 1998).

Carlson, D.R., 'Woodcut Illustrations of the *Canterbury Tales*, 1483–1602' *The Library* series 6, 19 (1997) pp. 25–67.

Carroll, Ruth, 'Recipes for Laces: An example of a Middle English discourse colony' in R. Hiltunen and J. Skaffari (eds) *Discourse Perpectives on English* (Amsterdam, 2003) pp. 137–65.

Carroll, Ruth, 'Middle English Recipes: Evolution of a Text-Type' in Irma Taavitsainen and Päivi Pahta (eds) *Medical and Scientific Writing in Medieval and Early Modern English* (Cambridge, 2004) pp. 174–91.

Carroll, Ruth, 'Vague Language in the Medieval Recipes of the *Forme of Cury*' in Matti Peikola, Janne Skaffari and Sanna-Kaisa Tanskanen (eds) *Instructional*

Writing in English: Studies in Honour of Risto Hiltunen (Amsterdam, 2009) pp. 55–82.

Carter, John, *ABC for Book Collectors* (New Castle DE, 1995, 7th edn).

Cassian, John, *Conferences*, trans. Colm Luibheid (Mahwah NJ, 2002).

Catalogue of the Second Portion of the Splendid, Curious, and Extensive Library of the Late John Dent, Esq., F.R.S. and F.S.A. (London, 1827).

Cayley, Emma, *Debate and Dialogue: Alain Chartier in his Cultural Context* (Oxford, 2006).

Cayley, Emma, '"Le chapperon tousjours dure": The Language of Ageing Desire in the *Debat de la damoiselle et de la bourgeoise* and *Debat du viel et du jeune*' in Rebecca Dixon (ed.) *Essays in Later Medieval French Literature. The Legacy of Jane H.M. Taylor* (Manchester, 2010) pp. 71–87.

Cayley, Emma, 'Debate after Alain Chartier: Authority and Materiality in the *Debat de la Noire et de la Tannee*' in Jean-Claude Mühlethaler and Jean-Yves Tilliette (eds) *Mythes à la cour, mythes pour la cour* (Geneva, 2010) pp. 311–21.

Cayley, Emma, 'Polyphonie et dialogisme: Espaces ludiques dans le recueil manuscrit à la fin du Moyen Âge. Le cas de trois recueils poétiques du quinzième siècle' in Tania Van Hemelryck and Claude Thiry (eds) *Le recueil au Moyen Âge. La fin du Moyen Âge* (Turnhout, 2010) pp. 47–60.

Cayley, Emma, '"Avoir puce en l'oreille": Voices of Desire in Alain Chartier's *Debat Reveille Matin* and Guillaume Alexis' *Le Debat de l'omme mondain et du religieulx*' *Cahiers de recherches médiévales et humanistes* 22 (2011) pp. 43–57.

Cayley, Emma, 'Machaut and Debate Poetry', in *A Companion to Guillaume de Machaut – An Interdisciplinary Approach to the Master* (Leiden, 2012) pp. 103–18.

Cayley, Emma, 'Coming Apart at the Seams?: Citation as Transvestism in Fifteenth-Century French Poetry' in Yolanda Plumley and Giuliano Di Bacco (eds) *Citation, Intertextuality, Memory in the Middle Ages: Text, Music, Image 29–30 January 2009, University of Exeter, Selected Papers vol. 2* (Liverpool, 2013).

Cayley, Emma, *Sleepless Knights and Wanton Women, Volume 1: The Debate Poems* (Tempe AZ, forthcoming).

Cayley, Emma and A. Kinch (eds), *Chartier in Europe* (Cambridge, 2008).

Chaganti, Seeta, *The Medieval Poetics of the Reliquary: Enshrinement, Inscription, Performance* (New York, 2008).

Chahin, M., *The Kingdom of Armenia: A History* (Richmond, 2001, 2nd edn).

Chandler, Alice, *A Dream of Order* (London, 1971).

Charlton, Edward, 'A Roll of Prayers Formerly Belonging to Henry VIII When Prince' *Archæologia æliana: or, Miscellaneous Tracts Relating to Antiquity* 2 (1858) pp. 41–5.

Christianson, C.P., *Memorials of the Book Trade in Medieval London* (Woodbridge, 1987).

Christianson, C.P., 'The Rise of London's Book-Trade' in Lotte Hellinga and J.B. Trapp (eds) *The Cambridge History of the Book in Britain III: 1400–1557* (Cambridge, 1999) pp. 128–47.

Classen, Albrecht, 'Heinrich Wittenwiler (before 1387–circa 1414?)' in James Hardin and Max Reinhart (eds) *German Writers of the Renaissance and Reformation 1280–1580* (Detroit MI, Washington DC and London, 1997) pp. 326–31.

Clemens, Raymond and Timothy Graham, *Introduction to Manuscript Studies* (Ithaca NY, 2007).

Clifton-Everest, John Michael, 'Wittenwiler's Marriage Debate' *Modern Language Notes* 90 (1975) pp. 629–42.

Cobb, Henry, Local Port Customs Accounts Prior to 1550' *Journal of the Society of Archivists* 1 (1959) pp. 213–24.

Cobb, Henry (ed.), *The Local Port Book of Southampton for 1439–40*, Southampton Records Series 5 (Southampton, 1961).

Cobb, Henry, '"Books of Rates"' and the London Customs, 1507–1558' *The Guildhall Miscellany* 4 (1971), pp. 1–13.

Cobb, Henry (ed.), *The Overseas Trade of London Exchequer Customs Accounts, 1480–1*, London Record Society Publications 27 (London, 1990).

Coleman, Olive, *The Brokerage Book of Southampton, 1443–4*, 2 vols, Southampton Record Series 4, 6 (Southampton, 1960–61).

Coleman, Olive, 'Trade and Prosperity in the Fifteenth Century: Some Aspects of the Trade of Southampton' *Economic History Review* 16 (1963) pp. 9–22.

Coleman, Olive, 'The Collectors of Customs in London under Richard II' in A.E.J. Hollaender and William Kellaway (eds) *Studies in London History Presented to Philip Edmund Jones* (London, 1969) pp. 181–94.

The Collection of Otto Schäfer, II: Parisian Books, Sotheby's (London, 1995).

Collier, John Payne, 'Reprints of Early English Poetry', *Notes and Queries* series 2:I (1) (1856) pp. 6–7.

Collier, John Payne, 'Lady Pecunia, or the Praise of Money' in *Bibliographical and Critical Account of the Rarest Books in the English Language, Alphabetically Arranged*, 2 vols (London, 1865) I, 58–62.

Comper, Frances M.M., *The Life and Lyrics of Richard Rolle as Gathered from Contemporary Manuscripts* (London and New York, 1928; repr. New York, 1969).

The Complete Peerage of England, Scotland, Ireland, Great Britain, and the United Kingdom (London, 1926).

Connolly, Margaret, 'Mapping Manuscripts and Readers of Contemplations of the Dread and Love of God' in Margaret Connolly and Linne R. Mooney (eds) *Design and Distribution of Late Medieval Manuscripts in England* (York, 2008) pp. 261–78.

Cooper, Lisa H. and Andrea Denny-Brown (eds), *Lydgate Matters: Poetry and Material Culture in the Fifteenth Century* (New York, 2008).

Contini, Gianfranco (ed.), *Poeti del Duecento*, 2 vols (Milan, 1960).

Cotton, Simon, 'Church Dedications' in Carola Hicks (ed.) *Cambridgeshire Churches* (Stamford, 1997) pp. 209–15.

Cré, Marleen, *Vernacular Mysticism in the Charterhouse: A Study of London, British Library, MS Additional 37790* (Turnhout, 2006).

Crotch, W.J.B., *The Prologues and Epilogues of William Caxton* (London, 1956).

D'Agata D'Ottavi, S., 'Melancholy and Dreams in Chaucer's *Troilus and Criseyde*' in G. Iamartino, M.L. Maggioni and R. Facchinetti (eds) *Thou Sittest at Another Boke ...: English Studies in Honour of Domenico Pezzini* (Milan, 2008) pp. 209–21.

Davies, Clifford S.L., 'Henry VIII and Henry V: The Wars in France' in John L. Watts (ed.) *The End of the Middle Ages? England in the Fifteenth and Sixteenth Centuries* (Thrupp, 1998) pp. 235–62.

Davies, W.G., *The Ancestry of Mary Isaac* (Portland ME, 1955).

Delsaux, Olivier, 'Du debat à l'esbat. Le debat de la noire et de la tannée: une définition en jeu' *Cahiers Moyen Âge-Renaissance 1: Jugement par esbatement* (2006) pp. 105–18.

Delsaux, Olivier (ed.), *Je meurs de soif empres le puys. Le debat de la noire et de la tannée* (Louvain-la-Neuve, 2006).

Delsaux, Olivier, '(D)ebat pour recueil en noir majeur. La supériorité du ms.-recueil sur le ms. d'auteur pour l'approche d'un texte poétique en moyen français' in T. Van Hemelryck and C. Thiry (eds) *Le recueil au Moyen Âge. La fin du Moyen Âge* (Turnhout, 2010) pp. 101–11.

Delsaux, Olivier, 'Le Debat de la noire et de la tannee. À la recherche d'un signalement' *Romania* (forthcoming).

Derolez, Albert, *Codicologie des manuscrits en écriture humanistique sur parchemin* (Turnhout, 1984).

Derolez, Albert, 'Observations on the Aesthetics of the Gothic Manuscript' *Scriptorium 50* (1996) pp. 3–12.

Derolez, Albert, *The Palaeography of Gothic Manuscript Books: From the Twelfth to the Early Sixteenth Century* (Cambridge, 2003).

Derrida, Jacques, *The Truth in Painting* trans. Geoff Bennington and Ian McLeod (Chicago IL, 1987).

Derrida, Jacques, 'L'Oreille de Heidegger: Philopolémologie (Geschlecht IV)' in his *Politiques de l'amitié* (Paris, 1994).

Derrida, Jacques, C. Lévesque and C.V. McDonald (eds) *L'oreille de l'autre: otobiographies, transferts, traductions. Textes et débats avec Jacques Derrida* (Montreal, 1982).

Di Stefano, G., *Dictionnaire des locutions en moyen français* (Montreal, 1991).

Dibdin T.F., *Bibliomania; or, Book-madness; Containing some Account of the History, Symptoms and Cure of this Fatal Disease, in an Epistle addressed to Richard Heber, Esq.* (London, 1809).

Dibdin, T.F., *Bibliomania; or, Book madness: a Bibliographical Romance in Six Parts* (London, 1811).

Dibdin, T.F., *The Bibliographical Decameron; or, Ten days Pleasant Discourse upon Illuminated Manuscripts, and Subjects connected with Early Engraving, Typography, and Bibliography*, 3 vols (London, 1817).

Dibdin, T.F., *The Library Companion; or, the Young Man's Guide, and the Old Man's Comfort, in the Choice of a Library* (London, 1824).

Dibdin, T.F., *Reminiscences of a Literary Life*, 2 vols (London, 1836).

Dibdin, T.F. and James Maidment, *Roxburghe Revels and other Relative Papers; including Answers to the Attack on the Memory of the Late Joseph Haslewood, Esq. F.S.A. with Specimens of his Literary Productions* (Edinburgh, 1837).

Dilling, Walter J., 'Girdles: Their Origin and Development, Particularly with Regard to their Use as Charms in Medicine, Marriage, and Midwifery' *Caledonian Medical Journal 9* (1912–14) pp. 337–57, 403–25.

Doob, P.B.R., *Nebuchadnezzar's Children: Conventions of Madness in Middle English Literature* (New Haven and London, 1974).

Doty, Brant Lee, 'An Edition of British Museum Manuscript Additional 37049: A Religious Miscellany' (unpublished doctoral thesis, Michigan State University, 1969).

Dove, Mary, *The First English Bible: The Text and Context of the Wycliffite Versions* (Cambridge, 2007).

Doyle, A.I., 'A Survey of the Origins and Circulation of Theological Writings in English in the 14th, 15th and Early 16th Centuries, with Special Consideration to the Part of the Clergy Therein' 2 vols (unpublished doctoral thesis, University of Cambridge, 1953).

Doyle, A.I., 'Books Connected with the Vere Family and Barking Abbey' *Transactions of the Essex Archaeological Society* 25 (1958) pp. 222–43.

Doyle, A.I., 'More Light on John Shirley' *Medium Aevum* 30 (1961) pp. 98–9.

Doyle, A.I., 'Remarks on surviving copies of Piers Plowman' in G. Kratzmann and J. Simpson (eds) *Medieval English Religious and Ethical Literature. Essays in Honour of G.H. Russell* (Cambridge, 1986) p. 45.

Doyle, A.I., 'The European Circulation of Three Latin Spiritual Texts' in A.J. Minnis (ed.) *Latin and Vernacular: Studies in Late-Medieval Texts and Manuscripts* (Cambridge, 1989) pp. 129–46.

Doyle, A.I., 'Stephen Dodesham of Witham and Sheen' in P.R. Robinson and Rivkah Zim (eds) *Of the Making of Books: Medieval Manuscripts, Their Scribes and Readers. Essays Presented to M.B. Parkes* (Aldershot, 1997) pp. 94–115.

Drewer, Lois, 'Saints and Their Families in Byzantine Art' *Deltion tes Christianikes Archaiologikes Hetaireias* 16 (1991–1992) pp. 259–70.

Driver, M.W., 'Women Printers and the Page, 1477–1541' *Gutenberg-Jahrbuch* (1998) pp. 139–53.

Driver, M.W., *The Image in Print: Book Illustration in Late Medieval England and Its Sources* (London, 2004).

Droz, E. and A. Piaget (eds), *Jardin de plaisance et fleur de rethorique*, 2 vols (Paris, 1910–25), I: facsimile; II: introduction and notes.

Duff, E. Gordon, 'A Bookseller's Accounts, c.1510' *The Library* series 2, 8 (1907) pp. 256–66.

Duff, E. Gordon, *A Century of the English Book Trade* (London, 1948).

Duffy, Eamon, *The Stripping of the Altars: Traditional Religion in England c. 1400–1580* (New Haven CT, 1992).

Duffy, Eamon, *Marking the Hours: English People & their Prayers 1240–1570* (New Haven CT, 2006).

Duneton, C., *La puce à l'oreille: anthologie des expressions populaires avec leur origine* (Paris, 1990).

Durrfeld, Eike Barbara, 'Toward a Historiography of Book Fastenings and Book Furniture,' in Ezra Greenspan and Jonathan Rose (eds) *Book History* (University Park PA, 2000) pp. 305–13.

Dutschke, C.W. and R.H. Rouse, *Guide to the Medieval and Renaissance Manuscripts in the Huntington Library*, 2 vols (San Marino CA, 1989).

Dutton, Elizabeth, 'Textual Disunities and Ambiguities of *mise-en-page* in the Manuscripts Containing *Book to a Mother*' *Journal of the Early Book Society for the Study of Manuscripts and Printing History* 6 (2003) pp. 149–59.

Dyer, Christopher, 'The Consumer and the Market in the Later Middle Ages' *Economic History Review* 42 (1989) pp. 305–27.

Earp, Lawrence, 'Scribal Practice, Manuscript Production and the Transmission of Music in Late Medieval France: The Manuscripts of Guillaume de Machaut' (unpublished doctoral thesis, Princeton University, 1983).

Earp, Lawrence, 'Machaut's Role in the Production of Manuscripts of his Works' *Journal of the American Musicological Society* 42 (1989) pp. 461–503.

Earp, Lawrence, *Guillaume de Machaut: A Guide to Research* (New York and London, 1995).

Ebert, Frederick Adolphus, *A General Bibliographical Dictionary* (Oxford, 1838).

Edler de Roover, Florence, 'New Facets on the Financing and Marketing of Early Printed Books' *Bulletin of the Business Historical Society* (December 1953) pp. 222–30.

Edmar, D. (ed), 'A Middle English Leech-book: MS Wellcome 405' (unpublished Lic. Phil. thesis, University of Stockholm, 1967) pp. 43–4.

Edwards, A.S.G., 'Continental Influences on London Printings and Reading in the Fifteenth and Sixteenth Centuries' in J. Boffey and P. King (eds) *London and Europe in the Later Middle Ages* (London, 1995) pp. 230–56.

Edwards, A.S.G., 'Decorated Caxtons' in M. Davies (ed.) *Incunabula: Studies in Fifteenth-Century Printed Books Presented to Lotte Hellinga* (London, 1999) pp. 493–506.

Edwards, A.S.G. (ed.), *Life of Saint Edmund, King and Martyr: A Facsimile* (London, 2004).

Edwards, A.S.G., 'John Lydgate's Lives of Ss Edmund and Fremund: Politics, Hagiography and Literature' in Anthony Bale (ed.) *St Edmund, King and Martyr: Changing Images of a Medieval Saint* (York, 2009), pp. 133–44.

Edwards, A.S.G. and C.M. Meale, 'The Marketing of Printed Books in Late Medieval England' *The Library* series 6, 15 (1993) pp. 123–4.

Edwards, A.S.G. and J.I. Miller, 'John Stowe and Lydgate's *St. Edmund*' *Notes and Queries* 228 (1973) pp. 355–69.

Edwards, Edward, *Memoirs of Libraries*, 2 vols (London, 1859).

Edwards, Edward, *Libraries and Founders of Libraries* (London, 1864).

Elias, Norbert, *The Civilizing Process: The History of Manners*, trans. Edmund Jephcott (New York, 1978).

Erdmann, Axel, *My Gracious Silence: Women in the Mirror of Sixteenth-Century Printing in Western Europe* (Lucerne, 1999).

Erler, Mary C., 'The Maner of Lyue Well and the Coming of English in François Regnault's Primers of the 1520s and 1530s' *The Library* series 6, 6 (1984) pp. 229–43.

Erler, Mary, 'Devotional Literature' in Lotte Hellinga and J.B. Trapp (eds) *The Cambridge History of the Book in Britain III: 1400–1557* (Cambridge, 1999) pp. 495–525.

Erler, Mary, *Women, Reading, and Piety in Late Medieval England* (Cambridge, 2002).

Fallows, David, *Grove Music Online* <http://www.oxfordmusiconline.com/subscriber/article/grove/music/15841>.

Farquhar, James Douglas, 'The Manuscript as a Book' in Sandra Hindman and James Douglas Farquhar (eds) *Pen to Press: Illustrated Manuscripts and Printed Books in the First Century of Printing* (College Park and Baltimore MD, 1977) pp. 11–99.

Fehrenbach, Charles G., *Marriage in Wittenwiler's Ring* (Washington DC, 1941).

Ferriar, John, *The Bibliomania: an epistle to Richard Heber, Esq.* (London, 1809).

Feydeau, Georges, *La Puce à l'oreille : Pièce en trois actes* (Paris, 1968).

Filieri, Maria Teresa, 'Proposte per il Maestro dei Santi Quirico e Giulitta' *Arte Cristiana* 83 (1995) pp. 267–74.

Fletcher, William Younger, *English Book Collectors* (London, 1902).

Fontaine, Jean de la, *Le Rossignol, contes et nouvelles en vers par Monsieur de La Fontaine* (Amsterdam, 1709).

Foot, Mirjam M., *Studies in the History of Bookbinding* (Aldershot, 1993).

Foot, Mirjam M., *The History of Bookbinding as a Mirror of Society* [The 1997 Panizzi Lectures] (London, 1998).

Foot, Mirjam M. (ed.), *Eloquent Witnesses: Bookbindings and their History: a Volume of Essays Dedicated to the Memory of Dr. Phiroze Randeria* (London, 2004).

Foot, Mirjam M., 'Bookbinding Research: Pitfalls, Possibilities and Needs' in Foot, *Eloquent Witnesses* pp. 13–29.

Ford, Margaret Lane, 'Importation of Printed Books into England and Scotland' in Lotte Hellinga and J.B. Trapp (eds) *The Cambridge History of the Book in Britain III, 1400–1557* (Cambridge, 1999) pp. 179–201.

Forrest, Denys, *The Making of a Manor: The Story of Tickenham Court* (Bradford-on-Avon, 1975).

Foucault, M., *History of Madness* (Paris, 1961; repr. London, 2006).

Fourrier, A. (ed.), *Plaidoirie de la Rose et de la Violette, 'Dits' et 'Débats'* (Geneva, 1979).

Françon, Marcel, 'Un Motif de la poésie amoureuse au XVIe siècle' *Publications of the Modern Language Association of America* 56, 2 (1941) pp. 307–36.

Frazee, Charles A., 'The Christian Church in Cilician Armenia: Its Relations with Rome and Constantinople to 1198' *Church History* 45 (1976) pp. 166–84.

Freedberg, David, *The Power of Images: Studies in the History and Theory of Response* (Chicago IL, 1989).

Freedman, Paul, *Images of the Medieval Peasant* (Stanford CA, 1999).

Freedman, Paul (ed.), *Food: The History of Taste* (Berkeley CA, 2007).

Freeman, Arthur and Janet Ing Freeman, *John Payne Collier: Scholarship and Forgery in the Nineteenth Century* (New Haven CT, 2004).

French, Katherine L., *The Good Women of the Parish: Gender and Religion After the Black Death* (Philadelphia PA, 2008).

Friedman, John Block, 'A Reading of Chaucer's *Reeve's Tale*' *The Chaucer Review* 2 (1967) pp. 9–18.

Friedman, John Block, '*The Nun's Priest's Tale*: The Preacher and the Mermaid's Song' *The Chaucer Review* 7 (1972) pp. 250–66.

Friedman, John Block, *Northern English Books, Owners, and Makers in the Late Middle Ages* (Syracuse NY, 1995).

Friedman, John Block, *Brueghel's Heavy Dancers: Transgressive Clothing, Class, and Culture in the Late Middle Ages* (Syracuse NY, 2010).

Fritz, J., *Le discours du fou au Moyen Age (XIIe–XIIIe siècles): Étude comparée des discours littéraire, médical, juridique et théologique de la folie* (Paris, 1992).

Furnivall, F.J. (ed.), *The Babees Book: Medieval Manners for the Young* (Colchester, 1923).

Gage, J., *Colour and Culture: Practice and Meaning from Antiquity to Abstraction* (London, 1993).

Gaier, Ulrich, *Satire, Studien zu Neidhart, Wittenwiler, Brant und zur satirischen Schreibart* (Tübingen, 1967).

Gair, Reavley, 'Rowlands, Samuel (fl. 1598–1628)' *ODNB*.

Gairdner, James (ed.), *Letters and Papers, Foreign and Domestic, Henry VIII*, VII (London, 1883).

Gaskell, Philip, *A New Introduction to Bibliography* (New York and Oxford, 1972).

Gaunt, Simon, *Love and Death in Medieval French and Occitan Courtly Literature* (Oxford, 2006).

Gaylord, A.T., 'Portrait of a Poet' in M. Stevens and D. Woodward (eds), *The Ellesmere Chaucer: Essays in Interpretation* (San Marino CA, 1995) pp. 121–42.

Gee, Stacey, 'The Coming of Print to York *c.* 1490–1550' in Peter C.G. Isaac and Barry McKay (eds) *The Mighty Engine: the Printing Press and Its Impact* (New Castle DE, 2000) pp. 79–88.

Gee, Stacey, 'The Printers, Stationers and Bookbinders of York Before 1557' *Transactions of the Cambridge Bibliographical Society* 12, 1 (2000) pp. 27–54.

Gellert, A., '"Abit ne makith neithir monk ne frere": Text and Pictorial Paratext in the Prioress's Tale' *Textus* 22 (2009) pp. 339–64.

Giaccherini, E., *Orfeo in Albione: Tradizione colta e tradizione popolare nella letteratura inglese medievale* (Pisa, 2002).

Gibson, Gail McMurray, *The Theater of Devotion: East Anglian Drama and Society in the Late Middle Ages* (Chicago IL, 1989).

Gifford, D.J., 'Iconographical Notes Toward the Definition of the Medieval Fool' *Journal of the Warburg and Courtauld Institutes* 37 (1974) pp. 336–42.

Gilissen, Léon, 'Un élément codicologique trop peu exploité: la réglure' *Scriptorium* 23 (1969) pp. 150–62.

Gillespie, Alexandra, *Print Culture and the Medieval Author: Chaucer, Lydgate and Their Books* (Oxford, 2006).

Gillespie, Alexandra, 'The Later Lives of St Edmund: John Lydgate to John Stow' in Anthony Bale (ed.) *St Edmund, King and Martyr: Changing Images of a Medieval Saint* (York, 2009) pp. 163–85.

Gillespie, Vincent, 'Vernacular Books of Religion' in Jeremy Griffiths and Derek Pearsall (eds) *Book Production and Publishing in Britain, 1375–1475* (Cambridge, 1989) pp. 317–44.

Gillespie, Vincent, 'Walter Hilton at Syon Abbey' in James Hogg (ed.) *Stand up to Godwards: Essays in Mystical and Monastic Theology in Honour of the Reverend John Clark on his Sixty-Fifth Birthday, Analecta Cartusiana* 204 (Salzburg, 2002) pp. 9–61.

Gillespie, Vincent, 'The Haunted Text: Reflections in The Mirroure to Deuote Peple' in J. Mann and M. Nolan (eds) *The Text in the Community: Essays on Medieval Works, Manuscripts, Authors and Readers* (Notre Dame IN, 2006) pp. 129–72.

Girard, R. (Y. Freccero trans.), *Deceit, Desire, and the Novel: Self and Other in Literary Structure* (Baltimore MD, 1972).

Glaister, Geoffrey Ashall, *Encyclopedia of the Book* (New Castle DE, 2001, 2nd edn).

Goldschmidt, E. Ph. [Ernst Philip], *Gothic & Renaissance Bookbindings, Exemplified and Illustrated from the Author's Collection*, 2 vols (Nieuwkoop, 1967).

Good, Jonathan, *The Cult of St. George in Medieval England* (Woodbridge, 2009).

Görlach, M., 'Text-types and language history: the cookery recipe' in M. Risanen, O. Ihalainen, T. Nevalaienen and I. Taavitsainen (eds) *History of Englishes* (Berlin, 1992) pp. 736–61.

Gottfried, Robert S., *Bury St. Edmunds and the Urban Crisis: 1290–1539* (Princeton NJ, 1982).

Gougaud, Louis, 'La prière dite de Charlemagne et les pièces apocryphes apparentées' *Revue d'histoire ecclésiastique* 20 (1924) pp. 211–38.

Gower, John, *Mirour de l'Omme*, trans. William Burton Wilson (East Lansing MI, 1992).

Grabes, Herbert, *The Mutable Glass: Mirror-imagery in Titles and Texts of the Middle Ages and English Renaissance*, trans. Gordon Collier (New York, 1982).

Gransden, Antonia (ed.), *Bury St Edmunds: Medieval Art, Architecture, Archaeology, and Economy*, The British Archaeological Association Conference Transactions 20 (Leeds, 1998).

Gransden, Antonia, *A History of the Abbey of Bury St Edmunds, 1182–1256: Samson of Tottington to Edmund of Walpole* (Woodbridge, 2007).

Gras, N.S.B., *The Early English Customs System: A Documentary Study of the Institutional and Economic History of the Customs from the Thirteenth to the Sixteenth Century* (Cambridge MA, 1918).

Green, P. (ed. and trans.), *The Poems of Catullus: A Bilingual Edition* (Berkeley CA, 2007).

Greenfield, Jane, *ABC of Bookbinding* (New Castle DE and New York, 1998).

Greico, Allen J., 'Food and Social Class in Medieval and Renaissance Italy' in Jean-Louis Flandrin and Massimo Montanari (eds) *Food: A Culinary History from Antiquity to the Present* (New York, 1999) pp. 302–12.

Griffiths, Ralph, *The Reign of King Henry VI: The Exercise of Royal Authority, 1422–1461* (Stroud, 1998, 2nd edn).

Gruchot, Christoph, *Heinrich Wittenwilers 'Ring': Konzept und Konstruktion eines Lehrbuches* (Göppingen, 1988).

Guglielmi, N., *Il medioevo degli ultimi* (Rome, 2001).

Gurevich, Aaron, 'Bakhtin and His Theory of Carnival' in J. Bremmer and H. Roodenburg (eds) *A Cultural History of Humour: From Antiquity to the Present Day* (Cambridge, 1997) pp. 54–60.

Gwara, Joseph J. and Mary Morse, 'A Birth Girdle Printed by Wynkyn de Worde' *The Library* series 7, 13 (2012) pp. 33–62.

Hahn, Cynthia, 'Peregrinatio et natio: The Illustrated Life of Edmund, King and Martyr' *Gesta* 30 (1991) pp. 119–39.

Hahn, Cynthia, *Portrayed on the Heart: Narrative Effect in Pictorial Lives of Saints from the Tenth through the Thirteenth Century* (Berkeley CA, 2001).

Hall, James, 'Desire and Disgust: Touching Artworks from 1500 to 1800' in Robert Maniura and Rupert Shepherd (eds) *Presence: The Inherence of the Prototype within Images and Other Objects* (Aldershot, 2006) pp. 145–60.

Haller, Margaret, *The Book Collector's Fact Book* (New York, 1976).

Halporn, Barbara C. (ed.), *The Correspondence of Johann Amerbach: Early Printing in Its Social Context* (Ann Arbor MI, 2000).

Hamel, Christopher de, *Catalogue of Western Manuscripts and Miniatures*, Sotheby Parke Bernet & Co. (London, 1980).

Hamel, Christopher de, *A History of Illuminated Manuscripts* (London, 1994, 2nd edn).

Hamel, Christopher de, *The Book: A History of the Bible* (London, 2001).

Hamer, Richard with Vida Russell (eds), *Gilte Legende*, 2 vols, EETS OS 327, 328 (Oxford, 2006).

Hamill, Francis, 'Some Unconventional Women before 1800: Printers, Booksellers, Collectors' *Papers of the Bibliographical Society of America* 49 (1955) pp. 300–14.

Hanham, A., 'The Stonors and Thomas Betson: Some Neglected Evidence' *The Ricardian* 15 (2005) pp. 33–52.

Hanna, Ralph, *IMEP Handlist XII: Manuscripts in Smaller Bodleian Collections* (Cambridge, 1997).

Hanna, Ralph, *A Descriptive Catalogue of the Western Medieval Manuscripts of St John's College Oxford* (Oxford, 2002).

Hanna, Ralph, 'Middle English Books and Middle English Literary History' *Modern Philology* 102 (2004) pp. 157–78.

Hargreaves, Henry, 'Some Problems in Indexing Middle English Recipes' in A.S.G. Edwards and Derek Pearsall (eds) *Middle English Prose: Essays on Bibliographical Problems* (New York, 1981) pp. 91–113.

Harris, Kate, 'John Gower's *Confessio Amantis*: the Virtues of Bad Texts' in D. Pearsall (ed.) *Manuscripts and Readers in Fifteenth-Century England: The Literary Implications of Manuscript Study* (Cambridge, 1983) pp. 27–40.

Harris, Kate, 'Patrons, Buyers and Owners: The Evidence for Ownership and the Rôle of Book Owners in Book Production and the Book Trade' in Jeremy Griffiths and Derek Pearsall (eds) *Book Production and Publishing in Britain, 1375–1475* (Cambridge, 1989) pp. 163–99.

Hellinga, Lotte, 'Importation of Books Printed on the Continent into England and Scotland before c1520' in Sandra Hindman (ed.) *Printing the Written Word: The Social History of Books Circa 1450–1520* (Ithaca NY, 1991) pp. 205–24.

Hellinga, Lotte, 'Peter Schoeffer and the Book-Trade in Mainz: Evidence for the Organization' in Dennis E. Rhodes (ed.) *Bookbindings and Other Bibliophily: Essays in Honour of Anthony Hobson* (Verona, 1994) pp. 131–83.

Henisch, Bridget Ann, *Fast and Feast: Food in Medieval Society* (University Park PA, 1976).

Herlihy, David, *Opera Muliebria: Women and Work in Medieval Europe* (New York, 1990).

Hertog, Erik, *Chaucer's Fabliaux as Analogues* (Leuven, 1991).

Herzfeld, George (ed.), *An Old English Martyrology*, EETS OS 116 (Oxford, 1900).

Hieatt, Constance B. and Sharon Butler (eds) *Curye on Inglysch: English Culinary Manuscripts of the Fourteenth Century (including the Forme of Cury)*, EETS ss 8 (Oxford, 1985).

Hobson, Anthony, *Humanists and Bookbinders: the Origins and Diffusion of the Humanistic Bookbinding 1459–1559, with a Census of Historiated Plaquette and Medallion Bindings of the Renaissance* (Cambridge, 1989).

Hodnett, E., *English Woodcuts 1480–1535* (Oxford, 1973).

Hodgson, Phyllis (ed.), *Deonise Hid Divinite and Other Treatises on Contemplative Prayer Related to The Cloud of Unknowing*, EETS OS 231 (London, 1955).

Hoey, Michael, *Textual Interaction: An Introduction to Written Discourse Analysis* (London, 2001).

Hoepffner, Ernest (ed.), *Oeuvres de Guillaume de Machaut* (Paris, 1908, repr. New York, 1965).

Hoffman, E.J., *Alain Chartier, His Works and Reputation* (Geneva, 1975).

Hohneke, Linda, 'Decorated Papers,' *Guild of Book Workers Journal* 37 (2002) pp. 2–13.

Horstmann, C., 'The Lives of Saints Edmund and Fremund', *Altenglische Legenden: neue Folge mit Einleitung und Anmerkungen* (Heilbronn, 1881) pp. 376–445.

Hudson, Anne, *The Premature Reformation* (Oxford, 1998).

Hult, David F. and Joan E. McRae (eds), *Le Cycle de la Belle Dame sans mercy* (Paris, 2003).

Hunt, Tony, *Popular Medicine in Thirteenth-Century England: Introduction and Texts* (Cambridge, 1990).

Huot, Sylvia, *From Song to Book* (Ithaca NY and London, 1987).

Huot, Sylvia, 'The Daisy and the Laurel: Myths of Desire and Creativity in the Poetry of Jean Froissart' *Yale French Studies* 80 (1991) pp. 240–51.

Husselman, Elinor M., 'The Martyrdom of Cyriacus and Julitta in Coptic' *Journal of the American Research Center in Egypt* 4 (1965) pp. 79–86.

Imbs, Paul (ed.), *Le Livre du Voir Dit* (Paris, 1999).

Incunabula from the Court Library at Donaueschingen, Sotheby's (London, 1994).

Inglis, Eric, 'A Book in the Hand: Some Late Medieval Accounts of Manuscript Presentations' *Journal of the Early Book Society* 5 (2002) pp. 57–97.

Jackson, William A., 'A London Bookseller's Ledger of 1535' *Colophon* new series 1 (1936) pp. 498–509.

Jacob, Ernest Fraser, *The Fifteenth Century, 1399–1485* (Oxford, 1961).

James, Montague R. *A Descriptive Catalogue of the Manuscripts in the Fitzwilliam Museum* (Cambridge, 1895).

James, Thomas B. (ed.), *The Port Book of Southampton*, 2 vols, Southampton Records Series 32, 33 (Southampton, 1990).

'Je chante ung chant: An Archive of Late Medieval French Lyrics', http://www. jechante.ex.ac.uk/archive/, part of the AHRC-funded project, 'Citation and Allusion in the Ars Nova French Chanson and Motet: Memory, Tradition, Innovation' led by Yolanda Plumley at the University of Exeter.

Jessop, Lesley, 'Pictorial Cycles of Non-Biblical Saints: The Seventh- and Eighth-Century Mural Cycles in Rome and Contexts for their Use' *Papers of the British School in Rome* 67 (1999) pp. 233–79.

Joldersma, Hermine, 'Modern Parodic Theory and Heinrich Wittenwiler's *Der Ring*' in Clive Thomson (ed.) *Essays on Parody* (Toronto, 1986) pp. 48–59.

Jones, Evan, 'Bristol 'Particular' Customs Account, 1503/04' in ROSE *Repository of Scholarly EPrints* <http://rose.bris.ac.uk/handle/1983/1296>.

Jones, Evan, 'Bristol 'Particular' Customs Account, 1518/17 [sic]' in ROSE *Repository of Scholarly EPrints* <http://rose.bris.ac.uk/handle/1983/1297>.

Jones, Evan, 'Bristol "Particular" Customs Account, 1525/26' in ROSE *Repository of Scholarly EPrints* <http://rose.bris.ac.uk/handle/1983/1298>.

Jones, George Fenwick, 'Heinrich Wittenwiler – Nobleman or Burgher' *Monatshefte* 45 (1953) pp. 67–9.

Jones, George Fenwick (trans.), *Wittenwiler's Ring and the Anonymous Scots Poet, Colkelbie Sow: Two Comic-Didactic Works from the Fifteenth Century* (Chapel Hill NC, 1956).

Jones, George Fenwick, 'Late Medieval "Realism" as exemplified in Heinrich Wittenwiler's *Ring*' in Sheema A. Buehne *et al.* (eds) *Helen Adolf Festschrift* (New York, 1968) pp. 86–98.

Jones, M., 'Folklore Motifs in Late Medieval Art I: Proverbial Follies and Impossibilities' *Folklore* 2 (1989) pp. 201–17.

Jones, Malcolm, *The Secret Middle Ages: Discovering the Real Medieval World* (Stroud, 2002).

Jonson, Ben, *The New Inn*, M. Hattaway (ed.) (Manchester, 2001).

Julian of Norwich: Revelations of Divine Love, trans. Elizabeth Spearing (New York, 1998).

Justice, Alan D., 'Trade Symbolism in the York Cycle' *Theatre Journal* 31 (1979) pp. 47–58.

Kadt, Elisabeth de, '"er ist ein gpaur in meinem muot, Der unrecht lept und läppisch tuot": Zur Bauernsatire in Heinrich Wittenwilers Ring' *Daphnis* 15 (1986) pp. 1–29.

Katzenellenbogen, A., *Allegories of Vices and Virtues in Medieval Art: From Early Christian Times to the Thirteenth Century* (Toronto, 1989).

Kay, Sarah, *Subjectivity in Troubadour Poetry* (Cambridge, 1990).

Keene, D., *The Summary Report on the Walbrook Study*, Economic and Social Research Council (London, 1987).

Keene, D. and V. Harding, *Historical Gazetteer of London before the Great Fire*, I *Cheapside* (Cambridge, 1987).

Keene, D., A. Burns, and A. Saint (eds), *St Paul's. The Cathedral Church of London 604–2004* (New Haven CT and London, 2004).

Keiser, G., 'Scientific, Medical and Utilitarian Prose' in A.S.G. Edwards (ed.) *A Companion to Middle English Prose* (Cambridge, 2004) pp. 231–47.

Keiser, G., 'Verse Introductions to Middle English Medical Treatises' *English Studies* 84 (2004) pp. 301–17.

Keiser, G., *A Manual of Writings in Middle English, 1050–1500, Vol. 10: Works of Science and Information* (New Haven CT, 1998).

Keitel, Elizabeth A., 'The Musical Manuscripts of Guillaume de Machaut', *Early Music* 5 (1977), pp. 469–72.

Ker, N.R., *Books, Collectors, and Libraries: Studies in the Medieval Heritage* (London, 1985).

Ker, N.R. and A.J. Piper, *Medieval Manuscripts in British Libraries*, 5 vols (Oxford, 1969–2002).

Kerby-Fulton, Kathryn, *Books under Suspicion: Censorship and Tolerance of Revelatory Writing in Late Medieval England* (Notre Dame IN, 2006).

Kerling, N.J.M., 'Caxton and the Trade in Printed Books' *Book Collector* 4 (1955) pp. 190–99.

Kerling, N.J.M. (ed.), *The Cartulary of St Bartholomew's Hospital. A Calendar* (London, 1973).

Kilby, Ken, *Coopers and Coopering* (Princes Risborough, 2004).

Kingdon, J.A., *Facsimile of First Volume of MS Archives of the Worshipful Company of Grocers of the City of London, AD 1345–1463*, 2 vols (London, 1886).

Kingsford, C.L. (ed.), *The Stonor Letters and Papers*, 2 vols, Camden Society 3rd ser. 29 (London, 1919).

Knühl, Birgit, *Die Komik in Heinrich Wittenwilers 'Ring' im Vergleich zu den Fastnachtspielen des 15. Jahrhunderts* (Göppingen, 1981).

Kolve, V.A., *Telling Images: Chaucer and the Imagery of Narrative II* (Stanford CA, 2009).

Kosmer, E., 'The "noyous humoure of lecherie"' *The Art Bulletin* 57 (1975) pp. 1–8.

Kosofsky Sedgwick, Eve, *Between Men: English Literature and Male Homosocial Desire* (New York, 1985).

Kowaleski, Maryanne, 'Port Towns: England and Wales 1300–1540' in Peter Clark (ed.) *The Cambridge Urban History of Britain*, 3 vols (Cambridge, 2000) I, 467–94.

Kreps, Barbara, 'Elizabeth Pickering: The First Woman to Print Law Books in England and Relations within the Community of Tudor London's Printers and Lawyers' *Renaissance Quarterly* 56 (2003) pp. 1053–88.

Lacan, Jacques, *Les Quatre Concepts fondamentaux de la psychanalyse : le séminaire XI* (Paris, 1990).

Lacan, Jacques, 'The Mirror Stage as Formative of the I Function as Revealed in Psychoanalytic Experience' in Bruce Fink (trans.) *Écrits* (New York, 2006) pp. 75–81.

Lackey, D.P., 'Giotto in Padua: A New Geography of the Human Soul' *The Journal of Ethics* 3–4 (2005) pp. 551–72.

Ladner, G.B., 'Homo Viator: Medieval Ideas on Alienation and Order' *Speculum* 42 (1967) pp. 233–59.

Lagorio, Valerie M. and Michael G. Sargent, 'English Mystical Writings' in *A Manual of the Writings in Middle English: IX* (New Haven CT, 1993) pp. 3049–137, 3405–71.

Laharie, M., *La folie au moyen âge: XIe–XIIIe siècles* (Paris, 1991).

Laidlaw, James C. (ed.), *The Poetical Works of Alain Chartier* (Cambridge, 1974).

Lamia, Stephen, 'The Cross and the Crown, the Tomb and the Shrine: Decoration and Accommodation for England's Premier Saints' in Stephen Lamia and Elizabeth Valdez del Álamo (eds) *Decorations for the Holy Dead: Visual Embellishments on Tombs and Shrines of Saints* (Turnhout, 2002) pp. 39–56.

Lane, Anne Marie, 'Notes on Libraries and Collections: Toppan Rare Books Library,' *Journal of the Early Book Society for the Study of Manuscripts and Printing History* 11 (2008) pp. 283–8.

Laumonier, P. (ed.), *Oeuvres complètes*, 20 vols (Paris, 1914–75).

Laurioux, Bruno, *Une histoire culinaire du Moyen Age* (Paris, 2005).

Lawton, Lesley, 'The Illustration of Late Medieval Secular Texts with Special Reference to Lydgate's "Troy Book"' in Derek Pearsall (ed.) *Manuscripts and Readers in Fifteenth-Century England* (Cambridge, 1983) pp. 41–69.

Le Maire, N.E. (ed.), *Poetae Latini Minores*, 8 vols (Paris, 1767–1832).

Leach, Elizabeth Eva, *Guillaume de Machaut: Secretary, Poet, Musician* (Ithaca NY and London, 2011).

Legge, William, 'A Decorated Mediæval Roll of Prayers' *The Reliquary and Illustrated Archaeologist* 10 (1904) pp. 99–112.

Lenky, Susan V., 'Printer's Wives in the Age of Humanism' *Gutenberg-Jahrbuch* (1975) pp. 331–7.

Leo, Domenic, 'Authorial Presence in the Illuminated Machaut Manuscripts' (unpublished doctoral thesis, New York University Institute of Fine Arts, 2005).

Lerner, Robert E., *The Heresy of the Free Spirit in the Later Middle Ages* (Berkeley CA, 1972).

Lewis, Flora, 'The Wound in Christ's Side and the Instruments of the Passion: Gendered Experience and Response' in Jane H.M. Taylor and Lesley Smith (eds) *Women and the Book: Assessing the Visual Evidence* (Toronto, 1996) pp. 204–29.

Lienert, Elizabeth, 'Das Tagelied in Wittenwilers 'Ring' *Jahrbuch der Oswald von Wolkenstein-Gesellschaft* 8 (1994–95) pp. 109–24.

Lloyd, T.H., *England and the German Hanse, 1157–1611: A Study of their Trade and Commercial Diplomacy* (Cambridge, 1991).

Lochrie, Karma, *Margery Kempe and Translations of the Flesh* (Philadelphia PA, 1991).

Loomis, G., 'The Growth of the St. Edmund Legend' *Harvard Studies and Notes in Philology and Literature* 14 (1932) pp. 83–113.

Louis, Cameron (ed.), *The Commonplace Book of Robert Reynes of Acle: An Edition of Tanner MS 407* (New York, 1980).

Lowden, John, 'The Royal/Imperial Book and the Image or Self-Image of the Medieval Ruler' in Anne I. Dugan (ed.) *Kings and Kingship in Medieval Europe* (London, 1993) pp. 213–40.

Lowes, J.L., 'The Loveres Maladye of Hereos' *Modern Philology* 11 (1914) pp. 491–546.

MacCracken, Henry Noble (ed.), *The Minor Poems of John Lydgate* (London, 1934).

McGrady, Deborah, *Controlling Readers: Guillaume de Machaut and his Late-Medieval Audience* (Toronto, 2006).

McGregor Jr., Rob Roy (ed.), *The Lyric Poems of Jean Froissart: A Critical Edition* (Chapel Hill NC, 1975).

Machabey, Armand, *Guillaume de Machault 130?–1377: La Vie et l'oeuvre musical*, 2 vols (Paris, 1955).

Machan, T.W., *Textual Criticism and Middle English Texts* (Charlottesville VA, 1994).

McKendrick, Scot, Kathleen Doyle and John Lowden (eds), *Royal Manuscripts: The Genius of Illumination* (London, 2011).

McKenna, J.W., 'Henry VI of England and the Dual Monarchy: Aspects of Royal Political Propaganda' *Journal of the Warburg and Courtauld Institutes* 28 (1965) pp. 145–62.

McKenna, J.W., 'Piety and Propaganda: The Cult of King Henry VI' in Beryl Rowland (ed.) *Chaucer and Middle English Studies in Honour of Rossell Hope Robbins* (Kent OH, 1974) pp. 72–88.

McKenzie, D., *Bibliography and the Sociology of Texts* (Cambridge, 1999).

MacKinley, James Murray, *Ecclesiastical Place-Names of Scotland: Influence of the Pre-Reformation Church on Scottish Place-Names* (Edinburgh, 1904).

Maclaine, Allen H., *The Christis Kirk Tradition and Scots Poetry of Folk Festivity* (Glasgow, 1996).

McMurtrie, Douglas C., *The Book: the Story of Printing and Bookmaking* (New York, 1989).

Madan, F., 'Day-Book of John Dorne, Bookseller in Oxford, A.D. 1520' *Collectanea* 1st series (Oxford, 1885) pp. 71–181.

Mahoney, Dhira B., 'Courtly Presentation and Authorial Self-Fashioning: Frontispiece Miniatures in Late Medieval French and English Manuscripts' *Mediaevalia* 21 (1996) pp. 97–160.

Manley, K.A., 'Brydges, Sir (Samuel) Egerton, first baronet, styled thirteenth Baron Chandos (1762–1837)' *ODNB*.

Marotti, A.M., *John Donne, Coterie Poet* (Madison WI, 1986).

Marks, Richard, 'Images of Henry VI' in Jenny Stratford (ed.) *The Lancastrian Court* (Donington, 2003) pp. 111–24.

Marks, R. and P. Williamson (eds), *Gothic Art for England 1400–1547* (London, 2003).

Martin, John, *A Bibliographical Catalogue of Books Privately Printed* (London, 1834).

Matthews, David, *The Making of Middle English, 1765–1910* (Minneapolis MN, 1999).

Maxwell, Kate, 'Guillaume de Machaut and the *mise en page* of medieval French sung verse' (unpublished doctoral thesis, University of Glasgow, 2009).

Meale, C.M., 'Wynkyn de Worde's Setting Copy for *Ipomydon*' *Studies in Bibliography* 35 (1982) pp. 156–71.

Meale, C.M., 'The Compiler at Work: John Colyns and BL, MS Harley 2252' in D. Pearsall (ed.) *Manuscripts and Readers in Fifteenth-Century England: The Literary Implications of Manuscript Study* (Cambridge, 1983) pp. 82–103.

Meale, C.M. (ed.), *Women and Literature in Britain, 1150–1500* (Cambridge, 1991).

Meale, C.M., 'The Libelle of Englyshe Polycye and Mercantile Literary Culture in Late-Medieval London' in J. Boffey and P. King (eds) *London and Europe in the Later Middle Ages* (London, 1995) pp. 198–202.

Meale, C.M., '"... Alle the Bokes that I have of Latyn, Englisch, and Frensch": Laywomen and their Books in Late Medieval England' in C.M. Meale (ed.) *Women and Literature in Britain: 1150–1500* (Cambridge, 1996) pp. 128–58.

Meale, C.M., 'London, BL, Harley MS 2252: John Colyns' "Boke": Structure and Content' *English Manuscript Studies 1100–1700* 15 (2011) pp. 65–122.

Mellinkoff, R., *Outcasts: Signs of Otherness in Northern European Art of the Late Middle Ages* (Berkeley CA, 1993).

Menjot, D. (ed.), *Manger et boire au Moyen Age. Actes du Colloque de Nice (15–17 Octobre 1982)*, 2 vols (Paris, 1984).

Metropolitan Museum of Art, *The Art of Medieval Spain, A.D. 500–1200* (New York, 1993).

Michel, P. (ed.), *Le Tiers Livre* (Paris, 1966).

Migne, J.-P. (ed.), *Patrologia Latina* 37 (Paris, 1845).

Miller, Elaine M., '"In Hoote Somere": A Fifteenth-Century Medical Manuscript' (unpublished doctoral thesis, Princeton University, 1978).

Miller, James, 'John Lydgate's Saint Edmund and Saint Fremund: An Annotated Edition' (Harvard University, 1967).

Miller, James, 'Literature to History: Exploring a Medieval Saint's Legend and its Context' *Literature and History: University of Tulsa Department of English Monographs*, Series 9 (1970) pp. 59–72.

Miner, Dorothy (ed.) *Walters Art Gallery, The History of Bookbinding, 525–1950 A.D.: an Exhibition held at the Baltimore Museum of Art, November 12, 1957 to January 12, 1958* (Baltimore, 1957).

Minnis, A., *Medieval Theory of Authorship: Scholastic Literary Attitudes in the Later Middle Ages* (London, 1984).

Mintz, Sidney W., *Tasting Food, Tasting Freedom: Excursions into Eating, Culture, and the Past* (Boston MA, 1996).

Moffitt, J.F., 'La Femme à la puce: The Textual Background of Seventeenth-Century Painted Flea-Hunts' *Gazette des Beaux-Arts* 110 (1987) pp. 99–103.

Montaiglon, A. de (ed.), *L'Amant rendu cordelier a l'observance d'amours* (Paris, 1881).

Montaiglon, A. de and W. Söderhjelm, *Anteckningar om Martial d'Auvergne och hans Kärleksdommar* (Helsingfors, 1889).

Mooney, Linne R., 'Practical Didactic Works in Middle English: Edition and Analysis of the Class of Short Middle English Works Containing Useful Information' (unpublished doctoral thesis, University of Toronto, 1981).

Mooney, Linne R., 'Lydgate's "Kings of England" and Another Verse Chronicle of the Kings' *Viator* 20 (1989) pp. 255–89.

Mooney, Linne R., *The Index of Middle English Prose, Handlist XI: Manuscripts in the Library of Trinity College, Cambridge* (Cambridge, 1995).

Mooney, Linne R. and Lister Matheson, 'The Beryn Scribe and his Texts: Evidence for Multiple-Copy Production of Manuscripts in Fifteenth-Century England' *The Library*, 7th series, 4 (2003) pp. 347–70.

Mooney, Linne R., David Mosser, and Elizabeth Sopolova, eds, *DIMEV: An Open Access, Digital Edition of the Index of Middle English Verse*. <http://www.cddc.vt.edu/host/imev>.

Moorat, S.A.J., *Catalogue of Western Manuscripts on Medicine and Science in the Wellcome Historical Medical Library*, 2 vols (London, 1962).

Moore, N., *The History of St Bartholomew's Hospital*, 2 vols (London, 1918).

Morant, P., *History and Antiquities of Essex*, 2 vols (London, 1768).

Morawski, J., *Proverbes français antérieurs au XVe siècle* (Paris, 1925).

Morse, Mary, 'Seeing and Hearing: Margery Kempe and the mise-en-page' *Studia Mystica* 20 (1999) pp. 15–42.

Moxey, K., 'Master E.S. and the Folly of Love' *Simiolus* 3–4 (1980) pp. 125–48.

Mueller, Rolf, 'On the Medieval Satiric Fictions of Neidhart and Wittenwiler: Fools for Their Theme: Let Satire Be Their Song' in Winder McConnell (ed.) *In hôhem prîse. A Festschrift in Honor of Ernst S. Dick* (Göppingen, 1989) pp. 295–305.

Mueller, Rolf, 'Die Forschung zu Heinrich Wittenwilers Ring 1988–1998' in Dorothea Klein *et al.* (eds) *Vom Mittelalter zur Neuzeit: Festschrift für Horst Brunnen* (Weisbaden, 2000) pp. 423–30.

Muzerelle, Denis, 'Pour décrire les schémas de réglure: Une méthode de notation symbolique applicable aux manuscrits latins (et autres)' *Quinio* 1 (1999) pp. 123–70.

Needham, Paul, *Twelve Centuries of Bookbinding 400–1600* (New York, 1979).

Needham, Paul, 'The Customs Rolls as Documents for the Printed-Book Trade' in Lotte Hellinga and J.B. Trapp (eds) *The Cambridge History of the Book in Britain III, 1400–1557* (Cambridge, 1999) pp. 148–63.

Nelson, Robert, 'A Thirteenth-Century Byzantine Miniature in the Vatican Library' *Gesta* 20 (1981) pp. 213–22.

Nichols, Ann E., '"O Vernicle": Illustrations of an Arma Christi Poem' in Marlene Villalobos Hennessy (ed.) *Tributes to Kathleen L. Scott: English Medieval Manuscripts: Readers, Makers and Illuminators* (Turnhout, 2009) pp. 139–69.

Nichols, Ann E., Michael T. Orr, Kathleen L. Scott and Lynda Dennison (eds), *An Index of Images in English Manuscripts from the Time of Chaucer to Henry VIII. c.1380–c.1509: The Bodleian Library, Oxford: I: MSS Additional – Digby* (Turnhout, 2002).

Nicolas, Nicholas Harris (ed.), *Privy Purse Expenses of Elizabeth of York: Wardrobe Accounts of Edward the Fourth* (London, 1830; repr. New York, 1972).

Nightingale, P., *A Medieval Mercantile Community. The Grocers' Company and the Politics and Trade of London 1000–1485* (London and New Haven CT, 1995).

Nolan, Maura, *John Lydgate and the Making of Public Culture* (Cambridge, 2005).

Norris, John, *Early Gunpowder Artillery 1300–1600* (Ramsbury, 2003).

O'Connor, J. (ed.), *Dr Faustus* (Harlow, 2003).

O'Connor, R.D., *The Weights and Measures of England* (London, 1987).

Oizumi, A. (ed.), *Complete Concordance to the Works of Geoffrey Chaucer*, 10 vols (Hildesheim, 1991).

Oliver, Leslie Mahin, 'A Bookseller's Account Book, 1545' *Harvard Library Bulletin* 16 (1968) pp. 139–55.

Olmert, Michael, *The Smithsonian Book of Books* (Washington DC, 1992).

Olson, M.C., 'Marginal Portraits and the Fiction of Orality: The Ellesmere Manuscript' in J. Rosenblum and W.K. Finley (eds) *Chaucer Illustrated: Five Hundred Years of Canterbury Tales in Pictures* (New Castle DE and London, 2003) pp. 1–35.

Olson, Todd P.,'La Femme à la Puce et la Puce à l'oreille: Catherine Des Roches and the Poetics of Sexual Resistance in Sixteenth-Century French Poetry' *Journal of Medieval and Early Modern Studies* 32, 2 (2002) pp. 327–42.

Onions, C.T., 'A Devotion to the Cross Written in the South-west of England' *Modern Language Review* 13 (1918) pp. 228–30.

Orme, Nicholas, 'Two Early Prayer-Books from North Devon', *Devon and Cornwall Notes and Queries* 36 (1991) pp. 345–50.

Orme, Nicholas, *English Church Dedications with a Survey of Cornwall and Devon* (Exeter, 1996).

Orme, Nicholas, *The Saints of Cornwall* (Oxford, 2000).

Orme, Nicholas, *Medieval Children* (New Haven CT, 2003).

Overty, Joanne Filippone, 'The Cost of Doing Scribal Business: Prices of Manuscript Books in England, 1300–1483' *Book History* 11 (2008) pp. 1–32.

Owen, C., 'What the Manuscripts Tell Us About the *Parson's Tale*' *Medium Aevum* 63 (1994) pp. 239–49.

Owst, G.R., 'Some Books and Book-owners of Fifteenth-century St Albans' *Transactions of St Albans and Hertfordshire Archaeological Society* [no vol. number] (1929) pp. 176–95.

Palmer, R. Barton, *Guillaume de Machaut: The Judgment of the King of Bohemia (Le Jugement dou Roy de Behaigne)* (New York and London, 1984).

Palmer, R. Barton, *Guillaume de Machaut: The Judgment of the King of Navarre* (New York and London, 1988).

Pantin, William Abel (ed.), *Documents Illustrating the Activities of the General and Provincial Chapters of the English Black Monks, 1215–1540* (London, 1933).

The Parish Church of St Cyr & St Julitta Newton St Cyres Exeter (no publication details, unpaginated).

Parkes, M.B., 'Layout and Presentation of the Text' in Nigel Morgan and Rodney M. Thomson (eds) *The Cambridge History of the Book in Britain, II: 1100–1400* (Cambridge, 2008) pp. 55–74.

Parkes, M.B., *Their Hands Before Our Eyes: A Closer Look at Scribes* (Aldershot, 2008).

Pasquier, Estienne and Catherine Des Roches, *La Puce de Madame Des Roches, qui est un recueil de divers poèmes Grecs, Latins et François. Composez pars plusieurs doctes personnages aux Grands Jours tenus à Poitiers l'an MDLXXIX* (Paris, Pour Abel l'Angelier, 1582).

Pastoureau, M., 'Formes et couleurs du désordre: le jaune avec le vert' *Médiévales* 4 (1983) pp. 62–73.

Patterson, A., '"The Human face Divine": Identity and the Portrait from Locke to Chaucer' in S. McKee (ed.) *Crossing Boundaries: Issues of Cultural and Individual Identity in the Middle Ages and the Renaissance* (Turnhout, 1999) pp. 155–86.

Patterson, Lee, 'Making Identities in Fifteenth-Century England: Henry V and John Lydgate' in Jeffrey Cox and Larry J. Reynolds (eds) *New Historical Literary Study: Essays on Reproducing Texts, Representing History* (Princeton NJ, 1993) pp. 69–107.

Patterson, R.B., 'Robert Fitz Harding of Bristol: Portrait of an Early Angevin Burgess Baron Patrician and His Family's Urban Involvement' *Haskins Society Journal* 1 (1989) pp. 109–22.

Pearsall, Derek, *John Lydgate* (London, 1970).

Pearsall, Derek, *John Lydgate (1371–1449): A Bio-bibliography* (Victoria BC, 1997).

Pearsall, Derek, 'The Manuscripts and Illustrations of Gower's Works' in Siân Echard (ed.) *A Companion to Gower* (Cambridge, 2004) pp. 73–97.

Pearsall, Derek, 'The Organisation of the Latin Apparatus in Gower's *Confessio Amantis*: The Scribes and Their Problems' in Takami Matsuda, Richard A. Linenthal and John Scahill (eds) *The Medieval Book and the Modern Collector: Essays in Honour of Toshiyuki Takamiya* (Cambridge and Tokyo, 2004) pp. 99–112.

Pecock, Reginald, *The Repressor of Over Much Blaming of the Clergy*, ed. C. Babington, 2 vols (London, 1860).

Pecock, Reginald, *Reginald Peacock's Book of Faith: A Fifteenth Century Theological Tractate*, ed. J.L. Morison (London, 1909).

Pecock, Reginald, *The Reule of Crysten Religioun*, ed. William Cabell Greet (London, 1927).

Peikola, Matti, 'The Wycliffite Bible and "Central Midland Standard": Assessing the Manuscript Evidence' *Nordic Journal of English Studies* 2 (2003) pp. 29–51.

Peikola, Matti, '"First is writen a clause of the bigynnynge therof ...": The Table of Lections in Manuscripts of the Wycliffite Bible' *Boletín Millares Carlo* 24–25 (2005–2006) pp. 343–78.

Peikola, Matti, 'Aspects of *mise-en-page* in Manuscripts of the *Wycliffite Bible*' in Graham D. Caie and Denis Renevey (eds) *Medieval Texts in Context* (London, 2008) pp. 28–67.

Peikola, Matti, 'Instructional Aspects of the Calendar in Later Medieval England, with Special Reference to the John Rylands University Library MS English 80' in Matti Peikola, Janne Skaffari and Sanna-Kaisa Tanskanen (eds) *Instructional Writing in English: Studies in Honour of Risto Hiltunen* (Amsterdam, 2009) pp. 83–104.

Peikola, Matti, 'Copying Space, Length of Entries, and Textual Transmission in Middle English Tables of Lessons' in Jacob Thaisen and Hanna Rutkowska (eds) *Scribes, Printers, and the Accidentals of Their Texts* (Frankfurt am Main, 2011) pp. 107–24.

Peikola, Matti, 'The Sanctorale, Thomas of Woodstock's English Bible, and the Orthodox Appropriation of Wycliffite Tables of Lessons' in Mishtooni Bose and J. Patrick Hornbeck II (eds) *Wycliffite Controversies* (Turnhout, 2011) pp. 153–74.

Piaget, Arthur (ed.), 'Chapel des fleurs de lis par Philippe de Vitry' *Romania* 27 (1898) pp. 55–92.

Piaget, A., 'La Belle Dame sans merci et ses imitations' *Romania* 34 (1905) pp. 416–23.

Pickwoad, Nicolas, 'Onward and Downward: how Binders Coped with the Printing Press before 1800' in Robin Myers (ed.) *A Millennium of the Book: Production, Design, and Illustration in Manuscript and Print, 900–1900* (New Castle DE, 1994) pp. 61–106.

Pickwoad, Nicolas, 'The Interpretation of Bookbinding Structure: an Examination of Sixteenth Century Bindings in the Ramey collection in the Pierpont Morgan Library' in Mirjam M. Foot (ed.) *Eloquent Witnesses: Bookbindings and Their History: A Volume of Essays Dedicated to the Memory of Dr. Phiroze Randeria* (London, 2004) pp. 127–70.

Piper, Alan and Meryl Foster, 'Evidence of the Oxford Book Trade, about 1300' *Viator* 20 (1989) pp. 155–60.

Plate, Bernward, *Heinrich Wittenwiler, Ertäge der Forshung* (Darmstadt, 1977).

Plomer, Henry Robert, 'The Importation of Books into England in the Fifteenth and Sixteenth Centuries: An Examination of some Customs Rolls' *The Library* series 4, 4 (1923) pp. 146–50.

Plomer, Henry Robert, 'The Importation of Low Country and French Books into England, 1480 and 1502–3' *The Library* series 4, 9 (1928/9) pp. 165–8.

Plummer, John, *The Glazier Collection of Illuminated Manuscripts* (New York, 1968).

Pollard, Graham, 'The Early Constitution of the Stationers' Company' *The Library* series 4, 18 (1937) pp. 1–38.

Pollard, Graham, 'The English Market for Printed Books' *Publishing History* 4 (1978) pp. 7–48.

Powell, Susan (ed.), *John Mirk's Festial*, 2 vols, EETS OS 334, 335 (Oxford, 2009, 2011).

Putnam, B.H., *Early Treatises on the Practice of the Justices of the Peace in the Fifteenth and Sixteenth Century* (Oxford, 1924).

Quinn, D.B. (ed.), *The Port Books or Local Customs Accounts of Southampton for the Reign of Edward IV*, 2 vols, Publications of the Southampton Record Society 37, 38 (Southampton, 1938).

Ramsey, Peter, 'Overseas Trade in the Reign of Henry VII: The Evidence of Customs Accounts' *Economic History Review* 6 (1953) pp. 179–81.

Rand Schmidt, K.A., 'The Index of Middle English Prose and Late Medieval English Recipes' *English Studies* 75 (1994) pp. 423–9.

Ransom, Will, *Private Presses and Their Books* (New York, 1929).

Raven, James, *The Business of Books: Booksellers and the English Book Trade* (New Haven CT, 2007).

Rawcliffe, Carole, *Medicine and Society in Later Medieval England* (London, 1995).

Reed, A.W., 'The Regulation of the Book Trade before the Proclamation of 1538' *Transactions of the Bibliographical Society* 15 (1917) pp. 157–84.

Renoir, Alain and David C. Benson, 'John Lydgate' in Albert E. Hartung (ed.) *A Manual of the Writings in Middle English 1050–1500* 11 vols (New Haven CT, 1980) VI, 1809–1920.

Rhodes, Dennis, 'Don Fernando Colón and His London Book Purchases, June 1552' in his *Studies in Early European Printing and Book Collecting* (London, 1983) pp. 163–80.

Ricci, Seymour de, *Census of Medieval and Renaissance Manuscripts in the United States and Canada*, 2 vols (New York, 1935–1940).

Rice, Nicole R., 'Profitable Devotions: Bodley 423, Guildhall MS 7114, and a Sixteenth-Century London Pewterer' *Journal of the Early Book Society for the Study of Manuscripts and Printing History* 10 (2007) pp. 175–83.

Richter, J.G., 'Education and Association: The Bureaucrat in the Reign of Henry VI' *Journal of Medieval History* 12 (1986) pp. 81–96.

Robbins, Rossell Hope, 'The "Arma Christi" Rolls', *Modern Language Review* 34 (1939) pp. 415–21.

Roberts, Julian, 'Importing Books for Oxford, 1500–1640' in James Carley and Colin G.C. Tite (eds) *Books and Collectors, 1200–1700: Essays Presented to Andrew Watson* (London, 1997) pp. 317–33.

Roberts, Matt T. and Don Etherington, 'Bookbinding and the Conservation of Books: a Dictionary of Descriptive Terminology' <http://cool-palimpsest.stanford.edu/don/dt/dt2850.html>.

Robinson, Michael Edward, 'Ornamental Gentlemen: Literary Curiosities and Queer Romanticisms' (unpublished doctoral thesis, University of Southern California, 2010).

Rogers, Nicholas, 'The Bury Artists of Harley 2278 and the Origins of Topographical Awareness in English Art' in Antonia Gransden (ed.) *Bury St Edmunds: Medieval Art, Architecture, Archaeology and Economy* (London, 1998) pp. 219–27.

Ronald, Paul, *The Basketmakers' Company: A History of the Worshipful Company of Basketmakers of the City of London* (London, 1978).

Roskell, J.S., L. Clark and C. Rawcliffe (eds), *The House of Commons 1386–1421*, 4 vols (Stroud, 1992).

Ross, Leslie, *Text, Image, Message: Saints in Medieval Manuscript Illustrations* (Westport CT, 1994).

Rowe, J.H., 'King Henry VI's Claim to France in Picture and Poem' *The Library* series 4, 13 (1932) pp. 77–88.

Roxburghe Club: List of Members 1812–1991, List of Books 1814–1990 (Otley, 1991).

Rudy, Kathryn M., 'Kissing Images, Unfurling Rolls, Measuring Wounds, Sewing

Badges and Carrying Talismans: Considering Some Harley Manuscripts through the Physical Rituals They Reveal' *eBritish Library Journal Article 5* pp. 1–56 at <http://www.bl.uk/eblj/index.html>.

Rundle, David, 'English books and the continent' in Alexandra Gillespie and Daniel Wakelin (eds) *The Production of Books in England 1350–1500* (Cambridge, 2011) pp. 276–91.

Rye, W., *History of the Parish of Hellesdon in the City of Norwich*, Rye Monographs of Norwich Hamlets 3 (Norwich, 1917).

Sargent, M.G., 'Walter Hilton's Scale of Perfection: the London Manuscript Group Reconsidered' *Medium Aevum* 52 (1983) pp. 205–6.

Sargent, Michael G. (ed.) *Nicholas Love: The Mirror of the Blessed Life of Jesus Christ. A Reading Text* (Exeter, 2004).

Sartre, Jean-Paul, 'Official Portraits' in Anne P. Jones (trans.) and Maurice Natanson (ed.) *Essays in Phenomenology* (The Hague, 1966) pp. 157–8.

Savell, Don Patrick, '"Meier Betz" and "Metzen Hochzit" as Examples of Peasant Satire in the Late Middle Ages' (unpublished MA thesis, University of Maryland, 1968).

Scanlon, Larry and James Simpson (eds), *John Lydgate: Poetry, Culture, and Lancastrian England* (Notre Dame, 2006).

Scase, Wendy, *Piers Plowman and the New Anticlericalism* (Cambridge, 1989).

Scase, Wendy, 'Reginald Pecock, John Carpenter and John Colop's "Common-Profit" Books: Aspects of Book Ownership and Circulation in Fifteenth-Century London' *Medium Aevum* 61 (1992) pp. 261–74.

Scase, Wendy, 'Reginald Pecock' in M.C. Seymour (ed.) *English Writers of the Late Middle Ages* III, nos 7–11 (Aldershot, 1996) pp. 86–91.

Scattergood, John, *Manuscripts and Ghosts: Essays on the Transmission of Medieval and Early Renaissance Literature* (Dublin, 2006).

Schapiro, M., 'On Some Problems in the Semiotics of Visual Art: Field and Vehicle in Image-Signs' *Semiotica* 1 (1969) pp. 223–42.

Schapiro, M., *Words and Pictures: On the Literal and the Symbolic in the Illustration of a Text* (The Hague and Paris, 1973).

Schirmer, Walter F., *John Lydgate; A Study in the Culture of the XVth Century*, trans. Ann E. Keep (Berkeley CA, 1961).

Schüppert, Helga (ed.), 'Der Bauer in der deutschen Literatur des Spätmittelalters – Topik und Realitätsbezug' in Heinrich Appelt (ed.) *Bauerliche Sachkultur des Spätmittelalters: Internationaler Kongress Krems an der Donau 21.bis 24. September, 1982* (Vienna, 1984) pp. 146–71.

Scott, Kathleen L., *The Mirroure of the Worlde. MS Bodley 283 (England c.1470–1480). The Physical Composition, Decoration and Illustration*, The Roxburghe Club (Oxford, 1980).

Scott, Kathleen L., 'Lydgate's "Lives of Saints Edmund and Fremund": A Newly Located Manuscript in Arundel Castle' *Viator* 13 (1982) pp. 335–66.

Scott, Kathleen L., 'Caveat lector: Ownership and Standardization in the Illustration of Fifteenth-Century English Manuscripts' *English Manuscript Studies 1100–1700* 1 (1989) pp. 19–63.

Scott, Kathleen L., *Later Gothic Manuscripts 1390–1490* (London, 1996).

Scott, Kathleen L., 'The Illustration and Decoration of Manuscripts of Nicholas Love's *Mirror*', in Shoichi Ogura, Richard Beadle and Michael Sargent (eds) *Nicholas Love at Waseda: Proceedings of the International Conference 20–22 July 1995* (Cambridge, 1997) pp. 61–86.

Scott, Kathleen L., *Dated & Datable English Manuscript Borders c.1395–1499* (London, 2002).

Scribner, Robert, 'Popular Piety and Modes of Visual Perception in Late-Medieval and Reformation Germany' *Journal of Religious History* 15 (1989) pp. 448–69.

Scully, Terence, *The Art of Cookery in the Middle Ages* (Woodbridge, 1995).

Seymour, Michael C., 'Some Lydgate Manuscripts: Lives of Saints Edmund and Fremund and Danse Macabre' *Edinburgh Bibliographical Society Transactions* 5 (1983–85) pp. 10–21.

Shailor, Barbara A., *Catalogue of Medieval and Renaissance Manuscripts in the Beinecke Rare Book and Manuscript Library Yale University* (Binghamton NY, 1987).

Shailor, Barbara A., *The Medieval Book* (Toronto, 1991).

Sharpe, R.R. (ed.), *Calendar of Wills Proved and Enrolled in the Court of Husting, London, A.D. 1258–A.D. 1688*, 2 vols (London, 1889–90).

Sherbo, Arthur, 'Utterson, Edward Vernon (bap. 1777, d. 1856)' *ODNB.*

Simpson, W. Sparrow, 'On a Magical Roll Preserved in the British Museum' *Journal of the British Archaeological Association* 48 (1892) pp. 38–54.

Siraisi, N.G., *Medieval and Early Renaissance Medicine* (Chicago IL, 1990).

Skemer, Don C., 'Amulet Rolls and Female Devotion in the Late Middle Ages', *Scriptorium* 55 (2001) pp. 197–227.

Skemer, Don. C., *Binding Words: Textual Amulets in the Middle Ages* (University Park PA, 2007).

Slootmans, C.J.F., *Paas-en Koudemarkten te Bergen op Zoom, 1365–1565* (Tilburg, 1985).

Smith, A.J. (ed.), *The Complete English Poems* (New York, 1986).

Smith, Jeremy J., 'Dialect and Standardisation in the Waseda Manuscript of Nicholas Love's *Mirror of the Blessed Life of Jesus Christ*' in Shoichi Oguro, Richard Beadle and Michael G. Sargent (eds) *Nicholas Love at Waseda: Proceedings of the International Conference 20–22 July 1995* (Cambridge, 1997) pp. 129–41.

Smith, Kathryn A., *Art, Identity and Devotion in Fourteenth Century England: Three Women and Their Books of Hours* (Toronto, 2003).

Smith, R., 'The Library at Guildhall in the Fifteenth and Sixteenth Centuries, Part I: to 1425' *Guildhall Miscellany* no. 1 (1952) pp. 2–9.

Smith, R., 'Part II. Inter-chapter: William Bury, John White and William Grove' *Guildhall Miscellany* no. 6 (1956) pp. 2–6.

Smith, Robert Howie, *The Poetical Works of Sir Alexander Boswell* (Glasgow, 1871).

Somerset, Fiona, '"Hard is with seyntis for to make affray": Lydgate the "Poet-Propagandist" as Hagiographer' in Larry Scanlon and James Simpson (eds), *John Lydgate: Poetry, Culture, and Lancastrian England* (Notre Dame, 2006) pp. 258–78.

Spiller, Elizabeth, 'Recipes for Knowledge: Maker's Knowledge Traditions, Paracelsian Recipes, and the Invention of the Cookbook, 1600–1660' in Joan Fitzpatrick (ed.) *Renaissance Food from Rabelais to Shakespeare: Culinary Readings and Culinary Histories* (Aldershot, 2010) pp. 55–72.

Stallybrass, Peter and Allon White, *The Politics and Poetics of Transgression* (Ithaca NY, 1986).

Stannard, J., 'Medieval Herbals and Their Development' *Clio Medica* 9 (1974) pp. 23–2.

Starr, Christopher, 'Fitzwalter family (per. 1200–c.1500)' *ODNB.*

The Statutes of the Realm, 1377–1504 III (London, 1900).

Steer, F.W., 'A Medieval Household. The Urswick Inventory' *Essex Review* 63 (1954) pp. 4–20.

Steeves, Harrison Ross, *Learned Societies and English Literary Scholarship* (New York, 1913).

Stephens, D., 'History at the Margins: Bagpipers in Medieval Manuscripts' *History Today* 19 (1989) pp. 42–8.

Stoichita, Victor, *The Self-Aware Image: An Insight into Early Modern Meta-Painting* (Cambridge, 1996).

Strohm, Paul, 'Hoccleve, Lydgate and the Lancastrian Court' in David Wallace (ed.) *The Cambridge History of Medieval English Literature* (Cambridge, 1999) pp. 640–61.

Strubel, Armand (ed.), *Le Roman de la Rose* (Paris, 1992).

Sutton, A.F., 'William Shore, Merchant of London and Derby' *Derbyshire Archaeological Journal* 106 (1986) pp. 135–6.

Sutton, A.F., 'Alice Claver d. 1489' in C.M. Barron and A.F. Sutton (eds) *Medieval London Widows 1300–1500* (London, 1994) pp. 129–42.

Sutton, A.F., 'Caxton was a Mercer' in N. Rogers (ed.) *England in the Fifteenth Century* (Stamford, 1994) pp. 118–48.

Sutton, A.F., 'The Tumbling Bear and Its Patrons: A Venue for the London Puy and Mercery' in J. Boffey and P. King (eds) *London and Europe in the Later Middle Ages* (London, 1995) pp. 85–110.

Sutton, A.F., *A Merchant Family of Coventry, London and Calais: the Tates, c. 1450–1515* (London, 1998).

Sutton, A.F., 'The Shopfloor of the London Mercery Trade, c. 1200–c. 1500: The Marginalisation of the Artisan, the Itinerant Mercer and the Shopholder' *Nottingham Medieval Studies* 45 (2001) pp. 43–5.

Sutton, A.F., *The Mercery of London: Trade, Goods and People 1130–1578* (Aldershot, 2005).

Sutton, A.F., 'Two Dozen and More Silkwomen of Fifteenth-century London' *The Ricardian* 16 (2006) pp. 49–50.

Sutton, A.F., 'The Hospital of St Thomas of Acre of London: The Search for Patronage, Liturgical Improvement and a School, under Master John Neel, 1420–63' in C. Burgess and M. Heale (eds) *The Late Medieval English College and Its Context* (Woodbridge, 2008) pp. 218–26.

Sutton, A.F., 'The Women of the Mercery: Wives, Widows and Maidens' in M. Davies and A. Prescott (eds) *London and the Kingdom. Essays in Honour of Caroline M. Barron* (Donington, 2008).

Sutton, A.F., 'Fifteenth-century Mercers and the Written word: Mercers and their Scribes and Scriveners' in J. Boffey and V. Davis (eds) *Recording Medieval Lives* (Donington, 2009) pp. 42–58.

Sutton, A.F., 'London Mercers from Suffolk c. 1200 to 1570: Benefactors, Pirates and Merchant Adventurers, parts 1 and 2' *Proceedings of the Suffolk Institute of Archaeology and History* 42, 1 and 2 (2009–10) pp. 1–12 and pp. 162–85.

Sutton, A.F., 'Alice Domenyk-Markby-Shipley-Portaleyn' *The Ricardian* 20 (2010) pp. 23–65.

Sutton, A.F., 'A Community in St Bartholomew's Close' (forthcoming).

Sutton, A.F. and L. Visser-Fuchs, 'The Making of a Minor London Chronicle in the Household of Sir Thomas Frowyk (died 1485)' *The Ricardian* 10 (1994–96) pp. 86–103, pp. 198–9.

Sutton, A.F. and L. Visser-Fuchs, *Richard III's Books* (Stroud, 1997).

Sutton, A.F. and L. Visser-Fuchs (eds) *The Book of Privileges of the Merchant Adventurers of England, 1296–1483* (Oxford, 2009).

Swanson, R.N., *Indulgences in Late Medieval England: Passports to Paradise?* (Cambridge, 2007).

Swift, Helen J., *Gender, Writing, and Performance: Men Defending Women in Late Medieval France (1440–1538)* (Oxford, 2008).

Szirmai, J.A., *The Archaeology of Medieval Bookbinding* (Aldershot, 1999).

Taavitsainen, Irma, 'Middle English recipes: Genre characteristics, text type features and underlying traditions of writing' *Journal of Historical Pragmatics* 2 (2001) pp. 85–113.

Taavitsainen, Irma and P. Pahta (eds), *Medical and Scientific Writing in Late Medieval English* (Cambridge, 2004).

Takamiya, Toshiyuki, 'Gawain's Green Girdle as a Medieval Talisman' in Richard Beadle and Toshiyuki Takamiya (eds) *Chaucer to Shakespeare: Essays in Honor of Shinsuke Ando* (Woodbridge, 1992) pp. 75–79.

Takamiya, Toshiyuki, 'A Handlist of Western Medieval Manuscripts in the Takamiya Collection' in James H. Marrow, Richard A. Linenthal and William Noel (eds) *The Medieval Book: Glosses from Friends & Colleagues of Christopher de Hamel* (Houten, 2010) pp. 421–40.

Taylor, Gary, 'Middleton, Thomas (bap. 1580, d. 1527)' *ODNB*.

Taylor, J.H.M., *Dies Illa: Death in the Middle Ages* (Liverpool, 1984).

Taylor, J.H.M., 'Embodying the Rose: An Intertextual Reading of Alain Chartier's La Belle Dame Sans Mercy' in B.K. Altmann and C.W. Carroll (eds) *The Court Reconvenes: Courtly Literature Across the Disciplines* (Cambridge, 2003) pp. 325–43.

Taylor, J.H.M., *The Making of Poetry: Late-Medieval Poetic Anthologies* (Turnhout, 2007).

Thomas, A.H. and P.E. Jones (eds), *Calendar of Plea and Memoranda Rolls ... of the City of London*, 6 vols (Cambridge, 1926–61).

Thomson, Rodney M., *Descriptive Catalogue of Manuscripts at Corpus Christi College Oxford* (Cambridge, 2011).

Thomson, Rodney M. (ed.), *The Archives of the Abbey of Bury St Edmunds* (Woodbridge, 1980).

Thomson, Rodney M., Nigel Morgan, Michael Gullick and Nicholas Hadgraft, 'Technology of Production of the Manuscript Book' in Nigel Morgan and Rodney M. Thomson (eds) *The Cambridge History of the Book in Britain*, II, *1100–1400* (Cambridge, 2008) pp. 75–109.

Toulmin Smith, L. (ed.), *York Mystery Plays* (Oxford, 1885; repr. London, 1963).

Trivedi, Kalpen, 'The *Pore Caitif*: Lectio through Compilatio. Some Manuscript Contexts' *Mediaevalia* 21 (2001) pp. 129–52.

Turner, Sam, *Making a Christian Landscape: The Countryside in Early Medieval Cornwall, Devon and Wessex* (Exeter, 2006).

Tuve, R., 'Notes on the Virtues and Vices' *Journal of the Warburg and Courtauld Institutes* 26 (1963) pp. 264–303, and 27 (1964) pp. 42–72.

Verville, B. de, *Le Moyen de parvenir* (Paris, 1896).

Voaden, Rosalynn, *God's Words, Women's Voices: The Discernment of Spirits in the Writings of Late-Medieval Women Visionaries* (York, 1999).

Wack, M.F., *Lovesickness in the Middle Ages: The Viaticum and Its Commentaries* (Philadelphia PA, 1990).

Wasyliw, Patricia Healy, *Martyrdom, Murder, and Magic: Child Saints and Their Cults in Medieval Europe* (New York, 2008).

Weidhaas, Peter, *A History of the Frankfurt Book Fair* (Frankfurt, 2003; repr. Toronto, 2007).

Welsford, E., *The Fool: His Social and Literary History* (London, 1935).

Wheat, Cathleen Hayhurst, 'Joseph Haslewood and the Roxburghe Club', *The Huntington Library Quarterly* 11 (1947) pp. 37–49.

Wiessner, Edmund, 'Der Gedicht von der Bauernhochzeit' *Zeitschrift für Deutsche Archiv* 50 (1908) pp. 245–79.

Wiessner, Edmund (ed.), *Heinrich Wittenwilers Ring, nach der Meiniger Handschrift* (Darmstadt, 1964).

Wiessner, Edmund, *Kommentar zu Heinrich Wittenwilers Ring* (Darmstadt, 1974).

Williams, Sarah Jane, 'An Author's Role in Fourteenth-Century Book Production: Guillaume de Machaut's "livre où je mets toutes mes choses"' *Romania* 90 (1969) pp. 433–54.

Wilson, Ben, *Decency and Disorder: The Age of Cant 1789–1837* (London, 2007).

Wind, Barry, 'Close Encounters of the Baroque Kind: Amatory Paintings by Terbrugghen, Baburen and La Tour' *Studies in Iconography* 4 (1978) pp. 115–22.

Winger, Howard W., 'Regulations Relating to the Book Trade in London from 1337 to 1586' *Library Quarterly* 26 (1965) pp. 157–95.

Winstead, Karen A., 'Lydgate's Lives of Saints Edmund and Alban: Martyrdom and Prudent Pollicie' *Mediaevalia* 17 (1994) pp. 221–41.

Wolf-Cross, Christa, *Magister ludens: Der Erzähler in Heinrich Wittenwilers 'Ring'* (Chapel Hill NC, 1984).

Wolfe, Richard J., *Marbled Paper: its History, Techniques, and Patterns, with Special Reference to the Relationship of Marbling to Bookbinding in Europe and the Western World* (Philadelphia PA, 1990).

Wolfegg, W., *Venus and Mars: The World of the Medieval Housebook* (Munich, 1998).

Wood, R., 'A Fourteenth-century London Owner of Piers Plowman' *Medium Aevum* 53 (1984) p. 85.

Woolf, Rosemary, *The English Religious Lyric in the Middle Ages* (Oxford, 1968).

Woolgar, C.M., Dale Serjeantson and Tony Waldron (eds) *Food in Medieval England: Diet and Nutrition* (Oxford, 2006).

Wright, Thomas (ed.), *Three Chapters of Letters Relating to the Suppression of the Monasteries*, Camden Society OS 26 (London, 1843).

Yandell, C., 'Of Lice and Women: Rhetoric and Gender in *La puce de Madame Des Roches*' *Journal of Medieval and Renaissance Studies* 20 (1990) pp. 123–35.

Young, M., 'The Web of Knowledge in a Medieval "Medical" Manuscript: An Examination of Two Representative Examples from British Library MS Royal 17.A.iii' (unpublished MA thesis, University College Cork, 2009).

Žižek, S., *Organs without Bodies: On Deleuze and Consequences* (London and New York, 2003).

Zupko, Ronald Edward, *French Weights and Measures before the Revolution: A Dictionary of Provincial and Local Units* (Bloomington IN, 1978).

Zupko, Ronald Edward, *A Dictionary of Weights and Measures for the British Isles: The Middle Ages to the Twentieth Century* (Philadelphia PA, 1985).

Zupko, Ronald Edward, *Revolution in Measurement: Western European Weights and Measures since the Age of Science* (Philadelphia PA, 1990).

Index

Printed and bound by CPI Group (UK) Ltd, Croydon, CR0 4YY

16/04/2025

14658574-0003